Richard Mulcahy (1886 - 1971)

A family memoir.

© **Risteárd Mulcahy, 1999**

ISBN-0-9535795-0-6

Published by the Aurelian Press, Dublin.
P.O. Box No. 6750
email: aurelianpress@tinet.ie

Design and production by e print Limited.

Printed by e print Limited, Glasnevin, Dublin 11.
email: books@eprint.ie

Tribute

These memoirs are written to celebrate the memory of that great generation whose faith and courage brought freedom and democracy to Ireland, and in the hope that their idealism and integrity will be a sword of light for succeeding generations.

Tiomnu

Scríobhadh na cuimhní cinn seo le ceiliúradh a dhéanamh ar chuimhne na glúine uasal úd ar éirí lena gcreideamh agus lena gcrógacht saoirse agus daonlachas a bhaint amach d'Éirinn, agus d'fhonn is go mbeadh a n-idéalachas agus a n-ionracas mar chlaíomh solais do na glúnta atá le teacht.

Fortiter et Fidiliter

Acknowledgements

I am grateful to Ulick O'Connor who gave me valuable advice and encouragement, and to Paddy Lynch who read the text and made important comments, particularly about the first Inter-Party government. Michael Adams gave valuable advice about layout and editing, while Professor Tom Bartlett gave guidance about publication. Thanks are due to Professor Jack Lyons for help with medical quotations.

I am grateful to Sean and Rosemarie Mulcahy, my sisters Elisabet Berney and Neilli Bacon, and my cousins Maura Mulcahy, Betty Glavey, Sheila Mulloy, Eoin Ryan and Joseph McCullough for their interest and recollections. I also thank my brother Padraig, Douglas and Dorothy Gageby, my cousins Domhnall and Mairtin McCullough, and Eithne Gaffney for photographs. My son Richard put his office facilities at my disposal where Denise O'Toole was prompt and highly efficient when photocopying earlier texts.

I am grateful to Michael Laffan, Seamus Helferty, Jennifer O'Reilly and the staff of the UCD Archives, and to the staffs of the National Library, the National Archives and the Military Archives. I wish to express my belated thanks to Maryann Valiulis's husband, Tony, who arranged to transcribe my father's original recordings to more modern and serviceable tapes. I thank my wife, Louise, for her patience.

Tugaim buíochas do Mhícheál O'Dómhnaill as Conradh na Gaeilge i dtaobh aistriúcháin na n-ailt i nGaeilge.

Deirdre McMahon was of immense help in providing sources of information, in guiding me along the narrow path of objectivity, and in painstakingly reading through the text and making important amendments. Margaret Hamilton of e print showed patience and understanding during the final stages of this book's gestation, as did Barry O'Brien.

CONTENTS

Introduction: 1 - 4

Chapter 1   Richard Mulcahy's background and family   5 - 15

Chapter 2   His career - a summary   17 - 23

Chapter 3   Richard Mulcahy's opinions and
                   writings about the period 1916-1924   25 - 92

                   3.1 The Rising, Knutsford and Frongoch   25 - 42

                   3.2 Return from Frongoch and army leadership`   43 - 56

                   3.3 The War of Independence : Army Policy.   57 - 75

                   3.4 First Dail and Sinn Fein   75 - 84

                   3.5 Truce   84 - 92

Chapter 4   Mulcahy writes about military and political
                   colleagues, with a reference to the genesis
                   of the civil war.   93 - 166

                   4.1 Michael Collins   93 - 122

                   4.2 Arthur Griffith   122 - 131

                   4.3 Eamon de Valera   131 - 153

                   4.4 Cathal Brugha   153 - 161

                   4.5 Dick McKee, Liam Lynch and others   161 - 166

Chapter 5   Further factors in the genesis of the civil war   167 - 184

Chapter 6   Post Treaty and the army Mutiny.   185 - 205

Chapter 7   The years 1924-1932   207-232

                 7.1 Political wilderness   207-218

                 7.2 Cumann na nGaedheal   218-223

                 7.3 The Irish language   224-232

Chapter 8   1932 and after: Opposition and
                 Inter-Party government   233-259

Chapter 9   Later Years and Last Days   261-273

Chapter 10   Min and the Ryan family   275-300

Chapter 11   Lissenfield   301-349

Appendix 1   Richard Mulcahy's homily
                 over Collins's grave   351-355

Appendix 2   His homily over the graves of Ashe,
                 Kearney and Beaslai.   357-360

Appendix 3   The Valiulis biography   361-365

Appendix 4   The Mulcahy papers, the annotation
                 and the tapes.   367-376

References   377-396

Index   397-422

Introduction

Letter to my son Richard

Dear Richard,

I am sending you a copy of a memoir about your grandfather, Richard Mulcahy, and about his family. As you are aware, he played a major role as a military and political leader in the freedom movement during the early part of this century. He subsequently played an important part in the evolution of our country as a free and democratic nation. You are already aware of the excellent biography about him which was published by Maryann Valiulis in 1992. This memoir is written with Dad as the central figure but many other aspects of our family history, both his generation and mine, impinge on his story and will be of interest to you and to your five siblings, to whom this memoir is dedicated.

An account of my mother, Mary Josephine "Min" Mulcahy, and her own family, the Ryans of Wexford, will also be of interest to you. Her family played an important part in the political and social life of our country and, despite political differences, both families remained close during my lifetime.

Dad died in 1971 and I have been acting as his literary executor since his death. I assisted him in putting his large collection of war of independence, truce, civil war and later personal and political papers in order, and to arrange their transfer to the archives of University College Dublin. I also provided him with the facilities and equipment to record his memoirs on tape and to write an important annotation of the Beaslai biography of Michael Collins. All this was done during the last ten years of his life.

I have made some comments about Maryann's biography [1] in appendix 2 which is attached to this memoir. The tapes and the annotation are an important and detailed source of his views about the people who took part in the independence movement and about the most significant events of the time. I have dealt in some detail with these sources in appendix 3. This memoir is largely complementary to Maryann's research and writings. I have not often referred to her text (except in appendix 3).

In writing these notes about my father, I am impelled to ensure that his contribution to Irish nationality and independence, and his wider contribution to the safeguarding of democracy, should be preserved in the national consciousness. I believe the biography by Maryann Valiulis needs some amplification. Maryann devoted her research and writing largely to the 1916-1924 period when he was destined to play such an important part in the military and, to a lesser extent, the political events of the time. The following pages are not designed to describe his career during that period, but to record his opinions of the participants and the events during his active lifetime, including the historic years of revolution. While the Valiulis biography conveys an accurate picture of his public image, I would hope to convey a more complete picture of his personality as perceived by his family and more intimate acquaintances, and as gleaned by an account of his extended family.

No historian or writer had made any attempt to resuscitate his reputation until Maryann Valiulis published her thesis on the army mutiny in 1985 [2] followed by her biography in 1992. Despite Maryann's scholarly contributions, his crucial role in the organisation of the Volunteers during the war of independence, his part in directing the war and his subsequent major influence in successfully establishing a professional peacetime army is obscured by the increasing attention to Collins. His qualities and attributes were not the sort to attract the media or to excite the public, unlike Collins with his overt and buoyant energy, his charismatic nature and his flamboyant self-confidence.

His contemporaries and my own immediate family were well aware of Dad's seminal contribution to the revolutionary movement and to the subsequent formation of a stable and democratic state. From an early age I too was aware of his achievements as one of the founders of the Irish Free State. I am also aware of how his military record, if not his reputation, had faded in the public mind, and how historians had neglected both his role and that of the general headquarters staff in the successful pursuit of the war of independence. Being familiar with his papers and with his accounts of the period, and the affirmation of his friends and contemporaries who were close to the family, I detected an imbalance in the military accounts of the war of independence, with the almost exclusive emphasis on the part played by Collins and his immediate adherents, and on the fighters in the field.

On questioning my father about de Vere White's statement in his biography of Kevin O'Higgins [3] that Collins was the supreme strategist during the war, Dad replies that this is so in relation to the intelligence side but that de Vere White knew little of what GHQ was doing in West Cork and elsewhere [4].

I believe that there were several reasons for the overshadowing of the part played by the the GHQ staff and the chief of staff. Maryann has alluded to some of these - the tarnishing of Dad's reputation as a result of his perceived draconian conduct of the civil war, the political, economic and social problems which existed after the foundation of the Free State, and which caused Dad such difficulties when faced with the demobilisation of the army after the civil war, the army mutiny and his own subsequent detachment from the army and temporarily from the corridors of power.

His reputation receded further as he survived the many dangers and problems of the post-revolutionary period. He was fortunate to elude capture by the British and later to escape the assassin's bullet. He lived to the age of 86 years, and was fortunate enough to die in his bed. His strained relations with his colleagues in the cabinet during and immediately after the civil war resulted from the difficulties in organising and subsequently demobilising the army. The army mutiny, leading to his resignation and that of the army council, certainly caused his colleagues to downgrade his former prominent role in military and political affairs. Their subtle antagonism and resentment may have been provoked by their unease at the cabinet's decision to force his resignation and that of such loyal army colleagues.

Despite his resignation in 1924, and his differences with his colleagues in the cabinet, he never expressed any bitterness about their actions nor their attitudes, nor did he desert the Cumann na nGaedheal party. Even O'Higgins, who was his greatest critic during the civil war and its aftermath, did not become an object of bitterness. Dad simply said that O'Higgins and the politicians in general did not understand the army and the huge problems he faced in establishing a peacetime army dedicated to defend the democratic institutions of the state after the disaster of the civil war.

There were other reasons why his reputation was overshadowed by the march of time and the activities of others. He lacked personal ambition and had none of the overt vanity which attracts attention. He was himself impatient with preoccupations about the past, at least until he had retired from politics ten years before his death. During his active years he refused to occupy himself in any way with the affairs and controversies of the past. As Maryann has opined, his personality was such that he became totally engrossed in his current work and interests. He often would say that Ireland had too many problems to allow us to occupy ourselves with affairs of the past. It was after his retirement that he first threw himself into the task of recalling and recording the past. He did so with the same dedication and undivided attention which he gave to his earlier work. His conversations with others, his recollections, and particularly the patient archiving and annotating of his extensive collection of papers, fitted well into the mould of his systematic approach and his orderly mind

I have used three documentary sources in writing about my father and the families. They are his papers lodged in the archives of University College Dublin, his 460 page annotation of Beaslai's biography of Michael Collins [5] and his tape recordings made between 1961 and 1969.

Chapter One

Background and Family

Richard Mulcahy was born at 70 Manor Street, Waterford, on 10 May 1886. This is a large double fronted building on one of the main streets leading to the west from the city. I paid a visit there recently and found that it is now a hostel housing 16 students attending the Waterford Institute of Technology. There were eight children in the family. He was the eldest boy and the second eldest child. His father Patrick was a post office clerk in Waterford when he met and married Elizabeth Slattery in whose house he was lodging. Although he appeared to have a modest occupation, he was obviously a well respected citizen if one is to judge by the size of his commodious residence and the fact that he was a burgess of the city. Patrick Mulcahy was later posted to Thurles in Co. Tipperary in 1901 as postmaster and he finally ended his career as postmaster in Ennis, Co. Clare. He died in 1923.

Dad attended the Christian Brothers school at Mount Sion in Waterford, the first school established by the founder of the Christian Brothers, Edmund Ignatius Rice. It was the forerunner of the many schools established widely at home and abroad, and which had such a profound influence on the nationalist movement in Ireland and on education here and in the wider western world. He was greatly influenced by the education he received in Mount Sion and in later years he kept in close and sympathetic touch with his former teachers, including some who subsequently emigrated to foreign lands as far away as Western Canada and Chile.

Richard Mulcahy's paternal grandfather was a tailor in Carrick-on-Suir. His maternal grandmother was a Quaker named Maria Harris from Waterford, whose father, Samuel, was a wealthy merchant and importer of wheat from the United States. The Harris family can be traced back to Thomas H. Harris, son of William Harris and his wife Hannah, who was born in 1663 in Parks Grove, Co. Kilkenny. There is a family tree recorded in the Harris bible printed in the seventeenth century and now in the possession of my brother Padraig. The family was well known and greatly respected in the business and social life of Waterford where they were members of every charitable board in the city.

Maria became a Catholic and was influenced in making this decision by a young Catholic girl who had been appointed her companion. Her father at first refused Maria's request to become a Catholic but when she claimed "But Jesus is calling me." he replied "If Jesus is calling you, his servant Samuel will not refuse to let you go."

The circumstances of Maria's conversion are of interest. Her young companion went to confession every Saturday. On each occasion she received the same penance, to say the Litany of our Lady. She confessed to Maria that she had not the courage to tell the priest that she was unable to read and asked Maria to do so. Maria continued with the service every week and was apparently thus influenced to joined the Church. This is the story as recalled by Dad's sister, Nell[1].

The Harris family was stunned by Maria's decision, according to Nell's account. She was ostracised by her family when she married a Catholic farmer, James Slattery, and never again had any contact with her parents or siblings. Such were the powerful prejudices which then existed in Ireland and which so sadly divided Christians of different persuasions. Dad's mother was Maria Harris Slattery's daughter, Elizabeth.

Dad moved with his family to Thurles in North Tipperary in 1898 when he was twelve. There his youngest brother, Sam, was born. Shortly after Sam's birth, his mother died from typhoid fever, leaving the eight young children without the comfort, security and solace she provided. Her place was taken by her sister who cared for the children for a few years until she too died of typhoid. Dad's five sisters graduated from the Catholic University, later University College Dublin, during the early years of the twentieth century. They trained as teachers and subsequently three of them joined the Ursuline teaching order.

Mary and Nell became well known to generations of girls who attended the Ursuline boarding school in Thurles. Mary (1884-1978), who took the religious name of Mary of the Sacred Heart, spent almost her entire lifetime in Thurles, where she was head of the community for many years. She did take leave for a year or two to establish a new Ursuline convent and school in Brecon, South Wales, after the World War. She remained active and in close touch with the affairs of her community, school and family until she died at the age of 94.

Nell (1895-1968), who took the religious name of Angela, subsequently went to Brecon in Wales where she took over the convent and school from her sister Mary. The school is still thriving today. Nell too remained active and devoted to her work and her vocation until close to the end. She, the youngest sister, was the sibling who was closest to my father. They conducted a regular and lifetime correspondence of an affectionate nature. She described the great enthusiasm for education which was a feature of their extended family.

Nano (1888-1945) joined the Ursuline Convent in Waterford where she became a teacher. She adopted the religious name of Otteran, after the patron saint of Waterford. Unlike her other sisters, she lived a life of reclusive spirituality. She was occasionally visited by my father with whom she maintained an occasional correspondence, but she was seldom seen by her other siblings nor I am aware that she was seen by her numerous nephews or nieces, except on one occasion by my brother Sean when he was taking part in a tennis tournament in Waterford. Indeed, our contact with her was so tenuous that the following event caused us little surprise: when Jim Monahan, married to Dad's sister Kitty, died in June 1945 while still quite young, one of his sons was instructed to send telegrams to the members of the family outside of the city. A telegram was sent to his aunt, Sister Otteran, in Waterford. It subsequently transpired that she had died two years earlier! It has to be stated that the story was recounted by an unreliable witness!

Otteran died early from what I do not know. Her deep spirituality and asceticism was in keeping with her frail and delicate constitution, and she apparently displayed all the attributes, including a cadaverous appearance, which qualified her for sainthood.

Elizabeth or Lil (1893-1976) took over the responsibility of caring for the younger children when her aunt died. When the last two boys had reached the mid or late teens she joined the Irish Sisters of Charity and adopted the religious name of Senan, the patron saint of Shannon fishermen. It was characteristic of her, and of her two sisters in Thurles, that she always appeared to be supremely happy in her life. She was deeply committed to her work and to her vocation in caring for the poor and the sick. She suffered none of the anxieties and preoccupations of the more independent and acquisitive laity.

Mulcahy family, c. 1896.

(left to right) Kitty; Elizabeth Slattery Mulcahy holding Nell; Nano; Richard; Lily; Patrick Mulcahy; Mary.

My sister Elisabet's first baby, who was born with severe congenital heart disease, died after six weeks in the Children's Hospital, Temple Street, where Senan was a member of the community. When my sister arrived hurriedly at the entrance to the Hospital, having received an urgent message to come, she was greeted at the door by a beaming Senan who rushed up to her, embraced her warmly and said "Congratulations, congratulations, your baby has gone to Heaven." I need hardly say that her exuberance was greeted by my sister's complete emotional breakdown. But life was wonderful for her and many of her colleagues in religion, a mere halting site which led to the perpetual joys of Heaven. Can we be as happy as they were in our secular pursuits of acquisitions and more tangible pleasures of life?

Kitty (1890-1981) also became a teacher. She was the exception in that she married a civil servant, lived in Donnybrook and, despite the limited financial resources available to most civil servants at that time, she reared a family of six children. Like their Mulcahy cousins, the five boys had the advantage of free primary education at a national school and free secondary education with the Christian Brothers. Kitty was a remarkably resourceful woman, determined, intelligent, dignified and hard-working, She was never discouraged by adversity. Despite relatively early widowhood and no provision for the widows of civil servants at the time, she was blessed with a successful family. Fortunately, and thanks to her boys, she lived long enough to enjoy a more comfortable and secure life at the end of her days. How she managed during the family's earlier years must remain a mystery, for she could claim no affluent relatives to support her in her trials.

In later years Kitty had this to say about her older brother [2]:

> I only remember Dick in Waterford as lively and a tease - the one boy among five girls, I suppose he had to get his own back somehow. We had two photos taken with his sisters at this time, in both he wears a stiff white winged collar (he was eight or nine years) and looks bored. In Thurles I remember him always laden down with a strap-load of books. When we did our lessons round the dining room table, Dick did his in his own room. I think he must have been a lonely boy. Being a stranger in Thurles and having the name of being clever - he had got intermediate scholarships and prizes - set him apart. His hobby was photography - there are still some specimens

9

extant! - the bathroom was frequently darkened and films developing in liquid in special trays lay on the floor.

He left school full of honours. Dick eventually went to Aldboro House, Engineering Department of the post office at Dublin, coming home at Christmas and Easter but spending holidays at some Irish speaking district. It was he influenced Nell to take up the study of Irish. Very generous always, his favourite gift was books - especially poetry - from a single poem like *Aideen's Grave*, daintily bound, to anthologies of Irish and other poets, Bulfin's *Rambles in Eireann*, Lady Gregory's *Gods and Fighting Men*, Hyde's *Legends*, etc, etc, etc.

He was making us national minded. Meantime *Sinn Fein* and Irish Freedom were posted to us lest we might not get them ourselves. We girls all went abroad at some period of our education, France, Germany, Belgium, Poland - *Sinn Fein* followed us everywhere. When at home we kept such papers out of papa's sight as he was fond of reminding us he was a servant of the British Government and he had done well by them. Certainly they had done well by him for he took his responsibilities very seriously. He knew Dick was a member of the Volunteers but realised there was nothing he could do about it. Easter 1916 stunned Papa but when at last he got a letter from Dick from Frongoch coolly giving instructions what he and we were to do, he took it calmly and with much relief.

There was no particular literary or artistic tendencies in either side of the family, but in both there was a great tradition of education and respect for religious practices and upright living that we were expected to carry on. Grandpapa Harris was a friend of Theobald Matthew and was one of the Cork Quakers who urged Father Matthew to take up the cause of temperance amongst the poor. Three daughters of John Slattery [the maternal grandfather] joined the Dominican Order at Sion Hill (in Dublin), two going out later to Port Elizabeth, South Africa, to teach. Joseph Slattery, a brilliant student of physics at Castleknock, joined the Order, going out to Australia where he taught in Stanislaus College. He died in 1931 and a tablet erected to his memory is inscribed 'One of Australia's foremost scientific workers'.

In the Mulcahy family a story of three teaching Mulcahy brothers (hedge schoolmasters?) was told with pride. Patrick Mulcahy's [Dad's father] eldest sister was a teacher married to a teacher. It is not then surprising to find that four daughters of Patrick and Elizabeth Slattery Mulcahy became secondary teachers or that, of the eight children, five became members of religious orders, but nothing in the history of the family would suggest that one would be chief of staff and later commander in chief of a revolutionary army!

Kitty was her family's historian, Her account of the family and their antecedents is lodged with the Mulcahy papers in the University Archives. Her reminiscences were recorded in 1965 on tape 35A [3] of Dad's collection. She talks about the various in-laws and cousins named Slattery, Harris, O'Sullivan, and Cremins, all from the South Munster area. She mentions her paternal great grandfather, Richard Mulcahy, who was apparently a farmer in the Carrick-on-Suir region of South Tipperary. However, unlike my mother's family in Wexford, whose lineage can be traced back to the early eighteenth century, the Mulcahy lineage goes no further back than Dad's great grandfather. The family clearly emerged from the poor Irish tenantry of the pre-famine days and there is little trace to be found of earlier generations.

The small landholders of her grandfather's generation became the artisans of the next generation and the petty officials of the next. By the end of the nineteenth century a great interest in education was stimulated within the emerging Catholic population by the better opportunities provided by the British and the local authorities, and particularly by the religious communities. The latter, by the mid-nineteenth century, were destined to play a major role in education and the welfare of the sick and the disabled. Dad was a great admirer of the religious orders in Ireland because of their crucial contribution to the education and mores of the native Catholic population during the nineteenth and twentieth centuries. His attachment to the religious orders almost certainly accounted for his conservatism when he became Minister for Education in the two inter-party governments. The establishment of the National University in 1907 with colleges in Dublin,

Cork and Galway was also a major fillip to the emerging Catholic people. Dad's father, like my mother's Ryan parents in Wexford, took advantage of the easier access to higher education for his five daughters, and, like many others, made major personal and material sacrifices to provide them with this privilege. Hence the next generation became teachers, doctors, lawyers and senior officials, and acquired the cultural, social and political thrust to lead the country to political independence. In their own way, Dad and his sisters and brothers made an important contribution to the social, academic, religious, political and military advancement in Ireland, and to the formation of the new independent state.

Kitty, in her conversations with my father and mother, refers to the great pride her immediate antecedents and her contemporaries took in their crafts [3]. She also refers to the high level of service which was a feature of the post office, the schools and other institutions. She talks about some of her female relatives in particular and refers to their dignity and to an element of grandeur, attributes which she herself shared with her four sisters. The emerging middle-class Catholic population was clearly emulating the grandeur and dignity of their middle-class Protestant brothers and sisters.

It is also clear from conversations with my father and members of his family that they, like many other Catholic middle-class families towards the end of the nineteenth century, were supporters of Home Rule but were otherwise not radical in their political views. Their nationalism did not conceive of the possibility of breaking with England nor with the Crown. Dad's participation in the 1916 Rebellion caused consternation in the family, and particularly in his father's mind, but this was soon changed to admiration and approval during his subsequent imprisonment and his later prominent role during the War of Independence Unlike his children, whose sense of nationalism was kindled by Dad's influence, Dad's father did not approve of any separatist ideas.

While father's five sisters went to university in Dublin and finished their third-level education, the three boys were not so favoured. Dad had an excellent academic record with the Christian Brothers in Thurles, achieving at the age of 14 one of the highest places in Ireland in what was then the Junior Grade examination. He describes in detail his days at school in Thurles, the boys he studied and played with, and the subsequent careers of a number of his contemporaries, some of whom distinguished themselves in the professions and in national affairs [4]. He describes how he was unable to accept an offer of free education in Rockwell College after his Middle Grade because of the family's difficult financial position, and of his leaving school at the age of 16 because the £20 exhibition money he had earned following the Junior Grade examination was needed to pay the family debts. Despite the austerity of their lives in Thurles and the frugal circumstances under which the family lived, they always appeared to be in debt. It was therefore necessary for the three boys to finish their education early and to relieve the household of unnecessary expense.

Major Paddy Mulcahy, 1936, in air-force uniform. Later Chief of Staff 1955-1959.

Dad was obviously admired by his siblings because of his academic record at school and, no doubt, because he was the eldest boy. He is described as a bit of a loner by his sister Nellie, who was his closest confidante. His hobby was photography, and poetry was also a strong interest. He enjoyed long walks on his own in the Thurles area which allowed him to indulge in opportunities to recall his favourite poems, a practice which stood him well during his three weeks of solitary confinement when he was in Knutsford Jail after the Rising.

His brother Paddy (1897-1987) left school to join the Post Office, having gained second place in Ireland in the entrance examination. He joined the British Army in 1915, spending the next three years in the trenches as a sapper. He survived despite carrying remnants of shrapnel in his body for the rest of his days. He returned to the Post Office in Ennis after the war where he had access to information which was of immense value to GHQ and the local Volunteers. When he was dismissed because of his clandestine actions, he joined the Tipperary IRA. He subsequently joined the Free State Army and became Chief of Staff (1955-1959), 35 years after his brother held the same rank. He died at the age of 89 years.

He was apparently the black sheep of the family, according to Kitty, and it required a long time for his sisters Kitty and Nell to shed their prejudices about him and to cease drawing unfavourable comparisons between him and his "famous elder brother".

Paddy married Josephine Barrett, whom he had known for some years. She was a member of a very prominent war of independence and anti-Treaty family from Co Clare. They married during the civil war at short notice. This must have caused consternation among her relatives because of the bitterness which prevailed between the two sides. Josephine died tragically after a minor operation while still in her mid-thirties, leaving behind her husband and five young children.

Dom Columban Mulcahy (Sam)
Abbot of Cistercian Monastery,
Nunraw, Scotland, 1948.

Sam (1901-1971), the youngest child, joined a seminary in Dublin at an early age too and later entered the Cistercian order. After many years as prior in the Cistercian Monastery in Roscrea, and a sojourn as the representative of the Cistercian Order in the Vatican, he travelled to Nunraw in Scotland in 1947 to set up Sancta Maria Abbey, the first post-Reformation Cistercian community in that overwhelmingly Presbyterian country. His monastery, now well established in the life of the people of mid-Lothian, received full support from the entire community, including the Presbyterians. Sam, as Dom Columban Mulcahy and Abbot of Nunraw, played a major role in the ecumenical movement in Scotland.

14

Writing in the Tablet (3 July 1971) on the occasion of Sam's death, George Scott-Moncrieff said:

> It was in the wider, national field that Dom Columban came to be a major figure in the ecumenical movement. His irresistible personality - he was half-pint size but brimmed over with dynamism - and 'sanctity, wisdom and cheerfulness' (to quote a tribute from Malcolm Muggeridge) made him a host of friends amongst other religious leaders in Scotland. In the twenty-two years before he resigned his abbacy he saw a remarkable change, which he himself had done perhaps more than any other individual to bring about, in the relationship between Catholics and Protestants in Scotland.

The welcome extended by the local Presbyterian community contrasts with the sad differences that divide some of the neighbouring population of Northern Ireland.

I find it remarkable that Dad and his seven siblings shared so many of the Christian virtues. They had a deep and unquestioned faith in God and themselves which sustained them in every aspect of their lives. Apart from their devotion to their Church, they showed an outstanding commitment to their work and vocations. I remember them as tolerant, even tempered and serene, and with no obvious sense of personal ambition or acquisitiveness. They shared a great sense of courtesy. Austerity and simplicity were the basis of their creative lives, and truthfulness was as much an intellectual as a moral virtue. Their motivation appeared to be based on service to their schools, their institutions and their country. Dad never sought power nor influence, and whatever position of power or influence he reached was thrust upon him by circumstances and not by his own will.

Dad refers to his family and his early life in his autobiographical notes in the University Archives and in several of his tape recordings [3,4,5-14].

Chapter Two

Richard Mulcahy - A Summary of his Career

Dad left school at the age of 16 in the autumn of 1902. He joined the Post Office as an unpaid learner in January 1903 when he spent his first six months with his father in the post office in Thurles before transferring to Tralee in Co. Kerry. Shortly after his arrival in Tralee he was transferred to Bantry post office in West Cork and his two years in Bantry were to play a seminal part in his social and intellectual development.

In Bantry he went for long walks in the hills and valleys of that beautiful part of West Cork. He came in close contact with the local people and found in Ballingeary, some 12 miles from Bantry, the place which was to have the greatest impact on his development. Ballingeary was and still is the centre of the West Cork Gaeltacht. There Irish was the functional language and it was in the house of Siobhan an tSagairt that he found the stimulus which was to implant the native Irish culture and traditions and the native language firmly in his mind. He had already acquired a basic knowledge of Irish when a teacher in Thurles offered voluntary classes to boys who wished to learn the language.

He called the house of Siobhan an tSagairt his "university". Here he met Irish poets and scholars, seanchai and singers, teachers and language revival enthusiasts. But, most of all, he met Siobhan and the local Irish population, still unaffected by the insidious approach of materialism, generous, hospitable and modest in their needs, and living their days steeped in the native culture which was their heritage. He was lyrical about the qualities of people there whom he described as "Biblical people" [1]. He shared their simple undemanding lives and their wonderful language, full of beauty, resonance and imagery. He soon became a fluent Irish speaker and continued to study and to savour the language up to his death [2-6].

In November 1998 I paid a visit to the wild and beautiful valley of Gougane Barra and stayed the night in nearby Ballingeary. By coincidence I lodged in the house of Sean Kelliher, the great grandson of Siobhan an tSagairt. Next door to Sean's house was the cottage where Siobhan lived and where she so inspired Dad and other Irish scholars. Her grandson's widow still lives there and the legend of Siobhan is still felt strongly by her and by her extended family

My father left Bantry after two years but returned to Ballingeary to his "university" during his summer holidays until, in 1915, he attended the Irish Volunteers training camp in Coosan, close to Athlone. Further visits to Ballingeary were less frequent afterwards but no less enjoyable. After the formation of the State he maintained close contact with the more westerly Gaeltacht in Kerry and to a lesser extent in Connemara, and as Chairman of the Gaeltacht Commission in 1925 and 1926 he had welcome opportunities of indulging in his passion for the Irish language.

His stay in Bantry was also to introduce him to Irish nationalism and to the separatist movement. Here he read papers published by Denis McCullough and Bulmer Hobson, who established the Dungannon clubs in Northern Ireland, and who were leaders in nationalist thinking in the North in the early years of the century. He also learned about Arthur Griffith and the Sinn Fein movement. His interest in nationalism continued during his later time in Wexford but his active life as a nationalist and separatist only started when, after his arrival in Dublin to join the engineering section of the post office in 1907, he was introduced as a member to the Teeling branch of the Irish Republican Brotherhood.

He describes at some length his days in west Cork and subsequently in Wexford where he was attached to the post office until his transfer to Dublin in 1907[7,8]. He found Wexford less exciting in terms of his interests in the Irish language and Irish culture, but he continued his reading and learning of Irish there, and he maintained a continuous programme of self-improvement through his eclectic reading, and his membership of the Wexford branch of the Gaelic League. He used his time there to prepare for the matriculation examination for which he took the four languages, English, Irish, French and Latin, as well as other subjects.

He continued his long, lone walks in the countryside but he clearly found the Wexford ambience less redolent of the rich Gaelic culture of Ballingeary, He described Wexford as "suitable for contemplation and work" and in one of his more philosophical moments he talks about the Wexford ambience in terms of culture, religion and companionship.

By the time he arrived in Dublin in 1907 he had become a fluent speaker of Irish. In Dublin he prepared for a number of examinations at the newly established vocational schools to advance his career as an engineer in the post office [9-11]. During his entire lifetime he continued his eclectic interests, as is evident from his extensive library, which includes books on history, philosophy, politics, economics, social affairs, personal health and self help.

In contrast to Wexford he found Dublin a most exciting and vibrant city. He took full advantage of the new third-level institutions which were becoming an important part of the city's academia. His days were spent at work but his evenings were passed at the technical college in Bolton Street where he continued his interest in languages and science, and where, among other interests, he learned shorthand. His shorthand was to prove of great value to him in his future political career. He recalls that he recorded Dev's speech in support of constitutional change at the Sinn Fein meeting in October 1921 [12]. He developed a most unusual hybrid form of shorthand with some elements of Pitman and others of Gregg. I have a signed copy of his Pitman's Shorthand which he must have acquired about 1908. How he managed to graft an element of Gregg on Pitman must remain a mystery. There are many samples of his shorthand in his papers in the University Archives but as far as I am aware it has not been possible to interpret his particular modification of the two standard systems.

He mainly attended the technical college in Dublin to study for the post office diploma in engineering. He was disappointed when, in the subsequent examination for the ten vacancies in the engineering department of the post office, he came 13th from an entry of about 250 from all parts of the British Isles.

His membership of the IRB from 1907 involved him in no political or military activities. He attended a monthly meeting of the Brotherhood but at best these were only roll-call meetings where an occasional application for new members was processed and the monthly shilling subscription was collected. This inactivity came to an end when he and the other members of his branch were advised to join the Irish Volunteers when this organisation was established in November 1913. Dad's orders from the IRB leaders was to join and "obey his superior officers", a precept which must have appealed to his orderly and disciplined mind. From November 1913 to the Easter Rising in April 1916 he continued in regular training with the Volunteers at weekends and at summer camp.

When Dad arrived in Dublin the great majority of the people of Ireland favoured the Irish Parliamentary Party and Home Rule. Home Rule was finally approved by both houses of parliament in Westminster in 1913 but its enactment was complicated by the overt resistance of the Northern Unionists and the Ulster Volunteers, and the support they received from many prominent Tories and some sections of the British army. Its enactment was postponed and the dilemma facing the British government was temporarily solved when the Great War started in August 1914. However, although the Rising of 1916 was promulgated by a very small group of separatists, it and its aftermath destroyed the Irish Parliamentary Party and made the very limited devolution enshrined in the Home Rule Bill unacceptable to a generation which was greatly influenced by the heroic sacrifice and radicalism of the 1916 leaders.

Irish Volunteers, Coosan Camp, Athlone, Summer 1915.
(left to right) William Mullins, Richard Mulcahy, Sean Lester, unidentified, Donal Barrett, Terence MacSwiney, John Griffen, Liam Langley, Pierce McCann, Austin Stack.

On joining the Volunteers he was appointed second lieutenant in the Third Battalion of the Dublin Brigade. Shortly before the Rising of 1916 he was elevated to first lieutenant. However, he did not join his battalion during the Rising. He had successfully cut the telephone and telegraph lines to Belfast and England on the Great Northern railway line in north Co Dublin on the

20

instructions of Sean McDermott, who was the principal organiser of the Rising. He was unable to get back to Dublin after he had completed his task because of road blocks erected by the British military. He therefore joined Thomas Ashe's Fingal Brigade in North Co. Dublin. There is a detailed description of this operation in his papers [13].

The Ashbourne action was the only "successful" action during the Rising but it has received little mention in subsequent recollections of 1916. Despite the Fingal brigade's success at Ashbourne, where they fought and captured a large body of armed RIC men, they were obliged to surrender on the orders of Patrick Pearse. Soon Dad was sent to Knutsford prison in Cheshire and, about six weeks later, to Frongoch in North Wales. His experience in these two camps is described by him in later paragraphs.

He returned to Dublin on Christmas Eve 1916 with the last batch of prisoners from Frongoch. The outlook for the returning prisoners seemed bleak, with little prospect of employment or assistance. Dad was appointed commandant of the second battalion of the Dublin Brigade on his return but there was little military activity at this time. He spent the spring and early summer of 1917 fundraising for the Gaelic League in Cork and Kerry, but had returned to Dublin before the summer to prepare for entry to the medical faculty of University College, Dublin, apparently with financial assistance from the Volunteer Dependents Fund. He became involved with the other leaders in reorganising the volunteers and was appointed commandant of the Dublin Brigade shortly after his return to the city. It was widely believed that he owed this important military appointment to the reputation he acquired as a military leader at Ashbourne, and to his role as the organiser of the Ashe funeral in September 1917. Ashe was one of the people involved in the political and cultural movement whom Dad greatly admired, and, as commandant of the Dublin Brigade in September 1917, Dad was given the responsibility of organising Ashe's public funeral. Ashe's death, caused by being force-fed while on hunger strike, and the subsequent public funeral, played an important part in forwarding the separatist movement in Ireland.

At the Volunteer Convention on 27 October 1917 a formal volunteer executive was set up with Dad as director of training, and in March 1918, just before the German Plot arrests and as the conscription crisis was looming, he was proposed by the other directors of the resident executive as chief of staff of the newly established general headquarters staff of the

Volunteers [14]. He and his colleagues on the staff were largely responsible for military policy during the subsequent three years before the Truce of July 1921, and it was GHQ which directed the war of independence from January 1920 to July 1921,

Dad became a member of the first Dail after the 1918 general election and was minister for defence initially in the first Dail cabinet. However, when the cabinet was reshuffled at the time of Dev's return from Lincoln in April 1919, Cathal Brugha became minister for defence while Dad remained as assistant minister and military head of the army. However, he had little time for political activities because of his heavy commitment to the military side and to the organisation of GHQ.

He remained head of the army during the Truce and until the ratification of the Treaty in January 1922. He retired as chief of staff when appointed minister for defence in the post-Treaty Dail cabinet. He spent the next six months organising the Free State army and making strenuous efforts to avoid the split in the army which was eventually to lead to civil war in June 1922. He returned to the army as chief of staff in June to lead the war on behalf of the provisional government and he became commander in chief on the 24th August 1922 after the death of Collins, who had returned to the army on the 13 July 1922. Dad retired finally from the army at the end of the civil war in May 1923 when he was re-elected to the third Dail, having decided to follow a career in politics. His role in leading the Free State army during the civil war was endorsed by the electorate at this election when he received a huge vote in his Dublin North constituency.

Dad continued as minister for defence in the Free State cabinet until March 1924 when he resigned in protest at the sacking of the army council by the government at the time of the army mutiny in March 1924. He remained in the political wilderness from 1924-1927. He was reinstated in the cabinet as minister for local government and public health after the first 1927 election and remained in this position until the advent of the Fianna Fail government in 1932. He was reinstated against the wishes of William Cosgrave who was obliged to yield to pressure from the rank and file of the Cumann na nGaedheal party, and some of his ministers, including Dad's earlier critics, Kevin O'Higgins and Paddy Hogan.

He remained out of the cabinet until the first election of 1927. During these four years he continued to support the government and he remained an active member of the Cumann na nGaedheal party. He states in one of the tapes that, without his support, it would have been difficult for the government to survive. If this is true, it was probably because of the important segment of the pro-Treaty group which perceived him as the major figure in the party who had contributed to the country's independence and as the person with the most advanced national record and outlook. It was this element in the party which forced Cosgrave to re-appoint him to the Cabinet in 1927[15]. There is a lengthy transcription of a tape recording of his views about the national success and the political failures of the Cumann na nGaedheal government during the period 1922-1932 [16].

From 1932 to 1948, during the 16 years of the Fianna Fail administration, he acted as the principal spokesman of his party and the opposition. He was elected President of Fine Gael when William Cosgrave retired in 1944 and spent the next four years in a hectic reorganisation of Fine Gael which was then at the lowest ebb of its history with only 30 members in Parliament. He also busied himself in the herculean but successful attempt to organise an inter-party government in opposition to Fianna Fail after the 1948 election. Although he was head of the main opposition party, he agreed to have a neutral Taoiseach because of the numerous small parties involved in the coalition, some with different political backgrounds and ideologies to those of his own. His four years of reorganisation followed by the change of government was to mark the revival of the fortunes of the Fine Gael party. He was minister for education in both inter-party governments (1948-51; 1954-57) and he remained head of Fine Gael until 1959 when he resigned, He retired from politics before the 1961 election. He died in 1971.

He spent his last 10 years revising and archiving his extensive collection of war of independence, Truce, civil war and Cumann na nGaedheal papers. He also lectured to various political and cultural groups about the 1916-24 period and he wrote a number of articles on the same subject for publication. He recorded numerous conversations on tape with colleagues, family members and the media about the period extending from before the Rising to the time of his retirement. He also recorded a 460 page annotation of Beaslai's *Michael Collins and the making of a new Ireland*. Like Beaslai's biography, his annotation is an important source document about the six years from 1916 to Collins' death in 1922.

Chapter Three

Richard Mulcahy's Opinions and Writings about the Period 1916-1924.

3.1 The Rising, Knutsford and Frongoch

Like most of the other participants in the Rising, Mulcahy had no knowledge of the intentions of the organisers until a few days beforehand, and then only because, being an engineer in the post office, he was needed to carry out the crucial cutting of telephone and telegraph communication with the North and Britain. On this matter he said:

> At the third training camp at Coosan, Athlone, in September 1915, I cannot recall any feeling of common gossip or common intention or expectation that a rising was in the air. We carried out our work there as a matter of pure training. We were very interested in it but all our comrade-like contact and the atmosphere that surrounded was that of persons engaged at volunteer work in the same way as we might have been engaged at learning Irish in Ballingeary with the various trimmings that went with that - talks and meetings in houses and excursions, walks in the hills.

> On Saturday the 15th April 1916, not only had I no idea that there was going to be a rising but that idea was so far from my mind that I had not the intention of being with the company on its manoeuvres on Easter Sunday about which we got a rather important urging at the officers' meeting in Dawson Street that night from Pearse. It was my meeting with Sean McDermott at the Banba Hall after the officers' meeting that caused me to know that the Easter Sunday parade was in fact going to be a rising [1].

Ashe appointed him second in command of the Fingals when he arrived from the outskirts of Dublin after interrupting telephone and telegraphic communications with the North and Britain. According to his comrades in the Fingal Brigade, he played a major role in planning the strategy which led to the defeat and capture of a large force of the Royal Irish Constabulary in Ashbourne [2]. It was his record in the Ashbourne affair which established Dad's reputation with his colleagues after 1916 and which led to his appointment as head of the Dublin Brigade of the Volunteers six months after his return from prison. The Ashbourne action has been described in detail by the late Col Joseph Lawless, who was attached to the Fingal Brigade. Lawless had this to say about Mulcahy:

> Early in the week, however, we had the very good fortune to be joined by a few stragglers from a city battalion, amongst whom was Dick Mulcahy, known already to the other members of the staff. It was soon apparent to everyone that his was the mind necessary to plan and direct operations; cool, clear-headed and practical, and with a personality and tact that enabled him virtually to control the situation without in any way undermining Ashe's prestige as the commander [3].

> .... Ashe, who had a hurried consultation with Mulcahy. The last mentioned then turned to us and assured us that the police had not a chance of success, and that we were going to capture or rout the whole force. The quiet confidence with which he made this statement had a very good effect on the ranks, and I listened intently whilst he explained to me the general idea of our attack and what he wanted us to do. It was significant that Ashe, who was nominally the officer in charge, appeared to place himself in Mulcahy's hands [4].

Lawless then proceeds to describe the plan of campaign which Mulcahy outlines and which eventually was instrumental in their capturing the large force of the Royal Irish Constabularly. There were 57 members in the police contingent, according to official sources, while there were 40 in the Ashe force. The latter number was somewhat inflated to 400 according to a subsequent report in the Constabulary Gazette! [5].

Several of his tape recordings deal with the Ashbourne action [6] and a further paper by Col. Joe Lawless, who took part in the action, testifies to Mulcahy's cool leadership and provides a graphic description of the battle [7]. During this action the armed RIC suffered severe casualties, including several who were killed, among whom were the chief commissioner and his next in command. The rest were captured and disarmed. There has been little reference to this sole military "success" by historians dealing with the Rising nor was it referred to as a significant action during the 50th and 75th celebrations of the Rising. I often wonder what my father, in my perception the most religious and least violent and aggressive of men, thought of his participation in the deaths of so many innocent people who were merely carrying out their duty as protectors of the peace. Perhaps his conscience about the deaths of the policemen was assuaged by his commitment to the Rising and to achieving the political independence and preserving the native culture of the Irish people:

> The harshness of the Rising idea itself was smothered to a large extent and the horror at the execution of the leaders was made more effective by the expounding and the growing understanding that the men who instigated the Rising were impelled by cultural, social and economic needs for the people, and had been deeply and variously active with regard to these [8].

Dad states that the Rising could not have been more politically successful, even if the whole country had risen and the arms had been successfully landed in Kerry [9].

Michael Tierney, in his biography of Eoin MacNeill [10] writes:

> Early in 1918 the Volunteer staff conceived the not-very-wise idea of court martialling officers and men who had not taken part in the rebellion.

I have never heard Dad refer to such a step, and he would have been firmly opposed to such an idea, although there is evidence that the IRB may have held an enquiry where Stack was the subject of interrogation about the failure to land arms in Kerry in 1916 [11]. Perhaps Brugha, as chairman of the resident executive, may have initiated this policy. There are several entries in the tapes and annotation where Dad emphasises that there were no recriminations, and no justification for recriminations, among the 1916 veterans in relation to those who failed to turn out in the Rising. In particular, he makes these comments about Cork City and Limerick, and the failures associated with the arms landings in Kerry. He deplores a few derogatory remarks on this subject, and he reminds us of the special care

Dev and others continued to take to honour MacNeill who had tried to stop the Rising [12].

On the question of recriminations he states:

Nobody ever wanted to question anything about anybody's actions in Easter Week and particularly all who knew anything of it maintained a generous and loyal silence [13].

Of critical remarks contained in the Beaslai Biography about the failure of the Limerick men to take part in the Rising he states:

.... but Limerick was very much affected by the Kerry situation, both as regards Casement and the Killorglin episode in which their own men were involved and the sentence about their inactivity etc. is inexcusable [14].

and he refers to the unfortunate criticism of the failure by the Cork people to take part [15]. Beaslai was quoting Colivet on the subject and Dad showed his fondness for metaphors when he had this to say of Colivet "he was never anything but a bubble in the gas pipe!"

No doubt Limerick and Cork were also influenced by MacNeill's notice cancelling the manoeuvres.

In a conversation about Easter Week, Dad, mother and I talk about Tom Clarke and Sean McDermott who were the organisers of the Rising, and Pearse who was the inspiration behind it, despite his earlier acceptance of Home Rule, which reflected the universally popular view before 1916 [16]. We talk about the failure of the arms landing in Kerry and the effect it had on McNeill's decision to stop the Rising. Mother recounts some of her experiences during the week, when, with her sister Phyllis, she visited the GPO every day until Thursday, and refers to the unusual gaiety of such normally solemn people as Tom Clarke at the time of their visits. Tape 116B (16) finally comes to an end as we discuss the "purifying" of the IRB, a process which was initiated by Denis McCullough, Tom Clarke and Sean McDermott in 1908.

Dad, mother and myself discuss Dev's performance in Boland's Mills and the possible cause of his nervous breakdown as described by one of his senior officers, Simon Donnelly, to Dr Tom O'Higgins* in Ballykinlar Camp during the Truce [17]. Dad also discusses the Bolands Mills episode in considerable detail with Sam Erwin [18]. Sam Erwin was with Dev in 1916 and he talks about their futile attempts to burn down Westland Row station. "There was nothing to burn"! The conversation finishes with:

> A final agreement that all the mistakes which occurred during the Rising were the result of inexperience and lack of professional training, and that all, including Dev, deserved perfect understanding!

We continue with a prolonged discussion of the Fenit arms landing, the background of its failure, and the decision not to proceed with the Rising; the American influence leading to the failure; some interesting facts about Roger Casement, including his alleged intention in returning to stop the Rising [17]. We talk about MacNeill's role in stopping the Rising and the hypothetical situation if German troops had taken part. It would have led to disaster and would have been inconsistent with the prime purpose of the Rising, which, according to Mulcahy, was always designed to be a symbolic action and was never thought likely to lead to a successful military outcome.

After the surrender on the Saturday of Easter Week Dad was sent with his colleagues to prison in Knutsford, close to Manchester, and later was transferred to the prison camp in Frongoch in North Wales. He gives the following accounts of Knutsford [19] and Frongoch [20] at the beginning of his Beaslai annotation.

Knutsford

> We arrived in Knutsford by daytime on Wednesday the third of May. It was a small jail, being used at that time for British soldiers who had been convicted of offences and were being

* [Dr. Thomas O'Higgins, brother of Kevin and later founder member of the medical corps of the Free State army. After the civil war he was appointed chief medical officer of Co. Meath and was a prominent member of the Fine Gael party when he was elected to the Dail].

punished there. They were down in the lower part of the prison; they appeared to have been very harshly treated; by day time we sometimes saw them going through a kind of torture drill in one of the prison yards, very heavily laden with their equipment; at night we very often heard them screaming under apparently very heavy physical punishment.

The prison was built with a number of wings consisting of three storeys of cells. The cells were arranged along both sides of the wing; a railed balcony ran around, and the open space left by the balcony was covered over with heavy wire netting to prevent prisoners jumping over or throwing things over. A narrow high slit of a window lit the cell (I don't think there was artificial lighting arranged for in the cell), a small triangle of wood was inserted in the wall at a corner near the door to serve as a table for taking meals; a wooden bed consisting of three planks joined together and raised about four inches above the floor together with one brown soldier's blanket, and a chamber pot was the only furniture in the place. Not only was there no mattress for the bed but there was no pillow. In the beginning, whatever leg you lay on 'went to sleep' and even lying on your back was no complete solution. The pillow problem was whether you were going to lie with your head flat on the board, or take off your boots and so tie them together with your boot strings as to make a kind of receptacle for your head, lifting it a couple of inches up. I used my boots as a pillow. Luckily I had leggings over a short knee breeches and my feet therefore didn't suffer too much from the cold.

For about the first three weeks we were in solitary confinement for twenty three and a half hours out of the day; we exercised for a half an hour a day by walking around in single file in a small circle around one of the prison yards; we just had the additional exercise of emptying our slops; and in an emergency we could ring a bell to get out. I am not sure if we could go for a shower bath once a week, but we did have shower baths now and then. On Sunday we had Mass in some kind of a prison church or large hall. When we stood up to leave after our first Sunday morning's Mass some of the boys started to sing 'Faith of our Fathers'.

The idea was taken up immediately and before a line or two had been sung, we were lifting the roof until we finished the whole of the hymn through all its verses. I think we frightened the life out of the warders and soldiers who were in charge of us. We liked the idea so well that we continued with "Hail Glorious Saint Patrick". It was a real feast of defiance and it was adopted as the regular Sunday procedure after that.

We were as hungry as anything. We received our meals in a tin can into which an inverted cover fitted. For breakfast in the morning and tea in the evening, little more than a cup of tea was received in the tin can. It was dark brown and turned almost black if you didn't drink it quickly, and in the receptacle on top there was a small lump of bread. Either in the morning or in the evening, but only once a day we got a small bit of margarine. This meal was taken on the little triangle of wood in the corner of the room. The approach to eating the bread was begun rather ravenously and it was only when the last bite or two remained that you remembered to chew it and chew it as much as you could, then you went around the table with a wet finger picking up the crumbs that had remained on the table.

When we first entered our cells there were three books in them, one a bible, the other a copy of Challenor's " Think Well of It", and some other pious book. We were allowed no writing material either paper or pen or pencil. I kept track of the day of the month by putting a pin prick into the leather band of my hat. I had one pin. After a day or so, the door of my cell was pushed in very urgently and a soldier stood inside and shouted at me something that appeared like "A.C". I could do nothing but look at the fellow. He repeated several times but I couldn't make anything out of it. Finally I tumbled to the fact that he was asking me was I a Roman Catholic - an R.C. When I said I was he stretched out his hand and made a glaum at the bible and was taking it away with him when I pleaded with him to be left it - I felt that it was a real Godsend for reading. But I was an R.C and there were prison regulations and that was that. Off he went with the bible.

Every week we were given a small octavo sheet of glazed paper upon which we might send one letter home. I don't recall how we were provided with a pen or a pencil for writing, that is in the early days of our solitary confinement, because my recollection of my row of pinpricks on the inside of my hat would show that I was dependent on the pin to mark the date for the greater part of the three weeks or so we were in solitary confinement. The hours of the day were indicated in various ways; those we were most interested in were indicated by the scurrying of feet on the ground floor, indicating that that particular activity which brought us our breakfast, our lunch and our tea were in train. In my cell after about noon, I had a kind of a sun dial formed by the split window where the sun traced a mark on that wall in which the cell door was. I had a particular interest in a particular spot down somewhat low to the left side of the door, it indicated that tea time was approaching. One of the Sunday afternoons there, I was watching it somewhat anxiously feeling that there was still a fair time to go before tea would arrive, when suddenly I was surprised by hearing the scurrying of feet that indicated that the tea movement was on. Right enough the tea came along. It was only some months afterwards that I realised that it was on that day that summer time was first introduced, so that tea arrived when the mark of the sun on the wall was an hour ahead of its normal point.

The problem of occupying the mind in relation to time was a very difficult one. The pros and cons of what had happened and what was likely to happen was in no way the occasion of any questioning of mind or cogitation of any kind. My mind was just in a state of waiting, it was looking for occupation and exercise. It very soon found that in a rather interesting and tantalising way. In the years 1913 and 1914 I had spent at least three weeks of the summer in Ballingeary. I had taken down from Siobhan an tSagairt a lot of pieces of poetry or rhyming, long and short. I had entered these carefully up in a good notebook, and to some extent I had memorised some of them. Also in connection with the attempt to begin to write Irish, I had taken some lessons in French from Bertha Dumay, later to become the wife of Dick Browne of the ESB; and working somewhat on the lines of studying Irish, I had been collecting passages and memorising such things as a couple of Aesop's fables or something by Lamartine. I began therefore to occupy my time trying to recollect some of that kind of material that interested me.

I found it very absorbing and very tantalising. On the Irish side there was plenty of material to try and work on, like *"Maidean aoíbhinn Fhómhair agus mé ag gabhall an róid tré choill"* or *"Seán de Búrca"* or *"Nat an bHacaig"* or *"Nat an Bhó"*. It might be that in the case of something that had about four verses in it, I would recall a line in the third verse, then the job was to complete that particular verse. While trying unsuccessfully to do that, I might recall the opening of the first verse or a line in the first verse, but meantime I had no paper or pencil with which to write down what I had got in the third verse and perhaps I would have to forget all about that particular piece for a day or two and get on with something else. This kind of thing occupied days, changing from one Irish piece to another or from Irish to French. Material on the French side would include something from Aesop, *"Une chene un jour dit au roseau"* or the fable of *"Le Corbeau"* and *"Le Fromage"* or something from, I think, Lamartine's *"Un Nom"* - *"Il est un nom cache dans l'ombre de nom amer"* or from I think, Moliere *"L'esprit doit sur le coeur prendre le pas devant"*. It was a great occupational find.

Naturally there was a great sense of personal isolation, but it was accompanied by the feeling that there was a great mass of humanity of a sympathetic and intimate kind all round in the personnel of the prisoners. There was no possibility of any communication with them except such as could be given by a glance or a smile or a whispered word in the occasional moments in which we moved together either in the passages of the wing or going out towards the exercise ground; there was no suggestion of dejection of any kind in either the faces or the demeanour of the men; there was a fierce sense of hunger which was felt very much by the country boys, and the cold of the cells, particularly at night, was very trying. There was largely, because of the presence of British military prisoners in the jail and the impression we got of their treatment, a suggestion of brutality about the place; you hesitated very much to ring your bell lest you would bring some element of that down on yourself for giving trouble; but only on one occasion had I any trouble with one of the soldier warders, and that was when for some reason or another, one of them in my cell threatened to beat the face off me as one of those bloody yankees who had come over here to create trouble.

The prison chaplain never made any impression on us except that of coldness. There was no sympathy between us. Different sections of the men exercised at different times of the morning. (One morning after about three weeks solitary confinement we were allowed to exercise in one of the yards). At certain times when they were exercising we in our cells could hear numbers being called out. We weren't very sure what it could mean. It could mean that prisoners were being called out for returning home either for trial or for release. Up to that time I had been under the impression that there was a likelihood that I might be returned to Dublin for court martial; both detectives and military had searched our room at Richmond barracks and surveyed all the men there in circumstances that could only mean that they were looking for the person who, on Ashe's behalf, had interviewed General Friend at GHQ on the Sunday [Dad was sent to interview Pearse in Kilmainham to receive confirmation of the surrender and was escorted there by British soldiers] When therefore after our "lunch", I found myself summoned to the Governor's office, I felt that the blow had at last fallen. I was utterly relieved when, on getting to the Governor's office, I found that he had a number of people with him who appeared to be friends.

Some of the Irish in Manchester with a Father Fogarty had made up their minds that they would visit Knutsford and see if they could see any of the prisoners, bringing gifts. There were two girls by the name of Mulcahy on the party, and looking over the lists from Dublin they found the name Mulcahy, so they asked to see me. They were able to get their visit for the reason that instructions had just come that the conditions of our confinement were to be changed and that we were to be treated as internees, so that, if not from that night at any rate, from the following day, the cell doors were open except for bedtime, and within limits the prisoners had the run of the place and complete association with one another.

The visitors from Manchester had brought fruit, biscuits, and cheese. These were all mightily welcome and in quantity and in value they appeared to be seven fold multiplied by reason of what they signified. There were seven or eight in all of the Manchester people - Father Fogarty and a couple of men, and two Mulcahy girls. One of them afterwards married Sean King, [I knew him in later years as a shopkeeper in Clare Street], another Mary,who afterwards married Sean O'Muirthile*, and a couple of others. This visit of the Manchester people was to open a regular periodic connection between the Manchester people and ourselves in Knutsford and later on in Frongoch; it re-established our complete connection with the world outside as well as providing that satisfaction and help that came of complete mutual association among the prisoners themselves.

The general make-up of one of the prison wings with its wire netting and its bars of various kinds was such, that on the following day when the full noise of intercommunication had got going, the prison became almost as intolerable as a monkey house, where all the animals had gone screeching mad. The noise and the clamour of talk and movement was almost unbearable. An interesting feature of this contact was the delight and surprise with which individual men met one another, very often very unexpectedly.

One of the earliest and most smilings that I got on our own landing almost immediately after the doors of the cells were open was from a young fellow who recalled the "awful dance" that I had led them a few Sundays before the Rising. On this Sunday morning, the second Battalion were going out on manoeuvres against the Fingal men. Tom Hunter was the O/C in charge of the

* [Later to be Dad's adjutant general in the Free State army during and after the civil war, and to be sacked at the time of the army mutiny].

35

battalion that day. Somewhere beyond Whitehall he had halted his men and he told me that he wanted me to take a party and go ahead on a reconnoitring expedition to find out the lie and the movement of the Fingal men. He marked off with his arm from one of the companies about twenty men, I was to take these. I said that, as I thought the work would be tough and might mean a lot of crosscountry work, I thought it would be better to have volunteers; my idea was that we would want to have a group of men who were all fit. So volunteers were asked for and I started off at a rather quick pace. When we had got a fair distance away from our own main column I started to move at a jog trot. It wasn't long until some of the men fell out and gave up. Then it wasn't long until in one way or another we got information that the Fingal men were not coming. So after moving into the fields a bit we decided that we would turn ourselves into an ambush party and ambush our own column. My prisoner friend complained appreciatively that morning "I went like a deer".

At Knutsford we never had that type of organisation of ourselves for management that was an integral part of our internment camp conditions [Frongoch]. We were all individual prisoners. I don't think that there was any particular person in charge of a wing or in charge of a row of cells, and if any work previously done by orderlies was now done by ourselves, such as the distribution of meals to the various cells, persons selected for this work were either self-selected or they were appointed by agreement with the military people who had been responsible for the direction of that work before.

The conditions of our stay at Knutsford until the time we left for Frongoch were not such as to induce any sense of organisation or control, and there was no element of that relaxation which would induce quiet intimacies between individuals or among groups. We were something like six weeks in all at Knutsford and (during) the last two or three (we) never got rid of the confusion of the first day of being released to internee conditions.

Father Fogarty became a regular visitor and heard confessions. The prison chaplain probably lost any work of that kind that he had. I don't think that razors were allowed, but it must have been by the assistance of some of the Manchester people and a safety razor that I got rid in time of a beautifully pointed red beard. A return to solitary confinement conditions might help me to recall individual prisoners of that time, but at the moment I have no such clear recollections. I just have one picture of Pierce McCann standing with a group of others on the ground floor on the day he was preparing to go off to Frongoch, distributing some copies of Messengers of the Sacred Heart and some holy pictures. Pierce was one of those who were at the training camp at Coosan, Athlone in September 1915. He afterwards died under internment conditions in jail in England in 1919.

We probably left Knutsford for Frongoch on the same day. I don't know how many of us were in it. Denis McCullough [who later married Agnes Ryan, my mother's sister] has in his home two photographs I gave him. They are hanging up framed. One shows himself and myself and some others coming out of the main gate of Knutsford, the other shows the railway station before we embarked. We might find some familiar faces in the first photograph. That was on the 17 June 1916.

There are a number of letters available written by me at Knutsford. I don't think they contain any evidence at all of any thought upon what the future was going to suggest to me in the line of any outlook on volunteer work or on political work. They would show that I was thinking of what kind of employment I might look for when release came and that that might be in some teaching work. I think they would suggest that I had a rather virgin outlook on a very virgin page suggesting that the future was entirely pathless by suggestion of any kind. But I think it will confirm that our minds were quite relaxed and unconcerned and waiting with a cheerful outlook for changes in the situation. There was nothing we could do about anything. We were all quite satisfied that something important had happened. We were all satisfied that there was a sufficient number of us in the position of prisoners to have a strength that could afford to feel quite peaceful, and there was a tremendous development of a feeling of satisfactory comradeship.

In Beaslai's account of Frongoch he [Beaslai] speaks of timidity and divided counsels and distinguishes between fighting men and those who weren't fighting men. There was no element at all of that in any way in the atmosphere at Knutsford nor do I recall that there was any element of distress which spread itself in any way as a result of men with troubles about domestic responsibility at home.

Frongoch

In his commentary on Beaslai's description of Frongoch, Dad said:

Beaslai has no impression as to what life in the camp and the circumstances of its organisation and its direction were. The south camp consisted of a distillery in which there were three large floors used as dormitories. About 200 men had sleeping accommodation in each of these three dormitories; the north camp consisted of about 30 huts capable of housing about 25 men each. In the south camp there was a camp commandant, Staines, and a couple of camp officers with him, and three officers in charge of a dormitory each. I was in charge of the dormitory at the top of the building; in the north camp there was a camp commandant with one or two officers, and an officer in charge of each one of the 30 huts. Each officer was only responsible for the discipline and minor matters connected with his own room and his own men. During the time in the camp Collins was rather a group man concerned with his own immediate colleagues, most of whom were apparently in his hut, and those who were refugees, that is, men from England who were liable to conscription if identified. Added to that he was part of the Kimmage group in Dublin rather than of the Dublin Brigade. I had a greater position of responsibility and a greater sense of responsibility as far as the general camp position was concerned. That arose from my position in the Dublin Brigade, heightened by the Rising experiences and my contact with Staines. Collins didn't come much generally in the picture nor take any very obvious responsibility for the general camp arrangements or policy. Looking back I would have to say that he probably confined himself, but very vigorously and attentively, to gathering together the threads of whatever IRB element there was in the camp, and preparing in this way to see that the IRB organisation and influence would be a very definite thing in the post rising political development in Ireland.

It is important to get a correct picture of the control situation in Frongoch. We will find that prisoners first went to Frongoch on the 9th June 1916. The batch from Knutsford arrived on the 17th June. At that time it is said there were about 200 persons in the camp. It is further said that before the north camp was set up the number in the south camp had risen to about 1,100.

Further dates that have to be kept in mind are the 26th June 1916, the date of the "Camp Orders" by Comdt J.J. O'Connell, commanding Irish prisoners of war. W.J. Brennan-Whitmore is associated with the order as Commandant and Adjutant. He had arrived with us from Knutsford nine days before, that is on the 17th June.

J.J. O'Connell* was one of the prisoners at Reading as recorded by Peadar(O'Donnell) on the 12th July. The following description of O'Connell from Peadar is a translation from page 129 of his *"Mar Mhaireas"* part one. "Ginger O'Connell is here also and is in great steam to direct everybody according to military ideas but he is not succeeding. He was the same way also in Richmond barracks but he found it difficult to make headway there. But Ginger is sensible and he did not go too far. He was trying to get us to understand in Dublin that we were prisoners of war and that therefore we should show respect to the officers (British) who came around, but when the question was put to him about the way in which Maxwell was carrying on and whether his treatment of the commanding officers of our army had been in accordance with the treatment of prisoners of war, he had no answer except to say "if they break the rules of war we should not imitate them". A good enough answer but it was not accepted. He himself however used to show respect to

* [J.J. O'Connell had been in the American army but returned to Ireland in 1914 when he joined the Irish Volunteers. He was on the GHQ staff in 1921, he supported the Treaty and subsequently had a distinguished career in the Army].

every officer (British) that came to us. He was a soldier and he conducted himself accordingly. There is no officer here who wants to make a matter of argument of it with him".

It is easy enough to understand how the first miscellaneous group of about two hundred prisoners with a man like John O'Mahony, no doubt the proprietor of O'Mahony's Hotel in Dublin, would set up an organisation based on messes and have a general council or civil government; and it is easy enough to understand that when people like Staines, McCullough, MacCurtain* MacSwiney** had arrived that they would make use of a man of whom they had such experience as O'Connell to set up a camp control on different lines. My earliest impression is that whatever kind of control there was within the first week or two of my being in Frongoch, there was a very placidly and generally accepted control, and that O'Connell was very active and very useful. He had been concerned with the original plans for the Rising in the Munster area, but in the circumstances of MacNeill's countermanding order and the non-arrival of the guns in Kerry, he had no part in the Rising. He could be regarded as being in the frustrated position that MacSwiney and MacCurtain in Cork were.

I had no responsibility of any kind in the earlier fortnight or so but I was in frequent and cooperative touch with O'Connell; one of the things he said to me during that period was that I appeared to have had established a great ascendancy over the Fingal men. I have no conscious recollection of there being anything like "civil government" or even a "military staff".

It is clear that the three weeks that elapsed between the 26 June and the 12 July, during which period apparently the North Camp was set up and M. W.O'Reilly appointed its commander, the

* [Active in Volunteers, was lord mayor of Cork when he was murdered by the Black and Tans in March 1920].

** [Active in Volunteers, teacher and lord mayor of Cork. He died on hunger strike in London. Dad had been his best man when he was married while under house arrest in England in 1919].

military staff personnel had largely been removed to Reading (jail), including O'Connell, and by the 16th or 17th July, M.W. O'Reilly, Commandant of the northern camp had gone there too. [M.W. was subsequently associated with Denis McCullough in the New Ireland Assurance Company]. It would appear that Michael Staines was the camp leader for the whole of Frongoch after that. It would have been in relation to such changes that I became the officer in charge of dormitory number three consisting of about 200 odd prisoners on the top floor of the distillery. I had plenty of work and responsibility to keep me going; the contacts and the acoustics of the camp were very good; I had the `closest hour-to-hour personal contact with Staines; and there were no matters to be discussed that had to be discussed at the level of anything like a military staff or a civil government's general council.

In the South Camp the whole working life of the place was directed to the dormitory leaders and the general plan and day-to-day direction of particular matters was ordered by Staines in counsel(sic) if necessary with the dormitory O/Cs. There would have been a regular series of camp orders and the arrangement of companies for company drill.

As far as the North Camp was concerned, each hut contained about twenty-five men and there was an officer in charge of each hut. I don't know who was the deputy in charge of it between the removal of M. W. O'Reilly to Reading about the 15th July and the latter part of August, by which time it was shut down.

In the remaining part of his account of Frongoch, Dad describes in some detail the organisation of the camp during the separate periods under different commanders and their "military staffs". He describes the movements of the men in and out of the camp, the early releases and the persistent attempts by the British to identify those who might be subject to conscription into the British army. He describes the recurring complaints and strikes which occurred as a result of disagreements with the camp's governor and his staff, troubles which simmered right up to the release of the remaining prisoners on the 23rd of December, 1916.

He differs strongly with Beaslai who inferred that a minority of the prisoners, who were seen to be fighting men and separatists, formed into a secret group to counteract the "timid and divided counsels" of the others.

He finishes his account with the following note about Collins:

> The period involves a certain number of stories general and personal, and calls for further reflections and discussions on the Collins activity in the camp. There were very many groups of kindred spirits in the camp, but I have no recollection of any group that made itself assertive (sic) or critical in any way of the camp controller or general camp organisation or activities. Collins was no doubt a very important centre of such a group or companionship as such. Based on a west Cork and an IRB centre, a distinctive group or part of his grouping would be the internees who were liable for conscription and some of their immediate friends, but in addition, he was very consciously pulling the threads of the IRB men together with a view to the situation which would develop politically and organisationally when all the prisoners, including the Lewes prisoners, were back at home and political life was beginning again in Ireland. The future politically in Ireland as far as organisation of the Volunteers or of political parties was concerned, was not a matter that got my concentrated thought in any way at that time; it was something that the future alone could take care of. I had no special group contact with Collins or those he was associated with and I never had any purely IRB discussions. I was apparently always accepted as an IRB man but was never 'involved'.

I have in my possession a "Universal" edition of the Works of William Shakespeare with three drawings dated 1916 by a T. McCartaigh. These drawings were done in Frongoch. They depict a Frongoch Siesta, three prisoners sleeping close together on the floor; a cell with a standing prisoner, described as a combined bedroom, diningroom, sittingroom and parlour; and a group of marching prisoners described as "Forward the Ration Party, Frongoch Camp". There are several signatures, including Tomás MacCurtain, Terence MacSwiney, Denis McCullough, J.J. (Ginger) O'Connell and Richard Mulcahy.

3.2 Return from Frongoch and Army Leadership

On his return from prison in Frongoch at Christmas 1916, Dad undertook fund raising for the Gaelic League in County Cork. He was there from March to August. He travelled the length and breadth of the county on his bicycle, including the Gaeltacht region of Ballingeary and Ballyvourney which he was so familiar with.

He was appointed commandant of the second battalion of the Dublin Brigade on his return from Frongoch but there was little volunteer activity during the early months of 1917. He was the principal organiser of the Thomas Ashe funeral in September 1917, immediately after which he was appointed the commandant of the Dublin Brigade. In September 1917 a meeting was held in the Keating Branch of the Gaelic League to discuss the setting up of Sinn Fein and Volunteer Executives. Present were a number of prominent nationalists and separatists, including Eamon de Valera, Arthur Griffith, Cathal Brugha, Sean McGarry, Michael Collins, Diarmuid O'Hegarty*, Michael Staines and Richard Mulcahy [1].

Shortly afterwards, on the 17th of October of that year, Dad became director of training in the newly established volunteer executive The volunteer executive was formed the day after the Sinn Fein executive was elected. There was a national volunteer executive, with 20 representatives drawn from the four provinces. De Valera was elected the nominal president. In addition, there was a smaller resident executive with Cathal Brugha as chairman, Six members from Dublin were co-opted to strengthen the resident executive, including four responsible for military affairs (1). They were:

> Michael Collins, organisation;
> Rory O'Connor**, engineering;
> Michael Staines, supplies;
> Richard Mulcahy, training.

* [O'Hegarty had been prominent in the IRB and IRA during the War of Independence, was a senior civil servant after the foundation of the state and his family was well known to us later when they lived in Brendan Road in Donnybrook].

** [Rory O'Connor was an engineer, He was an intractable opponent of the Treaty, a leader of the Four Courts garrison before the civil war, and was one of the four Mountjoy prisoners executed on 8 December 1922].

General Headquarters Staff, July 1921, by Leo Whelan.

Seated (left to right) Michael Collins, director of intelligence; Richard Mulcahy, chief of staff; Gearoid O'Sullivan, adjutant general; Eamon Price, director of organisation; Rory O'Connor, director of engineering; Eoin O'Duffy deputy chief of staff; Sean Russell, director of munitions,; Sean McMahon, QMG.

Standing: J.J. O'Connell, assistant chief of staff; Emmet Dalton, director of training; Seamus O'Donovan, director of chemicals; Liam Mellowes, director of purchases; Piaras Beaslai, editor of An tOglach.

Sean McGarry was appointed secretary of the resident group.

In March 1918, at the time of the conscription threat, the directors proposed the setting up of a general headquarters staff. This proposal was approved of by the national executive. Dad was appointed chief of staff [2]. The national and resident executives virtually ceased to function after the appointment of the GHQ staff. I do not have the names of the members of the two executives, apart from the names of the four directors who were appointed to quasi-military positions, and the names of the chairman and secretary. The formation and function of the volunteer executives is described by Dad in some detail [1].

Dad remained the military head of the army from March 1918 to the ratification of the Treaty in January 1922, and again from June 1922 at the beginning of the civil war to its end in May 1923 (except for the period from 13 July to 22 August 1922 when Collins was commander in chief).

The original GHQ staff appointed in March 1918 had the following members:

>   Richard Mulcahy, chief of staff.
>   Michael Collins, director of organisation and adjutant-general
>   Sean McMahon, quartermaster general.
>   Rory O'Connor, director of engineering and O/C Britain.
>   Dick McKee, director of training.
>   Austin Stack*, deputy chief of staff.(appointed but never acted)

By the Truce in July 1921 the staff had increased in number to thirteen. They were as follows:

>   Richard Mulcahy, chief of staff.
>   Michael Collins, director of intelligence.
>   Gearoid O'Sullivan, adjutant general.
>   Eamonn Price, director of organisation.
>   Rory O'Connor, director of engineering.
>   Eoin O'Duffy, deputy chief of staff.

* [Born in Kerry, a founder member of the Volunteers, Stack was associated with the failed landing of arms in Kerry in 1916. He was subsequently minister for home affairs in the 1919-1921 Sinn Fein cabinet and was strongly opposed to the Treaty but did not take part in the civil war]

Sean Russell, director of munitions.

Sean McMahon, quartermaster general.

J.J. (Ginger) O'Connell, assistant chief of staff.

Emmet Dalton, director of training.

Seamus O'Donovan, director of chemicals.

Liam Mellowes*, director of purchases.

Piaras Beaslai, editor of *An tÓglach*.

O'Donovan and Beaslai were appointed to the staff early in 1921. All the others and Austin Stack were named as being on the staff in the cabinet minutes of 25/11/1920. The nomination of Stack was not agreed by the GHQ staff. There are many references in the annotation and the tapes to the personnel of the GHQ staff during the period from the formation of the staff in March 1918 to the Truce in July 1921 [3-7].

In November 1920, on the night before Bloody Sunday, Dick McKee was killed when captured by the British. Mckee was a particular loss during this crucial period of the war.

Beaslai, in his biography of Collins, describes Mulcahy in several places as assistant chief of staff. Early in 1961, as I got more involved with Dad's writings and recordings, I called on Beaslai at the Catholic Commercial Club in O'Connell Street to question his reasons for describing Mulcahy as the assistant chief of staff. He replied that he thought Cathal Brugha was the chief of staff, an error which oddly enough appears in some of Collins' earlier correspondence. Brugha was, of course, chairman of the resident executive of the Volunteers and was never on the staff nor did he ever get involved in military activities after 1916.

Although Beaslai was the editor of *An tÓglach,* the clandestine organ of the Irish army, and he was a member of GHQ, his connection was almost entirely with Collins and the Vaughan's Hotel group. This group was made up of mostly IRB members who were with Collins on the intelligence side and who formed "the Squad", which was the active military wing under Collins's direction. Vaughan's Hotel was in Parnell Square and was a popular meeting place for Collins and his men. Many of the notices and articles which

* [Mellowes was born in England, and was a member of the Volunteers from 1913. He opposed The Treaty and was one of the four Mountjoy prisoners executed on 8 December 1922].

appeared in *An tÓglach* under the name of the chief of staff were written by Ginger O"Connell, Rory O'Connor or Dick McKee. Beaslaí told me at our meeting that he had little contact with my father during the war. As O'Muirthile states in his memoirs, he too was originally part of the Collins group but ultimately, when, as adjutant general and a member of the army council during the civil war, he came into closer contact with Mulcahy, he had this to say about him and the army council:

> The situation I stepped into then on 15 October 1922 was one of greater difficulty than I had expected - for the first time now I came into real association with two men I had never worked close to before, and outside of whose circle I had been up to then. I speak of General Mulcahy and General Sean McMahon. My school was that of Collins, O'Sullivan, Duggan, Boland, Tobin and others, and we were a happy carefree lot, who in the hardest of times could be found carelessly congregated at one or other of our various haunts. Collins was the 'boss' of a merry collection of subordinates. There was no side nor no aloofness or ceremony. Of Mulcahy and McMahon and their work, I knew practically all there was to know, but I had come to regard them as stern silent workers who scorned pleasure and frivolity and who had enslaved themselves to their respective tasks. My acquaintance with Mulcahy of course went back years, because through Gaelic League and Volunteer work we had occasion to associate. Sean McMahon I had known in more or less a distant way. Of the strenuous work he had been engaged in during the war with the British, when he so successfully received and delivered numerous consignments, large and small, of arms and ammunition at the Dublin Docks, I was well acquainted.

> As evidence of how false impressions and groundless opinions often lead to much mischief, I would like to say that had I remained in isolated and aloof subordination of these men, I might subsequently, as others did, regard them as a clique, and I too might have rebelled against their administration. In order to know men properly, you must live with them or work with them, and once I had begun to work and live within barrack walls with General Mulcahy and General McMahon, I realised the greatness of their outlook, their tireless devotion to their task,

and their fairness to all within the limits of their responsibilities. Their unqualified ardency and resolve to prosecute the task begun by Collins was ever visible. I settled down to work with them and we went through busy days and nights together, directing our respective departments throughout the day and sitting in council throughout the night, framing policy and regulations for an unorganised army (8,9).

Shortly after the Truce, Dad and my mother had afternoon tea in the Gresham Hotel. It was probably Dad's first appearance in public after being on the run. At the next table, they recognised the painter, Leo Whelan, who was with a priest. During the conversation with their two neighbours, my mother was inspired to suggest that Whelan should take the opportunity of painting the general headquarters staff while the truce lasted. Whelan apparently responded enthusiastically to the idea (10).

Hence the group portrait of the 13 members of the GHQ staff which is currently hanging in McKee Barracks. During the Truce and following the ratification of the Treaty, Whelan made individual portraits of each member of the staff. It was a busy time for Collins and Dad, and indeed for some of the others, and it was apparently with great difficulty that Whelan managed to get them all to sit. When he had completed the individual portraits, Whelan created the group portrait at a later date. The wherabouts of some of the individual pictures is known.

The group portrait measures five by nine feet. It was presented by me to the State in 1996 and will eventually hang as the centrepiece of the 1916-1921 section of the National Museum at Collins Barracks. It apparently had a chequered history. Little was known about its existence until it was exhibited at the RHA Exhibition shortly after the World War. Whelan hoped the government would buy it at the time. He was asking £1500 but there were no takers. It was exhibited again in the 1950s during the tenure of the second interparty government, but again no offer was made to buy it.

On the 11 March 1962, while talking to Dad and mother about the role of GHQ, I first heard of the picture when Dad showed me a short newspaper cutting which was published at the time of its second showing. I was immediately interested in seeking it out and offering to buy it if it was still available. With his usual efficiency, Dad contacted Whelan's two surviving sisters and within two days I had paid a visit to their house in Eccles Street. They were a rather prolix pair who were as faded and impoverished looking as the surroundings in which they lived. The picture too looked faded and neglected, straddled as it was across the top landing of the rather derelict looking five storey Georgian house. After much beating around the bush, they eventually mentioned the price they were seeking. I did not quibble, paid them a five pound deposit and, after my solicitor had drawn up an agreement, I had it moved to the Municipal Gallery of Modern Art. There the curator, James White, who showed a great interest in the picture, had it restored and hung it until he moved, with the picture, to the National Gallery a few years later.

Dad's appointment as chief of staff was proposed by the military directors who were members of the volunteer executive. It was subsequently approved by Cathal Brugha, the chairman, and the other members of the volunteer executive. Collins was the other nominee for the position but Mulcahy was preferred and the circumstances of the appointment were as described by Dad in his tape recordings and in his annotation, as follows:

> When on the night before the volunteer executive met to appoint the GHQ staff, the directors, about half a dozen of us, met at 46 Parnell Square to consider proposals to put before the executive, and when we had agreed that as between myself and Collins I would be the person recommended to the executive as chief of staff, McKee, as he came away from the meeting with me, expressed satisfaction and relief that Collins was not being recommended. The main reason for that was that in the light of what he knew of Collins's temperament, and the short period and the circumstances in which any information about him had been obtained, McKee - like the others - was a little bit wary of entrusting him with anything like complete control; in fact he did want time to disclose himself and his qualities, and even when so disclosed he was in a better position to use his energies and capacities over a number of concentrated and very important fields by a certain greater freedom of action as a result of his not being chief of staff and by the fact that I, as chief of staff, was in a flanking position of protection for him, and maintained complete and cooperative harmony in all our doings [11].

There were five active members on the GHQ staff at the time of its inception but this number had increased to 13 at the time of the Truce. Most of the new appointments were made towards the end of 1920 and the beginning of 1921, as the structure of the army became more formal, as the control of countrywide volunteer activity by GHQ increased and as the war became more intense. Other tapes and papers contain further details of the organisation and personnel of the GHQ staff from March 1918 to the end of the civil war [12-17].

During the war of independence decisions about the organisation and strategy of the Irish resistance were made by the GHQ Staff. Once the Irish volunteers adopted a more aggressive role towards the British police and military by the end of 1919, it was impossible for security reasons to hold formal meetings of the GHQ staff. By this time Dad met members of the staff individually or in groups of no more than three or four. His meetings with Collins provided the main focal point of army policy and organisation. And policy may have followed the various impulses which determined the progress of the war as much as giving a lead.

Dad talks about the role of the national and the resident executives of the Volunteers, set up in October 1917, as the political bodies controlling the army:

> The fact is that, set up as the GHQ staff was, on the eve of the practical development of the conscription issue, the only work that had to be done on the Volunteer side was actual military organisation, and the preparation of the Volunteer mind. The attitude of the Volunteers to the work of actual conflict was what had to be clarified and strengthened. Not only the general executive but the resident executive of the Volunteers had no function [after the appointment of the GHQ in March 1918]. On the military side this was strengthened by the fact that certain important members of the resident and general executive were members of the GHQ staff occupying the principal positions on it. The analogy between the cabinet and the GHQ Staff works the other way. Cathal as minister for defence, Collins as minister for finance and a member of the GHQ Staff, myself as assistant minister for defence and chief of staff, made it easier at that responsible level to feel that, while the work of the cabinet was

entirely distinct from the work of the GHQ staff, the work of the GHQ staff would be completely harmonised and subservient to cabinet outlook [18].

And he states:

> From the time the GHQ staff was set up, I kept in close personal touch with Cathal Brugha, who was the chairman of the Resident Executive, in practically the same way as I did later when he was the minister for defence, namely, I kept in complete touch with the civil representative of the Volunteer organisation until the Government was set up, and with the ministerial head after that. They were the same person.

And he states:

> I have suggested that from the time of the setting up of the general headquarters staff, the general volunteer executive had no particular function to discharge. The volunteer responsibility to the executive was fully discharged by the contact that I kept with Cathal Brugha, the chairman of the executive.
>
> When the Dail was established in January 1919 and a cabinet set up, apart altogether from the dovetailing of the personnel of members of the GHQ staff and the cabinet, and apart altogether from the fact that the minister for defence was the chairman of the executive of the Volunteers, and the head of the government the president of the volunteer organisation [Dev], the spirit in which the whole work was being pursued was that the GHQ staff and the army generally accepted the fact of government, and the authority of the cabinet and the expression of that authority through the minister for defence [19].

The role of the volunteer executive had largely atrophied following the setting up of the GHQ staff in March 1918. It was also likely that, for security reasons, meetings of the full general or resident executive would have been very undesirable following the Volunteers' change of policy to active aggression at the end of 1919. There was apparently one meeting of the resident executive in 1920 and one further meeting in 1921, which Dad refers to as follows:

I have in my mind the elements of the picture of the scene, but it was really nothing more than a formal coming together and looking at one another as a recognition, when the circumstances of the truce provided the opportunity, that there was such a thing as an executive of the Volunteer organisation. It had however completely atrophied, not only with regard to its function but with regard to any feeling that it existed; those who were active officers in the Volunteers throughout the country I'm sure never thought of it, and I'm sure that those who were not active volunteers throughout the country had no particular wish to think of it. There was probably expressed at the meeting full satisfaction and agreement as to the administration of the oath to the Volunteers in accordance with the decision taken by the Dail at its meeting on the 20th August 1919 [20].

By April 1919, when Cathal Brugha was appointed minister for defence, the political function of the general and resident executives was vested in the ministry and in the cabinet, such as it was. I have no information about the membership of either executive. The Sinn Fein standing committee did meet regularly during this time but, according to the minute books in my possession, no business of any political or executive nature was conducted by this body.

On the subject of the GHQ staff and of Mulcahy's functions as chief of staff, the following paragraph, based on material in his annotation on Beaslai's biography of Collins, was published by me in *An Cosantóir* [21]:

Each member of the GHQ staff had his own particular responsibilities of a full-time nature but it is clear that there was considerable overlapping in their work and in their contact with the army in the field. The circumstances of the time made it impossible to set up separate departments in a formal way, although by the spring of 1921 the different departments were clearly enough identified and demarcated to send in their own separate monthly accounts to the chief of staff's department. These accounts are now available in the University archives. Dad claims that the Volunteers were the hard core of the emerging political organisation of Sinn Fein, and he states that much of the organisation of the Volunteers in 1918 took place under cover of the by-elections of this time.

The war of independence could not have been sustained without the participation of the men in the field and without Michael Collins and his intelligence activities and widespread contacts in the country. Neither could it have taken place without the GHQ staff. They were the three points of the military tripod which supported the action against the British, and which lead to a Truce in July 1921.

Firstly, the achievements, initiatives, courage and sacrifices of the fighters in the field, particularly in Dublin, most parts of Munster, Longford and, to a lesser extent, in a few other scattered places, were such that, without these active men, no war could have taken place.

Secondly, Collins through his energy and talents, and assisted by his trusted men, provided an intelligence back-up and other essential services without which the central and peripheral units of the army could not have existed.

Thirdly, the GHQ staff, headed by Mulcahy and supported by such prominent figures as Rory O'Connor, Ginger O'Connell, Sean McMahon, Dick McKee, Gearoid O'Sullivan and others, provided a solid basis for an organisation which ensured progress towards a professional army with a good communications system, a structured command, a mature and ethical philosophy which must have been unusual in an insurgent army, and a commitment to parliament and to the will of the people [22-25]. The army's commitment to parliament was copperfastened by virtue of the fact that many of the army leaders, including Mulcahy and Collins, were elected to the first and second Dails [26]. Despite the work and influence of GHQ, as a body it maintained a low profile, which was probably essential for the survival of its members. This low profile is evident from the almost exclusive emphasis by the historians on Collins and the fighting men. It is understandable that Collins should dominate the history of the time from the historian's point of view because of his early death, his major political as well as his military role, his charismatic, flamboyant character, and the early publication of his biography by Beaslai in 1926, where no mention is made of GHQ.

C.C. Trench, reviewing my father's biography and referring to the development of the active service units, stated:

53

The main feature of the guerilla war - the use of mobile full time active service units and attacking soft rather than hard army targets - were not invented by the chief of staff but were devised perforce by the field commanders such as Liam Lynch. All Mulcahy did was to order others to do likewise [27].

This rather dismissive remark conceals a considerable degree of ignorance about the organisation and evolution of the Irish army. Many of the successful strategies which were adopted during the war of independence were, of course, initiated by those who were involved in the fighting in the field and who were face to face with the realities of the conflict. But the extension of these tactics to achieve an orderly strategy, the burning of the 300-400 police barracks, the organisation and training of the flying columns and the active service units - could not have taken place without the guidance and control of the GHQ staff. And this is not to mention a great number of other more mundane responsibilities which went to run a successful coordinated military campaign, such as the funding of the campaign, the divisionalisation of the army, the formation of companies, battalions and brigades, the appointment of officers, policies relating to spies and informers, the supply of arms and equipment, maintaining communications, and many other administrative, advisory and disciplinary procedures. This aspect of the war emerges clearly from the references quoted by Maryann in the Biography, and from a perusal of the extensive Mulcahy papers in the University archives.

Dad was by nature a "backroom boy", happiest when totally committed to a specific task of organisation, a characteristic which became more obvious as he got older. His commitment was to service, not only in his work as a soldier and a parliamentarian, but even in the smallest matters among his family and friends. He was not interested in power but, when thrust upon him, he was well capable of responding to it. Although he was elected to Dail Eireann in 1919, and did participate in some formal parliamentary activities, he devoted his entire attentions and energies to the army and its organisation during the period of the war of independence.

Like Collins, Mulcahy was on the run from the British authorities from January 1920 to the Truce in July, 1921, He had several narrow escapes from capture while staying in his various hideouts and he describes a few of these escapes in his annotation [28]. The following refers to a raid on his office in Paul Farrell's flat in South Frederick Street, which he had just left, leaving behind several incriminating papers:

> Paul Farrell used to do some acting in the Abbey Theatre and he now and then wore kilts. I say that they sent for bloodhounds and they gave them a smell of Paul Farrell's kilt and they sent them out on the roof to look for me. Meantime I was quite alright in UCD and just visited the cordoned area from the outside. It was a particularly difficult time for us. It would have been about February 1921.

He gives a list of his hosts and the 25 places where he did his office work, or where he slept at night during his eighteen months on the run [29]. He received food, hospitality and shelter from many courageous people during this difficult time, some of whom had no connection with the national movement, but all of whom showed intense loyalty to their fugitive guest:

> Sleeping accommodation was always to be an uncertainty; this October - November [1920 - RM] was a bad time; another bad time was to arise about March 1921 [29].

On another occasion he eluded capture by escaping on to the roof of Michael Hayes's terrace house on the South Circular Road and clambering from there into the house of a Jewish couple, who provided him with an early breakfast and advised him when it was safe to leave. His mode of transport was the bicycle, but it is not clear whether he always carried a revolver. On the question of being armed he had this to say:

> This question became really a problem in the latter part of the struggle. It wasn't a question easily settled.

and he continues by describing the following rather embarrassing experience:

> I ran into an awkward situation on one occasion when, being without a revolver, I went into one of our places in Westland Row, middle way in the street near the church, and on the church side. In the front room on the first floor, one of the QMG's young assistants named Harding had some kind of an office and I went

to him for a revolver; he gave me an automatic. I pointed it at the wall between two of the front windows and pulled the trigger; it went off. Harding just quietly said "You should come here oftener". However, with the noise of the traffic below, nobody came in from the next room to know what was up and I moved quickly away from the place - with lesson learned [30].

It was the critical security situation in Dublin in March 1921 that inspired the chief of staff and the GHQ members to decide on the divisionalisation of the army throughout the country. This was in case the GHQ staff might be wiped out, and the army in the periphery left rudderless, without coherent central control and coordination:

> The pressure in Dublin was such, that it was clear that there was no great security for the hope that we might be spared any further serious loss in the strength of the GHQ Staff or in the strong activists circle in Dublin; this led to thoughts for planning the divisionalisation of the country on the basis that there were very many areas in the country where the equivalent of a GHQ Staff could be set up, to maintain the morale and the initiative of the Volunteers in the area.

Despite his formidable reputation as a highly principled and unyielding head of the army, he was in private life an affable and friendly companion and colleague. He had little of the exuberance and public charisma of Collins, nor did he have Dev's aloofness and subtle detachment from his colleagues, attributes which are so frequently evident in the successful political leader. He did have the important ability as chief of staff to be totally committed to his task, and at the same time to freely delegate responsibility to his colleagues, and to encourage them in every way. As Collins's reputation advanced, so did the number of his critics, but Mulcahy was not one of these. His admiration for Collins is clearly and frequently expressed in his papers and tape recordings, and far from resenting Collins' increasing military and political reputation during the war, he did everything to encourage him in his multifarious activities, and to protect him from his critics.

3.3 The War of Independence: Army Policy

Mulcahy did formally direct the army during the entire period of the war. He was, as described by Maryann Valiulis, a forgotten hero in the sense that his reputation in later life had lost much of the shine it had during his military career. In an article *"The Lads who Freed Ireland"*(April 1922), and an article in *"Irish Indiscretions"*(1923), an American correspondent wrote of Dad's dominant role in organising the military resistance to the British, and referred to his outstanding qualities as a strategist [1]. He was responsible for army policy in the widest sense and for the activities and actions of the staff members and the commanders in the field. That is not to say that his colleagues on the staff and the commanders in the field did not play a part in formulating policy and in initiating action. His greatest and most seminal contributions, apart from his organisational role, was his insistence that the army should be organised on the ethical lines of a professional army, that unnecessary violence and killings should be avoided, and that the army must remain subservient to parliament and to the people.

His leadership was characterised by a policy of waiting and seeing rather than aggression, at least until the Dail was suppressed in September 1919 and war became inevitable. The earlier period was an important phase in the evolution of the Volunteers in the context of organisation and consolidation, as well as defensive policy.

P.S. O'Hegarty, in his *Victory of Sinn Fein* [2], writes:

> After 1916, there should not have been a shot fired in Ireland, nor a gun bought. They were totally unnecessary. We had the Sinn Fein policy, the men who made it, the enthusiasm and the support of the people. Without firing a shot we could have forced from England anything that we have forced from her by the gun policy, and more. We would at the same time have maintained our solidarity, escaped Partition, and avoided the irreparable moral disaster which has overtaken us [the civil war].

We discussed the justification for the war of independence and P.S. O'Hegarty's point that the war of independence contributed nothing to the advancement of Ireland's freedom [3,4]. Dad thought the O'Hegarty view was important but in his reply to my question he said:

> We have very very little conception of the forces that were
> operating in Great Britain at the time against this country.

He mentioned the Ulster Volunteers and the powerful Tory influence
supporting the Northern dissidents which led to Britain changing the rules
in relation to Home Rule in 1913. He mentioned the conscription issue and
the fabricated German Plot in 1918. He stressed the harassment of the Irish
political leaders as early as 1917 before the Volunteers were officially
reorganised in October of that year. Here he referred to Ashe's repeated
imprisonment for speaking in public about Ireland's right to freedom and
his death in prison in September 1917 from forced feeding as an example of
British intransigence. He held that the circumstances of British aggression
and harassment of the people and the members of the Dail was such that local
and eventually national reaction in terms of military aggression became
inevitable. It would be humanly impossible not to react to the cumulative
effect of British aggression which started as early as 1917, and which
continued for more than two years before the Volunteers adopted an active
policy of military resistance. Until the end of 1919, both the political head
(Cathal Brugha) and the military head (Richard Mulcahy) were committed to
a defensive policy on the part of the Volunteers, until the suppression of the
Dail in September 1919 was the final provocation [3]. The suppression of the
Gaelic League and the GAA about the same time was a measure of British
harassment.

He describes the British harassment, noted particularly during the Sinn
Fein loan campaign:

> Military and armed police breaking up meetings, suppressing
> newspapers, removing machinery, raiding individual people
> three or four times in one day, that is with persistency and very
> great pressure - it will be found that all this expresses itself in
> the daily papers of the time in spite of censorship, and in the
> pages of the official 'Irish Bulletin' [5].

> There were rather strong reasons why after the establishment of
> the Dail he (Brugha) would be strongly for controlling violence
> while keeping our powder dry; Cathal could very well, at that

time, be laying down principles encouraging the Volunteers to a sense of responsibility by the power, the duty and the function that was on them, and in the light of that power, seeking control and discipline and subservience to the Parliament.

In a local and spasmodic way, the violence of British agents in the country created individual occurrences in which there was bloodshed before September 1919. But it was when that tendency to violence by the British agents was crowned by the positive suppression of the Dail by the British Government, that the positive element of violence was introduced as a policy, to provide clearance areas in the country where the writ for the Dail could begin to run, and the smaller bodies of Volunteers, who were engaged in active hostilities, could have security and a certain freedom of movement [6].

On the question of the war, he maintained that the Volunteers, as late as the autumn of 1919, were still committed to their traditional defensive role, and that this policy was supported by the political as well as the military leaders. Indeed, strictly speaking, they were an apolitical force until the election of December 1918 [7]. A change to a more aggressive policy was brought about by the increasing harassment of the Sinn Fein leaders and the Dail by the police which I have already alluded to. And, although the conscription threat had passed by the summer of 1918, he believed that a more aggressive policy was inevitable, and was justified on moral grounds by the approbation of the Catholic hierarchy when they supported the anti-conscription campaign:

.... the Bishops' manifest(o) declared that 'The Irish people have a right to resist by every means that are consonant with the law of God.' Doctor McDonnell of Cork, lecturing to the Central Branch [of Fine Gael], made the point that this declaration gave the volunteers and their action the status and the justification of a national army under national control [8].

Dad deals with the defensive policy of the Volunteers and the change to a more aggressive approach at the end of 1919 in several tapes and in the annotation [3,6,9-17].

Dad was not infrequently criticised by battalion and field commanders for his prudence and conservatism, and what they perceived to be his undue caution in developing an aggressive policy. He was certainly a foil to the more flamboyant and aggressive approach of Michael Collins. For example, his condemnation of the Soloheadbeg episode contrasts with Collins's failure to condemn the action [18]. Collins states:

.... the fires of Easter Week,.... were blazing brightly again at Solohead, at Clonfin, at Macroom, ...

Dad says of Collins and the men who took part in the action that "Collins's attitude and manner would have been a comfort to them." However, the trust and friendship they shared were not impaired by such differences, as is apparent from Maryann's pages and from many of Mulcahy's papers, nor was Collins less concerned about the Army's reputation, despite his more tolerant acceptance of sporadic volunteer actions. Nor did Mulcahy object to any other action apart from the Soloheadbeg and Inishannon episodes, and in these cases his objection, and that of Cathal Brugha, was to the apparent cowardly and unnecessary loss of life [19,20].

He never expressed any reservations about allowing Collins to adopt such a prominent role in military affairs. I believe that, while he supported Collins in everything he did, his prudence and caution provided an important brake on the more impetuous people in the army. Without his control and the limitations he placed on what he perceived to be ill-judged, aggressive behaviour, or behaviour involving unnecessary risk, it is unlikely that the army would have evolved along such professional and ethical lines. It is also likely that the people of Ireland might have been less receptive and less supportive of the army's activities, particularly during the bitter days of 1920 and 1921. The shocked reaction of the people of Ireland to the Soloheadbeg episode would underline the danger of the population being alienated by excessive army aggression and brutality. It was a different matter when, later, the reign of terror was instituted by the British by the arrival of the Black and Tans and the Auxiliaries:

The decision to proceed with an active aggressive policy was taken in consultation between myself and the Minister for Defence, I imagine, but without any formal cabinet discussion, and it was discussed with the Cork people, and no doubt with

others in preparation for its extension in other parts of the
country for several weeks before Carrigtwohill* on the 4th
January 1920 [21].

The necessity for having a positive use of force policy was only
adopted under the compulsion of the suppression of the Dail in
September 1919. So engrained was the understanding of the
disadvantages of violence in the work that we were doing and the
message that we wanted to get across, that the new policy only
came into effective action and publicity with Carrigtwohill on
the 4 January 1920 [22].

In GHQ's contacts with the country, it was inevitable that some active and
independent spirits would take affairs into their own hands. This trend was
understandable in those areas where the British had been virtually cleared
out by the widespread destruction of police barracks. There were many
instances of peripheral impatience with the leaders in Dublin and this was
more evident in some areas than in others. Mulcahy refers, for example, to
the South Tipperary Volunteers who described GHQ in general and himself
in particular:

.... that GHQ representatives and particularly myself, were
mealy-mouthed in our instructions, both with regard to
sacrificing the lives of our own people, being careful not to keep
identity marks and even being careful in not unnecessarily
taking the lives of members of the enemy. In the whole of our
policy, these things were matters of conscience with us. They
were also matters of political expediency, they were also matters
with common sense and in accordance with the spirit in which the
Volunteers were first founded as a defence (force) [9,10,17,23-25].

His cautious attitude to unnecessary killings, even among the enemy, is
reflected in Dad's reference to "the Compton Smiths" in his speech during
the Treaty debate when he deplored the necessity of killing innocent men
during the war of independence. Major Compton-Smith was an Englishman
who was taken hostage and executed by the IRA when the British authorities

* [Carrigtwohill was the first of the many police barracks to be attacked and
destroyed].

refused to reprieve the death sentence on three Volunteers whom they had captured [26].

Another example of peripheral criticism is to be found in Sean Treacy's biography by Desmond Ryan [27] where, in referring to excessive Volunteer quiescence, Treacy comments about the disintegration that threatened the laboriously built-up Volunteer force. He is quoted: "If this is the state of affairs we'll have to kill someone, and make the bloody enemy organise us" [28]. Treacy, with Dan Breen, was involved in the killing of the two policemen at Soloheadbeg in January 1919.

When writing about the Volunteer policy of non-aggression, Dad gives a list of episodes in Dublin, Meath, Clare, and one or two in other counties which preceded the change to a more aggressive policy at the end of 1919 [29]. He mentions the shooting of a few detectives in 1919 [30]. None of these events were arranged by headquarters but were invariably initiated locally in response to local harassment. With one or two exceptions, they were subsequently approved by headquarters.

He had this to say on the matter:

> Some of the 'fighting spirits' would look at this kind of thing, coming from me, as being office-chair-and-table kind of business. I was saved from being too thin skinned about this by Diarmuid O'Hegarty's remark in certain circumstances that 'Mulcahy was the only one who came out of Easter Week with a military reputation.'

He also had this to say on the matter of prudence in conducting an aggressive policy:

> Our general hesitancy both as a matter of humanity and as a matter of policy to taking life or risking our own people's lives has been used in various ways from time to time to discredit the policy of offensive resistance after circumstances had demanded that it be embarked on and to imply disagreements in policy in respect of it. Desmond Ryan implied in his lecture (number 54) that Griffith was at variance with Collins and ourselves on the point; and Hayes-McCoy implies that there were similar disagreements on the part of members of Dail Eireann and

members of the Volunteer Headquarters, stating something like,
'In fact these bodies still share the public dislike of activities
which caused casualties to either side [31].

As one example of his prudence, he was requested to agree to a public
funeral for Michael Savage who was killed during the unsuccessful ambush
on the Lord Lieutenant, Lord French. He refused and defended this decision
on the grounds of security but he attempted to console Savage's colleagues by
stating his resolve that the British would be pursued to the end [10]. In the
same tape he states that the more ardent spirits were kept under control by
GHQ, "thus leading to much of the success of the Volunteers".

Apart altogether from the expressed opinion of Cathal Brugha
and others to the effect that the Volunteers could never be
anything but a threat to Britain, it would not have been
reasonable or useful to encourage an attitude of aggression as
long as the Dail was there for propaganda appeal purposes [32].

What can we deduce from the general evidence about relations between
headquarters and the country units? It is that, under the circumstances and
severe constraints of the times, and bearing in mind the total lack of
traditional military and political discipline among the people of Ireland up
to the early 20th century, there was a remarkably cordial and harmonious
relationship between country divisions and GHQ which manifested itself
progressively from 1918 to the end of the Truce in December 1921. It is
evident from the Mulcahy papers that country activities and pressures
required to be restrained at times and that headquarters held these powers
of restraint. It is evident that no action was ever disapproved of by
Headquarters, apart from the Soloheadbeg and Innishannon episodes in early
1919, actions which were not initiated by GHQ. Indeed headquarters'
acceptance of subsequent spontaneous country activities and innovations
may have been an important factor in ensuring a stable and cohesive
relationship between the Dublin military and political leaders on the one
hand and the country brigades on the other.

The Soloheadbeg incident was initiated by the North Tipperary brigade
without the approval of GHQ. Two policemen were killed without provocation
in the course of their routine duties when they were delivering explosives to
a quarry. It was unfortunate that the action occurred on that day of

celebration when the first Dail met. It was widely condemned and particularly evoked the condemnation of both Cathal Brugha and the chief of staff [33,34].

Dad discusses the event in detail when he states that "bloodshed should have been unnecessary in the light of the type of episode it was, ...", and "it pushed rather turbulent spirits such as Breen and Treacy into the Dublin arena from time to time, where their services were not required and their presence was often awkward." He described the effect the incident had on the Archbishop of Cashel:

> The effect on Dr Kinnane, the Archbishop of Cashel, who many years after told me that he had regarded Soloheadbeg as part of official policy and that after it he withdrew his mind from such things and concentrated entirely on the religious and the moral aspect of his responsibilities and work, when, later, a monument was being erected at Soloheadbeg to mark the episode, he intimated to those concerned that he did not wish any priest in his diocese to be associated with it, and that as far as the parish priest was concerned, into whose parish the President, Sean T. O'Kelly, was going for the occasion of the unveiling, he was to receive the President with all due courtesy but not to be associated with the official proceedings. Sean T had asked the Executive Council at the time [the second Inter-Party government] what action he should take in reply to an invitation to be present. The Executive Council told him that they had no advice to offer him. He went there [35].

Headquarters was apparently willing to compromise and to be tolerant of local intransigence but there is no doubt, as David Fitzpatrick states in his *Politics and Irish Life 1913-1921* [36] that central control by headquarters became more manifest as the war continued. On this subject Fitzpatrick wrote:

> During 1918 and 1919, however, headquarters began to show greater adeptness at directing and supervising the Volunteers [37];

and

Headquarters provided advice, instruction, a little equipment and a welcome sense of national togetherness. In return provincial units accepted the dismissal and appointment of commandants, provided the families of local influence were not seriously inconvenienced; and to some extent they modified their military activities to accord with headquarters' preferences [38].

The greatest source of conflict between GHQ and the provincial units during the war remained the shortage of arms However, Dad states that there is a general failure to appreciate the large part played by GHQ in imposing national policy on and in achieving control of the Army as well as creating a more formal military structure. The great amount of material in the University archives testifies to GHQ's increasing influence as the war progressed without at the same time impairing the initiatives and energies of the local units.

Many actions were initiated locally without consultation with GHQ, usually in response to local pressures, but such actions usually received the approval of headquarters because they conformed to the military and ethical policies of the Army and the Dail. Despite these local spontaneous actions, the documentary evidence available to us confirms that headquarters, through its policy of divisionalisation, through its control and integration of the destruction of the police barracks and tax offices, and of the activities of the flying columns, through its control of the appointment of divisional, brigade and battalion officers, through its effective imposition of discipline and ethical standards, through its regular distribution of orders on a wide variety of military and organisation matters, and through its responsibility for supplies and training, gave us an army which evolved in an orderly and disciplined way. The army's orderly evolution under the circumstances and difficulties of the time was little short of remarkable. Not the least of these difficulties was the size of the British Forces, which, during Lloyd George's intensified war in the Spring of 1921, were made up of Black and Tans, the Auxiliaries, the remnants of the RIC, and 80,000 British regular soldiers.

The Mulcahy papers contain a great amount of material in the form of communications between the GHQ Staff and the active units. The material testifies to the close and improving communication between the leadership and the army in the field up to and including the Truce. The material covered by the general orders also testifies to the same situation. For example, a perusal of GHQ general orders covers at random such subjects as recommendation about actions in military situations and in civil situations, advice about conducting correspondence within the organisation, the boycotting of the RIC, the medical treatment of the wounded, the seizure of arms by the enemy, the functions of the volunteer police force, emigration as a form of desertion, the organisation of the courts, the handling of women spies, the procedures as regards the death penalty, the treatment of deserters, association with the enemy, the management of records, the recognition of bravery, publicity, information to the enemy, purchase of war material, reprisals, etc.

The Valiulis biography underlines the important part the GHQ staff played in the evolution of the insurgent army and the subsequent army of the Irish Free State, an emphasis which is necessary in view of the general neglect by historians of the important and less obtrusive infrastructure which it provided and extended during the Anglo-Irish War. Without the stabilising influence and the prudent policies of the GHQ staff, sometimes resented by the fighters in the field, military initiative during the war could not have been maintained and expanded, nor would the subservience of the army to parliament and the people have been necessarily so certain if and when independence was achieved. Dad more than once underlined the control GHQ had over the country brigades, particularly in the later phase of the war when different areas of country activity were formed into divisions which were designed to be self contained in the event of the elimination of GHQ by the British forces [39].

Dealing with the relations between the various members of the staff, Dad refers to the excellent spirit which existed among them. There was never the slightest disagreement and the work dovetailed and interlocked in a satisfactory way _ "no suspicions, no withdrawings, no waste of time" and speaking of attitudes which prevailed about the shortcomings and failures of soldiers and politicians during the war of independence, he maintains that criticism was exceptional and recriminations were rare and unworthy.

It was obvious that Brugha became more involved with the army and its policies after De Valera's return from America [40] and that this was one source of Dad's problems which I deal with elsewhere [41]. It was probably Brugha's initiative and possibly that of de Valera that the attack on the

Custom House was organised shortly before the Truce in July 1921. There is no mention of the proposed action in the minutes of the Cabinet but at no stage in the entire period was there a mention of a military action in the minutes. Writing of the decision to attack the Custom House, Dad said:

> Certainly, the initiative for such an action at this stage did not come from the GHQ staff. I was fully in on the discussions in connection with the proposal. Mrs Kilkelly, sister of Colonel Moore, had a house in Fitzwilliam Street near the corner of Baggot Street. For some time I had been using a room on the hall floor as an office. The discussions on this matter, as far as I recall, took place in the back drawing room upstairs. Cathal Brugha and De Valera were present at the discussions, and my recollection is that they were there with me on the day of the attack on the Custom House, while we were standing by waiting to see what the result of the operation was going to be.
>
> I think that it is Nowlan [Prof Kevin, historian] who, in his lecture, points out that an action of this kind indicated a serious departure from previous policy on the part of the army. My feeling with regard to the destruction of the Custom House was the same as my feeling with regard to the sending of men to London with Cathal on an assassination policy - it was the feeling of being "dragged". There was no hesitancy on the part of the Volunteers in Dublin to undertake the job, nor was there any hesitancy at the level of the GHQ staff to pursue it or to argue against it in any way. Once the project had formulated itself in minds, whether inside or spanning the threshold of the cabinet, as in the case of London, the men were provided and unlike London, the job was done [42].

And he added:

> This article inevitably raises the question, whether the Custom House was not burned as a propaganda matter, however effective it might have been in dislocating the 'taxing departments', and the Local Government administration [42].

On another occasion, I had the following conversation with Dad

> **RM:** The burning of the Custom House was an action which you
> say was not initiated at GHQ staff, and, if it received approval
> from you, it was only because de Valera was keen about it. I take
> it then that it was de Valera initiated the idea of the Custom
> House. You say you weren't keen but you cooperated in the
> matter. In fact you and Collins and the people in the GHQ Staff
> must have had very little to do with it. Did you do anything about
> the planning of it?

> **R:** I had nothing to do with the planning of it. It was all in
> Traynor's* hands and the 2nd Batallion. I wouldn't say that
> Collins had anything to do with the planning of it. Collins
> would have been interested in it from the point of view that this
> was a kind of a blow that would affect the administration. I can't
> at all understand, if Collins was effectively interested in it,
> that the Active Service Unit and the Squad wouldn't be fully
> used in it [43].

Seventy men were captured in the Custom House action, including several
killed. The loss of such a large number seriously depleted the forces in
Dublin, and might have had catastrophic effects on the Dublin campaign were
it not for the early cessation of fighting with the Truce of July 1921.

Army/Sinn Fein Relations

The cabinet papers, stretching as they do from March 1919 to December
1921, contain only a few references to the army and then mainly to moneys
provided to the department of defence. There are four mentions of sums of
£1,000 and one reference to a grant of $1,000,000 but no other details to
explain the latter act of generosity. Dad was paid £350 annually but

*[Oscar Traynor, as commandant of the Dublin Brigade and successor to Dick
McKee, was in charge of the operation. I have seen Traynor's detailed description
of the planning of the action and its results in his private memoirs, *Oscar Traynor:
A Record of his experiences in the War of Independence*, which are unpublished
but are in the possession of his family].

officially he was paid as assistant minister of defence and not as chief of staff [44]. The army was referred to twice only during the 32 months of cabinet meetings and then only in connection with the proposal about its reorganisation in November 1921.

Dad provided the vital link during the war of independence between the GHQ staff and the representative of the political section of the movement, Cathal Brugha. Brugha was chairman of the resident executive of the Volunteers since its inception in November 1917, and, from April 1919, minister for defence in the Dail cabinet. Dad also kept in touch with Arthur Griffith and Eoin MacNeill, both of whom were important figures on the political side and with whom there was considerable mutual trust and respect. His contact, and that of Collins, with Brugha and Griffith in particular was an important factor in maintaining an agreed policy and an understanding between the military and the civil authority, although it must be apparent that the main thrust of policy came from the military.

It is sometimes suggested that there was a lack of understanding between the army and the political wing of the independence movement, and that the army acted as an independent and unauthorised force. My father would strenuously deny that any such dichotomy existed in the situation and he was highly sensitive to such assertions. There is a wide ranging discussion about the army/Dail relationship [45]. The following are only a few of the comments he makes on tape and in the annotation where he underlines the close association between army and the politicians:

> If there was any weakness in the situation, it could come from the fact that, so far from being too far apart and being autonomous of one another, the army chief, so-called, and the members of the Government had relations more closely dove-tailed into one another than would be normal between the heads of an army and the heads of a government [46] ;

and

> ....there was no clash of any kind either of thought or feeling or action between any of the members of the government or members of the parliament, and those who were conducting the Volunteer work, either at top or throughout the country [46].

If there was any other weakness in the situation, it was the depletion by imprisonment of the Sinn Fein leaders from 1918 to the end of 1920, when de Valera returned from America, and the ineffective role of the Sinn Fein standing committee and possibly the Dail cabinet. Cathal Brugha was the only formal political link with the GHQ staff, although he never appeared to attend the Sinn Fein standing committee and his department and the army were seldom referred to in the Dail cabinet minutes. He played little part in formulating military policy, apart from approving of Mulcahy's conservative approach to aggression up to the end of 1919, and the more aggressive policy subsequently. The Dail had no influence on the war - it rarely met and was also severely depleted in numbers - but Griffith and Eoin MacNeill, who were in close contact with Mulcahy during the hostilities, did not oppose the army in its policies. Dad attended the standing committee from October 1918 to March 1919, so clearly he had some contact with the residue of the Sinn Fein membership, and during this short period he was elected a member of the subcommittee to prepare a submission on Ireland's demand for independence for the forthcoming Peace Conference [47].

Nothing written by him of the revolutionary army could be construed in any way as suggesting disloyalty or an independent attitude on the part of the soldiers. In his later notes on Cathal Brugha he emphasises the close contact which existed between himself, as chief of staff, and Cathal Brugha, as the minister for defence. Perhaps Dad's attitude to the question of the army's relationship with the civil authority is best summed up in the following letter he wrote to Bishop Fogarty of Killaloe after the publication of P.S. O'Hegarty's book *The Victory of Sinn Fein* [48]:

> When you said on Friday that you were sending a copy of P.S.'s book to a few influential friends in America, I said that there was a comment I would like to make on it for their information, so that at least one very serious misrepresentation contained in the book would be offset to some extent. And the comment is this: one of the main things that it does is - it paints a picture that suggests that 'the greatest achievements of any Irish generation was brought about by a military terrorism in which a civilian government existed merely as a machine for registering military decrees and under which every argument, save the gun, was eliminated' [49] in a situation in which the 'political machine became a tool in the hands of the military side of the

70

movement so that in the end the whole thing was moulded by men who were incapable of regarding democratic government seriously only in so far as it could be manipulated or forced to do what the military mind wanted'.

We can only imagine that ordinary people reading the book will read that the 'military mind' is the general headquarters staff of the time, and that the 'political and democratic machinery of government' is the cabinet and the Dail.

If P.S's painting of the position is accepted as he has put it, it contains to my mind a very great danger to the State on some possible future occasion.

The fact is that his painting of the situation is entirely wrong, and the inferences that ordinary people would draw from his painting, if anything, more wrong. I feel that it is of very great national importance that the names of the old members of the GHQ staff should not be invoked by some future decade or generation to show that national progress can only be made in any doubtful national situation by taking the 'Civilian Government' by the throat. It is my personal opinion that no group, pre-Truce, realised the necessity for building up and making as effective and as prominent as possible our Civil Departments than did the individual members of the General Headquarters Staff. And no people suffered more by the more or less ineffective work of some of those departments than did the General Headquarters Staff and the Volunteers generally.

I have told P. S. O'Hegarty, with whom I discussed the matter, that the time has not yet come when it is either desirable for some of us to "look back", but that I personally have a considerable lot of material that would support this latter statement of mine, and would give the lie to the very serious suggestion of his that I refer to.

For instance, I attach for your Lordship's information a copy of a letter sent by me on the 4th of June 1921 to Cathal Brugha, the Minister for Defence, which is typical of our attitude on this

matter. I have papers to show that the Military Authorities felt
it was not right that civilians should be tried by court-martial,
that the work should be done by the Home Affairs Department -
that the Military Authorities saw danger in "allowing people to
feel that the Defence Department was, perhaps, trying to run the
Government" in connection with matters that should have been
done by the Local Government Department, and where we
considered that the prestige of the Local Government Department
itself demanded that they should do particular work. The papers
dealing with the organisation and development of the police, and
police work, show a very serious attitude towards civil
administration on the part of the military authorities, and a very
irresponsible one on the part of the civil departments.

In May, 1921, the military authorities made complaint of the fact
that there was no conception of any organisation extra-military,
and that military work was suffering as a result of that fact. And
in the autumn of 1921 the position was such that I asked of one
of our senior officers that he crystallise into a memorandum, for
the information of the Dail Cabinet, the disabilities and the
weaknesses that the military organisation suffered under
through the absence of effective civil administration for a large
number of matters that were proper to be dealt with by the civil
authorities*.

It is absolutely untrue that the guerilla warfare was not fully
approved of by the Volunteer Executive and by the Dail Cabinet.
It must be perfectly obvious that there was good reason why it
should not be publicly made clear that the Dail Cabinet was
responsible for the guerilla warfare. Members of the Dail
cabinet had to take public action, and be in public, in
circumstances that very often involved arrest, and we could not
send the members of the Cabinet into their captor's hands with
a rope tied round their necks, as would have been the position if
it had been in any way publicly made clear that they held
themselves responsible for the conduct of the War. The
published report of the Dail Proceedings for 1919 and 1921

* [This was one of the factors which led to the disagreements between Mulcahy
and Collins and the Dail minister in charge of home affairs, Austin Stack].

72

showed that the Dail supported the Volunteers by monies, and imply entire support of their action. At the very first private meeting of the Dail, after the public meetings in January 1919, I, personally supplied a report on the condition of the Volunteers at the time as Minister for Defence. There was no explicit authority from the Executive of the Volunteers to do so, but the implication must be accepted as the Volunteers put themselves at the disposal of the Dail once the Dail was elected. The proceedings, however, do not report that such a report was made.

O'Hegarty's statement with regard to Griffith's attitude to the military mind is utterly misleading. I was, personally, in the most close contact with Griffith and there was a very great sympathy and understanding between the two of us - and O'Hegarty's whole representation of Griffith's last days are utterly absurd and untrue. It is worth mentioning too that O'Hegarty, who considers that a shot should not have been fired after 1916, was of the opinion in February or March 1919, when we called off the reception for de Valera at Mount Street Bridge after his escape from Lincoln, and the release of the other prisoners there, because of a Proclamation issued and action intended by the British Military Forces in Dublin - O'Hegarty considered that our calling off of the reception was 'the biggest blow that Ireland had ever received since O'Connell called off his Clontarf Meeting and was, in fact, a much bigger blow than that'.

To deal adequately with the points I touch on would take a very deep going into certain matters, but what I have said will, perhaps, serve some kind of offset to some of his statements.

Dad complained that the Volunteers were caught up in matters which rightly were the responsibility of the department of home affairs and other civil bodies [50,51]. He attributed the military involvement to the fact that the Volunteers were the only body with any semblance of an organised structure, and that, up to the end of 1919, while the army was maintaining a defensive role, members of the army were available to deal with civil matters. Their involvement, according to him, led to "certain weaknesses on the civil administration side" [50].

The IRB and the Army

The role of the IRB during the war of independence is a subject of controversy. The IRB, with Brugha, spearheaded the revival of the Volunteers as early as November 1916 after the Rising [52] and was an important influence during the war. Its members were active in the Volunteers and in particular they were associated with Collins in his military and intelligence work. However, it is emphasised in the Mulcahy papers that the council of the IRB, and the leaders of the IRB as such, had no part to play in formulating military policy during the war [50,53-58]. Military policy, whether it was arrived at electively or in response to circumstances, was formulated by the leaders of the Volunteers and approved by Brugha representing Sinn Fein and parliament, and not by any other group.

Dad was conscious and appreciative of the part the IRB members played in Collins's intelligence work before and during the war of independence, and in establishing communication channels with the country forces and with contacts in Great Britain. As far as I can ascertain from his papers and recordings, Dad had no formal contact whatever with the IRB during the entire period from 1913 to 1924, although he was always thought of as an IRB man, even as late as 1924. His remoteness from the Brotherhood is apparent from the conversation he had with Sean MacEoin about the IRB on the telephone which is recorded on tape [57,58]. Unfortunately it is difficult to understand MacEoin's contribution to the conversation because his voice is poorly transmitted on the phone.

However, it is clear from Dad's responses to MacEoin's comments that the IRB was alive and well up to the time of the mutiny in 1924, and that Dad was unaware that both Sean McMahon* and Sean O'Muirthile, who were on the army council during the civil war and until they were sacked at the time of the mutiny, were also leaders of the IRB. They were attempting to resuscitate the Brotherhood "to further the national and cultural aspirations of the country", whatever that may mean. Dad at all times in his papers denies that the IRB had any significant presence during the war and immediate post war years. It is likely that, because of his unique position as political and military head of the army, those members of the IRB who were closest to him

* [Active in IRB and IRA during the war of independence, chief of staff during the civil war after Collins's death and sacked by cabinet at time of army mutiny].

were reluctant to inform him about their connection with the secret organisation nor was such a revival by the senior officers of the Free State army in any way a sinister development in relation to the new state or the role of the army in defending the state.

The following is a note he makes about the role of the IRB. It is a good example of Dad's propensity as he got older to indulge in long sentences and metaphors!

> The secret organisation remained as a kind of humus in the political ground on the one hand, and on the other it was the core of the kernel of the intelligence organisation effectively built up by Collins and controlled by him, that disrupted and outwitted the secret service, destroyed its murder arm, and on the other hand, manipulated the machinery that so controlled the "water ways" that De Valera could be brought from Lincoln to Ireland and then to the United States and then back home again, and was the basis of the security which prevented the country ever having to feel that either its parliament or its executive government had been destroyed by enemy action [59].

3.4 The First Dail and Sinn Fein

Dad had little to do with politics up to the time of the ratification of the Treaty although he had been a member of the Dail since its inception, and minister for defence in the Dail cabinet from January to April 1919. He was appointed assistant minister for defence on Dev's return to the cabinet in April 1919 and remained so to January 1922 although at no time did he attend cabinet meetings.

Dad was one of those chosen as a candidate for the first Dail in December 1918 but his choice was made only at the last moment when the chosen candidate for Drumcondra/Clontarf constituency, Harry Boland, was transferred to his home constituency, Roscommon [1]. Dad was at the time a second year student of medicine at University College Dublin, as well as being chief of staff, but as his staff duties increased during 1918 he was obliged to abandon a medical career. His success against the Parliamentary Party candidate could be partly attributed to his fellow students who came out in force to canvass and speak on his behalf. His contact with University College was important subsequently because one of his offices and an important retreat for him when he was on run between January 1920 and July 1921 was the department of physiology at Earlsfort Terrace.

Dad was the last of ten speakers at a Sinn Fein election meeting in the Mansion House. In a report afterwards P.S.O'Hegarty, writing of him, said "the last speaker would have been interesting but he spoke in a monotone."

Dad made some comments on the occasion of the fiftieth anniversary of the first Dail meeting The text is fairly characteristic of his last few years in that he is wordy, allusive, and tortuous in his allusions and metaphors. Nevertheless, he deals in considerable detail with the significance of this first meeting of a native and democratic parliament, particularly in terms of the wishes of the population, the rejection of British control of Irish affairs by the people, and their willingness to face up realistically to British aggression. He goes on to say how the meeting marked the beginning of a process which had its successful conclusion in the Truce agreement in July 1921. At all times he emphasises the crucial role of the people. He obviously and perhaps a little naively attributes to "the People" sentiments which reflect his own strong democratic idealism [2,3]. Dad talks about the achievements and triumphs of the first Dail [4].

He describes in detail the transferring of power from the standing committee of Sinn Fein to the Dail in January 1919 and the procedures and meetings whereby this process was brought about. Committees were formed for specific tasks, such as the preparation of a declaration of independence, and a group to visit London to influence the representatives of other countries to support the Irish cause in the peace negotiations. He provides the names of the members. A liaison group (Mulcahy and Harry Boland) was, at Dad's suggestion to the standing committee, organised to protect political meetings from British police and army aggression, and to press for the release of the german plot and other prisoners after the overwhelming success of Sinn Fein in the 1918 general election.

He talks about the democratic programme which he proposed in the Dail, and Griffith's very positive response to the policy it contained. This programme was drawn up by members of the Labour Party (Thomas Johnson and William O'Brien) at the behest of Sinn Fein [5]. Griffith saw in this programme support for his own belief in the innate qualities of energy and talent of the Irish people, whatever their religion, politics, or gender.

Much of what Dad records is redolent of his own idealism and political philosophy when he talks about the Irish people and their struggle for independence [5,6]. He refers to Pearse and to his support of Home Rule in 1912, and to his change of outlook by 1916, a change Dad attributed to the fact that the Irish Parliamentary Party followed the British rules during the years of the Home Rule movement, but that, when the Irish were about to achieve their political objectives, the British changed the rules. He likens the thrust towards independence to a river which becomes turbulent when it meets the turning tide at the estuary. This is one of his most sustained metaphors and he continues to rely on it for several sentences.

He finishes this subject by referring to the meeting of the full Dail in April 1919, made possible by the release of all the prisoners in early March, after the escapes of Dev, McGarry, Milroy and Barton from jail. The full Dail met on the 1, 2, 4 and 10 April, 1919, and was followed by a Sinn Fein Ard Fheis on the 11th [2,3].

Apart from his attendance at the infrequent Dail meetings and his participation in certain formal political activities, such as attending the American delegates to the Peace Conference while they were in Ireland [7], formally proposing the democratic programme when the Dail first met in January 1919, and proposing, with Sean MacEoin*, Dev as President of the Dail in August 1921, he was totally absorbed in his military responsibilities. He claims that he had little knowledge of the intricacies of the political situation from the time Dev came back from America in December 1920 to the time of the Truce in July 1921 because he was so heavily committed to the organisation of the army. He also was sufficiently removed from the political scene during the Truce in the autumn of 1921 to be able to say that he failed to appreciate the longterm implications of the rift which was occurring between the leaders at this time [8]. However, he was obviously a close observer of the political as well as the military scene if one is to judge from his writings and his papers. Because of his intimate contact with the revolutionary movement and its principal architects, and

* ["The Blacksmith of Ballinalee" famed for his military exploits as commandant of the Longford Brigade during the war].

his unique collection of papers, he may well have been the most authoritative and knowledgeable to have survived the period. Many of his associates thought that he was the survivor of the war of independence and civil war best qualified to write about these turbulent times [9].

Sinn Fein

The original Sinn Fein organisation was established in 1905 by Arthur Griffith, with the dual monarchy as his constitutional solution to Ireland's aspirations for self determination. Its precursor was the Irish National Society of London. Its early history is dealt with by my mother and father in discussion [10,11]. The post-1916 party was established in October 1917 with the coming together of a number of individuals and organisations with nationalist aspirations. It had a constitution which included a most complex system of committees and councils which need not be described here, except to say that its standing committee was the only body which met regularly before, during and after the war of independence and which was responsible for conducting the regular business of the party. Its annual convention or Ard Fheis met each year except for 1920 and was the party's legislative body. Students interested in the history of Sinn Fein and its evolution will find a detailed description of its post-Rising structure in Michael Laffan's *The Resurrection of Ireland: The Sinn Fein Party 1916-1923* [12].

It might be appropriate at this stage to record some of Dad's views of the part Sinn Fein played, through its standing committee, in the struggle for independence between 1917 and the Treaty. He refers to Sinn Fein frequently in his tape recordings and the annotation, confirming the apparent indolence of the political wing of the movement during the period of the War. He refers to the constitution of Sinn Fein [13,14] and to its influence on the Treaty issue and the ineptitude of its members in dealing with the divisions which occurred following the ratification of the Treaty.

According to Dad, Sinn Fein and the Dail had little effect on the struggle against the British, apart from some of its individual leaders. The Volunteers were the only organised body which was effective and without them the courts and other services organised by the Dail could not have functioned [15].

Wherever the political strength of the people came from in the country, it apparently did not come from any drive from on top of the purely political organisation [16].

I have in my possession two Sinn Fein minute books [17]. These were given to my father by Paidin O'Keeffe. O'Keeffe recorded many conversations with my father [18]. He was the paid secretary of Sinn Fein and continued in that capacity during the war, except for his year in prison from March 1918 to March 1919. The first book records the seven page proceedings of the eighth annual congress at 6 Harcourt Street on 4 October 1912 with Arthur Griffith in the chair. There were 23 further meetings of the national council up to and including the 10 July 1913. The minutes of the first meeting were unsigned but the subsequent meetings were signed by Arthur Griffith, Constance Markieviez or Jenny Wyse Power.

The second book includes the minutes of the standing committee of Sinn Fein from 5 June 1919 to the 24 March 1922. The committee had 78 weekly meetings during this latter period but, according to Dad and Paidin O'Keeffe, its main characteristic was its low key activities and its concern with minor matters of detail rather than matters of policy or organisation [8,9,13,19,20]. At times Parkinson's law prevailed. It had no semblance of the functions or powers of an executive body of a dominant political party. It was unwieldy because of lack of clear leadership. The meetings during the war up to the Truce were mostly brief and poorly attended, and were suspended entirely from November 1920 until February 1921, after Dev's return from America.

The attendances after Dev's return improved greatly and the proceedings lasted longer. However these meetings were not concerned with any political matters of great import, apart from approving the nominations for the 1918 election and making the necessary arrangements to transfer some of its functions to the first Dail which met in January 1919. Certainly Dev kept all political matters to himself. The army and the military were not mentioned once during the entire 78 meetings nor did Cathal Brugha, who had been a member of the standing committee, attend any meeting from March 1919 until 22 March 1922. At the meeting on 22 March 1922, he acted as proxy for the joint honorary secretary, Austin Stack, and may therefore have resigned from the committee and simply confined his business to the cabinet. Brugha had attended eight meetings up to March 1919. [The minutes of the standing committee before 5/6/1919 are available in the National Library - RM]. Apropos of his earlier attendances, O'Keeffe said "(I) never saw Brugha doing anything except attending meetings of the standing committee and saying nothing." and "....but Cathal had no work to do, he never did anything."

From March 1919 onwards the cabinet of Dail Eireann obviously assumed many of the political functions of the standing committee of Sinn Fein. It is not surprising therefore that few matters of a political nature were on the standing committee agenda nor is it surprising that Cathal Brugha failed to attend being a member of the cabinet from January 1919. His department's affairs were clearly a responsibility of the cabinet. Throughout the 21 months up to December 1921, when 115 meeting of the cabinet had taken place, the army was never discussed except twice in relation to the its proposed reorganisation in November 1921 [21,22] nor was the department of defence mentioned except to confirm financial support on a few occasions. Brugha continued his business activities and he refused his salary of £500 as minister for defence [23].

Neither was much else of a significant political nature discussed at cabinet, at least if one is to judge by the records of the meetings. Attendances were only mentioned at later meetings during the Truce and opinions were never voiced. There was some discussion about the early negotiations between Dev and Lloyd George [24] and about the appointment of the plenepotentiaries [25] but how much these meetings influenced de Valera is impossible to measure. I expect that, like the Dail, the cabinet rubber-stamped most of Dev's proposals.

A few conclusions may be reached from a perusal of the standing committee and cabinet papers. Firstly, it seems that Dad had little conception of the activities of the cabinet while he was beavering away organising the army. Despite his appointment as assistant minister of defence he never attended cabinet meetings nor do I think that he was ever informed of the meetings or of its proceedings. During the three months from January to April 1919, when he was minister for defence, there was only one cabinet meeting and that was only just before the reshuffle in early April when Dad was replaced by Cathal Brugha as minister.

Secondly, I believe that Brugha was not greatly involved in political or military activities, at least until Dev's return from America in December 1920, but following this date his presence as minister gradually became more intrusive and on some occasions his actions as minister were inappropriate. Thirdly, it seems that Dad was not the only one to be remote from cabinet activities. The entire military campaign up to the truce seems to have been little influenced by the cabinet or by the Sinn Fein party.

One can understand the contention by Dad and by Beaslai that the army provided the major and probably the only effective role in the fight against the British and that the absence of the available cabinet leaders from the standing committee, with the exception of Griffith and Stack, reduced the influence of Sinn Fein. Of Austin Stack O'Keeffe said "Of course Stack was not capable of doing anything." [19]. He implied that Stack had the Casement cloud on his mind since the Kerry debacle at the time of the Rising.

The small attendances and the rather trivial matters dealt with at earlier meetings of the standing committee were not surprising in view of the president's absence in America. However, despite Dev's presence at most of the later meetings, no matters relating to the Truce, Treaty and the Treaty disagreement were raised. It confirms that de Valera kept things close to his chest, at least from the organised Sinn Fein party. It is not surprising that during one conversation Dad complained about Dev's failure to keep him and his staff informed of political progress during the Truce. Elsewhere Dad implies that Dev's only confidante and advisor was Erskine Childers. One would expect that Collins would have kept Mulcahy up to date on political matters during the Truce and immediate post-Treaty period. Whether he did is not clear nor is it clear that he met Dad during his many visits to Dublin during the Treaty negotiations. I suspect that Dad was too absorbed in army matters to concern himself with political developments at the time, nor do I think that Collins was particularly communicative with him as Collins drifted out of army activities coming up to the Truce of July 1921.

Dad was in full agreement with O'Keeffe that the standing committee had little influence on matters of political, social or economic importance. One of the subjects on its agenda was the Belfast boycott [26]. According to O'Keeffe he as secretary of Sinn Fein had the unwelcome task of being involved in organising the boycott. The boycott was supported by the Dail cabinet and apparently by Griffith and Collins. Griffith's support is surprising and seemed a lapse of political judgement but according to

P.S. O'Hegarty's view expressed in his *The Victory of Sinn Fein* [27] Griffith supported the measure and was influential in opposing some of his Dail colleagues who were not in favour of the boycott. It is perhaps less surprising that Countess Markievicz, the minister for labour, declared in the Dail on the 17 August 1921 the she had taken charge of the boycott earlier in the year and that since then the work was going forward well. She refers to the twelve organisers and the 400 committees under her control, and said "it was almost impossible for a Belfast merchant to sell a pennyworth of goods in any part of Ireland."

The cabinet first discussed the subject on the 13 November 1920 when it proposed the setting up of a Belfast committee under the control of Michael Staines to direct the boycott. There is no evidence that any member of the cabinet, including Arthur Griffith and Michael Collins, were opposed to the boycott, but the cabinet records are scanty and do not mention the names of those who attended nor do they include the discussion which ensued. Nevertheless, it is likely that O'Hegarty was correct in his view. It is difficult to believe that they would have proceeded with the campaign against the wishes of Griffith who was then acting president.

The boycott was mentioned again in the cabinet on the 21 October 1921 [28] and there appears to have been no objection to its continuing. It was finally suspended by agreement between Collins and Craig [29]. It was originally imposed in response to the vicious attacks on Catholics in Belfast in July and August 1920. The boycott had a hugely divisive effect on relations between North and South, and apparently was a factor in influencing many loyalists in favour of partition who were initially uneasy about this British solution of the Irish problem. I have no idea if Dad supported the policy or had any thoughts about it at the time but he had this to say about it in 1961:

> The opportunity for disorderly interference with the goods of
> others and for pillage afforded by the boycott was an important
> element for detonating irregularism, which probably brought all
> the robbers over on the side of the anti-Treaty forces. A book
> was published "*The Green Fool*" (I think) which gave a rather
> lurid account of civil war robberies in story form; and there was

a whole area around Ferbane and the Shannon which earned a notorious name. The Belfast boycott was a very disturbing influence of this kind, particularly in the civil war days. Even in pre-truce days it may be found to have encouraged 'commandeering' by reasonably disciplined volunteer units [30].

The failure of the standing committee to have a meeting between October 1920 and February 1921 during and after the Clune truce initiative* suggests that it had little part to play in political matters [9]. The February meeting was only convened because of de Valera's return from America. It may be that political initiatives were confined to the members of the Dail cabinet who were still in Dublin or perhaps solely to Griffith as acting president, and to Collins after Griffith's imprisonment in November 1920. The cabinet papers of 30 November and 18 December 1920 refer to peace negotiations and on the second date the matter was left in the hands of Griffith. The Clune negotiations failed in December 1920 but from that date up to the Truce of July 1921, there were recurring background activities through various unofficial channels aimed at a truce. During this time de Valera was granted immunity from arrest by the British in the hope of providing an effective link on the Irish side, and it is also believed that this immunity was granted to Collins in the later months of the war.

Apart from his regular weekly contact with Cathal Brugha, the chief of staff and the army had little contact with the Sinn Fein party, and were little influenced by the politicians in terms of army policy. Dad was apparently sufficiently reassured and comforted by his close contacts with Arthur Griffith and Eoin MacNeill, who approved of the army policies during the war, and who were supportive of the decision to adopt a more aggressive policy after the suppression of the Dail in September 1919, and the earlier suppression of the GAA and the Gaelic League. Dad makes many references to the relationship between the army and the civil authority as represented by Sinn Fein initially and later the Dail [4,28,31-36]. There was considerable overlapping in personnel between the two bodies, with six of the 13 members of the GHQ staff members of parliament in July 1921, and with Collins and Mulcahy having cabinet responsibilities. In Dad's case these responsibilities were nominal. At no time from March 1918 to the Truce in July 1921 was there any evidence of disagreement between the

* [Archbishop Clune from Australia was sent to Dublin by Lloyd George in November 1920 in an attempt to arrange a truce].

military and civil authorities, although, in effect, the military provided the main national initiative, at least until de Valera's return at Christmas 1920.

Dad also underlines the little influence the Dail had during the struggle [15]. From its inception in January 1919 to the Truce in July 1921, it had only met on a few occasions, and was without its priomh aire (Dev) for 19 of its 30 months and was usually severely depleted of members, who were either in jail or on the run.

While there was no obtrusive political influence apparent in the formulation of army policy or tactics up to December 1920, when Dev returned from America, the situation showed a distinct change at this juncture [37]. Dev was initially critical of army policy after his return, although he got little support for his views either from the army or the Dail. However, the year from January 1921 to the ratification of the Treaty in January 1922 saw a good deal more involvement by Dev and Brugha, although this involvement had little effect on the work of the army. An example was the sacking of the chief of staff on two occasions by Brugha during the Truce [8] which, under the circumstances of the time, was an academic gesture and would have received no support from either politicians or army leaders.

3.5   The Truce

The Mulcahy biography makes a valuable contribution to our knowledge of the six months period of the Truce. It underlines the difficulties which were created for the army in general and for the chief of staff in particular during this time. The frustrations, antagonisms, and personality clashes during this uncertain time contributed, in Maryann's analysis, to much of the divisions which were to occur after the Treaty was ratified. It would be hard not to agree with Maryann's views about the adverse influence of the circumstances created by the Truce. However. Dad qualified this opinion when he claimed that the Truce period would have had little adverse influence on subsequent events if Dev had not so promptly and savagely attacked Griffith and Collins after the Treaty agreement had been signed in London.

Brugha's antipathy towards Collins commenced towards the end of 1920 and worsened during the following year. It was sustained during the Truce although what was equally important from the point of view of the

left to right: Sean MacEoin, Richard Mulcahy, Sean Moylan, Eoin O'Duffy.
Truce 1921.

relationship between some members of the Cabinet and the GHQ staff was the less obvious antagonism between Brugha and Mulcahy. This subject is dealt with in some detail by Maryann and it is almost certain that Brugha's antagonism to Mulcahy was related not only to Mulcahy's determination to protect Collins from Brugha/Stack criticism but also to his resentment that the army's unique role in bringing about a Truce was so clearly in the minds of the people, and to the obvious public perception that the army leaders were the outstanding figures in achieving British recognition of the Irish demands.

Dad deals in considerable detail with the conflict which developed between Brugha and Stack on the one hand and Collins on the other [1-3]. This conflict inevitably led to the wider division which developed between some members of the cabinet and the army leaders and which became more manifest on 25 November 1921 when de Valera at a cabinet meeting attempted, without success, to found a "new army". All members of the GHQ staff attended the cabinet meeting by invitation. The main purpose of the exercise appeared to be the attempt by Brugha and Dev to have Stack appointed to the staff. In the words of Dev, Stack would hold a watching brief for the minister of defence, Cathal Brugha. Such a reason was unlikely to appeal to the chief of staff and his colleagues.

The members of the staff resented Dev's intrusion, having little confidence in Stack as a suitable addition to the army leadership. Each member of the staff expressed his opposition to the proposal and they left behind them an irate president who shouted after them "Ireland will give me a new army" (4-7). The resentment of some of the staff was such that both Eoin O'Duffy*, the assistant chief of staff, and Liam Lynch, the senior commanding officer in the South, sent letters of resignation to Mulcahy in protest at Dev's intrusion. Needless to say, their resignations were ignored by Dad and the cabinet (8). Sean Russell, who was soon to become passionately anti-Treaty and to continue his military struggle for a republic long after de Valera's new constitution was adopted in 1937, said to Mulcahy after the meeting "I didn't think that there was a man in the country who would speak to my chief [Mulcahy] like that" (9). Russell had been appointed director of munitions on the GHQ staff late in the war of independence. His later IRA activities brought him to Germany during the World War. He died in a German submarine when he was returning to Ireland.

The "new army' had already been discussed at cabinet on two occasions before the 25 November meeting. On the 15 September 1921 it was decided to put the army on "a regular basis" with Austin Stack to attend staff meetings and Cathal Brugha to chair the meetings on special occasions. On the 4 November it was confirmed that the arrangements to "recommission" the army were to go ahead, and all GHQ and other heads to be re-appointed. On this occasion there was no mention in the minutes of Austin Stack. The staff's unanimous opposition to Stack was almost certainly related to his reputation as an inefficient minister of home affairs and the army's resentment that so many of the responsibilities proper to his department had to be adopted by the Volunteers. It is somewhat surprising that Griffith and particularly Collins would, as cabinet members, agree to such interference with the army but I expect that their heavy responsibility as plenipotentiaries left them no time to attend to other cabinet matters apart from the negotiations with the British, and that they may not have been present at the two meetings. The basis of the conflict about the appointment

* [IRA leader in Monaghan and subsequently member of GHQ and the 1919 Dail. He was noted for his success in organising the civic guard after the Treaty. He headed the Blue Shirts and Fine Gael for a brief period in the 1930s].

of Stack was certainly symptomatic of the widening divisions which were developing between the army heads and certain members of the cabinet.

Despite the failure to get agreement with GHQ at the cabinet meeting on the 25 November, the minute of the meeting gives a uncharacteristically long account of the proceedings and fails to mention GHQ's attitude [10]. It provides a list of the newly appointed GHQ staff, with no changes apart from the addition of Stack as joint deputy chief of staff with Eoin O'Duffy, the latter to be chief of staff in Mulcahy's absence. It states "The supreme body directing the army is the cabinet" and that all commissions derive from the government and must be sanctioned by the minister for defence. The minister can nominate or veto members of the army but "He must produce a working army". "The chief of staff is the professional or technical head of the army, and when in command is supreme on the field of battle as regards the disposition of his forces"! I need hardly say that Griffith and Collins were not present at the time of these proceedings. They were on the boat back to London having attended the earlier part of the meeting.

Of course it was reasonable of the cabinet to adopt this policy towards the army and I am sure that Dad was in full agreement with the principle of civilian control. However, the circumstances were hardly likely to be accepted by the army leaders where a successful and efficient staff was being asked, without prior consultation, to accept an unpopular addition who was deemed inefficient and who was already on poor terms with some of the army leadership. And the rationale of the appointment was to say the least undiplomatic where Stack was "to act as Brugha's watchdog". In a proper army/cabinet relationship I would have thought that the link with the minister for defence was one of the chief of staff's functions.

Intervention in military affairs without consultation with GHQ by Brugha and Mellowes was particularly evident during the Truce, which the chief of staff resented, believing that certain of these interventions were matters which concerned the military heads of the army and were not of concern to the civil authority [11-13].

Maryann, writing about the Truce, noted that the chief of staff was not invited to meet the head of the British Army in Ireland, General Macready, to arrange the Truce terms. She implies from Mulcahy's comments that the failure to invite him may have been related to "the British refusal to recognise the IRA" and/or "It was not yet time for the members of the army to come out in the open". Neither reason seems plausible to me. My father's note on the subject tends to hedge on the matter:

> There was no necessity, from my particular point of view, to stand on any ceremony in the matter; it was sufficient for me that a truce was being arranged, and that full responsibility was being taken and an effective truce was being arranged at the political level of responsibility [14].

It would seem to me that the politicians who attended the Truce talks, Dev and Brugha, might have been anxious to emphasise the status and equality of the two military forces by insisting that Macready was met by his counterpart from the Irish side. I suspect that Dad was excluded by Brugha for personal reasons and because Brugha by this time was determined to play a more active role in controlling the army, a trend which started with de Valera's return from America and continued right up to the signing of the Treaty. This suspicion is strengthened by Brugha's action in appointing Duggan and Barton, two junior officers of the IRA, as liaison officers without consulting with the chief of staff. These two relatively junior officers apparently attended the truce negotiations. This could only be interpreted as a casual dereliction of protocol at best or as a deliberate discourtesy at worst. Later, other liaison officers were appointed without consultation with the chief of staff.

Dad refers to the appointment of Barton* and Duggan** as liaison officers in his papers [14]. He stresses in these notes that they both continued as liaison officers with the British military authorities during the Truce without his acquiescence and without consulting him. Barton had been in jail until a few days before the Truce and was immediately appointed a commandant in the army on his release. Although he was only a few days back in the army, he was appointed one of the two to represent the Irish military authorities. Dad thought that his subsequent appointment as one of the plenipitentiaries on the Treaty delegation was "bizarre". At no time does Dad speculate about the influences which accounted for Barton's unexpected appointments, but his

* [Wicklow born, ex-British army officer; TD for Wicklow and minister for agriculture in first Dail. Later signatory of Treaty but eventually opposed it and retired from politics.]

** [Solicitor, TD for Louth/Meath in first Dail, signatory to Treaty].

cousin, Erskine Childers, may have been involved or Collins may have recommended him. He had always been a close friend and admirer of Collins. The only cabinet reference to the liaison officers was to discuss their payment (15). A further action of Brugha's was to set up a Commission of Defence during the Truce without discussing the proposal with the chief of staff. When Dad wrote to Brugha to enquire about the proposal, he received a rather dismissive letter of explanation from his minister (16). Nothing appears to have come out of the Commission.

It was rather typical of my father that he would not allow such breaches of protocol to become a contentious issue. He was certainly justified in resenting Brugha's increasing activities during the Truce in contacting individual members and groups of the army, and in conducting business with them, without the knowledge and the acquiescence of the chief of staff or other senior officers.

That Brugha's involvement in army affairs was not on major questions of policy but on more mundane matters is suggested by the following comment by Dad on the Robbie affair, which was an administrative one:

> The Robbie papers and the developments in relation to myself that flowed from them indicate that the things about which Cathal was at variance either with Collins and ultimately with myself were not matters of policy or of principle, nor were they matters of the kind that normally come for discussion at a higher level of political or executive level.Cathal's correspondence with me about the Robbie case begins about the 10 July. It continues until the 13 September, when I am told 'you will hand over to the deputy chief of staff all monies, papers, books and other property of the Department in your possession.' And two items of monies are specifically referred to; a suspence (sic) account of £996 odd, and another £500 'transferred from your account to that of the Director of Purchases, but which amount the latter yesterday reported he had no record of having received from you' - the deputy chief of staff intended to be Austin Stack and the director of purchases being Mellowes - and on the above instructions being carried out,'I shall have your salary up to date paid to you.' (17).

My father may have been too tolerant of Brugha and others who failed to deal with him according to normal protocol. Dad was deeply committed to maintaining the army as the servant of parliament and the people, and on all occasions he maintained a formal and proper approach to those whom he recognised as the representatives of the electorate. I feel that, in dealing with people who had no greater claim to prominence in the national movement than himself, he was perhaps too deferential to his senior political colleagues and that he may have diminished his own influence in this way. He was at fault in not protesting about some actions taken by Brugha (and later by O'Higgins) in matters which were clearly the remit of the head of the army, and not of the civil authority. To appoint military liaison officers without consultation with the head of the army, to arrange a military truce with the head of the British military without consulting the head of the army, to maintain contact with army officers on military matters without the knowledge of the chief of staff, such breaches of protocol by political leaders should have evoked a more vocal and indignant response from Mulcahy. Indeed, if he had been more protective of the privileges of his office, he might have avoided some future misunderstandings.

Other problems were to occupy him during the Truce. There was a massive increase in the number of young men who wished to join the Volunteers during the Truce, nicknamed the "Trucileers". This was a pejorative term applied in particular to those who joined in parts of the country where little activity was evident during the War of Independence. Two counties stand out in particular. Kerry and Wexford caused the chief of staff a lot of frustration because of incompetent leadership and inactivity during the war of independence. Both counties were to provide some of the more vicious atrocities during the civil war. It was for this reason that the term Trucileers was perceived to be a pejorative word.

Maryann in the biography suggests that the problems created during the prolonged truce was a contributory cause of the army split and the civil war.

The members of the IRA who were in concentration camps during the time were in some cases subjected to intimidation and harassment by the British in charge. Trouble was particularly evident at Spike Island in Co. Cork where the officers were offensive to both the prisoners and to the IRA liaison officer, Tom Barry. Barry* was, according to Mulcahy, temperamentally unequal to his task [18]. Dad believes that the treatment meted out to the prisoners may have alienated them to the point of refusing to accept the Treaty.

Problems were also caused by Brugha and others during the Truce, according to Mulcahy, which may have damaged the rank and file attitude to Mulcahy and Collins. He had this to say on the subject:

> In addition to this, that during the Truce Cathal, minister for defence, had opportunities of being in touch with all kinds of visiting officers from the country to Dublin during the Truce period. It would be almost impossible that there would not leak out from him, to some of his more intimate contacts of that time, something of his antipathy to Collins, and perhaps some of his differences with myself; this might easily have operated during the Truce to weaken the prestige and the position of the GHQ staff as such with some of the men in the country. There is no doubt that they came to them [Brugha and Mellowes] appealing for assistance and sympathy in relation to the inadequacy of the arms situation in the country; and there is no doubt that neither Cathal nor Mellowes would hesitate to join in any criticism of the GHQ men in relation to such a complaint" (19,20).

However, the influence of the Truce should not be exaggerated. It was a difficult time, lasting more than five months, and full of uncertainties about the future role of the army and the likely outcome of the negotiations with the British. But in general discipline and adherence to the conditions of the Truce were maintained. Local and foreign newspaper correspondents, who were invited to one of the training camps in the Dublin mountains during the Truce, were loud in their praises of the organisation of the camp and the disciplined behaviour and training of the 800 volunteers who were there to receive the chief of staff and his visitors. They were impressed by the chief of staff's address to the troops and the Volunteers response which confirmed their clear commitment to the army and the nation.

*[Tom Barry was a prominent leader of the Volunteers in Cork during the war of independence. He subsequently opposed the Treaty as did the other Cork leaders. However, he did not participate in the civil war.].

Despite the difficulties experienced by the chief of staff and GHQ during the Truce, both in their relations with the political leaders, and with the soldiers in the field, Dad states that, without Dev's intervention immediately after the signing of the Treaty, the effects of the Truce would not have led to a split in the army.

Chapter 4

Richard Mulcahy Writes about Military and Political Colleagues, and refers to the Genesis of the Civil War

Dad refers to many of his colleagues who were involved in the independence movement. The following paragraphs deal with Collins and the three political leaders, de Valera, Griffith and Brugha. He also refers briefly to other military figures.

4.1 Michael Collins

Collins was in the GPO as a junior officer during the 1916 Rising and was appointed secretary of the National Aid Association after his return from Frongoch. He was director of organisation on the volunteer executive, October 1917. He was director of training and adjutant general on the GHQ staff from March, 1918; subsequently director of intelligence until the Treaty. Commander-in-chief of the army from the 13 July to his death on the 22 August 1922. Minister for home affairs and later minister for finance in the first and second Dala, and chairman of the Provisional Government from January to July 13 1922.

Dad first became closely associated with Collins when they were appointed to the volunteer executive in October, 1917. He has recorded extensive memoirs of this association. Among these memoirs I have included a number of comments of my own which may throw further light on the relationship between the two leaders.

My father's relationship with Michael Collins has always intrigued me. As chief of staff and therefore Collins' military superior, he had an intimate association with Collins during the entire war of independence. This is clear from the following paragraphs. That he admired Collins for his many attributes is evident, just as he never showed any resentment as Collins's military reputation soared during and after the war, as did his political reputation before and after the Truce. At all times he showed an extraordinary sensitivity to criticism of Collins (as he also did to criticism of Griffith), particularly on the Treaty issue and its aftermath [1]. For instance, he reacted furiously to the suggestion that Collins was a drinker

Michael Collins, Commander in Chief, August 1922.

and that he was philandering during the negotiations in London [2]. It is clear from the tape recordings that he believed Collins could do no wrong [3,4]. If Collins had any faults, Dad was blind to them [5]. The deaths of Griffith and Collins in August 1922 at the height of the civil war was in his view the ultimate tragedy for the new Irish State.

As an example of his sensitivity to criticism of Collins, during the Truce he was outraged when he received a letter from Sean O'Hegarty, the IRA leader in Cork, reporting that Collins was drinking and carousing during the Treaty negotiations in London [6]. Despite the chief of staff's vigorous demand for evidence, it was not forthcoming.

It was typical of Dad that when Constantine Fitzgibbon described Collins getting out of a prostitute's bed in the first page of a novel he had written, he became so irate that he pressed the then minister for justice, John Kelly, to refuse Fitzgibbon his naturalisation papers [7-10]. Despite several approaches by Mulcahy to the minister, he failed to stop Fitzgibbon becoming an Irish citizen. He described Fitzgibbon's "foul penmanship" [9]. While Collins was widely admired for his extraordinary achievements, not many people would share my father's extreme sensitivity about him. His robust personality would hardly evoke such sentiments.

Dad remained chief of staff until the ratification of the Treaty in January 1922. As such he was the head of the army during the entire war of independence. He describes elsewhere that while the members of the staff had clearly defined roles and duties, at least during the later stages of the war, there was of necessity much duplication of activities and responsibilities. Nowhere was this more evident than in the case of Collins, who was given a free hand which he took with alacrity and great energy to undertake a multitude of commitments, including many which might appear to be the responsibility of the chief of staff or of his assistants. Indeed, apart from his intelligence work, Collins was involved in other areas, including contact with the commanders in the field. However, he was obviously assured that his initiatives would have received the chief of staff's support and would have conformed to general staff policy. Collins's intelligence work was organised through a network of colleagues, most of whom were members of the IRB. His extensive links with the country brigades were also probably maintained by IRB contacts

Collins's wide ranging activities and his soaring reputation were never a source of resentment or irritation to my father. On the contrary, his energy, his organisational ability, his great capacity for work and his powerful influence on his colleagues was a great source of satisfaction and admiration to his chief who shared with Collins the same dedication to work and to meticulous organisation. A lesser man in his senior position might have felt resentment towards his colleague in such circumstances, but the following quotations from his annotation clearly confirm Dad's appreciation of Collins and his great contribution to the foundation of the state.

I have a strong impression from discussions with my mother and her sister, Phyllis O'Kelly (second wife of Sean T O'Kelly) that the Ryan sisters had certain reservations about Collins in relation to Mulcahy - that his boisterous, flamboyant and charismatic nature tended to eclipse Dad's more muted role during the war and that he did not sufficiently show his appreciation of Dad's contribution to the struggle [11]. Such sentiments were certainly not expressed to Dad to the best of my knowledge. He would have reacted angrily to any criticism of Collins. Phyllis, who met Collins frequently when he visited the chief of staff at his home at 19 Ranelagh Road during and after the war, said to me "He was a rough type and more or less ignored the women" - not surprising in view of his preoccupation with his multifarious military and political commitments. There is little doubt that Collins was by nature a rugged individualist and may have been driven by the vanity which is so often at the basis of such a personality. Mother may have been right in believing that he was less conscious of the standing of his chief of staff colleague than he should, that he was prone to act too independently of his chief and in the later phase of the struggle did not keep him fully acquainted with political developments.

Dad's appointment as chief of staff allowed Collins that freedom of action which was fundamental to the success of his intelligence work and to the survival of the army. Dad not only encouraged Collins in every way but he provided him with that vital protection from his critics on the political side, who responded adversely to Collins's military and political successes, and to his rather flamboyant and sometimes abrasive behaviour and personality. It was an extraordinary and fortuitous partnership, not the least because his chief never showed a trace of resentment as Collins became more prominent both nationally and internationally. His admiration of Collins's role was the result of Dad's commitment to the success of the revolutionary movement. Dad was totally committed to army organisation and its good reputation and had little interest in his own public image.

Although in the early years Dad was apparently as well known as Collins for his military role in the war of independence, he had a largely administrative role coordinating the headquarters staff, as indeed did Collins. His profile has obviously diminished over the years. Unlike Mulcahy's, Collins's reputation has advanced with the years and with increasing media and literary attention, so much so that nowadays we hear little of any other military figure in the war.

Dad wrote about their association during the war but there is little direct correspondence between them available nor is there any evidence that there was much. They apparently met regularly and committed little or nothing of their decisions or conversations to paper. They met at Dad's apartment at Oakley Road at the beginning of the war and later at 19 Ranelagh Road where Dad went to live in 1920. The nature of their relationship is probably best described in his characteristically conversational, almost poetic, style in the following quotation:

> I opened and kept open for him all the doors and pathways that he wanted to travel - our relations were always harmonious and frank and we didn't exchange unnecessary information. We each knew what the other was at and particularly in his domain of intelligence - I had no occasion to be questioning him. Over many matters we exercised a constructive and practical Cistercian silence [12].

And Collins needed the protection of his military colleague, particularly after Dev's return from America. Historians have paid too little attention to the antagonisms which Collins evoked and which developed after this time, particularly among the politicians [13]. Nor have the reasons for these antagonisms been properly evaluated. Collins did not suffer fools gladly and was inclined to be abrasive with the incompetent. Whatever about any tendency for Collins to be abrasive, Dad had this to say about him:

> It can be seen that there was never on Collins's part any note of mere domineering or anything but the offer of the most effective service in a most reasonable manner and terms. Without in any way overpowering or wanting to overpower their judgement in any matter, where their judgement might differ, he would in fact in matters of practice have earned in practical affairs a certain ascendancy over them [14].

Dad refers on several occasions to the antagonism shown towards Collins by Brugha and Stack, and speculates about the cause or causes of their antipathy, an antipathy which appeared to surface in early 1921 when de Valera returned from America.

> In my joint dealings with Collins and Brugha together, I could not say that there was any friction between them until it developed over the question of the Scotch accounts in the end of 1920 [15].

Various factors may have been responsible for the antagonism, including Brugha's criticism of Collins's handling of certain financial transactions in relation to the supply of arms from Glasgow - the Scotch account. There were many who thought that jealousy of Collins by Brugha and Stack may have been a factor and such an opinion was expressed by Dev early in 1921 when Dad complained that Brugha's quarrel with Collins was endangering the security of the members of the GHQ staff. On that occasion Dev said to Dad:

> You know I think Cathal is jealous of Mick. Isn't it a terrible thing to think that a man with the qualities that Cathal undoubtedly has would fall a victim to .... jealousy [16].

Stack was a close associate of Brugha, and his antipathy to Collins may have influenced Brugha. Stack had disliked Collins and his dislike was attributed to Collins's dismissive remarks to Stack when, at the time of the Easter Rising, Stack and other local Kerry people failed to land the arms from Germany, and when Roger Casement was captured. Fionan Lynch, in a conversation with me, referred to Collins's lack of diplomacy with Stack as a likely cause of the rift between the two [17]. Paidin O'Keeffe, in his conversations with Dad, also refers to Collins's propensity to offend [17].

On this matter Mulcahy said:

> I find it difficult to think that the resentment spoken of is related to the 'fame and power' side of Collins. It could easily have been originally generated from Stack, that is, there was the same element of reaction in Cathal Brugha as in Stack but only to a smaller extent. It would arise from Collins's manner, from Cathal's feeling that the IRB membership had not come out in the Rising, from Stack's apparent failure in Kerry in the Rising, and from whatever feeling might have been generated by the way in which any IRB inquiry into the 1916 Kerry episode might have rubbed Kerry the wrong way. When Cathal (Brugha) became the public exponent of this hostility to Collins, he spoke with the joint figure of himself and Stack. I'm not clear what kind of public attack on Collins Stack ever made - look up the Dail discussions on the Treaty [18].

In another place my father states of Brugha:

> .... he was however bitterly critical of the supposed members of the IRB who didn't turn out during the Rising .....

and Brugha may have perceived Collins as having a leading role in the IRB.

There is also clear evidence that Brugha had been for a long time antagonistic to Griffith, if one is to accept the account of Paidin O'Keeffe, who had been close to the two men as the paid secretary of Sinn Fein during the War of Independence, and who recounted his experiences of the many political and military leaders in his conversations with Dad recorded on tape. The full O'Keeffe/Mulcahy conversations are listed on tape 64A. Collins's close association with Griffith may have been an added factor in provoking Brugha's antipathy.

On the question of the Scotch accounts, my father said:

> Cathal did definitely imply that monies that Collins had control
> of, at any rate in his position as a member of the GHQ staff, and
> which were supposed to be used for the purchase of arms, were
> being wasted or mis-spent or unlawfully made use of by Collins
> or by persons to whom Collins distributed these funds [19].

When Dad discussed the situation with Brugha in attempting to defuse the
disagreement, Brugha replied "As long as the ordinary laws of accounting
are attended to, that is all I require." Dad goes on to say:

> He wanted for some particular reason to have Collins removed
> (from) his position on the GHQ staff. Apparently he gave no
> consideration at all to what Collins's work meant, not only to the
> staff, but to the Government ...." [19].

And he adds:

> A glance at some of this correspondence revealing the accidents,
> disappointments, dangers and achievements in this line of
> purchasing and transporting arms would reveal also the
> pettiness and the mean lack of imagination on the part of men
> like Stack and Brugha and perhaps Mellowes. The mentality is
> not understandable.

And in a further comment about Stack, he says:

> .... it is impossible to envisage what kind of a spirit, a heart or
> a mentality Stack could have had or have developed that would
> bring him so bitterly and so disastrously against Collins and
> drive the country into civil war [20].

It is difficult to quantify the effect of these various factors, but the attitude
towards Collins was sufficiently strong for Brugha to ask for Collins's
resignation from the army [19]. It is surely likely that the divisions which
existed in 1921 between Brugha and Stack on the one hand and Collins and
Griffith on the other (and later Dad was included) had some influence in
leading to the Treaty divisions and the civil war, even if this view is largely

discounted by my father, who said that such differences as the cabinet divisions and army problems during the truce would not have led to a serious political or military split on the Treaty if Dev had not so aggressively, disastrously and promptly rejected the settlement in public.

Throughout the annotation one finds an impression of a deep sense of mutual trust, harmony and respect between Dad and Collins. They shared a number of attributes. Dad was trained in the British civil service and Collins had the same type of training in London. Despite the contrast in their personalities, they shared the same boundless energy and flair for organisation. In one of his personal remarks about Collins he states:

> He was the person who, by his approach and by the contacts he made, prised open the whole system of the British Intelligence system and enabled it to be destroyed; in that, his character has its place; a vast amount of stuff could be assembled associating his smiling buoyancy, his capacity for bearing tension, clearness of mind, perfectly controlled calm and a devil-may-carishness completely concealed. His clarity of mind and his whole manner and demeanour, together with his power of concentration on the immediate matter in hand, gave him a very great power over men. There was little doubt that his position in the IRB and what he apparently wished to make of the IRB and its tradition gave him, in relation to those people that he was most responsibly and closely dealing with in matters of high secrecy, some kind of mystique which was a kind of cement in matters of loyalty and service; it probably helped particularly to penetrate, and to make as effective as it was, the group of his associates inside the detective force and the police [21].

His character, his ability and his impulses and tendencies spurred him to make use of his associations. His IRB associations stemming from Frongoch, the further extension of his contacts through the work of the National Aid Association, of which he was secretary, his position of director of organisation [on the resident executive], his contact with the Sinn Fein organisation which became more powerful and important after the German Plot arrests, all widened the base over which he could use his great energy and stimulate activity in other individual persons and in groups. He was effective with pen and tongue. When, in correspondence and instructions, he was dealing with sluggish material, he has been known to make five copies of a letter, sending out if necessary periodically the third, fourth, fifth copy, as an effective reminder with considerable labour-saving elements [22].

Speaking of Collins's administrative approach:

This sample of Collins's correspondence is important and interesting and what has to be understood is the type of control that such correspondence exerted over the people in the country who received it, and who in relation to individual letters, had to answer details arising out of the questions asked and who, in relation to the somewhat very elaborate forms that had to be returned monthly or so, were forced to keep in touch with the actual details of their whole area over a rather wide field of observation. A number of these forms, for the greater part of the country, are available over a substantial period of time.

The scheme of things provided a very important link between the person at the receiving end of Collins's correspondence and various other people all through his area, with whom he was required to keep in authoritative contact, directing their efforts in assembling information on the one hand and in carrying out activities on the other.

This technique can be reviewed in relation to wider aspects of the situation in my own correspondence and papers. There were similar lines of contact and direction coming from the adjutant general, the QMG, the director of organisation, the director of training.

Some of the "fighting spirits" would look at this kind of thing, coming from me, as being office,chair and table kind of business. but when Collins wrote 'for God's sake, buy a pen and a bottle of ink,' they knew what he meant, and they knew that he was telling them very plainly that they weren't being asked to do anything that wasn't fully within their power [23].

From the point of view of public recognition and appreciation, the Collins that stood by the grave of Ashe in September 1917 and the Collins of January to March 1920 were two figures of very different dimensions. If, internally, he had grown in power, strength of will and flexibility, as he had, he had done it by tireless, vigorous, almost turbulent hard work, applied to his office work as much as to his widespread and general personal contacts. The impulse to make the necessary movement from place to place, and to meet an increasing number of different people to deal with various facets of work, added to his daring, gave him enormous momentum [24,25].

A few pages later, in an account of Collins's recreational activities and of his character, Dad talks about his propensity to horseplay:

There were very many reasons why Collins indulged in a certain amount of rough and tumble, and, of course, a little of that particularly encountered by people 'on the fringe' can be very much exaggerated. He was capable of an intense amount of concentration over what might be called documentary or office work; his own natural capacity, his early office schooling contributed to this; he was intensely interested in contact with persons - for a purpose - his purpose carried his concentration into these contacts as zealously as his concentration was carried into office work, or what might be called his personal planning and contemplation related thoughts; he couldn't slow down, he was entirely geared for action. It would be an exaggeration to say, however, that "horseplay" was his recreation, but in part it provided perhaps a substitute for that and was a kind of escapism; it was also a definite part of his diplomatic technique. It is unnecessary to say that in those times Collins necessarily had a lot of contact with people of all kinds who as a matter of inquisitiveness or self-importance would like to know some of the things in his inner mind; some with Volunteer or political responsibilities might like of know something which Collins might have reason for considering that they should not know; others might want to know something from the point of view of being able to gossip and boast in a human way about what they knew; a list of his "joints" would indicate the type of places in which he had occasion to meet people, very often of a mixed kind, where light banter, indulged in to protect himself against serious conversation, could easily develop into a little rough and tumble. The basis of this is a natural kind of desire not to slow down, continually exercised energy of some kind, mental protection against awkward or inquisitive persons, escapism [26].

And in another comment he said:

(Liam) Deasy, who was a leading guerilla commander in Cork, gives in his notes an account of a visit to Dublin in March 1921. He tells us of the dance that Collins led them to the Phoenix Park Races, to Vaughan's Hotel, up the Dublin Mountains to the Lamb Doyles, and a final visit to O'Sullivans, Palmerston Park (an American) where they had "for four hours, a serious discussion on the IRB part in forcing activities in the area [Cork]". When some of them, at midnight, went off to bed he recalls, 'Collins was now relaxing and in turn, went to every room and started a pillow fight. By four o'clock, when the last dropped off from sheer exhaustion, there was nothing to be seen in any bedroom but feathers from floor to ceiling.' Collins apparently felt that he was really amongst his own then - yet they were the people that were afterwards to kill him [27].

Collins dealt particularly with the aggressive activities of urgent and spot intelligence in relation to enemy activity. There was a kind of a 'quick-silver' instinct about his mind and action in moving about [28].

In the light of this it is worth recording that at this moment i.e. October 1920, Collins was on the eve of (1) The 21 November 1920, which marked the climax of his great intelligence work which on that date enabled a great spy offensive on the part of the British to be exterminated by the Dublin volunteers, and (2) on the arrest of Griffith immediately after that, to assume in addition to his volunteer work, his work as minister for finance (and) the responsibility of acting president. The appreciation of Collins and his work and their mutual association expressed by Griffith in the Treaty debates wasn't germinated in London; it had grown progressively since Griffith and Collins became associated in the work of Dail Eireann after its establishment. The only time probably that Griffith had any anxiety with regard to Collins was when he thought it possible that he was endangering the safety of the Treaty by the length to which he appeared to be prepared to go to placate the antitreatyites and to shepherd them away from preventing a general election in 1922 or avoiding anything like civil war [29].

As regards their specific roles on the GHQ staff he writes that Collins was in full control of intelligence work which started before the setting up of the staff when Broy first contacted him indirectly in the Summer of 1917. More than once he refers to Collins's enormous capacity for work, his genius for organisation and his ability to stimulate others. He states that, as regards work outside Dublin or large scale work of any sort, there was the closest possible consultation between himself and Collins.

> Through Collins's system of keeping contact with companionable groups, and his system of JOINTS [clandestine meeting places] for meetings with such as these, he could exercise a very considerable amount of executive power, and he would never be out of reach when wanted, if Boland or anybody else thought there was a matter that he should come in personally on [30].

> It is quite true that Collins always moved with the most easy freedom wherever his many activities required him to move. For him as for the rest of us the bicycle provided mobility, this was our main protection. He wore no disguise, moved with an assurance that disarmed everybody, and bluffed his way through almost impossible situations [31].

> Beaslai is perfectly correct in saying that Collins 'remained unshaken in his loyalty to his chief', that is to De Valera [after the ratification of the Treaty]. Following one of the occasions upon which he was home [from London] and had some talk at the Cabinet and with De Valera, he remarked to me that one of the things that De Valera had said to him was something like 'when a settlement does come it is only the people who are no good will be against it.' [32-34].

I have never known anything but the greatest cooperation and cordiality between Collins and Griffith during the whole period. It must have been with the greatest possible confidence that Griffith accepted him as a colleague to go to London with him. I am certain that there is no one whom he would most wish to have with him in such circumstances, than Collins. That he would be justified in such a feeling is shown by the result of the negotiations, and Collins's attitude after the Treaty was signed. Not until the question of an election pact with De Valera, into the discussion of which and the planning of which, Collins was forced by circumstances, did I see Griffith disturbed - and seriously disturbed. Griffith was concerned with giving the people a chance of declaring unequivocally, whether they accepted the Treaty or not; he knew very well that they wanted to accept, but he also knew that what was possible to achieve through the Treaty, could be very prejudicially affected by the firmness or otherwise with which the people's acceptance was expressed. At that particular time, Collins, suffering under his stresses, could speak rather testily about Griffith and Griffith, under his strains, was alarmed and disappointed in Collins [35].

Having referred to the sacrifice made by the leaders of the 1916 Rising, Dad had this to say about Collins:

Collins was making an analogous sacrifice in his capacity as chairman of the Supreme Council of the IRB, when he went to London as a negotiator. But as MacDermott and Pearse didn't sacrifice their lives without some hope and some faith of definite achievement and progress towards Irish freedom and the road to an Irish Republic, so Collins didn't go to London without hope and faith and with a lot more assurance perhaps than the 1916 men had of progress towards Irish freedom - and on the road to an Irish Republic, though no one even at the Supreme Council of the IRB level would have assured him that he could get a republic agreed to by the British, or that, even if they demanded that he should, would have persisted in that demand on the light of Collins telling them, prior to his going to London, that he couldn't get it for them [36].

Referring to Collins's visit under an assumed name to Stack in Manchester jail, while he, Collins, was on the run, Dad said:

This is typical of his audacity [37]; and on the Treaty

When Beaslai suggests that Collins did not think that he was the right man for the task, it is that Collins's difficulty was that De Valera should have led the delegation. With De Valera and Griffith members of the plenipotentiaries group, Collins would not necessarily have thought that his presence on the group would not be an additional strength. He would feel however, if he were not one of the plenipotentiaries, that he had complete confidence in such a pair and that he would be in a stronger position to help them in their consultations and outside discussions, but more particularly, that he would be in a stronger position to support them ultimately in the work of getting accepted whatever decisions they might come to in terms of Treaty. He would then have been pleading for the acceptance of work done by the leaders who had done their best [38].

Collins went as a soldier 'at the orders of a superior officer' although against his own judgement. He objected strenuously against De Valera's decision not to go to London. He considered that his military position and military record debarred him from being a suitable member of the negotiating body. The fact is that after De Valera and Griffith, Collins was the outstanding personality who should be with them; and the question cries out for understanding why these three names were not the first selected, and the persons most willing to serve and most able to guarantee complete confidence and support [39].

And in relation to the antagonism shown by Brugha and Stack to Collins during the Truce and the negotiations:

There is the temptation to ask, what on earth did either Stack or Brugha think they were sending Collins with his incurable desire to work and serve into the middle of the London negotiations, while bedaubing him in this particular way, either in relation to the efficiency of the organisation in Britain that he was depending on for this work, or in relation to dishonesty on the part of either himself or persons in Britain in relation to money matters. [This refers to the Scotch Account controversy]. The question arises as to what Collins thought of it all. He pushed it all from him as something that would be smothered out of existence in coming achievements; the true answer would be that he did not think of it at all; all his energies and all his thoughts were absorbed with the many works in hand and now particularly with work bearing on the negotiations in London. All the circumstances of the time were vigorously dynamic. He was now associated with Griffith in very definite pin-pointed responsibility and power to take the possibilities shown by Lloyd George's approach in his letter of the 20th of July, explore them, expose their realities and help to formulate the proposals in a way for presentation to acceptance by the Dail. I doubt if he bothered to consider what kind of a group he was leaving behind as the remnants of the Cabinet. I feel that he still trusted De Valera, felt that he was out for making peace and that he understood the necessity for it, and that he left out of his mind any unnecessary doubts that would interfere with the freedom of his thought or his consultations and work at the Irish plenipotentiary level [40].

He talks about Collins and the immediate impact of the Treaty crisis:

It is somewhat humiliating to find ourselves considering these things in the light of the terrible moments that had to be faced by so many people at the end of the year 1921. The crisis breaks particularly around Griffith and Collins, and the decision that was taken on the night of the 5/6 December. Collins, in the light of all he meant in terms of work, development and achievement in so many areas previously, and his astounding exertions and activities from the beginning of January 1922 to the date of his death, appears a particular figure in the light of his character and doings and sacrifices ...... But in the light of what Griffith meant back to 1899 and in relation to the beginning of everything, a special poignancy attaches to him [41].

De Valera's suggestion, soon after his return to Ireland from America, that

Collins should go to America to complete Dev's unfinished work and to patch up the divisions Dev had left behind, may partly have been motivated by a conscious or subconscious resentment of Collins' public noteriety and his dominance of the political scene. At least Dev must have felt that he could do without Collins, even at this crucial stage of the War of Independence. It seemed an extraordinary suggestion and Dad had this to say about it (with his latter day long sentences and verbal tortuosity!):

It was possible for us to hear of the proposal by De Valera that Collins was to be sent to America with a long list of things to be done and to smile at the pungent if laughing word of Collins to his pals that, 'the long .... wont get rid of me as easy as that'. But it is fantastic now to look back over notes and to think that in the many sided crisis that existed for the people generally and such institutions of the government, including the Dail and the army, as were at work, the president, returning after an absence of more than a year and a half in America and practically another year absent before that in English jails following the arrests in May in connection with the German Plot, would, in relation to Collins have nothing else to suggest but that he should go away on the kind of work set out in pages 1-5 [vol 2 of Beaslai's biography]. It was only a person living in fairyland and having no sense of action or what, in the carrying out of action, mutual and seasoned trust among men mean, who could think that even in the military arena alone, Collins could be spared at such a moment. The Minister of Defence was concerning more with an examination of what were called the "Scotch accounts" with, I fear, a certain amount of cooperation from Mellowes, also returned from America, in the development of an antagonism against Collins and with a view to damaging him by surrounding him with mean insinuations; pursuing the matter in such a way as to endanger the safety of the members of the GHQ Staff by requiring them to attend meetings to discuss these things at a time when, normally, I wouldn't allow more than three or four of them to meet at one time .... [42].

De Valera's letter to Collins about going to America is dated the 18th January 1921. That, in a fortnight after his return to Ireland, and he should have contemplated the idea of sending

Collins to America, and drafted the actual details of the letter of the 18th is a thing that nobody immersed in the home circumstances of the time could possibly understand. And if Mick's [Collins] reported comment on the suggestion cannot be regarded as just a word of one syllable, it must certainly be regarded as just a compound word, because he couldn't express anything but just 'surprise' - surprise at something beyond understanding, and at a time too busy and too full of pressure to feel that it was necessary to understand it. Any understanding could afford to wait in the development of his contacts with the man whom he had been out of personal contact with for 19 months, although he remained in close communication by letter with him. Collins's cooperation with Dev and his confidence in his person as leader never developed any weakness or questioning [43].

The coming of Craig* and (Lord) Derby and the movements and talks of other persons with peace feelers had stirred the atmosphere a good bit [June 1921]. The submission of 'the Hearst' man of a number of questions to Collins emphasises the fact that, apart altogether from Collins's general work and activity, the arrest of Griffith in November 1920 had put the final touch to bringing Collins into the forefront of the political sphere of importance and contact. Even if De Valera had not gone to America, Collins's position as Minister for Finance, balanced by his equally important position in army matters, would always have held him on the level with both De Valera and Griffith.

Collins was fortunate (in the historical sense) to have died at the height of his fame, and to have his reputation enhanced by subsequent historians and writers, so that he has become a legend. He is perceived by many as a lost saviour to his country, but he, like other heroes who had the good fortune to survive the revolution, would have found himself facing the realities of a political and social situation where the gilt of his fame might easily have worn thin with the passage of time and the interpersonal problems and conflicts which are inseparable from the rough and tumble of political life, particularly at a time of profound change. Collins raised many antagonisms

* [Sir James Craig, prime minister of Northern Ireland from 1921 to 1940]

during his time, which are referred to by Paidin O'Keeffe in his conversations with Dad [44,45]. It is likely that, if he were faced with the many difficulties of the fledgling new state, he would experience the same problems encountered by his surviving colleagues.

It was Dad's belief, consistent with his admiration for the man, that Collins would have been the saviour of the country if he had survived. Mother and I, in commenting on Dad's view, took a somewhat more pragmatic view of the hazards to one's reputation of survival in politics, particularly in the bitter post-civil war milieu, with its severe recession, and with massive unemployment, aggravated by the post-war demobilisation [46,47]. However, Dad may have had a point in that Collins's influence in the cabinet might have eased the demobilisation problems and might have prevented the O'Higgins' intrusion into army affairs with the consequent army mutiny and its adverse influence on the government and its supporters. How Collins would have coped with the rough and tumble of political life in the Ireland of the 1920s, with its recession and the aftermath of the civil war, is anybody's guess [48].

Dad was still alive, and living in the mundane political world of post-Treaty Ireland with its chronic problems of recession and reconstruction, made worse by the bitter political divisions. His reputation, which during the war of independence was closely linked with that of Collins, slowly atrophied as he faced the problems of the Truce and the civil war, and its aftermath of bitterness and disillusionment, and as his admirers and those contemporaries who thought so highly of him gradually departed the scene. Collins died at the right time for himself and for his reputation, although perhaps not the right time for Ireland. Apart from his outstanding military role, he deserved to be remembered for his seminal contribution to the political evolution of the Irish State. However, his reputation might have suffered too if he had survived to face the rigours of post-Treaty Ireland. After 1924, Dad's reputation began to yield to the influence of the commonplace. He himself, because of his tendency to self effacement, his lack of political mystique and personal ambition, and his inability to have recourse to the devices that make a politician popular with the crowd, was at least partly responsible for his own declining reputation. Collins is a folk hero, at least in the minds of the media and among some of his biographers, because of his military exploits and not so much because of his great administrative skills during the War of Independence. John Regan, in his article on Collins [49] underlines this point when he writes:

> But like the seldom published photograph of Collins at his
> department desk, the Michael Collins of the Department of
> Finance does not have the same appeal as Collins the gunman.

Collins shared with Dad the most important attributes of a winning leadership in war, good organisational and administrative abilities.

Despite the reputation Dad acquired as a result of the Ashbourne action in 1916, he was a desk man He certainly never fired a shot after the Ashbourne affair, which explains the remark of one reviewer of his biography who stated that he could safely predict that no film would ever be made of Mulcahy.

I have referred earlier to my instinct that mother and a few others of the Ryan siblings resented Collins because of his flamboyant and extrovert character, his charismatic public persona, his involvement in all aspects of the military campaign which may have appeared to them to impinge on the domain of the chief of staff, and particularly, perhaps, because, rather than resent his prominent and dominant role, Dad did everything to encourage and support Collins, and, ultimately, to protect Collins against people who did resent his prominence and his soaring reputation [11]. The remarkable thing about Dad was his commitment to the army and to its vital role in serving the cause of Irish freedom and democracy. His complete absence of any personal ambition, attributes which served the army and the country well, but which were not likely to enhance his own reputation and political career, bordered on political altruism. He was to show the same spirit of abnegation in 1948 when he gladly and enthusiastically encouraged the nomination of Costello as Taoiseach of the first Interparty Government.

As for Collins, Padraig Colum, who like many others admired him, wrote:

> And there were others who disliked the brusque ways of a young
> man who at times was so intent on one or another of his
> multifarious jobs as to be unmannerly [50]. And "Darrell Figgis,
> who had no love for Collins ...." [51].

I am reminded again of the constant theme in my father's writings and conversations which is his sensitivity to criticism of Collins and Griffith (2,3,4,52). In his opinion they were the two great architects of the independence movement, and their deaths in August 1922 at the height of the civil war was the ultimate tragedy for the new Irish State. During a recorded conversation he reacts strongly to implied criticism of the two leaders, and during the same conversation he expresses his dislike of Prof Desmond Williams who was Professor of Modern History at University College, Dublin and who, during a Thomas Davis lecture, said that both Dev and Collins shared the blame for the civil war [52]. Dad disagreed profoundly with Williams's conclusions on the genesis of the civil war, but perhaps Williams may have had a point.

Several references are contained in the tape recordings to the influence Michael Collins may have had in provoking resistance to the acceptance of the Treaty and thus to the subsequent split in the army. These references are quoted from conversations Dad had with Paidin O'Keeffe. O'Keeffe was the paid secretary of Sinn Fein from October 1917, at the time the Sinn Fein executive was elected, until the ratification of the Treaty, except for one year he spent in jail from March 1918 to March 1919. He came into intimate contact with all the leaders during this time. He talks about the various personal problems and stresses which arose among leaders. He was pursued relentlessly by my father in the early 1960s to record his experiences during his tenure of office with Sinn Fein. He equally was well informed about Sinn Fein, the IRB, and the background to the formation of the Sinn Fein and Volunteer executives in 1917. He refers to these in several of the tapes.

O'Keeffe had a prodigious memory and he was an observant and uninhibited critic of those whom he served. On several occasions he spoke about Collins, particularly in relation to his frenetic activities and the effect his dominance had on his colleagues. He maintained that part of the vote against the Treaty was an anti-Collins vote, and that Collins first caused a degree of antagonism because he, with Harry Boland and Diarmuid O'Hegarty, three Volunteers and prominent IRB men, had the choice of candidates for the 1918 election, a fact which was resented particularly by those who had aspirations to be invited to enter the Dail but who failed to be nominated [53-55].

The whole thing about Collins was, he did too much, he was too much to the fore and he had the selection of the bloody first Dail, which was a bloody curse ...." [54].

And O'Keeffe goes on to name a number of prominent Sinn Fein people including P.S.O'Hegarty, Joe McDonagh, John O'Mahoney and Father O'Flanagan and adds that there were hundreds in the country who had aspirations to join the first Dail. It is possible that the influence of Collins, Boland* and Diarmuid O'Hegarty led to more Volunteers being proposed than the non-military members of Sinn Fein and that this bias may have increased the politicians antipathy towards the Volunteers and the IRB. O'Keeffe implies that the IRB, the "secret organisation", operated effectively throughout the country to select the candidates. Hence his statement in answer to Dad's query that there was an anti-Collins vote on the Treaty based on an antagonism to Collins which had its origin in the choice of candidates for the 1918 election, virtually all of whom were re-elected at the 1921 election.

In another comment O'Keeffe said:

> Collins was a right eegit because he took on so much that, when Dev came back from America, the only person whom people wanted to contact about affairs was Collins, thus apparently leaving Dev out in the cold [56].

O'Keeffe's objective analysis of Collins might imply some criticism but Dad was certainly blind to any weaknesses in the Collins character or actions which may have ruffled the feelings of some of his acquaintances [5].

It is generally acknowledged that Collins could be abrasive at times, particularly with the incompetent, and that he did not suffer fools gladly. O'Keeffe, although an ardent admirer of Collins, refers to his propensity to offend, although Dad did not join in O'Keeffe's strictures. However, both Mulcahy and O'Keeffe agree that the antagonism which developed between Brugha and Stack on the one hand, and Collins on the other, (and which previously included Griffith [57,58] and was subsequently to involve Dad) was a disaster and must have contributed to the divisions which existed in the cabinet coming up to the signing of the Treaty. The antagonism to Dad was to lead ultimately to his twice attempted sacking as chief of staff by

*[Harry Boland, close associate of Collins's during the war of independence and joint secretary of Sinn Fein. He opposed the Treaty and fought and was killed in the civil war].

Brugha during the Truce, and to the attempt by Dev and Brugha to appoint a new army at the cabinet meeting of the 25th of November, 1921.

A further factor which may have contributed to an anti-Collins move in the Dail was his perceived association with the IRB, already referred to by me. By 1921 there was a degree of antipathy towards the IRB among other politicians, as well as Dev, Brugha and Stack [59,60]. There may also have been some generalised jealousy of Collins among a few deputies because of his dominance, some of whom may have been influenced by Brugha and Stack [61].

Michael Collins died towards the end of the engagement at Beal na mBlath. Because of testimony at the time, it was believed that he was killed by one of the last bullets fired by the irregulars which ricocheted off the armoured car or off the road before it entered his head. However, occasional suggestions have been made that he was shot by one of his own men, but the circumstances of his death makes such a possibility highly unlikely.

He was laid out in 58 St Stephen's Green, a private wing of St Vincent's Hospital. According to Fletcher of the department of anatomy at UCD, who was a young attendant in the department at the time, a postmortem examination was carried out by Jimmy Redditch, the head porter at the anatomy department of the Royal College of Surgeons, with St. John Gogarty in attendance. It is likely that the procedure was confined to a superficial examination of the head wound and to preparing the remains for embalming and the lying in state at the City Hall from 25-27 September, 1922. Fletcher told me that the embalming fluid used was formalin, and that eosin was added to retain a pink colour in the face. This would be confirmed by Lavery's painting of the dead Collins, which shows him with normal or even a slightly exaggerated lifelike coloration [62].

Perhaps Calton Younger, in his "Ireland's Civil War" [63] is correct when he states that no postmortem was carried out. Unfortunately, despite enquiries with the College more than forty years ago, I was unable to obtain any record of the examination, nor was such information available from the hospital.

Beaslai, in his biography of Collins [64] quotes Emmet Dalton who was with Collins when he was killed "There was a fearful gaping wound at the base of the skull behind the right ear" And Calton Younger writes that the body was examined by a Dr Leo Aherne in Cork who "like Dr Gogarty later, was sure that the wound was caused either by a ricochet or a spent bullet." [63]. Ulick O'Connor, in his life Oliver St John Gogarty [65] writes of Gogarty "With fine skill, he was able to hide the gaping wound in the back of the head." The photograph in Younger's book of Collins' body lying on a bed in Cork with a wide white bandage around his head was consistent with his having an extensive head wound.

However, in a conversation recorded by Dad with Gerry Ryan of Tipperary, it is stated by the latter that the body was inspected by a British army officer. According to Ryan, the officer described a small entry and a large exit wound [66]. The absence of an entry wound would strongly support the view that he was killed by a ricochet bullet and not, as the unsubstantiated opinion of a few suggest, that Collins was killed by one of his own men. The presence of an entry wound would suggest that the forensic evidence was irrelevant to the question. However, the circumstantial and strategic evidence, and the unquestioned loyalty of his own companions, clearly contradicts the possibility of his being killed by one of them, nor was such a possibility ever suggested at the time or for many years afterwards. There is not the scintilla of evidence that Collins was killed by one of his own men.

Kathleen Galvin, who was acting night matron on the morning of the 24 August, gave me a most poignant account when I was a young consultant there in 1951 of the arrival of Collins's horsedrawn guncarriage. The remains arrived at the North Wall very early on that morning. She described the moment, about four in the morning with the sun just rising and shortly after rain had fallen, and with the cobblestones glistening in the early light, when the gun carriage appeared and moved slowly from the Shelbourne Hotel to the hospital steps, preceded by a makeshift army band playing the moving and evocative Scottish dirge "The Flowers of the Forest". She talked about the emotional turmoil of that moment, and of the intense sadness which prevailed.

Dad spoke with two colleagues who were in the Free State army at the time of Collins' death [66]. One was Frank Holland who was leader of the pipers' band before the advent of Fritz Brase as head of the army school of music. Frank was with the pipers at the North Wall when the Collins' remains arrived in the early morning. It was he who said that the dirges played were the *Flowers of the Forest* and *Lord Lovett's Lament*. At the end of Dad's

To the Men
of the Army —

23.8.22
3.15 am

Stand calmly by your posts.

Bend bravely and undaunted to your work

Let no cruel act of reprisal blemish your bright honour.

Every dark hour that Michael Collins met since 1916 seemed but to steel that bright strength of his and temper his gay bravery

You are left each, inheritors of that strength, and of that bravery

To each of you falls his unfinished work

No darkness in the hour — No loss of comrade will daunt you at it.

Ireland! the Army serves — strengthened by its sorrow.

Risteárd Ua Maolchatha
Chief of the General Staff

Message from General Richard Mulcahy to the army on the occasion of the death of Michael Collins. 23 August 1922.

interview with the two ex-soldiers, they all three attempt to sing *Lord Lovett's Lament*. I remark in my abstract of the tape:

> Holland's description was followed by an atrocious rendering of the latter dirge by Dad and his two visitors, confirming that the larynx undergoes the same functional deterioration with age as the other organs of the body!

I also had a description from Kathleen Galvin of Kitty Kiernan's arrival at St. Vincent's Hospital later in the day. She was dressed in a dark grey suit and a white hat. She "was swooning and behaving in a most dramatic way" before she laid a lily on the coffin, and then sat beside it for a prolonged period in a trance.

My father talks about Collins's death on tape (66). His death evoked Dad's well known message to the army which was aimed at preventing reprisals, and which was published immediately after the news of Collins' death reached Dublin:

> To the men of the Army
> Stand calmly by your posts.
> Bend bravely and undaunted to your work.
> Let no cruel act of reprisal blemish your bright honour.
> Every dark hour that Michael Collins met since 1916 seemed but to Steel that bright strength of his and temper his gay bravery.
> You are left each inheritors of that strength, and of that bravery.
> To each of you falls his unfinished work.
> No darkness in this hour - No loss of comrades will daunt you at it.
> Ireland! the Army serves - strengthened by its sorrow.

This message was followed one week later by Dad's homily delivered over Collins' grave. (See Appendix 1).

Dad's deep commitment to his religion, his spirituality, his interest in Irish history and Ireland's culture and language, is clearly evident from this homily. A later panegyric over the graves of Thomas Ashe, Peadar Kearney and Piaras Beaslai is equally full of references to God's Providence and the Christian path to perfection, to the Kingdom of Peace on earth, to recent Irish heroes and the spirit of Fenianism. He speaks with confidence about the nation's hopes and resurrection, and his quotes in the Irish language bear witness to his idealism [67]. The Beaslai homily is in its own way a tour de force but, although it was delivered fifty one years after 1916, it is hard to reconcile its contents with his military performance at Ashbourne. Perhaps it is not surprising that Kevin O'Higgins called Dad a soldier saint.

General Mulcahy delivering the homily at the grave of Michael Collins,
29 August, 1922.

Writing of the Dail debate on the Treaty, Nichevo (R.M."Bertie" Smyllie) of the *Irish Times* gave a pen picture of several of the leaders, including Collins and Mulcahy:

> The two legendary figures of the Dail were Messrs. Collins and Mulcahy. One had heard all sorts of stories about these two men during what is known euphemistically as 'the trouble.' ....

Whether these and similar stories are true, I do not know. But they made me very anxious to see these two men in the flesh. Neither of them looks the part. Each, in a sense is the antithesis of the other, but they both are very prosaic looking individuals whom you never would dream of crediting with hair raising exploits.

Michael Collins, Richard Mulcahy and senior army officer at Arthur Griffith's funeral, August 1922.

Mr Mulcahy is one of the most interesting men in the Dail. Mr Collins fairly oozes energy; he is what the Americans would call a "kinetic' type. Mr Mulcahy, although he walks with a jaunty gait, is remarkable for his repose. I have watched him sitting for an hour on end in the Dail while deputies raved at one another and half a dozen were on their feet at the same time. He never stirred. Sitting with his arms folded he might have been listening to an interesting sermon in church. He has a very impassive face. It is deeply furrowed, and suggests a well-balanced mind, and his long nose gives him an almost aristocratic appearance. When he is speaking he purses up his lips, and has a knack of using uncommon words, which he chooses with the utmost care. He always seems to be tracing something with his finger on the desk in front of him, and never raises his eyes. His speech in favour of the Treaty was a remarkable utterance. He was virtually the only member of the Dail whose words did not contain a trace of bombast. There was no sabre rattling or beating of drums. He ignored the 'gallery' and made his appeal to the intellect rather than to the sentiment of his listeners. I tried to think of some non-Irishman with whom Mr Mulcahy might be compared, but his type is very rare. *Mutatis mutandis*, he has much in common with Colonel Lawrence, of Arabian fame. If he wore silk socks, and were a Fellow of All Souls, the resemblance would be even stronger.

He then goes on to talk of Collins. He refers among other characteristics to his leonine energy, and his love of action which "makes him impatient and easily provoked". "But he did his very best not only to restrain himself, but to induce his fellow-members to maintain the dignity of the Dail".

Nichevo then brings us down a peg when he finishes on the rather mundane note that "It is a pity that he (Collins) did not exert his influence to prevent the members from smoking; cigarettes and pipes should have no place in the vital councils of a nation"!

Among many letters and telegrams Dad received after Collins death [68] the following extracts are quoted:

Frank Aiken, by September a prominent irregular leader, wrote to Dad after Collins was killed, expressing extreme sorrow on his loss. In his letter he states that it was particularly tragic because he believed that Collins was about to change his mind at the time of his death, realising that he was wrong in opposing the irregulars. He would, according to Aiken, have stopped the civil war and supported the republic:

You alone now can save the nation! I think if you believed absolutely in the sincerity of the men opposed to you, you would stop the struggle. If that is true, I prove to you if you wish. I die in order to prove to you if you guarantee to me that you'll stop this civil war if I do so. For God's sake, Dick, agree to this and let one death end it all.

He signs the letter *"mise do naimhid agus do chara"*. I am your enemy and your friend.

This letter sums up the tragedy and the poignancy of the civil war, of the shattering and passionate break among those who fought side by side against the British, a break which was made all the more tragic because of the patent sincerity of those on both sides of the struggle. It also underlines the strange loss of realism among the irregulars when such stalwart men as Aiken asked my father to stop the civil war, when Liam Lynch, in November 1922, asked that all pro-Treaty supporters should be ostracised, and when, at the very end of the war, with only a few of his companions left with him in the Knockmealdowns to fight the Free State army, Lynch seriously believed that victory was in his grasp.

It was also part of the Irregulars' propaganda after Collins' death to say that he was disillusioned with the Free State and that he was critical of the Four Courts attack which marked the commencement of the formal civil war [69],

George Gavan Duffy wrote to Dad on the 23 September 1922, the day after Collins died:

> I have never known a man so great, with that combination of magnetic personality and dominating will and character, (and) far seeing judgement. And to you, who were his intimate friend, the tragedy must be beyond words. But it is on you pre-eminently that the shouldering of his burden will lie, and your lead and your example must now be our beacon. I feel that you will turn to Eoin MacNeill as the one fitting counsellor left to you in the big things of life. I pray that our responsible men will smother in their own hearts the intense bitterness they must feel against the irregulars; there will be acrimony and recriminations enough anyway without any prompting from our propagandists; and your dignified address to the army was in the very note to strengthen the situation that was wanted. With your cool head to direct the military mind, I have no fear of the outlook there ....

And the telegrams he received included such exhortations as "Trusting you will be spared to carry on his work to a finish, and may God spare you for a good cause". and "Fight on for free Ireland in memory of our gallant commander in chief"

Mrs Katherine Tynan Hinkson, in a letter in The Times after Collins' death, writes:

> Your Dublin correspondent, writing of the calamitous death of Michael Collins, said of Richard Mulcahy that he is 'handicapped by the temperament of a philosopher'. Well, he may have the temperament of a philosopher - though I should not call that a handicap in Irish politics - but he has also the temperament of a poet, without which no Irish genius is complete. I listened at the Dail meetings last autumn to speech after speech which seemed to me, brought up on the traditions of Irish oratory, deliberately commonplace and dull. Then came Mulcahy and the whole thing was changed. He was not ashamed to put his emotions into oratory; listening to him one was back in the great days. His address to the army on the death of Michael Collins seems to me admirable as poetic prose. Nothing could be finer   There is no higher type of man in our history than the man who is at one a poet and a man of action, as witness the great men of the Elizabethan days. Ireland has suffered a terrible calamity in the death of our two leaders [Griffith and Collins] but while such men as Richard Mulcahy, and the Brennans of Clare, lead her army, we may lift up our heavy hearts [70].

4.2 Arthur Griffith

Founder of Sinn Fein in 1905, minister for economic affairs in the first and second Dala. Acting President of the first Dail during Dev's time in America and President of Sinn Fein from 10 January 1922 after the ratification of the Treaty to his death on the 12 August 1922. Despite beliefs to the contrary, he was not a member of the cabinet of the Provisional Government but was chairman of the co-existing Dail cabinet, a body which in fact had no political standing following the ratification of the Treaty.

Arthur Griffith
1922

Griffith was an active member of the Sinn Fein standing committee during the 1917-1921 period:

> From about the 15 April 1919, after Griffith came out from Lincoln, he systematically attended at all the meetings of the standing committee of Sinn Fein up to the 15 October 1920 when he was arrested. He presided at most of these meetings to the number of about 50 in all [1].

Dad makes many references to Griffith in the annotation, particularly in relation to his political role while de Valera was in America, and to his role during and after the Treaty negotiations. If Collins was Mulcahy's military hero, Griffith was his political hero and his philosophical mentor [2,3]. His political philosophy, based on self-determination for Ireland but retaining a link with the Crown, and therefore with Great Britain, appealed to Mulcahy's pragmatic view of things. It was in keeping with the attitudes of the people in the early part of the twentieth century, and indeed right up to the Treaty, where the great majority did not conceive of or support the concept of an independent republic, and when Ireland was so close to Britain in economic, cultural, social and professional affairs.

Padraic Colum in his biography of Arthur Griffith [4] quotes Griffith as saying:

> Though I am a believer in the republican system of government, I am ready - as I believe is every other Irish Nationalist - to accept any form of native government in preference to alien rule.

Dad admired Griffith for his political realism, for his modesty, for his lack of personal ambition, and for his firm adherence to the Treaty agreement. He was appalled by the treatment Griffith received after the Treaty negotiations, particularly as he had been reluctant to take part in these without De Valera. He was saddened by the bitterness and vituperation of the Treaty debates and by their impact on Griffith, and by Griffith's differences with Collins, when the latter was, in Griffith's perception, compromising the Treaty agreement later in 1922. Dad was saddened too by Griffith's untimely death. His death, like that of Collins, in his opinion was an important destabilising factor during the difficult months of the civil war. Griffith had a high opinion of my father as a young military and political leader with a part to play in the foundation of the new state [5].

In connection with Griffith's attitude to De Valera, Mulcahy had this to say:

> Both as a matter of principle and as a matter of full and
> voluntary agreement, Griffith (was) to maintain full confidence
> in De Valera. A story by Denis McCullough of a discussion in
> Gloucester (jail) at a time when Griffith and a number of others
> were there under the German Plot arrests, epitomises Griffith's
> whole philosophy and attitude; the point he made there, when
> asked for his opinion after a long discussion on certain aspects
> of things that might be going to happen was that, 'whatever De
> Valera does, I agree to that' [6].

Despite considerable pressure on Griffith from Paidin O'Keeffe and others
in early October 1917 to accept the presidency of Sinn Fein before the
convention arranged later in the month, Griffith refused on the grounds that
he was not a leader, that he was simply a teacher and writer. He thought de
Valera was the best choice, particularly because of his 1916 record and his
recent election to parliament in Clare, He stated that he would propose Dev
subject to Dev satisfying him on three points of policy [5-8]. Griffith was also
concerned that, if he went forward against Dev, the votes would be split and
Count Plunkett might be elected, which he, Griffith, thought would be
disastrous. Paidin was also concerned about the possibility of Plunkett's
nomination and it was this possibility which induced him to go to Griffith.
One of the three questions was whether Dev would break on the Crown in the
event of a settlement. Dev apparently reassured Griffith on the three points,
including saying that he would not break on the crown. According to
O'Keeffe, Dev's assurance was crucial in receiving Griffith's support [9,10],
although it does seem that it was early days to have considered the crown as
a crucial matter in people's aspirations.

My father spoke as follows about Griffith, the Treaty and the Treaty
negotiations:

> He had fully supported De Valera's election as President of Sinn
> Fein in October 1917. On one occasion, probably during the
> approach to the conscription issue in March 1918 (though it
> could have been shortly after April 1919 when the full cabinet
> had been set up), I had occasion to go with Griffith to visit the
> Archbishop of Dublin, Dr. Walsh. We went up by tram and

entering the gates to the Archbishop's palace on foot, Griffith
was telling me that nearly all his life he had been looking for a
young man to lead the political movement (in the early days no
doubt he regarded Rooney as this), and he was expressing his
great appreciation of the fact that, in De Valera, they had now got
the kind of young man they wanted. It is possible that even in his
great disappointment of having to face the London negotiations
without having De Valera with him, and De Valera shouldering
the responsibility of chairman of the plenipotentiaries, he still
clung to his early hope and principle that 'whatever De Valera
does I agree with'. To the very end I feel he (Griffith) relied
confidently on Dev to lead though quite surprised and
distressed that he declined to lead the plenipotentiaries [11].

M.J. MacManus in his *Eamon De Valera* [12], referring to details of the Treaty
conference held in London at 3 o'clock on the afternoon of the 5th December,
reports:

Lloyd George proceeded to deliver his hammer blow .... The
British could concede no more and would debate no further. The
Treaty must be signed or else.....
Griffith surrendered. 'I will give the answer of the Irish
Delegation at 9 o'clock to-night,' he said. 'but Mr Prime Minister
I will personally sign this agreement and recommend it to my
countrymen.'
'Do I understand Mr Griffith that, though everyone else refuses,
you will nevertheless agree to sign?' 'That is so' replied Griffith.

Dad continues:

The question arises to my mind as to whether these are not the
most valiant words ever spoken in the course of Irish history.
They were the words of a man who, in an unquenched gaiety of
spirit, had suffered poverty and degradation and apparently
fruitless labours for years, entirely devoted to the service of
the uplift of the people in terms of spirit, economic well-being,
social happiness, political strength.

Pakenham* thinks that, before he spoke to them, he should have got on the telephone to De Valera. I don't know what Pakenham may have known about De Valera or the position of the others around De Valera in Dublin; or what he can have known about the mentality of Lloyd George and the circumstances around Lloyd George affecting his strength to do things or support for anything that he might want to do - support from his colleagues. There are some pages in *The Decline and Fall of Lloyd George* by Lord Beaverbrook[13], that give some idea as to what the difficulties there were, in coming to and holding fast to a decision on anything like satisfactory Treaty terms. Griffith must have, by the 5th December, been fully aware of the dangers that were inherent in the inconsequential approach of persons like Stack and Brugha, and he must have been fully aware of the internal difficulties among the most important British members of the negotiating group. I cannot feel that, in his most wearied, his most frustrated, his most disappointed moment, Griffith would yield to any element of despair either personally or for the Irish people, but I feel that these words represent a supreme valour that in another might have to be called despair or recklessness [14].

And later on the next page, Dad states, speaking of the problems posed by De Valera and his cabinet colleagues at home:

What we apparently have to do here is to examine their weaknesses, their pettinesses, and see to what extent they contributed to the circumstances that Griffith found himself in when he had to make such a declaration on the 5 December 1921 [15].

He went to London. He strenuously objected to being required to go there without De Valera. He had borne the burden of acting President of the Cabinet during De Valera's absence in America. He would always have regarded it as his duty to undertake the responsibility for partaking in such a mission as the London mission [16].

* [Lord Pakenham, Earl of Longford, was joint author, with Thomas P. O'Neill, of *Eamon de Valera*, Gill and Macmillan, Dublin, 1970].

I have already referred to the anomalous situation facing Griffith while Dev was in America in relation to the difficulties and lost opportunities of negotiating with the British [17]. Despite Griffith's disabilities as regards initiating truce negotiations, Dad had this to say about him and his role as acting president:

> If in fact de Valera were able to do this, that is to go to America at that time without injury to our morale, it is a tribute to the character of Griffith and to his past, and the confidence that his work of the past had inspired in us, that we had a sound political approach for a people who had a strong national tradition and a warm fruitful culture to maintain. Given that Griffith was there, I didn't at the time feel any weakness in the situation. My position as the military head of the army probably suffered a diminution of importance politically, in that I had no head of government between whom and myself to sandwich the minister of defence [18].

> As for myself, I have never heard from Griffith and I am sure that Collins never did either, anything but what expressed complete understanding and sympathy with what we were doing, the job that we had and the spirit in which we were facing it. My contacts with Griffith, which were not infrequent, were such as to make me feel very consoled that the person whom I most regarded as being the political intelligence and the political conscience in the general situation, was completely at home with me in our discussions. and quite unruffled about any of the matters we were dealing with. Oliver Gogarty in the memorial issue *Arthur Griffith and Michael Collins* [19] writes 'The man he looked to of the younger men was Richard Mulcahy' can be taken as an expression of the type of relationship that existed between us [20,21].

On the question of Griffith's attitude to armed intervention, on page 62 of Padraic Colum's biography of Griffith [2], the old Fenian O'Leary, in a conversation with Griffith, speaking of the prospect of Irish Freedom, said:

> 'I answered that it would need baptism of blood to make it prevail. Blood alone will sanctify,' O'Leary said. Griffith

128

answered 'I have counted on that, sir. The spirit of Fenianism will respond at the right moment' [22].

Nevertheless, Griffith was not in favour of insurrection under the circumstances prevailing in Ireland, according Colum on page 135 of the biography.

Colum also refers to Griffith's commitment to a pluralistic society on page 95 [2], and he refers to Griffith's views on the mutual dependence of Capital and Labour, and to the nation's responsibility to protect both. And speaking about Griffith's contribution to the economic advancement of Ireland, Dad states:

> The fact of the 'Commission of Enquiry into the resources and industries of Ireland' is a monument to the vigour and the persistence of Griffith's purpose in the economic side of all his long years of teaching. It has to be remembered that this commission was set up in the teeth of the suppression of the Dail. To the people generally, and particularly to the type of people who were concerned with the economic situation in Ireland, the fact that this committee was working and getting the cooperation of many witnesses, was a very great steadier and a contribution to the morale of the people. Among the reports actually printed and issued, were reports upon:
>
> (1) Milk (March 1920)
> (2) Industrial alcohol (March 1921)
> (3) Coal (March 1921)
> (4) Fish (July 1921)
> (5) Peat (December 1921)
>
> I think another report was issued on water power, and another on dairy cattle or stock [23].

Griffith and Collins died early and at the height of the civil war. Their deaths were described by my father as the ultimate tragedy for the emerging young state, a tragedy which underlined what he described as the "compound disaster" of the civil war.

Griffith's death was attributed by some people at the time to a broken heart, but, with a little more realism, it was generally accepted that he had died from a stroke. The diagnosis entered on the death certificate was a subarachnoid haemorrhage (caused by an artery rupturing into the brain and its surrounds). He was cared for in the private wing of St Vincent's Hospital at 95, Lower Leeson Street by Oliver St John Gogarty who signed the death certificate. There is no record of a postmortem examination.

I always had reservations about the cause of Griffith's death. The circumstances were more suggestive of a sudden heart attack the result of coronary heart disease. It occurred after he was admitted to the hospital for treatment. Padraic Colum, in his biography of Griffith on page 373 [2] writes that Dr Gogarty admitted him because of insomnia and "an imperceptible stroke." However, there was no evidence of a stroke or of its precursors while he was in hospital. He was mobile at the time, visiting his office every day, and about to be discharged when it is recorded that he collapsed.

Kathleen Galvin, who was a nurse attending him at the time, informed me that his death was instantaneous:

> On the day of his death he was out on the corridor and he appeared to bend down to tie his shoelace and he collapsed. There was general panic but nothing could be done for him.

After his collapse, he was seen immediately by Dr Jim Magennis and surgeon Harry Meade, who had been finishing an operation in the private theatre closeby. A few minutes later St John Gogarty arrived, but he was pronounced dead by the time the doctors got to his side.

Instantaneous death must be very rare in stroke or subarachnoid haemorrhage, and, in the latter case, a severe headache usually precedes unconsciousness. Nor is there any record that he showed any signs of a stroke before his unexpected end, except for Gogarty's rather tentative diagnosis before admission. In the early years of the century, and as late as the last world war, it was common to classify sudden unexpected death from a heart attack as a stroke. In fact, this misclassification remained a feature in Eastern European countries until quite recently. The role of ventricular fibrillation, a fatal irregularity of the heart which is the commonest cause of sudden death, and its association with underlying coronary heart disease, was not understood until the work of the American physician, Bernard Lown, and others in the late 1950s and early 1960s.

The fact that Griffith was a cigarette smoker is another circumstance which might support a diagnosis of death from coronary heart disease. At a reception in his honour in the Mansion House in March 1921, de Valera presented him with a fountain pen and "a smoking cabinet or jacket." [24], and there is a photograph of Griffith at Croke Park on page 58 of the Griffith/Collins memorial issue [19] referred to above, which shows him smoking a cigarette. The relationship between cigarette smoking, coronary disease and sudden death is now established beyond doubt.

4.3 Eamon De Valera

Eamon de Valera first came into prominence as commandant of the fourth Dublin brigade in the Rising. He was elected president of Sinn Fein and president of the national volunteer executive in October 1917 and remained in these positions until the ratification of the Treaty, 7 January 1922. His presidency of the volunteer executive was an entirely nominal position. He was priomh aire (first minister) of Dail Eireann from April 1919 to January 1922, and was elected president of the Republic by the Dail in August 1921.

While my father had numerous meetings with de Valera during the years from 1917 to 1922, his relations with him appear to have been formal and in keeping with his position as head of the army in the presence of the head of state. There certainly appeared to be no sense of intimacy between them and dad's description of some meetings presents Dev as a rather patronising colleague - advising him to study economics and to read the Prince [1], or asking the rhetorical question why, as assistant minister of defence, he did not attend cabinet, but adding, before he got a reply, "you are as well not to, you would be as bad as the rest of them if you did!"

My first main contact with Dev would have been about the end of
August 1917 in the Keating Branch of the Gaelic League, when a
small group of us, including Ashe, De Valera, Collins, Cathal
Brugha and others - about eight or ten - met to consider the
approach to the reorganisation of the volunteers and the calling
of a Convention. Dev would have been much more involved on the
political side of things and in relation to the organisation of the
Sinn Fein Convention; the next contact would be in connection
with the holding of the Volunteer Convention in Jones's Road on
the 27th October; the next serious meeting would be when he and
others came up to Fernside (dad's home) in April 1918 (I had
lumbago) when the first real excitement about conscription
began.

Dev was arrested in May 1918 and from that time until he
returned from America on the 24 December 1920, the only
revealing contact I had with him was at 3 Fitzwilliam Square,
before he went to America, that is say, April or May 1919, when
out of the blue in a casual conversation for a few minutes in the
hall of the house at Fitzwilliam Square, the president, soon to
depart for the States, said to the chief of staff of the army "You
are a young man now going in for politics, I'll give you two pieces
of advice, study economics and read the Prince [2].

Dad became interested in economics in his later parliamentary years but
probably never read "The Prince". At least there is no copy of the book in
his library!

Two particular meetings with Dev during the Truce were the cabinet meeting
with the GHQ staff on the 25 October 1921 to discuss and to disagree with
Dev on the "new army", and the meeting of the staff with Dev alone on the 10
December where, in answer to Dev's question, the members of the staff were
to swear loyalty to him if he were to win the vote against the Treaty in the
Dail [3]. He had many casual meetings with Dev during the post Treaty period
but his only meeting with him during the civil war was in Dr Farnan's house
in September 1922. Dr Farnan was a gynaecologist and was a close friend and
confidant of de Valera's. This meeting finished in a matter of a minute or two
when they were unable to reconcile their views on the Treaty and the
acceptance of the people's decision on the matter [4].

Mulcahy appeared to think that Dev made little contact with any other leader during the Truce and the run up to the Treaty negotiations, and that his strategies were the result of his own initiatives and were just rubber stamped by Dail Eireann. He may of course have discussed matters with Childers or other confidantes, but certainly not openly with the other political or military leaders. That Childers was particularly close to Dev is referred to by Dad when, in a reference to Griffith's association with Darrel Figgis, who was joint secretary of Sinn Fein, Dad said:

Griffith kept up a very close working friendship with him (Figgis) but only to a very minute degree would he have been to Griffith what Childers was to De Valera [5].

Mulcahy wrote of Dev's apparent lack of communication with others before and after the Truce:

We are concerned with two periods of such communications. First, the approaches and the correspondence leading up to the actual acceptance of a truce position, and secondly, the considerations and the correspondence that led up to the taking of the decision which brought about at Downing Street on 11 October 1921 the first meeting of the peace conference that ultimately concluded the Treaty agreement. I get the impression from the story here that there is less personal contact for the discussion of these things between the principals, even between Collins and DeValera, than would have been possible and desirable [6].

De Valera had four preliminary meetings with Lloyd George in July 1921, after the Truce. They lasted in all seven and one half hours. Although he had a substantial group of others with him in London, including Griffith, he attended all the meetings on his own. Surely he was one to keep things close to his chest!

Under the title "National Unity" Mulcahy excuses the members of the Dail for their unanimous and uncritical support of Dev's decisions:

Was there anything unnatural in the show of "national unity" that was made by the Dail by the reserve of criticism? It can hardly be said, given the type of lead that De Valera was giving with apparently the cabinet supporting him, that there was anything unreasonable in the absence of criticism made in the Dail: it was rather a demonstration of national unity and strength intended to give confidence to the leader and the cabinet in facing up to the work that was going to fall on them. De Valera's proclamation to the people of Ireland dated the 10th October 1921, was an appeal almost to the people to copperfasten their mouths as a protection against division and in the maintenance of "an unwavering faith in those who have been deputed to act in the nation's behalf [7].

It is also possible that the cabinet itself merely rubberstamped Dev's decisions, at least if one is to go by the paucity of information in the cabinet minutes during the war and the subsequent Truce.

Maryann states that Mulcahy had an obsession about Dev's responsibility for the civil war. I quote the relevant paragraph on page 87 of the Biography:

Mulcahy's analysis reflected his obsession with de Valera's responsibility for the Civil War - an obsession which would be a dominant motif for the remainder of his life and which obscured from him the fact that, despite a degree of culpability on the part of de Valera, a section of the army was determined to revolt.

Maryann's opinion is supported by Professor John A Murphy in his review of the Mulcahy biography [8]. I quote:

As Dr. Valiulis stresses in her fine study, antagonism to de Valera was an obsession with General Mulcahy. Like all obsessions it completely clouded his judgement where his adversary was concerned. Thus in September 1922 he expressed the egregious opinion that 'de Valera could stop the civil war by writing a letter to the Evening Mail'!

134

Deirdre McMahon, who is currently writing a biography of Dev, recently expressed the view that the pro-Treaty prejudice against Dev was largely the result of his being in power for so long after 1932. However, Dad and his pro-Treaty colleagues' views about Dev in relation to the genesis of the civil war were as strong in the 1920s as they were afterwards, although Dad's resentment about Dev's role was undoubtedly aggravated by the latter's dominance of the political scene since 1932. Dev's long tenure of power, his Messiah-like control of affairs, and perhaps his and his colleagues claim to be the only legitimate and effective political party in the state must have rankled with him and copperfastened his conviction. Maryann Valiulis refers to the evidence confirming the conviction of the rank and file of the Cumann na nGaedheal party in the mid 1920's that Dev played the key role in precipitating the civil war [9].

There is no doubt whatever that my father laid the primary blame for the civil war on Dev's shoulders, although the description of his opinion as an obsession has a pejorative ring and suggests an abnormal preoccupation with such a view. Perhaps it might be worth considering the matter in more detail by examining the basis of his views which he has recorded in the annotation. Before quoting relevant passages, let me try to encapsulate what he thought in a few lines.

De Valera became the leader of the Irish separatist movement in October 1917, when he was elected president of the newly elected Sinn Fein executive and of the general executive of the Irish Volunteers. He received unswerving loyalty from all his colleagues from this time to the ratification of the Treaty in January, 1922. This loyalty was extended to him despite the fact that he was absent from the country for two and a half years during the three and a half years between his election as president and the Truce of July 1921. This loyalty was, according to Dad, confirmed by the desire to maintain unity and, despite some inconsistencies in his character and problems created by his actions during the time, he was accepted as a moderate who would best lead the country to independence. De Valera, in his initial contacts with Lloyd George after the Truce, proved to be a stubborn and difficult negotiator, but whatever understanding he had with Lloyd George which led to the Treaty negotiations, he was aware that the British would not yield on the Crown and that the inclusion of the six northern counties of Ireland with the twenty six counties as an independent state was not a reality. Indeed, partition was already a *fait accompli* since the

Government of Ireland Act in 1920. At the time Dev was quoted by Collins as saying that only the extremists would oppose a settlement.

When the plenipotentiaries were appointed in October 1921, he refused to join them, despite objections by many of his colleagues, and more strenuous objections since. He did, however, ask the people of Ireland to trust them in their endeavours, to await patiently the outcome of their task, and he pleaded for reticence about the final settlement, at least until the terms were discussed by Dail Eireann.

On the question of the genesis of the civil war, Mulcahy also believed that Dev had betrayed the cause of democracy by his political ineptitude in failing to prevent a split in the army, despite the assurances from all the members of the GHQ staff, conveyed to him at a meeting on the 10 December 1921, that, in the event of the Treaty being defeated in the Dail, they would continue to support him as the army of the Republic. This support was qualified by both Mulcahy and Collins who stated that, under such circumstances and because of their political commitment to the Treaty, they would have to resign their leadership positions in the army and revert to being ordinary soldiers. Everyone else said that they would stand as soldiers supporting the Dail and the Government [10,11]. Nine of the GHQ staff subsequently supported the Treaty while four opposed it. Dev, who attended the meeting with the staff at the suggestion of Griffith, stated: "If he lost the vote on the Treaty, he would not stand for mutiny" [12].

This meeting with the GHQ staff was arranged because Griffith advised de Valera that he should consult the army if he intended to oppose the Treaty. The attitude of the army and its leaders facing a return to war needed to be ascertained if the Treaty were to be rejected by the Dail.

If I was regarding myself as the brass hat responsible for the army, here now you have come to peace and we must not go back into war and I must see what is going on about the peace. (If) I would have taken up that attitude, it would have been a reasonable attitude to take up because here you have de Valera in December after the Treaty was signed preparing to go back if necessary into the danger of war without consulting the GHQ at all about the matter .... [13].

De Valera's reputation as a moderate was shattered, as were his earlier pleas that any settlement should be considered dispassionately by the people until it was approved or otherwise by the Dail, when, on the day after the terms were announced, he publicly rebuked Griffith and Collins, his colleagues in the cabinet, and when two days later he published his opposition to the Treaty in the newspapers. It seemed odd to me that during the discussion of the Treaty in the cabinet on 8 December 1921, where Dev, Brugha and Stack stated their opposition to the Treaty that Dev should say at the meeting that he intended to announce their opposition publicly by writing to the newspapers. I would have thought that the other members favouring the Treaty, Cosgrave, Collins, Griffith, Barton and O'Higgins (who had no vote) would have insisted that the cabinet discussion should first be brought to the notice of the Dail members in view of previous undertakings by de Valera that the Dail should be the first authority to consider the settlement.

In my father's opinion, Dev's precipitate action had a disastrous effect on the army. It also had an adverse effect on the many people who would otherwise have accepted the Treaty, at least as a stepping stone to a republic free from the symbolism of the Crown. Dad held that Dev's intransigence provoked many of the inflammatory anti-Treaty speeches in Dail Eireann which had a further and final adverse effect on army unity. Finally, he believed that if Dev had supported the Treaty, if he had joined in preventing the split in the army, and if he had not played a part in preventing an election immediately after its ratification, and thus preventing the people from expressing their opinion about the Treaty, the more seriously disaffected members of the IRA would have had little chance of precipitating a civil war. De Valera admitted that the majority of people in Ireland favoured the Treaty.

He particularly condemned de Valera because of his proclamation during the civil war advocating a policy of assassination of pro-Treaty deputies and other prominent supporters of the Treaty. It was this act which led to the shooting of deputies Hales and O'Malley, and to the government's illegal execution of four irregular prisoners. It is a constant theme throughout all his writings that Dev had failed as a leader during the vital four years from 1918 to 1922 [14-17]. He concludes that Dev had a "blind pride in seeking power" [17]. Was this his Messiah complex, his ability to look into his heart and to know what was best for the Irish people?

These are, I believe, the reasons he laid the primary blame for the civil war on De Valera. His view was shared by many of the pro-Treaty leaders, including Cosgrave, MacNeill, McGilligan, O'Higgins, Michael Hayes, Desmond FitzGerald, Fionan Lynch and James Dillon. And, oddly enough, despite the view expressed by Maryann Valiulis in the biography, she states in her article *After the Revolution: the formative years of Cumann na nGaedheal* [9], speaking of the dissident and more nationalistic elements in the Cumann na nGaedheal party in 1924-1925, "De Valera, the man they held responsible for the civil war, remained an anathema to them."

Maryann stated that "his obsession was to remain with him to the end of his life". Undoubtedly, Dev was never far from his mind in his last few years, but, if one were to ignore his writings and his recordings of the last years of his life, one would find little evidence of such an obsession, despite his acknowledged views about Dev's culpability. He never criticised Dev during his many public lectures to the 1916-1921 club, to Fine Gael groups, and to other organisations in his later years, nor did he ever discuss his views about Dev and the civil war in his earlier years, unless on the rare occasions when he might have been questioned on the matter in private conversation. The various tape recordings of his public lectures are notable for the absence of any criticism of any colleagues, whether friend or foe, and his charitable sentiments about so many of them.

He was of course appalled by the tragedy and the human, economic and political consequences of the civil war, which he describes on tape as a "compound disaster" It is perhaps understandable that he was critical of those who fought against the new government, many of whom he admired for their contribution during the war of independence. As a person dedicated to the democratic ideal, he could not understand how the anti-Treaty forces refused to accept the will of the majority.

Dad states that Griffith and Collins, while they reluctantly accepted the task of negotiating with the British without Dev, believed that he was a moderate and that his influence would contribute to the acceptance of a compromise on the constitutional settlement agreed with the British [18].

Apart from the fact that Dev said that he was not a doctrinaire republican, Mulcahy had this to say to justify the faith Griffith and Collins had in Dev as a moderate:

On the question of the Treaty and the Crown: De Valera had, over his four meetings between himself and Lloyd George alone on the 14, 15, 18 and 21 July, 1921, at least seven hours talking with plenty of time in between for thinking and discussion. As early therefore as the 21st July, he knew several very definite things:

That a Parliament had been established in Belfast to deal with affairs of the six counties and a Government had been set up there. He knew that that would continue so to act, and in a subordinate position to the British Parliament, until those who had vested interests in that parliament were argued out of their position or persuaded or coaxed in some other way than by insult or arms or threats of any kind.

He knew that, in a scheme of definite order, as between representatives of the six counties and representatives of the rest of Ireland, the door would be open for the fullest and the most orderly discussions of whatever was involved by way of problem or otherwise that required conciliation or consultation or change.

He knew that the rest of Ireland was being offered all the power of a sovereign state, internationally recognised, and, as against any British interference, guaranteed and secured by four other dominions of whom Canada was being pointed to as the prototype of the sovereignty that existed.

Nothing of this that he knew from his conversations with Lloyd George was undermined or pared down in any way by any references to 'empire' or anything else in Lloyd George's letter to him of the 20 July, 1921.

It is not easily conceivable that, at any moment after understanding this or hearing this, De Valera could have visioned his leading the Irish people or the Dail into such a position that they would go back into a war situation with Great Britain." [19].

There is a fourth point that should be added to the three

mentioned above as a thing which De Valera knew by the 21st July following his four talks with Lloyd George and that is, that there was not the slightest doubt that as far as Britain itself was concerned, the British negotiators would resist, to the very last, any implied interference with the prestige, the mystique or the picture of the Crown as a linchpin idea in the constitution of Great Britain itself, of the individual dominions existing and its position as a connecting mystique for the commonwealth group as a whole: on two headings he knew that there had to be some acceptance of the Crown, (1) on the aforementioned grounds and (2) on the holding, under any scheme, of any hope of giving a link of unity with the Northern counties [20].

Mulcahy does not at any point mention the Dail motion passed unanimously on the 26 August, 1921:

"That if plenipotentiaries for negotiations be appointed by the Cabinet or the Dail, such plenipotentiaries, be given a free hand in such negotiations and duly to report to the Dail'." [21].

He recalled Dev's proclamation before the negotiations started:

In connection with these proceedings [the appointment of the plenipotentiaries] the 'A proclamation to the people of Ireland' was issued by De Valera on the evening of the 10th of October, which he winds up as follows, 'The power against us will use every artifice it knows in the hope of dispiriting, dividing, weakening us. We must all beware. The unity that is essential will best be maintained by an unwavering faith in those who have been deputed to act in the nation's behalf, and the confidence manifesting itself as hitherto in eloquent discipline. For this I appeal'.

It remains to be considered whether he was asking for unwavering faith in those who had been deputed as negotiators and plenipotentiaries, or whether he was thinking of himself as 'those who have been deputed to act in the nation's behalf' [7].

140

Dad also refers to Dev's motion proposed at the Sinn Fein convention on the 27 October, 1921. It was a proposal to add to the constitution of the party the following clause, one which Dev introduced after a preamble in which he emphasised that the declaration of the republic in 1916 was the basis of the independence movement:

> Dail Eireann, the duly elected parliament of Ireland, in the exercise of all its legitimate functions and in all the steps it legitimately takes to maintain public order, to provide for national defence, to secure good government, and to ensure the general welfare of the people of Ireland [22].

This amendment to the Sinn Fein constitution was discussed by the standing committee at a meeting earlier on the day of the Ard Fheis. Dev, who had proposed the amendment, had included the phrase "and to the President and Cabinet of Dail Eireann, the lawful Executives of the State" after the words "Dail Eireann, the duly elected parliament of Ireland", but this phrase was eliminated by the unanimous decision of the members.

Dad also quotes Dorothy Macardle on the issue of the crown. She in her book *The Irish Republic,* [23] quotes de Valera as saying in regard to the plenipotentaries:

> (The problem is to devise a scheme that will not detract from Irish freedom) They may come back having found what seems to them a way and recommend it to us. When they come, we in the Cabinet will have to decide our policy with respect to the scheme, and Dail Eireann will then have to consider it. (I am not able to judge, but I am anxious that you should realise the difficulties that are in the way, and the fact that) the best people might legitimately differ on such a scheme. The worst thing that could happen would be that we should not be tolerant of honest differences of opinion. I believe that if such differences of opinion arose and were carried to the country, it would mean disaster for our hopes. As sure as the nation is divided, the nation will be tricked [24].

Dad, in reading page 305 of the Beaslai biography [25], makes a note about the different definitions of the oath which might or might not be acceptable.

He writes:

The reference suggests that the Crown and the manner of its acceptance was the only big obstacle that remained to be faced. This raises the question, 'Was it on the question of the acceptance of the Crown that the break between Griffith and De Valera came.' If not, what was it on?

We compare the relative clauses, THE TREATY Clause 4: The oath to be taken by members of the parliament of the Irish Free State shall be in the following form: 'I _____ do solemnly swear true faith and allegiance to the constitution of the Irish Free State as by law established, and that I will be faithful to His Majesty King George the fifth, his heirs and successors by law in virtue of the common citizenship of Ireland with Great Britain, and her adherence to and membership of the group of nations forming the British Commonwealth of Nations.'

DOCUMENT NUMBER 2, Clause 6: That for purposes of the association, Ireland shall recognise his British Majesty as head of the association.

The following additions are made under Clause 6 in pamphlet 132 (E):- Mr De Valera also agreed that: 'As a token of that recognition, the Irish legislature will vote an annual contribution to the king's Personal Revenue.'

(The) oath approved by Mr De Valera in December 1921 before the Treaty was signed: 'I do swear to bear true faith and allegiance to the constitution of Ireland and the Treaty of association of Ireland with the British Commonwealth of nations and to recognise the King of Great Britain as head of the associated states.'

And in document B 194 presented to the British on the 22nd November 1921, Clause 2 reads:- 'Ireland agrees to be associated with the British Commonwealth for purposes of common concern and in respect of those purposes to recognise the Crown as the symbol and accepted head of the association.'

The tragedy of the political differences and the subsequent army split was that the oath, which was the main stumbling block in reaching an agreement, was of no consequence in terms of freedom but became a major issue because of the Sinn Fein rhetoric preceding the Treaty and the inflammatory statements of Childers and the anti-Treaty members of the Dail.

Maryann Valiulis, in the Biography, believed that problems arising in the army during the Truce contributed to the army split after the Treaty ratification. Dad had this to say on this subject:

> It is true that the prolonged Truce was very bad in every way, and that excesses of one kind or another arose out of the relaxation of strain, and that a certain amount of demoralisation took place, but don't let us think that there was anything in the situation of that particular kind that would not have been completely arrested and corrected at the time of the signing of the Treaty, if even at that late hour De Valera had accepted and supported the Treaty signed by Griffith and Collins. That checking would have been much more secure if the country was in the position of realising from the start that he was leading the delegation of plenipotentiaries to London himself [26].

> I don't accept at all that either disorder or revolt was inevitable. There was no element of inevitableness in the situation up to the 5th December 1921, and none would have come into the situation, but for the manner in which De Valera so savagely attacked the Treaty before Griffith and Collins even got home. It is quite irresponsible to relate to any Truce relaxation among Volunteers, the idea of the inevitability of disorder or revolt in relation to the establishment of regular government [27].

On the question of Dev's attack on Griffith and Collins when the terms of the Treaty were announced, and of his letter to the press on the 9th of December condemning the Treaty terms, Dad had this to say:

> It was really an infamous performance on the part of De Valera, as the leader of the nation that he was appealing to, to issue this letter at this time. For all practical purposes it was tantamount to his meeting Griffith at the boat at Dun Laoghaire and slapping

him publicly across the face. For, although between the time he had received the terms of the Treaty, let us say the morning of the 7th December (in view of his preoccupation with Dante on the night of the 6th), and his writing a letter on the 8th for publication on the 9th, he must have had a session of the Cabinet with all members present; it cannot have been a session to consider in any kind of a reasonable way the terms of the document brought home*.

For political purposes the slap in the face was administered from the time that De Valera met Griffith on his return. The contents of the letter can be examined from the point of hypocrisy, dishonesty, incitement, but it is the immediate effects of the publication of the letter that challenges examination with the whole nation's spotlight turned on him, the man who had been the leader of the country over the dramatic years announces monumentally a split in the Government, and announces it in an explosive irretrievable way. The fact that so many of us could not believe it, probably made the happening all the more irretrievable.

As far as the people generally were concerned, they got the terms of the Treaty in the press on the 7 December, and the president's letter in the press on the 9 December, with the information that a public session of Dail Eireann was being summoned for Wednesday the 14 December. The Dail meeting that day did nothing but add to the confusion, and emphasise how disorderly and impassioned the split in the Cabinet was going to be made. The public silence of the Dail from the 14 until the meeting on Monday the 19 December added to the public distress and confusion: the reports of the Dail meetings on the 19, 20, 21 and 22 helped to make the position in the country worse. The vote in support of the Treaty on the 7 January and the

---

* [The cabinet minutes of the 8 December were not available to Dad when these notes were written. The minute (CPs 8/12/1921) is exceedingly brief and simply records the voting intentions of the members in relation to the Treaty and Dev's proposal to write an immediate letter to the press announcing his opposition to the agreement with the support of Brugha and Stack [28]. There is no record of any discussion].

election of Griffith on the 10 January as President of the Dail, caused a kind of a pause for breathing and for hoping, but the main thing looked for in the hope, was not to come - that is, peace [29].

I have said already that of the two sides to the national movement from 1916 to the end of 1921, the military side of the movement, the Irish Volunteers, had completely discharged their function under the direction of the GHQ Staff by the 11 July 1921, when the people had been able to declare with unexampled strength and unity of voice, in the general election of May 1921, that they then stood for, and continued to stand for what they took for in the general election of 1918, as a result of which, they established Dail Eireann in 1919 [30].

The following are some extracts of his views on the subject of De Valera's sojourn in America as recorded in his annotation of Beaslai's biography of Collins. These views were recorded in the early 1960s. The first ten pages of his commentary on Volume 2 of Beaslai's biography contain some interesting notes about Dev's stay in America which extended from May 1919 to December 1920.

Beaslai records that within eighteen months of his going to America, Dev had brought about a split, leaving two open organisations and two rival *Clann na nGaedheal* (sic) bodies. The original *Clann na nGaedheal* was the associate of the IRB and it was the organisation which stood in our minds in our early days for Irish organisation in America [31].

Clann na nGaedheal , in the person of John Devoy,* meant for us the accumulation of tradition (of) mind and men, that from the Fenian time had found refuge in America to develop organisation and purpose directed towards Irish freedom [31].

*[John Devoy was a veteran Fenian and after a long and eventful career as a separatist he retired to the United States where he spearheaded American support for the cause of Irish independence] .

The old Clann, as well as being closely connected with and helpful to the Rising of 1916, had in the circumstances ranging from 1916 to 1919 mobilised public opinion in favour of Ireland by a number of race convention meetings. The new open organisation, established as a result of De Valera's activities, was the American Association for the Recognition of the Irish Republic, which was launched on the 16 November, 1920 [31].

That it(that is, Dev's absence in America) had no effect on us - the sentries - was no doubt due to the fact that we had been accustomed to do without De Valera and to see the situation in Ireland developing and going along without him [32].

His going to America after his release from Lincoln and the setting up of the full Dail Cabinet in April 1919 was a very great surprise to us - and in many ways a disappointment. However, again the position was that we had no experience of having him with us, there was nothing in particular we wanted him for, except that we must have been looking forward to a situation in which the head of the government would be in the country [33].

Looking back now, it might appear a very remarkable thing that the national leader would leave the country immediately after the parliament had been set up and before the discussions that had taken place in the parliament had formulated for the people the lines upon which the parliament was going to conduct itself and endeavour to effect national, social and economic policy, while making at the same time its case for representation at the Peace Conference and making there the case for its freedom [33].

And in referring to Dev on his return from America on Christmas Eve, 1920:

De Valera was back early that morning. I saw him at Farnan's at about 8 o'clock a.m. In the back return room, without sitting down - in just a stand up conversation - his line to me almost directly was, after just a mere word of greeting, something along these lines   'Ye are going too fast. This odd shooting of a policeman here and there is having a very bad effect, from the propaganda point of view, on us in America. What we want is, one

146

good battle about once a month with about 500 men in each side'. That was the essence of our talk [34].

Coming back after a long absence you would feel that he disparaged our military efforts - at any rate he had no words of compliment or praise to give to it; our 'shooting of odd policemen' was bad from the propaganda point of view and theirs in America; he had nothing more to say of any detail, of the type of resistance that had been carried out over the year 1920 from the beginning of the offensive on police barracks; he had an idea that we could have spectacular encounters with 500 men on each side [35].

And in his address to Dail Eireann in January 1921 after his return from America he advocated a less active military policy:

All Ireland had was the power of moral resistance. They ought to make up their minds to hold out, they should not seek a decision. This policy might necessitate a lightening off of their attacks on the enemy [35].

According to Mulcahy, the Dail had no sympathy for such an attitude and the military view at the time is expressed in the following paragraph:

As far as we were concerned, the circumstances outside made the pace for us. It demanded all our attention and all our energies. We were involved in a machine and in work that had developed and had gone on without him. There was no particular assistance that he could give us except by leaving us alone and encouraging us; for all his prestige and power in America he had done nothing to get even a small supply of arms from there. Collins was to try and do something about that from America; Collins was to patch up the broken unity that he had left behind him in America; Collins was to get American Government policy on the right path in relation to the League of Nations when Harding became President in March, 1921 [35].

147

And continuing the same theme:

> There must have been a great distortion of mind and balance in
> this particular matter arising out of the length of time and the
> absorption of De Valera in the US and the effect that had on
> taking the eyes of those in Ireland off the diplomatic and the
> negotiation side of things in Britain [36].

De Valera was absent in America from May 1919 to December the 24 1920.
Previously he had been in a British prison from March 1918 to March 1919.
From October 1917 he was the acknowledged leader of the Sinn Fein
separatist movement. He adopted the mantle of authority with ease, and his
leadership received the most complete support from all his political and
military colleagues. Dad believed that Dev's prolonged absence, particularly
in 1919 and 1920, created a political vacuum at home which seriously
militated against any possible peace negotiations with the British earlier
than July 1921 [37]. He believed the prolongation of the war of independence,
with the increasing bitterness engendered during the last months of 1920
and the first six months of 1921, created an atmosphere which increased the
likelihood of political polarisation and the development of more radical
aspirations in relation to the eventual constitutional settlement. My father
and O'Keeffe, in discussing the factors which caused a delay in reaching a
truce with the British, underline Dev's absence in America, and Griffith's
reluctance to adopt the mantle of leadership in Dev's absence [38].

Griffith replaced de Valera as acting president of Sinn Fein while the latter
was in the United States. Despite Griffith's seminal contribution to the
separatist movement, and despite the high regard in which he was held,
particularly by Mulcahy and Collins, he never had, nor wanted to have, any
ambition to supplant de Valera's authority in such a crucial area as
negotiating with the British.

My father had this to say about Dev's absence in America:

> But while all kinds of conventions and meetings and all that kind
> of thing had been contacted in the US by De Valera personally ....
> it would appear that no contacting of any kind had been done in
> either Great Britain or in the North of Ireland or among the

Unionists here in Ireland to prepare for the day when such contacts as close to negotiation points would have been made as Craig, Derby, Smuts. As far as De Valera was equipped in the matter, he was apparently relying entirely on the heart and the eyes of Childers .... While Griffith was left with the responsibility as acting president from the time De Valera went to America in May 1919, he was overshadowed on the one hand by the leadership of De Valera and the glorified diplomatic level at which the leader had elected to go to work, the companionship of Collins on the Cabinet was very supporting and dynamic in its effects, but may have operated to close Griffith's mind to the desirability of trying to see what diplomatic contacts could be made in Britain. It was possible that the circumstances of the times here were such that he or nobody else could risk that. But there must have been some element of impulse in that direction on his part, when P. Moylett, was doing his probing - apparently shortly before Archbishop Clune came over here [5].

The following conversation took place between myself and my father after I had read the above paragraph:

RM. Are you making this point that, because de Valera was away so long and so far away, and because of the quality of the people who made up the Sinn Fein executive at the time, that there was virtually nobody in the country who could explore possible peace plans at diplomatic level except Griffith, and that Griffith himself was under a serious disadvantage in this regard because he wasn't in fact the leader, that the leader was 2,500 miles away from him and that any contacts he might make might lead to trouble between himself and De Valera or trouble in the Sinn Fein organisation generally? What I'd like you to do is to summarise this aspect of De Valera's going to America, and being so long away that you think it created serious difficulties in establishing diplomatic contacts from the point of view of establishing peace feelers and eventually of establishing peace.

R. Yes, and as a matter of fact I don't think that anybody here, Griffith or Collins or Brugha or anybody else, was in a position to get feelers or enquiries going in Britain leading up to a kind

149

of preliminary diplomacy getting some kind of an idea under what headings a peace could be arranged with de Valera over on the other side, because Dev had been put to such a high level and he had got so completely away from the situation here, completely above as the leader and the final power, that Griffith or any of these could easily find themselves in the powerless position of Father O'Flanagan, when Fr. O'Flanagan in his blundering way came out in the open.

RM. In other words Fr. O'Flanagan took on the mantle of leadership and he in fact created embarrassment for everybody.

R. If, in an underground way, Griffith or anybody else were trying to make contacts or to have feelers set abroad, they might easily feel that they were weakening the situation.

RM. Cathal Brugha and Stack hadn't sufficient stature and sufficient sense of responsibility and sufficient poise as political leaders to have helped Griffith there or to have taken over themselves in the matter?

R. They wouldn't have thought of it for a moment because Cathal Brugha or Stack would not take the position of acting President when Griffith went into jail in November.

RM. Were Griffith and Collins the only two with any real sense and feeling of leadership whilst De Valera was away?

R. On the cabinet, yes.

RM. And all this crowd in the Sinn Fein executive had none at all - none of them showed any promise of leadership in any way apart from Collins and Griffith?

R. No. And to some extent they were handicapped even in lifting or moving Griffith to the point of decision or to the point of initiative by reason of the fact that Dev was away.

RM. What about Eoin MacNeill or Plunkett? Had they any influence approaching that of Griffith at all?

R. Plunkett - none in the world. MacNeill would always be a man whose counsel would be appreciated very much, but he wasn't in the position of power nor was MacNeill attempting to use any power at all.

RM. Reading the histories of the time you get the impression the Clune negotiations and the general negotiations of that time broke down because of a certain amount of dishonesty on the British side in eventually making it a condition of truce that the Irish Republican Army would have to give up their arms, and the impression you get is that the truce idea broke down then because of this single demand by the British. Is it possible that, if Dev were in Ireland at that time and had been in Ireland for some months before that, the Clune negotiations would have succeeded?

R. It is possible that it would. I wouldn't have any strong views one way or another about it [39].

In my opinion the Truce of July, 1921 could have been secured in December 1920 at the time his Grace Archbishop Clune endeavoured to mediate, but the opportunity was lost through the too precipitate action of certain of our public men and public bodies. The actions taken indicated an over-keen desire for peace, and although terms of Truce were virtually agreed upon, they were abandoned because the British leaders thought those actions indicated weakness, and they consequently decided to insist upon surrender of our arms [38].

The latter circumstance, the British last minute insistence on the surrender of arms, was clearly brought out by Collins in *The Path to Freedom* [40].

Dad raised the question of why the truce was delayed in his conversations with Paidin O'Keeffe [38]. O'Keeffe stated that he had no idea but said in his response that Dev had been approached towards the end of his stay in the

United States and told by the British consul there that the British were anxious for a truce The British consul urged him to return to Ireland where he would be granted immunity from arrest.

Perhaps Dev's presence was not that essential to achieve a truce in view of this important opinion expressed by Collins, an opinion widely accepted at the time by the army and political leaders in Ireland. Dad may have been exaggerating the influence of Dev's absence although clearly if Dev had remained in the country and had actively sought some accommodation with the British a truce might have been easier to achieve at this early stage. Father O'Flanagan* and the Galway County Council were the agents who precipitated the breakdown.

The cabinet did discuss the possibility of a truce on two occasions in late autumn 1920. A Mr Henderson apparently wished to explore the possibility of peace but was refused an interview without first securing the release of Griffith from prison [41]. Two weeks later the subject was again discussed [42] and it was decided to leave the matter in the hands of Arthur Griffith. It appears that the cabinet at the time had little concern with the Clune intervention and that the affair was largely in the hands of Griffith and Collins

Mulcahy wrote of the possible influence of the failed truce in November/December 1920:

> It could very well be considered that civil war would have been impossible. The inflation of spirit, caused by the fine summer [during the truce in 1921] and the long dragged out negotiations and the irritations developed at liaison level such as between the British command in the southern area and our liaison and other officers there, would either not have arisen or not have had time to inflame the situation. And the Brugha-Stack and Collins

*[Father Michael O'Flanagan was a teacher in Sligo and was vice-president of Sinn Fein. He retired from his church duties for a long period during which he was active in Sinn Fein. He opposed the Treaty and remained a committed republican well into the 1930s. His intervention in the Clune episode was considered to have encouraged Lloyd George in the view that the IRA were a beaten force. He eventually retired from politics and resumed his ministry].

conflict might not have been so strong, nor their influence have
time to affect Dev. The particular type of murder situation that
developed in Belfast would probably not have had time to develop
either [43].

Lloyd George terminated the negotiations with the remark "we have murder
by the throat", implying that the army would soon defeat the rebels. The
following excerpts show how wrong he was:

> Figures are given comparing the activities against the British in
> the month of May 1921, with that of October 1920. Attacks on
> British forces, 192 as against 42 in October. British forces
> killed, 76 as against 38 in October. British forces wounded, 106
> as against 48 in October. It had been suggested in the early part
> of the year that, after the dropping of the peace feelers, Lloyd
> George was going to have another six months of it; it was
> expected that that would reduce the resistance and prepare the
> country for some such basis of peace negotiations as Lloyd
> George was pressing for in December 1920. There appeared to be
> no such weakening in the country [44].

> Reviewing the first four months of 1920 and the first four
> months of '21, in weekly comparisons, the totals figures given
> are, for the first four months 1920. Attacks 52; killed 63;
> wounded 30. Totals for the same period 1921, attacks 509; killed
> 160; wounded 353 [45].

The increasingly bitter war which continued for the six months following the
Clune negotiations was also a factor in leading to the intransigence of those
who opposed the Treaty.

4.4 Cathal Brugha

Brugha was born in Dublin and was the owner or manager of Lalor's, the
candlestick makers in the city. It was generally believed that his father
came from England but his son, Rory, claims that he was descended from an
old Carlow family. Brugha was seriously wounded during the Rising. He was
an active separatist long before 1916. He had been a member of the IRB, and
was opposed to the Griffith concept of a dual monarchy. He was an Irish

speaker and member and one time president of the Keating branch of the Gaelic League, whose members generally were active in the IRB and later in the Volunteers*.

Dad gives an interesting account of Brugha's activities in the few years before 1916. As early as 1912, before the Volunteers were established in November 1913, Brugha and some of his colleagues in the IRB had organised rifle practice. Paidin O'Keeffe describes how he with Brugha, Eamonn Kent, and Sean MacDermott (the latter two were to be signatories of the republic proclamation) practised regularly on Sunday mornings at the old Greenmount Oil site at Harold's Cross Bridge. The owner or manager of the site allowed them to use the area and gave them a present of a gun. On one occasion he presented a prize of five pounds for the best shot. It was won by Cathal Brugha who according to O'Keeffe "made a bull's eye every time" [1,2].

Brugha was the first to encourage the reorganisation of the Volunteers in the autumn of 1916, when he was approached by two members of the IRB, Diarmuid O'Hegarty and Sean O'Muirthile. He was elected to the executive of Sinn Fein and appointed the chairman of the resident executive of the Volunteers at the two conventions in October, 1917. He was appointed temporary priomh aire of the Dail from January to April 1919 in the absence of de Valera and minister for defence from April 1919 to the ratification of the Treaty in January, 1922. He was implacably opposed to the Treaty and died from gunshot wounds sustained in the early days of the civil war.

Dad, in his capacity of chief of staff, had very close contacts with Brugha during the war of independence. His recollections of Brugha are included in considerable detail in various parts of his annotation on Beaslai's life of Collins, and in his tapes [3-6]. Brugha continued to manage his candle making business up to the time of his death. Dad met him for the first time and then only casually at the Keating branch of the Gaelic League. Brugha played an active role in the 1916 uprising. Because he had suffered severe gunshot wounds during the Rising he was not arrested nor was he deported by the British. He emerged from the Rising as an heroic figure [7].

*[Brugha's biography, *Cathal Brugha: a Shaol is a Threithe*, FNT, Dublin, 1969, was written by Tomas O'Dochartaigh].

Brugha subsequently played a leading role in bringing the threads of the shattered Irish Volunteer movement together again after the Rising, [8,9] so that there was a nucleus of volunteer activity when the deportees and surviving leaders later returned to Ireland between Christmas 1916 and June 1917. Dad writes about this early reorganisation of the Irish Volunteers by Brugha and a few IRB members, and he describes the setting up of the volunteer executive in October 1917 [10].

Referring to relations with Brugha during the war of independence, Mulcahy said:

> Cathal, I don't think ever clashed with us, Collins or myself, in any aspect of the positive (army) policy that was being pursued. Beyond the one element of clash between himself and myself, when he challenged me about some violent action that took place between some Volunteers, including Tom Hales, in the Bandon area, and the RIC in respect of which he said he would call the volunteer executive together for the purpose of dealing with whoever was responsible for it, there was no other occasion of any other complaint of this kind; and although both Collins and myself disagreed with Cathal's impulse to go on an assassination expedition to England, we not only did nothing to impede him in any way, but I provided, from the country and Dublin, the volunteers to go on that work, and others to intimate that they would be ready to go on that work if wanted [11,12].

He adds:

> None of us on the staff appreciated at all the idea of Cathal's mission to London [to assassinate the British Cabinet ministers]. I got the volunteers who were to go with him. Collins was here putting him in touch with an IRB contact in Liverpool who supplied more men there. He was there for quite a number of weeks. I think that I had the feeling that we were glad that Cathal had something to concentrate on and occupy him, leaving us free to feel and act about the situation in Dublin and in Ireland as we wanted to do in our own way [13].

There is a rather oblique reference in the cabinet papers of 6 November 1920 to some plan Brugha had in relation to Britain which may have had a connection with one of his two sorties to go to London to assassinate British ministers. He was advised to discuss it with the president who was still in America. Brugha did stay away for some weeks on such a mission but fortunately nothing came of it.

My father as head of the GHQ staff kept in close touch with Brugha who was the minister for defence. These visits kept Brugha informed of Volunteer activities and provided an opportunity to discuss matters relating to military policy. Apart from such discussions, Brugha played no part in military activities, did not attend staff meetings (despite Beaslai describing him as chief of staff), and at no time did he have any conflict with the policies initiated by the staff, except in relation to one or two minor occurrences. It was not until the end of 1920 or early 1921, after Dev's return from the United States and when rumours of Truce were in the air, that Brugha began to become more involved in army affairs.

Neither did Brugha appear to be very occupied on the political side until Dev returned. He attended the cabinet although whether he did so regularly is not clear. He did not attend the standing committee of Sinn Fein and he refused the acting presidency when Griffith was arrested in November 1920. Dad states that, after his return from America, Dev and Brugha were intent on wresting power and influence from those, like Griffith, Collins and himself, who had led the struggle while he was away [14].

It was about the time Dev returned from America in December 1920 that Brugha's antipathy to Collins began to manifest itself [2,8,15,16]. This antagonism had become a major cause of discord by the time of the Truce in the autumn of 1921, when Dad also found himself the object of Brugha's antagonism. I have already referred to the effect of Brugha's antagonism to Collins and Mulcahy in contributing to the political and army split after the Treaty. According to Paidin O'Keeffe, Brugha was also antagonistic to Griffith for a much longer period, and probably from the early days before 1916 [2,17]. This antagonism was probably based on Griffith's Sinn Fein policy advocating a dual monarchy as part of the constitutional settlement with Britain, which did not appeal to Brugha and the more separatist IRB members. Dad, however, states in response to O'Keeffe's assertion, that he had never noted any animus between Brugha and Griffith [1].

156

Despite being sacked by Brugha twice during the Truce, and despite Dev's demand for a "new army" in November 1921 [18,19] Dad remained chief of staff until he resigned the position after the ratification of the Treaty in January 1922 to become minister for defence in the Dail cabinet. He had this to say to Paidin O'Keeffe about his sacking:

> Mind you, I had a job of my own to stick to too, and it did you no good to be suspicious of people or to be questioning them. You had to go along ..... Actually I was sacked twice by Cathal from being chief of staff during the Truce, but also I thought that a very strange thing, you see, ... and you thought it would make me suspicious and difficult, but you didn't mind it. You simply went on and you felt you had trust in everybody ....

Brugha's antagonism to the two military leaders continued up to the ratification of the Treaty, when Brugha opposed the Treaty and resigned his ministry after its ratification. Dad refers to Collins's attitude to Brugha during these bitter times of discord, when he confirms that Collins retained his admiration and affection for him, and appeared to show no animosity or resentment at any time, nor did Dad, despite his difficulties with Brugha during the latter days of the war of independence and the Truce.

> A definite element in Collins's make-up was that no matter what was developing even up to a worst moment between Dev and Cathal and himself, he had a very definite established sneaking regard for whatever good was in them. He had a particular regard for Cathal in the same way as you would have for a difficult but natural child [20].

He refers to Brugha's brusque and impetuous character:

> .... Cathal Brugha was a very intense person, but he never sat down to any working councils of ours. My impression is that from the setting up of the GHQ Staff in March 1918, he took no part in the discussion of any matters that could be regarded as purely staff or military matters. And that would almost refer even to the development of policy. I kept in the most constant personal touch with him, visiting him at his working office in Lalor's the candle makers' place at Ormond Quay, or at his own

home in Upper Rathmines Road. Normally, talking to him was never a great pleasure. You were never sure when some intensity of mind on his part about something or another was disturbing his atmosphere. But in the developing of the situation, our appreciation of it was very much a common one and my experience of him was that as we progressed in policy from one step to another, his agreement flowed naturally and readily with us.

He was naturally blunt and frank and was no more tending to intrigue than he was to diplomacy. I had a couple of experiences of his brusqueness, but in the light of his broad agreement, and his tendency not to interfere in any way in the absence of some intenseness about something on his part, I found it easy to discharge my duty of keeping in touch with him, and there was never any necessity on my part or on the part of the members of the staff to feel that we were not in all matters pursuing a policy entirely approved of by him and by the Government. Beaslai's phrase "He was hopelessly out of touch with our army and the realities of the situation" means nothing. If it did mean anything, it would mean that I, who was assistant minister for defence as well as chief of staff, was out of touch with Cathal or keeping things from him; that is not so; and that Collins, who was his colleague on the cabinet as well as being deep in very responsible work in the army, was likewise neglectful [21].

On the question of agreement on policy it can be said: our whole approach to the aggression and reaction period pre-September 1919 was one on which there was entire agreement between the staff and Cathal; our approach to the attacks on barracks, begun as a result of my discussion with the Cork people, had his entire approval; the natural development subsequent to the evacuation and burning of barracks, and the development of columns was similarly agreed on; similarly with regard to the shooting of spies and detectives.

He describes Brugha as "tending to crush both communication and manners" and he was not "a tete-a-tete man" [22]. Unlike others, Brugha would not allow himself to be captured without putting up a fight. "As brave as a bull and as brainless" is a quote from Griffith [23].

158

Dad describes the night he spent with Brugha after they had met with Collins and McKee (OC of the Dublin Brigade) to discuss the shooting of the detectives in November 1920, the night before Bloody Sunday [24]. Dad was on the run at the time and, rather than cross the city to one of his haunts on the south side at such a late hour, he decided to stay the night with Cathal at a haunt of the latter's near Mountjoy Square. Apparently because of a lot of military activity following the shootings of the detectives, they stayed on during the following morning. At one stage when there was a particular commotion, probably when the military were arriving at the nearby Croke Park where the Bloody Sunday event was to occur, they must have felt threatened and:

> ....what does Cathal do but went up to his room, pulled up the window, pulled over a chair alongside it, pulled out two revolvers and put them on the bed beside him, and took off his boots! .... Now, my tactics would have been entirely different. I would have my bicycle out and been out of the gate at the back, and I would have been off up Drumcondra, but, noblesse oblige, I had to sit alongside my minister on the side of the bed there praying at whatever was going to pass [24].

Dad quotes, as appropriate to Brugha, a comment by John XXIII

> In the daily exercises of our pastoral office we sometimes have to listen much to our regret to voices of persons who, though burning with zeal, are not endowed with too much sense of discretion or measure [23].

The circumstances of his death in 1922, and the description of his reaction to possible British interception on the night of the 21 November, 1921, would support this view of his personality.

Brugha died "as brave as a bull" on June 19 1922, when he refused to surrender to the Free State forces at the start of the civil war. He died as he lived, impetuous and passionate. and a victim of his own idealism. He was a symbol of those who were committed to the immediate attainment of a political ideal which had not yet been demanded by a pluralistic Irish society. He died full of "passionate intensity".

Dad also wrote of Brugha and his death sacrifice:

> Cathal Brugha, who considered in 1917 that, because a policeman
> was killed in Cork, somebody was irresponsibly bringing
> destruction on the people and ruining the country, and who
> could in March 1921 be sending one of our most brilliant
> sustainers and leaders of the people generally to do a Japanese
> act of self-sacrifice in assassinating a British Minister* was
> throwing away his own life in O'Connell Street to stain our work
> in blood.

Whether Dad spoke about Brugha with resentment or with compassion is hard
to say, but he often spoke to me of him with sympathy and respect. When he
was invited by the 1916-1921 Club to speak about Brugha in 1965 he refused
on the grounds that he did not wish to be seen to be critical of him[4,25]. Dad
felt that Brugha, like many others who opposed the Treaty and fought against
it, had been misled by De Valera, and had been influenced by Dev to take up
arms against the democratically elected government of the Free State.
Whether this is true cannot be confirmed but might be considered unlikely
in view of Brugha's rather uncompromising character.

Indeed, could Brugha have influenced de Valera when he, Dev, showed such
anger towards Griffith when he first met the public at the Dante Exhibition
on the evening after the terms of the Treaty were announced? What might
have transpired between Brugha and Dev when, just after hearing of the
settlement, the news of which was received by Dev in Limerick with a non-
commital verbal nod, they travelled alone by train to Dublin on the 6th of
December. I would be tempted to exchange my worldly goods to have a
transcript of the conversation which took place in that railway compartment.
Dad had been in Clare, Limerick and Galway reviewing the troops with de
Valera and Brugha at the time of the Treaty settlement [19,26,27] but, as a
matter of courtesy to Stephen Rynne, who was accompanying them, he
travelled back to Dublin in the next compartment to Dev and Brugha.
Apparently no comment was made at any stage in his presence during the
visit to Clare and Galway about the negotiations which were taking place in

---

* [Brugha wanted Sean MacEoin, the renowned Volunteer leader from Longford,
to go to London to lead a party to assassinate British cabinet ministers, a proposal
which Dad refused to countenance].

London, nor did Dad ask any questions.

It seemed typical of dad's perception of his relationship with the political leaders that he would not feel it proper to question them on such important political matters. It was equally typical of Dev that he would not discuss any political matter, however topical or related to the military situation, with the head of the army. His only comment when he heard the news of the settlement was to say "I did not think that they would settle so soon" [27].

4.5 Dick McKee, Liam Lynch and others

While most of his references were to those who had leading roles in the struggle and its aftermath, Dad recalls his contact with many of his less prominent colleagues in the course of his conversations on tape and in his annotation. Typical are his references to Teeling, Ernie O'Malley and Simon Donnelly:

> An interesting thing about this general Kilmainham episode is the fact that after three successive nights of frustration and the attempt to escape then failing by reason of the rope breaking, Teeling, O'Malley, and Donnelly, without any outside assistance, succeeded in escaping on the following night. There is plenty of room for story telling here and Simon Donnelly is still alive; he was a great 3rd batallion man, would be very loyal to De Valera because of that and his association with Stack in relation to police matters pre Truce copperfastened him on the irregular side. He is mentioned here (Page 189 of Beaslai's biography) as becoming the commanding officer of the "Dublin" Republican police [during the war of independence]. I always regarded him as being, as it were, the chief commissioner of the republican police. I may have correspondence to indicate that. If he wasn't, then Stack had done nothing to put a headquarters top to the direction of his police and it shows how much the matter of police work was being left on the shoulders of the Volunteers.
>
> Frank Teeling was a rather interesting and very definite type of the fighting man, quite fearless and concentrated but with no just mere flamboyancy [1].

Ernie O'Malley

From the time Ernie O'Malley was with me in Tyrone he must have been engaged as an organiser with the Volunteers. We will find his tracks in the documents relating to many areas. At a time when the Auxiliaries had established a headquarters at Inistiogue in Kilkenny, a county where there had not been any great sense of aggressiveness or resistance shown, I sent O'Malley down there lest the presence of the Auxiliaries would reduce the Kilkenny men too much. I found him in Dublin about a week or so after I thought he had gone down, but I could find excuses for that. In his book, however, he appears to have criticised the Kilkenny people with the result that for a number of days in the *Irish Press* at one particular period, he ran a long series of articles on O'Malley and his doings in Kilkenny. At one particular part they seem to suggest that he did a lot of sitting by the fire and reading, mentioning "Mr Britling Sees it Through," as one of his guide books. He was apparently always very much at home with the south Tipperary men, Seamus Robinson and Co, but over a fair part of the midlands, Limerick, South Tipperary, perhaps North Cork area, he did a good lot of work.

When the Treaty division came there was no particular reason why he should be against the Treaty .... he was one of a group talking in (Paddy) McGilligan's house in Leeson Street, and is recorded as saying that, 'there would be nothing to do for a fellow like him in Ireland now after this Treaty, that there would be no more fighting and people like him would have to go off to India or some place like that.' The idea was that he could do fighting there [2].

In fact, O'Malley joined the Irregulars, was in the Four Courts with O'Connor and Mellowes, but escaped when they were captured by the Free State forces. He became one of the leading (members) of the Irregulars during the rest of the civil war. He wrote one of the earliest and most popular books on the war of independence *On Another Man's Wound* [3].

And in another part of the annotation he speaks of Florrie O"Donoghue, the Cork IRA leader, and the biographer of Liam Lynch:

> I placed him as one of the impeccables (sic) without whom the civil war could not have arisen.

Dick Mckee

Dick McKee he placed only second to Collins in the struggle against the British [4]. He was head of the Dublin Brigade, a position he inherited from my father. As head of the Dublin Brigade he provided invaluable support to Collins and to the Squad. He was also held in great esteem by some of the country brigades which he had visited and left his mark as director of training. Dad quotes Liam Deasy, the IRA leader, who remembered McKee organising a training camp in Glandore, Co Cork:

> Deasy speaks of the camp as an event which 'was to have far-reaching and decisive results. This was the six day training camp at Glandore under the command of the late Dick McKee who was then O/C of the Dublin Brigade. In all about fifty officers attended that camp. For six days an intensive course of training under the most rigid discipline was given under the stern command of Brigadier McKee. It is hard for me to attempt after such a lapse of time to tell in cold words what Dick McKee meant to those of us who were chosen to undergo that course of training.

> The cumulative effect of Dick McKee's training and leadership was evident in the fighting record of every unit of the third Cork Brigade in the succeeding two years when attacks, raids and ambushes were carried out with a verve and competence that would have done credit to the elite corps of any army in the world. In Dick McKee the fighting men of West Cork had found a mentor worthy of their metal.'

Mckee was captured on the night before Bloody Sunday, and was killed that night "trying to escape". No other loss during the war of independence affected Dad more than the loss of McKee. He was highly regarded by those who came in contact with him and knew him best. As director of training, he played a vital role in organisation, particularly in those parts of the country where the army was to prove most effective [5]. He carried out a number of brilliant actions, including the raid on the military airfield in Collinstown, when 75 rifles and 6000 rounds of ammunition were captured and sent to some country units which were seriously short of arms [6,7].

Liam Lynch

In the annotation [8] Dad writes about Liam Lynch the commandant of the First Southern Brigade. He mentions Lynch in his references to the West Cork activities during the War. Dad describes West Cork as the O'Donovan Rossa country, after the great Fenian patriot who was born there. This part of the country had a special place in dad's affection since he had spent two or three years in Bantry as a post office learner. There he first became immersed in Irish culture and nationalism, and it was there he attended the "university" of Siobhan an tSagairt in Ballingeary. He was also aware that West Cork was the birthplace of some of his volunteer colleagues, including Collins, O'Muirthile, Gearoid O'Sullivan and Diarmuid O'Hegarty.

Liam Lynch, Chief of Staff
of Republic forces

Liam Lynch was the leader of the First Southern Division which was formed in the later stages of the war. Dad thought him the most competent, reliable and inspiring of all the southern leaders. He appeared to have a special sense of trust in and admiration for Lynch which made it all the more difficult for him to understand why Lynch proved such an implacable opponent of the Treaty. He also found it hard to comprehend how Lynch's apparent fanaticism in support of the Republic, as chief of staff of the irregular forces, led to his futile and lonely death in the Knockmealdowns after the struggle was obviously seen to be lost to all except Lynch himself.

....it was Liam Lynch's leadership and work in the north Cork
Brigade number 2 that I found most impressive and orderly [8].

Dad's confidence in Lynch's maturity and good sense was such that, just before the assault on the Four Courts, when Lynch was already under arrest, he was released on dad's specific instructions. Dad believed that he would have a moderating effect on the recalcitrant Four Courts garrison. He was to be sorely disappointed when Lynch joined the Irregulars after the Four Courts attack and proved to be the most implacable opponent of the Provisional Government.

It was Lynch who wrote to Dad shortly after the signing of the Treaty on behalf of many of the southern volunteer leaders stating that the Treaty was unacceptable to them on the grounds of the oath (they wanted an oath to the Commonwealth and not to the King) and because of the retention of the ports by the British. They also stated that partition was not acceptable to them [9]. It was the early adverse reaction to the Treaty by Lynch and his West Cork colleagues which prompted Maryann Valiulis and others to think that even de Valera's acceptance of the Treaty would have made little difference to the extent of the subsequent army split.

Speaking of Lynch's outlook on the Treaty, Dad said:

> .... as an outlook that would perhaps not reasonably have led him into the fighting of the civil war or into any development like it if the reaction of De Valera to the Treaty had been different or even if De Valera had stopped short of approving of the use of arms by the Irregulars, whether after the Four Courts or before it [10].

This is a further repetition of Dad's prevailing view that Dev's immediate, unexpected and trenchant reaction to the Treaty was a major factor in provoking others to oppose the Treaty:

> Liam Lynch, who had been a lion of the resistance movement in the heart of the supreme British effort against the people, had left to serve with Cathal Brugha, whom on the 6 December on pre-Treaty grounds he had declined service with, to become by August or so 1922 a person so bedevilled with his position that he was telling De Valera that he would have to look in future to Childers as his leader, - and dying deserted on the Knockmealdowns [11].

I assume what Dad meant here was that by August 1922 even Dev was not extreme enough in his opposition to the Provisional Government to satisfy Lynch. Lynch would have to look to Childers, the leading anti-Treaty propagandist, as his political leader. And Lynch was literally deserted when he died on the Knockmealdown mountains through the capture of many of his republican colleagues and the retirement of the rest as they saw their cause was lost. But even at the end, when Lynch was holding out on his own, he believed that the war would be won by the republicans. This unrealistic optimism was a feature of the irregular campaign during the later days of the war, and is alluded to by Dad [12].

Chapter 5

Further Factors in the Genesis of the Civil War.

It is evident that the attitude of the rank and file of the Volunteers to the Treaty was largely determined by their leaders. An important factor in creating the split in the army was the intractable attitude to the Treaty on the part of the West Cork leaders who had been so active and successful during the war of independence. They had achieved a military success in the South West which was sufficient to clear the British police from the greatest part of the province. They may have been sufficiently isolated in their independent domain to be unaware of the political realities in the country, where the great majority of the people wished or at least had no objection to maintaining some link with Britain and the Crown. They may have thought that the great majority of people in Ireland, apart from the unionists, were in favour of an independent republic. It is likely that the independent spirit of the Cork IRA, and the implacable attitude of the Four Courts group,were important factors in finally creating the army split.

The failure of those who took up arms against the Treaty to accept the democratic decision of the people may be difficult to understand and accept, but the devotion to democracy may have been less strong then, particularly among people who had only a short history of participating within such a political system. A number of the IRA leaders who opposed the Treaty, some of whom fought against it, were clearly aware that the majority of the people favoured the settlement.

> In view of subsequent events it is well to notice that, Dan Breen, South Tipperary, Tom Hales, West Cork, Humphrey Murphy, Kerry, and Sean O'Hegarty and F. O'Donoghue, Cork City, made public their feeling that the fact should be accepted that 'it was admitted by all sides that the majority of the people of Ireland are willing to accept the Treaty' and that it should be possible to have an agreed election: with the result being a government that would have the confidence of the whole country: and that this would secure army unification [1].

The leaders referred to in this quotation by Mulcahy were united in their opposition to the Treaty, but to my knowledge none of the five took part in the civil war. Their willingness to await the will of the Irish electorate was in contrast with the uncompromising attitude of Rory O'Connor, Liam Mellowes and the other leaders in the Four Courts garrison.

Dad goes on to discuss other aspects of the army split and the effect of the Treaty debate on the army's attitude:

> The effect of the proceedings [in the Dail] since its first assembly on the 14 December 1921 to discuss the Treaty, following Mr de Valera's repudiation of them on the 8 December, had been to spread confusion and dismay through the country as a whole. The vast majority of the people were completely in favour of the Treaty. They were appalled by the fact that De Valera challenged it, and by the way in which he did it, in his statement to the people generally, before the Dail met, and in the manner in which he did it in the Dail. They were shocked and frightened by the obvious development of disorder and strife. There was nothing however that the great majority of people could do about it only talk, and develop opinions, and wait.
>
> The Volunteers, the army generally, were in a very different position. They had heard from the highest possible level that the plenipotentiaries had, as it were, behind the backs of De Valera and other members of the Government, broken their word in London and had done something that they should not have done; with the implication that they would not have been allowed to do it if, having obeyed what were alleged to be their instructions, they had consulted their colleagues at home before taking action; they were told that in future they would be the King's army, and that the King himself or his Governor-General in Ireland would be the person who would permit and sign all their commissions; and that while the British Army could go out now, it had every legal right to return where and whenever it pleased. They had had painted to them by a person who knew all about the King and the inside of British Government working [Erskine Childers, who had been in the British civil service and army] and he was supported by De Valera and other members of the cabinet and

other members of the Dail, the contention that the King had power over every scrap of legislation in Ireland and that his power could be decimal pointed in its effect by the use of the telephone. The binding and immobilising influence of the oath to the Republic was pressed home on them; and the inflexibility of any possible interpretation of that word in practice, except in accordance with some brainwave of De Valera's or some aspect of De Valera's conscience, was pushed home. The eyes of their dead comrades were turned upon them, and the eyes of important people like Stack and Sean T. O'Kelly etc. who were ready to sacrifice their lives, either deliberately or in terms of a bet, against the idea of De Valera ever doing wrong (Stack had said that he would commit suicide if he thought Dev would do anything wrong) [2].

As far as the general rank and file of the people were concerned with the challenge in all this, all they could do was think and pray and wait for the opportunity of saying what they thought, when they could go to the polls. For the army it was different. They were being challenged to stand to attention and in the face of all this, to humiliate themselves by acquiescence, or to take active steps to prevent, in one way or another, at the polls or otherwise, the bringing about of such a situation as would impose all these indignities on the country. With the varied experience of the days in which they were struggling against the British, the situation offered and suggested very many varied types of opportunity to various types of people for obstruction, incitement and aggression towards the new 'Dublin Castle Government' [3].

Dad also expressed the view to me that the volunteers in Cork, who were so successful in clearing the British police and the British presence from that part of Munster, were particularly influenced by the commitment to a republic and to a total break with Britain. In their isolation, induced at least to a degree by their successful campaign, they may have had an inflated conception of the volunteers' military success in the war, and perhaps of the prospect of continuing the war to a successful conclusion if hostilities were to resume. They may have been unaware of the obstacles to achieving a republic in a country where the majority wished to accept the Treaty and to retain some link with Britain and the Commonwealth. They were also unaware of or at least indifferent to the reality that partition and the Northern settlement was no longer a negotiable issue. It is historically understandable that, in resisting parliament by arms, they were less committed to the principles of democracy which we so readily accept to-day. Some of their leaders in their public statements admitted that the majority of the people wished to accept the Treaty settlement. But, no doubt, they were of the same opinion as de Valera that "the majority had no right to do wrong"!

Mulcahy includes in his annotation a number of the statements made in the Dail by the anti-Treaty deputies which he considered had an inflammatory effect on the army [4]:

> The King representing the British Government or the Governor General will have power to give or refuse assent to Irish legislation.

> Every act of legislation done by Ireland will be read in the light of that inflexible condition that Ireland is virtually a protectorate of England, for under this Treaty she is nothing more.

> What the King means is the British Government, and let there be no mistake under the terms of this Treaty the British Government is going to be supreme in Ireland.

> Pass that Treaty admitting the King to Ireland, or rather retaining him as he is in Ireland now, retain him while recognising him, recognise the British Government in Ireland and your rights and independence are lost forever.

> And the King and the Government behind the King would be barely 200 miles away and capable of exercising immediate control over what is done in Ireland.

> Every Commission held by every officer in the army of the Irish Free State will be signed either by His Majesty or by his deputy in Ireland.

Are we, by our own act, to abandon our independence? I hold that is impossible. I hold this assembly neither will nor can do that.

That document makes British authority our masters in Ireland.

I say they are subverting the republic. It would be a surrender which was never heard of in Ireland since the days of Henry the Second; and are we in this generation, which has made Irishmen famous throughout the world, to sign our names to the most ignoble document that could be signed?

I regard the Provisional Government as Dublin Castle for the moment - as Castle Government.

We are now in the position of Grattan and Flood. If Grattan had not permitted the Volunteers to be disbanded, the Act of Union would never have been passed. Now you cannot - this government of the Irish Free State cannot control the Army of the Irish Republic.

They never saw one Treaty signed by England with Ireland that England did not dishonour. Have they any assurance that this Treaty will be honoured either? [5].

Some of these statements were made by Erskine Childers, and a few by Sean MacEntee*. Dad considered that Childers's inflammatory attack on the Treaty was an important factor leading to the intransigence of the IRA, and particularly may have influenced those members of the army in Munster. Perhaps it is little wonder that the leaders of the Provisional Government were so bitter about Childers's intervention and his subsequent inflammatory publicity campaign on behalf of the Irregulars in the civil war. Childers, MacEntee and other speakers might have had little influence with

* [Sean McEntee, born in Belfast, was a member of the volunteer executive during the war of independence but I have no record that he was active on the military side. He was a founder member of the Dail and later of the Fianna fail party. He and his family were well known to us when they later lived in Leeson Park. Socially he was gracious and soft spoken but he had a sharp political tongue and was active as a hatchet man in the Dail debates].

the army, but these statements, if conveyed to the army from Dail Eireann, would undoubtedly have influenced the soldiers. At least that was Mulcahy's opinion.

If Dev had supported the Treaty, he would have been joined by most of the leading anti-Treaty TD's, including subsequent influential Fianna Fail members such as Jim Ryan, Sean Lemass, Frank Aiken and Oscar Traynor. A number of these were reported to have responded initially in a favourable way to the terms of the Treaty. Mary Josephine Ryan, my mother, was a member of the Wexford Ryan family, a family intimately involved in the Sinn Fein movement. She was a member of Cumann na mBan and was close to the political leaders. In her recollections on tape she states that her family, including her brother Dr Jim Ryan and several of her sisters, and many others who opposed the Treaty, responded enthusiastically at first to its terms but later must have been influenced by de Valera's outspoken opposition or by Sean T O'Kelly, who married mother's sister, Kate Ryan [6-9].

It is hard to believe that a section of the army could have effectively opposed the Provisional Government or prevented an election on the issue of the Treaty if a substantial majority of the Dail had accepted the settlement. It is very unlikely that the type of contributions to the Treaty debate by Erskine Childers and others which served to inflame the anti-Treaty section of the army, would have taken place if the politicians had accepted the Treaty as a stepping stone to the Republic. In such an event, it is unlikely that the real hard line anti-Treaty members of the IRA, such as O'Connor and Mellowes, would have had sufficient support to resist the provisional government in arms, or at least to create a resistance of the magnitude of the civil war.

If Dad appeared to be unrealistic in saying to Dev in September 1922 that he could stop the war by writing a letter to the Evening Mail, as is suggested by Professor Murphy in his review of the Mulcahy biography, he meant that even at that late stage of the war if Dev had called for a truce and proposed an amnesty, it was likely that the war would have ended earlier and with less bitterness, and less political and material damage to the country. And certainly the later and disastrous assassination policy promulgated by de Valera and the Irregulars, which intensified the execution response of the provisional government, would not have occurred.

Perhaps the most important questions are, to what extent did Dev's early and outspoken antagonism to the Treaty ensure that "a section of the army was determined to revolt," as asked by Mulcahy's biographer, and to what extent did he thus influence leading anti-Treaty politicians who might have otherwise supported the Treaty? To what extent would a more substantial majority in favour of the Treaty have influenced the more ardent republicans to accept the Treaty as a stepping stone? and to what extent did the more inflammatory contributions to the Treaty debate encourage so many members of the IRA to oppose the new state in arms, when the supporters of the Treaty were dubbed as traitors to the country?

My father, in answering the above four questions, was speaking as the person most intimately associated with the army, and close to all the political and military leaders. He was convinced that there would have been no split serious enough to lead to civil war if Dev had not set up the devastating chain reaction of aggressive opposition to the Treaty before it had been discussed by the Dail. By the time the Treaty was ratified, and all had spoken, it was too late for Dev or anybody else to influence the dissidents in the army. By then the damage was done, and anyhow Dev's continued equivocation merely served to further confuse the situation, and certainly did not help the maintain army unity. Tom Garvin wrote:

> Irish people have always sensed that a great disaster occurred
> between the signing of the Anglo-Irish Treaty on December 7th,
> 1921, and its ratification on 7 January 1922 [10].

Dad would say that the disaster was Dev's intemperate and violent reaction to the news of the signing.

Whatever influences may have led to the post-Treaty army split, and ultimately to the civil war, it is certain that the antagonism which was shown by Brugha and Stack towards Collins and Mulcahy must have had serious long term consequences. It may have dragged Dev into the Brugha camp and it must have led to discord between the military and political wings of the independence movement which did not exist before the end of 1920. I suspect that Dad would qualify this opinion by saying that the basic cause of Brugha's continued intransigence was Dev, because of Dev's failure to intervene when the chief of staff complained in the Spring of 1921 about the demoralising effect Brugha was likely to have on the army because of his open antagonism to Collins [11].

I questioned Dad on several occasions about the divisions between the army leaders and some of the cabinet which developed during 1921. He would not agree that the differences between Dev, Stack and Brugha on the one hand and Collins and himself on the other played any significant part in the disagreement about the Treaty. However, I cannot believe myself that the circumstances which existed in 1921 were not at least significant factors in the split. Brugha's increasing interference with the army, his less than proper recognition of and consultation with the chief of staff on matters of military responsibility, his open antagonism to Collins on apparently trivial matters, his later antagonism to Mulcahy, his longstanding antagonism to Griffith, and, in addition, Stack's implacable hostility to Collins, must have sown the seeds of later political and military divisions. These tensions among some of the leading participants in the national movement cannot be ignored when studying the genesis of the civil war.

In a paper which I read to the Army Club at McKee Barracks on the 22 March 1996, I spoke about my father's views about the genesis of the Civil War. In describing the war as a "compound disaster" [12], he attributed many of the political, economic, social and psychological problems which faced the new state to its consequences. In particular, he states that the civil war had a disastrous effect on Craig's attitude and on possible Northern conciliation [13].

Prof J.J. Lee, in his history *Ireland 1912-1985, Politics and Society*, reminds us of the deterioration in Ireland's economic status compared to Britain and other European countries which occurred after we had gained our freedom [14]. Apart from the senseless destruction of lives and property, there were other reasons for the adverse economic change, but it must have been largely caused by the divisive effects of the disagreement about the Treaty and the subsequent civil war. Few of our politicians after the foundation of the State had a strong and enlightened interest in the economic and social progress of the country, when much of the energies of our leaders was dissipated in the prolonged and bitter divisions which followed the civil war, nor would those interested in such aspects of politics have been easily heard above the tumult of acrimony and recrimination.

I am struck by the extraordinary polarisation which occurred among intelligent and responsible people in relation to the Treaty and the tragic consequences of their irreconcilable differences. It was particularly poignant to hear Dad mention about the internees in the Curragh who were loud in their cheering and jeering when they heard of Collins's death [15]. I wonder whether we should be studying conflict as a human problem, one which is so evident in the world to-day with all the civil and military conflicts which are taking place everywhere. How otherwise will we ever achieve a state of universal peace and security? The language, opinions and abstractions that surrounded the concept of the Republic, in the light of the pluralistic nature of Southern Irish society and of the Northern dilemma, created problems that even transcended the tragedy of the civil war. In practical terms what was needed was to achieve concrete objectives which would grant full self determination, the ability to change our constitution when and as we would wish, and the opportunity to exist in peace and harmony with our neighbours, to the mutual advantage of our two countries. Surely this was all granted by the Treaty, as was proved by subsequent events. The tragedy lies in the baleful influence the Treaty divisions and the civil war had on our relations with the North and on our own political, social, economic and psychological development. It also may have created a political vacuum which allowed the Catholic Church to exert too much political and social influence on the citizens of the Free State.

Clearly, the civil war had a multifactorial origin, and it would be difficult to quantify the influence of each factor, although there are some which were more significant than others in the sense that the war would not have taken place without them. According to Dad, the outstanding factors were the strait jacket of the republic imposed by the policies and rhetoric of the Sinn Fein movement, and de Valera's immediate reaction to the Treaty agreement. Some of these have already been dealt with.

The Strait Jacket of the Republic

Without the sustained commitment to a republic, the civil war would not have taken place. The declaration of the republic by the signatories in 1916 left a relic for the succeeding political movement which nurtured the ideological myth of a republic rather than the achievable reality of a constitution encompassing self determination and the will of most of the people to retain some connection with Britain and the Commonwealth. The myth was sustained from 1917 to 1922 by the rhetoric of the leaders of Sinn Fein. Dad discusses the stated republic of 1916 and the notional republic of the IRB [16].

175

He believed that few participants during and immediately after the war of independence had any real concept of the final constitution of a free Ireland [17]. Michael Hayes, a close friend and political associate of dad's, refers to the concept of the State's future constitution as perceived by the many participants in the freedom movement [18]. His views correspond closely to Dad's.

Dad's views on this subject were shared by other leaders. Michael Tierney, in his biography of Eoin MacNeill [19] quoted MacNeill as follows:

> For my own part, as well as being a Gaelic Leaguer, I am a Nationalist in politics. My politics are very simple and amount to this, that the less connection we have with Great Britain the better for us in every way. Still I do not believe in carping and finding fault with those who are trying to gain us a limited but effective amount of self-government. In theory I suppose I am a separatist, in practice I would accept any settlement that would enable Irishmen to freely control their own affairs, and I would object to any theoretical upsetting of such a settlement. If the truth were known, I think that this represents the political views of 99 out of every hundred nationalists.

Griffith, in a letter, advised that it would be unwise at this stage (November 1920, while he was in prison) to define the constitutional position of the new Irish state [20,21]. At this time of the Clune intervention he may have been concerned about the possible consequences of a commitment to the republican ideal which was the stated policy of Sinn Fein.

There are several comments in Maryann's biography implying that Dad was lukewarm about the Treaty and that his motivation to support it was largely based on his loyalty to Collins. I must confess that I am surprised by the suggestion that he might otherwise have been lukewarm about the Treaty. Nothing in his early or subsequent political outlook and nothing in the nature of the man would suggest to me that he could be anything but enthusiastic about the terms of the Treaty settlement. Although a separatist by conviction, he was a pragmatist by nature, and on several occasions, in discussing the circumstances of the Treaty settlement and the unhappy outcome, he told me that despite the notional republic which was promulgated by the Dail and the army during the war of independence, the driving force behind his separatist ideas was self determination. He claimed to have only a superficial idea of the final constitutional settlement which might be achieved. He was apparently no doctrinaire republican nor did he think that the doctrinaire republicans were anything but a small minority of the Irish population. He had a great regard and admiration for Griffith, and would expect him to put matters of practicality and common sense before matters of principle. He was greatly influenced by Griffith's political philosophy, particularly by his early proposal for a dual monarchy. I believe that Mulcahy, like Griffith and MacNeill, would always put matters of practicality and common sense before those of principle. He was not a person to be polarised about issues which were capable of being solved by compromise.

It was his opinion that many of his colleagues who were active politically and in the army during the war of independence were equally vague about the exact status of the constitutional end-point they envisaged. I believe that Dad was totally committed to the Treaty from the beginning by personal conviction, and that it embodied all the criteria of self determination which he aspired to, including the capacity to evolve constitutionally in any direction a democratic electorate might decide. If at any time during the spring and early summer of 1922, when he was so completely involved in preserving army unity, he gave any impression of being lukewarm about the Treaty, I would say that it was for diplomatic reasons and as a means of mollifying the antagonisms of the anti-Treaty section of the army. Apart from any impression of being lukewarm about the Treaty arising out of his efforts to mollify the more recalcitrant members of the army, there is no other evidence, so far as I am aware, to suggest that he was anything but enthusiastic about the settlement.

Speaking of his election campaign in December 1918, when he was a candidate for the post-war election, he said:

> The whole of my election comment was based on the self-determination principle, and not until MacEoin and I were required to nominate de Valera as President of the Irish Republic at the Dail meeting in August 1921, did I ever in a public speech refer to the Irish Republic in any way [22].

Neither do I believe that his later and influential role in reconciling the more radical members of Cumann na nGaedheal, despite the perceived anti-republican policies of the first Free State cabinet, was evidence of his inherent republicanism, as suggested by Maryann, although, from listening to his tape recordings, it is evident that he was more committed to Irish culture, Irish traditions and the Irish language than his political colleagues, with the exception of Eoin MacNeill and, possibly Ernest Blythe. I believe that he was as committed to the Treaty as Cosgrave, O'Higgins, and the other members of the cabinet, but that he was less identified with their apparent "pro-British" political philosophy because of his military role before the Treaty, because he was no longer a member of the cabinet after the army mutiny, and because of his fluency with the Irish language and close contact with Gaelic Ireland through his chairmanship of the Gaeltacht Commission in 1925.

Certainly, his shortlived detachment from the mainstream of political power following his resignation from the ministry in 1924 absolved him from some of the pro-British opprobrium which the cabinet at the time attracted. In my view, he would have approved of the Treaty as a permanent settlement with the United Kingdom, subject to such modifications as the taking over of the ports, and the intent to achieve eventual Irish unity with the agreement of the people in the North. As late as 1944 his views about Ireland and the Commonwealth were crystallised when, in his first address to Fine Gael as their newly elected president, he pledged his party to support and to remain in the Commonwealth.

We need to be reminded of the people who were elected to the first Dail in December 1918. Sixty-eight Sinn Fein deputies were elected, all chosen, not by the democratic choice of their constituents, but by Michael Collins and Harry Boland, and possibly a few other colleagues close to them, and ratified by the standing committee of Sinn Fein. The 68 deputies (representing 73 constituencies) were all members of Sinn Fein or the Irish Volunteers, although obviously not all were doctrinaire republicans. There were six Parliamentary Party and 26 Unionists elected [23,24].

The 121 Sinn Fein deputies in the second Dail of May 1921 were elected without contest. They included almost all the original 68 Sinn Fein deputies elected to the first Dail. The rest were chosen by the local Sinn Fein cumainn nationwide, with a strong influence from the army [24]. The second Dail was the parliament which by 64 to 57 votes ratified the Treaty in January 1922, a narrow majority. But the members of the Dail were not representative of the Irish electorate. Every voter in the country who desired self-determination had no choice but to vote for Sinn Fein. The Parliamentary Party by May 1921 was completely discredited and had not put forward any candidates. The Labour Party had not contested the 1918 and 1921 elections by agreement with Sinn Fein and in order not to split the nationalist vote [20,25]. No other party went forward with a less radical self-determination policy than that of the republic. It is not surprising, therefore, that, while the Dail passed the Treaty by a narrow majority, the country approved the Treaty by a very substantial majority. The history of the Labour Party and the agreement not to contest the first and second Dail is discussed on tape [25].

Because of the non-representative nature of the second Dail, it was probably not correct of de Valera to justify the republican claim in an interview with the *Irish Bulletin* representative in the Spring of 1921 [26] when he was challenged by his interviewer about the moral right of the Volunteers to fight the war of independence. Dev makes the point that this was the army of a government which was legitimised by the decision of the people in the election of 1918, and that, because of the sacrifice of the leaders of 1916, who proclaimed the republic, this republic was confirmed by the people at that election. Under the circumstances Dev's response was understandable even if not based on the realities of the situation. Dev's arguments must have been most convincing to the masses, even to some of the British readers, and it is not surprising that many members of the army in Cork and Kerry, who were remote from the political realities of the time, were so committed to the republican ideal when the Treaty issue arose, particularly when they were aware of the opposition of Dev and other leaders to the Treaty.

It was also naive if not disingenuous of de Valera when, two days after the Treaty was signed in London, he wrote to the newspapers rejecting the settlement with the following words:

A chairde Gaedheal,

You have seen in the public press the text of the proposed Treaty with Great Britain. The terms of this agreement are in violent conflict with the wishes of the majority of this nation as expressed freely in the successive elections during the last three years.

179

I feel it my duty to inform you immediately that I cannot recommend the acceptance of this Treaty, either to Dail Eireann or the country. In this attitude I am supported by the ministers of home affairs and defence. A public session of Dail Eireann is being summoned for Wednesday next at 11 o'clock. I ask the people to maintain during the interval the same discipline as heretofore. The members of the cabinet, though divided in opinions, are prepared to carry on the public services as usual.

The army, as such, is, of course, not affected by the political situation and continues under the same orders and control.

The great test of our people has come. Let us face it worthily without bitterness and, above all, without recriminations. There is a definite constitutional way of resolving our political differences. Let us not depart from it, and let the conduct of the cabinet in this matter be an example to the whole nation" [27].

In discussing the genesis of the civil war, Dad also mentions the failure of the politicians and the influence of the women.

The failure of the politicians

Mulcahy makes several references to the failure of the politicians to support the efforts of the military leaders to prevent a split in the army. Despite his strenuous efforts, and those of Collins and the more moderate elements on the republican side, no agreement could be reached between January and June 1922 to prevent the army split. Attempts at agreement failed because of the recalcitrance of O'Connor and Mellowes, and their colleagues in the Four Courts, and some of the military leaders in the country, particularly in the south-west counties of Cork and Kerry. Dad refers to the failure of the politicians to support the efforts of the army leaders. He records the failure to reach decisions about working the Treaty by the Sinn Fein party at its Ard Fheis in March 1922 [28], and in May 1922 in the Dail he complained about the failure of the politicians' efforts. He said "This is the 47th time we have discussed the issue without any prospect of agreement or compromise"

Dad muses at length about the influences which caused Dev, Brugha and Stack to oppose the Treaty so vehemently [7-9]. He describes in great detail the negotiations to prevent the split between January and June 1922 [29].

In a conversation I had with Dad, we discuss the hypothetical situation if the Treaty had been defeated by Dail Eireann [30]. We conclude that it would have created an anomalous situation where the majority of the people would not support their parliament and where perhaps the British government would adopt the role of supporting the people against its own elected representatives. We speculated that a number of the deputies who voted against the Treaty through lack of moral courage would have voted otherwise if they thought that it was likely to be defeated. This is a valuable and detailed exposition of dad's opinion of Dev's and other politicians' failure to provide leadership at this crucial juncture in Irish affairs.

The influence of the Women

It has been stated that the extreme anti-Treaty attitude of the women played a part in causing the army split. The six women deputies in Dail Eireann voted against the Treaty, a few of whom made personal attacks on Collins, Griffith and Mulcahy. Twenty-eight of the 30 members of the standing committee of Cumann na mBan were opposed to the agreement. So how would we do if we had a matriarchal system of government? Mrs Jenny Wyse Power was one of the two members to support the Treaty. Many of her letters can be found among dad's papers [31]. They contain material dealing with the attitude of the women TD's and the members of Cumann na mBan to the Treaty, and interesting material about the Treaty conflict and about the author's forebodings during the increasing crisis in the spring of 1922.

In the same file there is a letter from Phyllis Ryan, mother's youngest sister and later to become the second wife of Sean T O'Kelly, announcing severance of all family relations by herself and the other sisters opposing the Treaty with mother following her husband's betrayal of the Republic [32]. Happily the initial bitterness which afflicted the Ryan family was dissipated, at least overtly, within a few years.

P.S. O'Hegarty, in his book, *The Victory of Sinn Fein* [33] states "he had the strongest condemnation of the women who were affected by the moral deterioration induced by the war of independence."

Brian Farrell, in his Thomas Davis RTE lecture on the occasion of the fiftieth anniversary of the Rising, quoted O'Hegarty "....Turned them into unlovely destructive-minded arid begetters of violence" [34] and Bishop Doorly, at a confirmation ceremony in 1925, described the same women as "furies".

Richard Mulcahy meets old comrades in 1968 to discuss genesis of civil war.
Seated (left to right) : Michael Brennan*, Sean MacEoin*, Richard Mulcahy*,
Peadar McMahon*, Joe Sweeney*.
Standing (left to right): Gen. Michael Costello, Professor O'Connell (Cork),
Michael Hayes, Chairman of the Dail (1922-1932), Liam Archer*.

In a conversation with five surviving chiefs of staff in 1966, when many aspects of the civil war were discussed and recorded on tape, Dad quoted the above comments. However, he was himself more charitable in believing that the influence of the women was the consequence rather than the cause of the divisions among the politicians and the army [36]. I think that his views were more from the heart than the head. He indulges in one of his poetical flights of fancy when he talks of the women of Dublin [37]. After he had referred to the people of the West Cork gaeltacht "with a biblical stature of

* Former Chiefs of Staff.

182

mind, character and disposition" he went of to say of the plain people of
Dublin:

> I found the same stature in places like the cul-de-sacs of
> Gloucester Street and places like that. They had a matriarchal
> system there where the mother was the queen of the place! [37].

Clearly, whatever faults he may have had, he could never be accused of being
a male chauvinist!

There is an important parallel between the situation in Ireland from January
to June 1922, and the situation as it existed in the North of Ireland until
recently. The first ceasefire in the North continued from September 1994 to
February 1996, a period of more than seventeen months. During this time the
leaders of the different parties failed to agree to meet. And this situation
continued until the first meeting of the Northern leaders arranged by the
new Labour government after the second ceasefire. The political failure in
1922 is reflected in the Northern situation a short while ago. The actions of
the politicians in 1922 failed to reflect the wishes of the great majority of
the Irish people. In failing to meet over the 17 month period, at least some
of the politicians charged with settling the Northern problem were probably
not reflecting the wishes of most of their constituents.

In defence of the Treaty, Collins spoke about it as a stepping stone to a more
acceptable final constitutional solution. His instincts and those of many
others were subsequently proved to be correct. I believe the same stepping
stone opportunity has now been grasped in the North. If we de-emphasise the
concept of a final constitutional solution, but encourage greater cooperation
between North and South in economic, social, cultural, sporting and artistic
affairs, we shall certainly reach a political settlement, albeit not overnight,
which will satisfy the great majority of the Irish, North and South, and the
British. Such an approach will immediately benefit both parts of the
country, for many of the fundamental social, economic and human problems
we are facing are common to both Irish communities.

Finally, the question of the decommissioning of arms bedevilled the earlier
Northern negotiations. The abortive truce in November 1920 in the South
failed on the rock of decommissioning, but the successful truce of July 1921
was arranged without mention of any such precondition. It seemed to be

accepted by both sides in 1922 that commitment to a truce was sufficient evidence of a sincere wish to reach a settlement. So the Good Friday Agreement was reached without preceding decommissioning.

Chapter 6

Post-Treaty and the Army Mutiny.

Perhaps one of dad's most difficult and frustrating periods between 1916 and 1924 was after the ratification of the Treaty, when he and Collins made the most strenuous efforts to prevent the army split and the civil war. Between January and June 1922, he devoted his time and energies to reconciling the different elements of the army, while, as he complained, the politicians did nothing but squabble and incite the soldiers to lawlessness. At times he and Collins sailed dangerously close to offending the supporters of the Treaty in their efforts to mollify their opponents, although this did not imply that they were not fully supportive of the Treaty. In retrospect, it seems that their efforts were never likely to overcome the intransigence of O'Connor and Mellowes, and the other anti-Treaty army members who occupied the Four Courts from March to June 1922.

Collins and Mulcahy were not alone among those who did all in their power to avoid an army split. A number of the moderates on the anti-Treaty side of the army were involved in finding an amicable solution but were unsuccessful in overcoming the intransigence of their colleagues who had an inflexible commitment to the Republic. Tragically, the army failed to remain united and the civil war, with all its ghastly consequences, became inevitable. At least the army tried while the politicians procrastinated. Maryann, in her biography of my father, gives a detailed account of the frustrating negotiations which took place between the two sections of the army between the ratification of the Treaty in January and the start of the civil war in June 1922.

Dad had a great pride in the army. It was an integral part of his own brand of idealism and nationalism. He believed the army held the key which would ensure that Ireland would emerge as a free, prosperous, christian and pluralistic democracy, with a culture combining the old gaelic traditions with those of the Anglo-Irish community [1,2]. His idealism extended beyond the function of the army as a military force. Even at the height of the civil war he was already laying down plans, with his brother-in-law, Denis McCullough, and John Larchet, professor of music at University College, Dublin, to establish an army school of music. Jack Larchet and his family

The last of the Dublin of Parliament days - the funeral of General Michael Collins 29 August, 1922.

were close friends of my parents, and it was he and McCullough who travelled to Germany in late 1922 or early 1923 to find a bandmaster to organise the school.

Dad believed an army training would prepare young men to be better citizens. In a speech Dad made to the troops on the 8 October 1922 during the civil war, he thanked the army for its excellent work in restoring the roads and railways, and bringing a state of peace and normality to many parts of the country, and he said:

> In the same way they looked forward to making the army a national institution through which the young men of Ireland would pass to be much better men and citizens.

Well before the civil war ended Dad had engaged Fritz Brase, one of the ex-Kaiser's bandmasters, to head up the army school of music [3-6]. The German brass bands had a different pitch from the British. Dad favoured the higher continental pitch, advice he had received from a Mr O'Beirne, who was in the Board of Works. O'Beirne must have had some knowledge of music as subsequently he was justified in this advice when the British army bands made the same change. Dad's stated object in setting up the army school was to train musicians who would continue in a musical career after discharge from the army and who would enhance the musical traditions of the country. The history of the Army School of Music has been published [7].

As early as October 1923, the first army band, under the baton of Fritz Brase, gave its first public concert in the Gaiety Theatre to a crowded audience, including W.T. Cosgrave and members of the Executive Council [8,9]. Dad, as minister for defence, and the members of the army council, occupied a special box in the theatre. It must have been a proud moment for my father, particularly as the band played the Mulcahy March, composed by Fritz Brase, for the first time in public. However, the aftermath may have proved a little embarrassing because of dad's decision, supported by his army colleagues, that they would not stand during the playing of the national anthem. Dad had already proposed to his ministerial colleagues that, with the war with Britain over, the bellicose tone of the national anthem *Amhrán na bhFiann* was no longer appropriate. He proposed instead O'Donnell Abú (the words of which, I think, are equally bellicose although perhaps less topical) and it was to make this point that the minister and army leaders

187

decided to sit out the Soldier's Song [9]. I expect their action misfired and may have given an undesirable impression of arrogance to the audience (or possibly some of the audience thought it was part of strict army protocol to sit out the national anthem!).

In the same tape he criticises Dev for "dipping his dirty fingers" into the Irish version of the anthem to name his new party Fianna Fail in 1926.

Dad had other ideas for the peacetime army. He believed the soldiers after demobilisation at the end of the civil war should be employed in reafforestation and other public works. Whether such projects were practical at the time is questionable. Proposals along these lines were made to the cabinet as early as September 1922 but received no support from his colleagues [7,10,11]. Because of the overriding effects of the civil war and the grim political situation, such economic policies had a low priority. Anyhow, the major political problems associated with demobilisation which led to the army mutiny and dad's resignation from the ministry put paid to such high minded plans.

The 1916 to 1924 period in dad's career ended with the army mutiny and his resignation from the ministry of defence. He resigned from the army in May 1923 at the end of the civil war, and decided to devote his life to politics. He retained his position as minister for defence in the cabinet and was returned to the 4th Dail in Augusts 1923 with a whopping vote of 22,203, a figure which has not been reached by any candidate before or since, and which was surely a powerful endorsement by the electorate of Clontarf constituency of his leadership of the army during the civil war.

The Irish Times, on the 22 September 1923 wrote:

> General Mulcahy has cast aside the sword, to resume once more the legislator's toga. He, too, has been through the fires within the past twelve months, and, if one does not notice such a marked change in his personality, it is because he is a philosopher. He was a wise head long before its time and today he is the same curious mixture of gentleness and relentless purpose, the same strange amalgam of dreamer and man of decisive action and one of sympathy, and compelled our respect when first he stood up in the Mansion House, a frail and somewhat pathetic figure, and spoke in lyric phrases about Cuchulann at the ford [12].

Much was written about Dad and his dominant role during the 1922-1923 period in the national and international press after the civil war ended [12]. He was described as "the most interesting man in Europe" by a correspondent in *Colliers Magazine* [13]. The correspondent went on to say "Michael Collins was the bold charging front of the rebellion: Mulcahy was the organising and planning brain. When I learnt of Collins's death, it seemed to me that he rather than Mulcahy should have been killed. The task in hand required a Mulcahy type." The correspondent writes at length about the organising of the Free State army and he asks "What was Mulcahy's task? (he) was a man with a hand of steel who offered the volunteers uniforms and regular pay in return for unceasing drill and absolute obedience".

The taking over of Beggar's Bush Barracks, January 1922.

Dad's role in the civil war is described in detail by Maryann Valiulis in the biography. In view of Maryann's account, it is not my intention to deal in any detail with dad's involvement. In his speech at the Treaty debate, he stated that the army did not have the capacity to carry on the military struggle against a determined military effort by the British. The best they could do was to attack a fair sized police station. He agreed with General Macready's view expressed to Lloyd George that the (British) army, if given a free hand, could suppress the rebellion but this would not solve the Irish question [14]. In dad's view, if extensive army sweeps throughout the troubled areas had been employed, the thinly spread guerillas would not have survived. The British army was under-utilised during the war of independence because the British authorities did not wish to consider the conflict to be anything more than a local disturbance and not worthy of the army's total participation. However, Dad noted increasing army involvement during the last few months of the war and hence his anxiety to divisionalise the volunteers to give each area a greater degree of autonomy in the event of major British army successes in the field.

The taking over of Collins Barracks, November 1922.

His papers in the university archives contain a vast amount of material - correspondence and newspaper comment - about the period [15]. They provide a background to dad's character and reputation, to his deep commitment to the discipline, efficiency and integrity of the army, and to the highest professional standards during the many months he was leading the fight against the Irregulars It is said that every morning at 7 o'clock, when he met the army council in Portobello Barracks during the war, he opened the proceedings with the exhortation "Decisions, decisions, decisions!"

Despite the tragedy of Collins' death while travelling in hostile country, Dad apparently visited several parts of the country during the war. On one occasion in January 1923 when he was visiting the south of Ireland, a note on file states "Exceptional precautions were taken for General Mulcahy's protection, and two aeroplanes accompanied him"! [16]. Whether the planes could have helped in the event of an ambush in wooded areas or of a strategically placed land mine must be open to some doubt. I would have thought that the aerial activity might have given valuable information to his adversaries about his wherabouts.

The army mutiny occurred ten months after the ending of the civil war. I interviewed Dad about the circumstances which led to the mutiny, and the role of the IRB in the army at the time [10,11]. The presence of renewed IRB activity among the senior officers of the Free State army was a contention of the officers who mutinied and who believed that the IRB people were being retained in the peacetime army while the old IRA were being discharged, despite their service during the war of independence. The presence of renewed IRB activity was also one of the complaints of O'Higgins about the army at the time. Although I seemed to do most of the talking in this tape, Dad managed to deal with some important matters in his replies. He talks about the relationship between himself and Kevin O'Higgins before, during and after the Treaty, and in particular with his contention that O'Higgins and his department of home affairs interfered to an unacceptable degree with the army from the end of 1922. He names some of the army officers who were in contact with O'Higgins, unknown to him at the time. These officers were disaffected for various reasons and were critical of certain aspects of the army's activities and its policies.

O'Higgins's increasing criticism of the control of the army during the civil war and its aftermath, caused Mulcahy justifiable irritation. While he never showed any personal animosity to O'Higgins, he said that neither O'Higgins nor any other member of the cabinet knew anything about the army and the difficulties it faced during the civil war and its aftermath. O'Higgins's complaints included a charge that venereal disease was rife in the army and was not been dealt with properly. Mulcahy denied this and spoke of the high standards of the medical services in the fledgling army, staffed by members of the medical profession who distinguished themselves afterwards in the medical services of the country. Dad mentioned the names of "Pops" Morrin, Tom O'Higgins and Matt O'Connor as a few of his medical officers. Morrin became a well known surgeon at St Vincent's Hospital and had been trained as a trauma surgeon in the British army during the Great War. O'Higgins, a brother of Kevin O'Higgins, was later appointed chief medical officer for Co. Meath, and O'Connor became the pathologist to the Richmond Hospital.

O'Higgins criticised Mulcahy because of lack of discipline in the army and he complained about atrocities in Kerry. He claimed the civil war was allowed to drag along without reason, and that there should have been more executions as a deterrent [10,11,16-19].

O'Higgins's criticism of Mulcahy and the army continued after the end of the civil war, when Mulcahy had the formidable task of demobilising 40,000 or more of the army in his efforts to establish a professional peacetime force. Efforts at demobilisation led to serious disturbances among the soldiers, culminating in a serious episode when a large number of officers defected from the Curragh with arms in 1923. It eventually culminated in the mutiny of 1924. These events were a serious threat to the stability of the government.

It is likely that despite the high ethical and disciplinary standards the Free State army leaders aspired to, it was impossible to mobilise a new and raw army, and to pursue a difficult military campaign without some breakdown in discipline and control. Indeed, it seems almost miraculous to me that the army succeeded in maintaining such high standards of discipline and control under the circumstances of such a bitter and prolonged conflict, and against adversaries who did all in their power to reduce the country to a state of chaos. Yet O'Higgins and his friend, Paddy Hogan, the minister for agriculture, became increasingly critical of the conduct of the civil war by the army and, according to Mulcahy, O'Higgins undermined the force's morale because of his association with the officers who kept him informed of army details without the knowledge of the commander in chief and the army council.

His attempts to ease the problems of demobilisation after the civil war, by finding jobs for those thousands who were discharged from the army, received, according to him, little sympathy or support from the cabinet. The problems associated with his efforts to change what had been an insurgent army to a professional peacetime army involved him in many tensions with those of his old colleagues who were no longer suitable for peacetime duties.

Dad's relationship with his cabinet colleagues is discussed in detail in his papers [20].

He discusses his unsuccessful efforts to have Cosgrave and the other cabinet ministers solve his demobilisation problems by providing extra employment in housing, road building, forestry, and other constructive works, although he does admit elsewhere that he might have made a greater effort to consult Cosgrave about his problems. As early as September 1922, while the civil war was at its height, he raised this question with the cabinet, so that he appeared to have some foresight of his subsequent demobilisation difficulties.

The demobilisation difficulties led to the army mutiny and its aftermath, and to a serious rift in the Cumann na nGeadheal party. In making the point about consulting Cosgrave, he may have been implying that Cosgrave might have had a restraining effect on O'Higgins and might have shown greater sympathy for the army council at the time of the mutiny.

In response to my question about the Government's efforts to deal with the demobilised soldiers, Dad answered as follows: "I fell down in not forcing them to realise that better ...." [21]. (The tape came to an end at this stage and I was unable to find the sequel).

He remarks about the stultifying effect on the cabinet of being confined to Government Buildings during the early months of the civil war, and their neglect of economic and social problems while the Dail debated the new constitution and indulged in "gossipy" type of work during the autumn of 1922. Their continued preoccupation with the newspaper accounts of the disturbances in the country had the effect, according to Mulcahy, that they had nothing better to do than criticise the army while it was undertaking the mammoth task of beating the Irregulars [10,11,22].

When I questioned him about a possible breakdown between himself and the cabinet during and after the civil war (underlined by Maryann in her biography as a factor leading to the mutiny), this was not denied but he maintained that he was too preoccupied with pursuing the war to spend time sitting around talking to his cabinet colleagues [10,11].

Dad talks about the various stresses and crises which occurred in relation to the army and the government during and after the civil war. Despite difficulties for himself and the army council, he states that he did not let these interfere with his personal relations with his colleagues.

One of the stated reasons for the tarnishing of Mulcahy's reputation proposed by Maryann Valiulis was his draconian conduct of the civil war. He never expressed any regrets about the illegal execution of Rory O'Connor, Liam Mellowes, Richard Barrett and Joseph McKelvey in November 1922 in response to the shooting of deputies Hales and O'Malley. However, he did state that he regretted having to take such draconian action and blamed the proclamation by de Valera and Lynch in November 1922 which advocated a policy of assassination aimed at the members of the Dail and other leading pro-Treaty figures.

He and the members of the army council were the main instigators of the executions, although Kevin O'Higgins suffered the greatest opprobrium subsequently. Indeed, O'Higgins was the last member of the cabinet to agree to dad's proposal and apparently only did so reluctantly [19]. Dad deplored Dev's support of the policy of assassination of the members of the Dail and other prominent pro-Treaty supporters, and he believed that democracy in Ireland was under imminent threat because of this republican policy [23]. He believed the execution of the four prisoners and threats of further executions brought a sudden cold sense of realism to his opponents, as did the execution of Childers and of many other Irregulars who were found to carry firearms.

There was serious public reaction to the shooting of the four prisoners. Certainly from a distance of seventy years or more it seemed a very extreme reaction. I, like most others, would think the execution of the four prisoners was unnecessary, as indeed may have been the prolongation of the execution policy into the Spring of 1923. But it is easy to say now what should or should not have been done. It is less easy to assess the necessity of these actions at that critical time.

There was the same political and public reaction to the execution of Childers, who was found to possess a small hand gun when he was captured in his home [10,11,24-27]. Dad includes a note about the reasons and circumstances under which he proposed the execution policy and the military courts to the cabinet in September 1922, and why he approved of the decision to execute Erskine Childers in November 1922 [10].

Childers, a member of a well-known Anglo-Irish family had been in the British civil service and the British army. He fought in the Boer and later in the great war. He became passionately committed to the republic, and masterminded the Howth gun running episode in 1914. He was particularly disliked by the Free State leaders because of his bitter and telling propaganda which was circulated widely at national and international levels during the civil war. Childers also made some inflammatory and misleading statements during the Treaty debates which were perceived by my father and others to provoke many of those who took up arms against the Treaty. It is easy to understand why Cosgrave and his colleagues did not want to make an exception of him.

*The Commander in Chief with officers in Kilkenny
during the Civil War.*

However, the pressure to commute the death sentence was such that Cosgrave was reluctantly obliged to consider a reprieve. The night before the execution a message was conveyed to Childers that if he would agree to cease all further opposition to the democratically elected parliament of the Free State, the death sentence would be withdrawn [18]. According to Terence de Vere White, writing of Kevin O'Higgins on the 40th anniversary of his death,

Diarmuid Coffey saw Mr Cosgrave on the day before the execution and got him to agree to pardon Childers if he would sign an undertaking to keep out of politics [28]. Childers apparently answered that he would make a decision after he had spoken to his wife.

Later that night he replied that he could not agree to the conditions imposed on him. There is a conversation recorded between Dad, mother and another when they spoke about Childers [29]. The unidentified discussant states that Childers was dominated by his wife, and that she was particularly extreme and rigid in her views, which may be relevant to his refusal to accept the offer from Cosgrave. However, this view is not supported by Deirdre McMahon who is familiar with the Childers papers.

Frank Holland was a private in the Free State army in 1922 and had been active during the war of independence. He was the soldier in charge of Childers after his arrest, and was constantly with him until his execution. Holland describes the extraordinary courage of Childers. He apparently thanked his executioners, expressed forgiveness to his opponents and refused to be blindfolded. In fact, he eventually agreed to a blindfold when the officer in charge explained to him that it would cause undue distress to the firing party if his eyes were not covered. The order to fire was given by dropping a handkerchief and not by the usual verbal order (O'Connor, personal correspondence in author's possession).

There is a graphic account of the Childers execution on dad's tapes [30,31]. He was housed in a large shed in Beggar's Bush Barracks, where he exercised three times a day by walking one measured mile inside the shed. In between he slept for a few hours and spent the rest of his time writing. There was maximum security to prevent any possible rescue, either by outsiders or by members of the army. Paddy O'Connor was the officer in charge. When he was told about his execution the evening before, Childers thanked O'Connor, and, according to Holland, the information did not cost him a thought. At midnight he asked to see the Church of Ireland Bishop Gregg, who arrived promptly and spent the night with him. The bishop, according to Holland, wept at times.

There were fifteen men in the firing party, but only five had loaded rifles. Paddy O'Connor arranged secretly that the five with the loaded rifles were ex-great war soldiers, apparently because of their superior markmanship.

The execution took place in the early morning at first light, and was so arranged that Childers was placed at the end of a shed where part of the roof had been removed to leave him in the light. The firing party were in the dark where they could not be easily seen by Childers. His death was instantaneous and the markmanship apparently very accurate.

Only a man with a profound belief in his principles could have behaved as Childers did. He died a martyr to his cause. The tragedy of Childers's death is a sad reminder of the consequences where principle conflicts with pragmatism, where passion overcomes all sense of realism, and where a man will die for what others may perceive to be an empty formula. One wonders if we shall ever solve the problems of human conflict.

The continuation of executions for the possession of arms and other crimes by the early months of 1923 has often been criticised, even by supporters of the army. While there may be some justification in such criticism, it is difficult to appreciate 75 years later the state of the country then where the war had deteriorated into widespread but isolated vandalism, murder, robbery, arson and intimidation, and where law and order were difficult to apply in many places. Perhaps it was felt that the possession of arms by many irresponsible individuals, without any central military control, was the primary reason for the continuation of the conflict, and that draconian measures were required to discourage the perpetrators.

There is a conversation between Dad, mother and myself on various aspects of the circumstances leading up to the army mutiny, and about dad's relations with his cabinet colleagues [21, 32]. During this conversation Dad said:

> The situation I was dealing with and the circumstances and, if you like, the technique or the absence of technique that I had to adopt not to increase the area of conflict or to inflame that contact which was there, (meant) I never attempted to enter into detailed dissection of (the) O'Higgins mind ..... It wasn't my makeup to try and examine what kind of a man Joe McGrath was, what kind of a person Kevin O'Higgins was, what kind of a person Paddy Hogan was ..... There was developing in the army evidence that Hogan and people like that were out to undermine the position of myself at any rate and others in the General

Headquarters Staff. .... as far as the cabinet was concerned I relied on Cosgrave to handle any cabinet situation that was there, and I didn't either discharge my feelings by analysing O'Higgins or by analysing Joe McGrath and I didn't even discuss with Cosgrave, perhaps to the extent which I might, the developments of antagonism to us in the army.

I had just read the biography of Kevin O'Higgins by de Vere White [32] when this tape was recorded. The book dealt in some detail with the relationship between O'Higgins and Mulcahy, and the difficulties which emerged as a result of O'Higgins's criticism of the army and its leaders during the civil war and the post-civil war period of demobilisation leading up the the mutiny of 1924.

It was clear from this conversation, and from other conversations and documents, that, as the military head of the army from March 1918 to the end of the civil war in May 1923 (with the exception of the periods January-

The Army School of Music group at Lissenfield, 1923.
Front: Mrs Mulcahy, Col. Firtz Brase, Richard Mulcahy, Mrs Larchet.
Back: Prof. John Larchet, Comdt. Sauersweig, Denis Mc Cullough.

198

June, and 13 July to the 22 August 1922) and the political head from January 1922 to March 1924, Dad had a gargantuan task in trying to reconcile the various political and military interests and conflicts which were inevitable during this rapidly changing time. The bitterness of the civil war and the intractable attitude of the members of the irregular forces, the vandalism which destroyed so much property and disturbed vital services, created problems for the Free State army in terms of discipline and control, when a rapidly mobilised army of 50,000 or more, mostly inexperienced recruits, had to cope with the urgent and stringent conditions leading up to and including civil war.

These problems, allied to the increasing impatience of the population with the military on both sides, as a result of more than four years of civil strife, was at the basis of O'Higgins's criticisms. He felt that the war was unnecessarily prolonged, and was not being pursued with sufficient urgency and energy.

Dad had reason to resist the interference by Brugha in affairs which were strictly matters for the chief of staff during the Truce. But despite his difficulties with Brugha, he never allowed these to interfere with their formal relationship as the military and political heads of the army, nor did he allow these differences to affect the welfare and morale of the army by sharing his problems with his colleagues.

As with Brugha, his personal relations with O'Higgins were not affected. His refusal to condemn O'Higgins in public or to speak adversely of his character, while criticising his actions; his continued relationship with all his former cabinet colleagues; his resignation rather than confront the government, and his continued loyalty to Cosgrave and his political party, testify to the fact that he always put the welfare of the army and the state, including its democratic institutions, before his own career or self-interest. He has stated more than once that his continued support of the government through and after the mutiny was vital for its survival, and that it would never have occurred to him to jeopardise the government for reasons of personal gain or of resentment.

It is clear from our taped conversations that, while Dad greatly resented the way O'Higgins interfered in army affairs, and resented the government's action in dismissing the senior officers who had simply been doing their

Richard Mulcahy at the hustings, before the 1923 elections.

duty in arresting the mutineers, he did not allow his personal feelings to interfere with his loyalty to the pro-Treaty party in the Dail and he was careful to ensure that the army should remain loyal and subservient to the democratically elected parliament. It is also clear that he never allowed his feelings to affect his personal relations with any of his opponents, and, even as late as 1963, when this conversation took place, he was unwilling to respond to my questions by making any criticism about O'Higgins' character. Nor was he willing to speak to de Vere White, O'Higgins's biographer, about him, as he did not wish to impair the O'Higgins reputation by being critical of him [33,34]. It is obvious that his continued contacts and good relations with his colleagues in the 1924 cabinet and his continued loyalty to the party were important factors in his successful return to the cabinet in 1927.

Dad and O'Higgins had a lot in common. They were both dedicated to democracy and the survival of the new state. They both felt impelled to adopt a draconian approach to the Irregulars as the turmoil of the civil war disrupted the nation, and each projected a public persona of dedication, austerity and perhaps aloofness. O'Higgins differed from Dad in his propensity to the sharp and wounding retort, and to a certain bitterness, attributes which must have affected his foes more than the more measured approach of my father. O'Higgins was also perceived to be more committed to retaining a close association with the British during his last few years. To the rank and file of the party and perhaps to a wider audience, he was less "national" than my father.

Dad continued as minister for defence in the cabinet following the 1923 election, and remained in that position until the army council was sacked by the government after the mutiny affair. He resigned in protest at the government's action, but O'Higgins stated that he would have called for Mulcahy's resignation if he had not first resigned. Apparently the only minister in the cabinet to support his defence of the army council was the minister for fisheries, Fionan Lynch [35].

There is little point in my discussing the details of the army mutiny and its genesis. Maryann Valiulis's account in *"Almost a Rebellion"* [36] gives the definitive account of this episode as does her biography. The Mulcahy papers and the report of the government's commission of enquiry are in the University archives and provide a comprehensive background to the affair. There is a detailed discussion about the mutiny on tape [10].

The following conversation was recorded on tape [21,37]:

> **RM:** To what extent was this increasing intrigue and conflict between these two groups of the military movement [the IRB, alleged to be the army council, and the old IRA, by which the mutineers described themselves], affecting the army during 1923 and 1924? If you had decided to oppose O'Higgins it is very likely that you would have had a serious bloodbath. Is that true?

> **R:** Oh you could have had a burst-up but you couldn't have controlled it. I couldn't have controlled a situation in which you have McGrath on the one side and a section of the army on the other, opposed by McGrath, and (another) section of the army supported by O'Higgins. Any kind of reasonable attitude by me other than what I did, I would have been simply squeezed between two very distuptive forces.

> **RM:** There were three sections in the army ....?

> **R:** .... and the IRB was not one of them. You have the pure volunteer spirit that was just serving and serving in the traditional spirit ..... there was no clash between an IRB section and any other section. It was a figment created by the Tobins and these, and used by O'Higgins.

Dad believed that Tobin was the main instigator of the Mutiny [38, 39]. There was no evidence that the attempts to revive the IRB by the senior officers had any sinister significance nor that it was related in any way to the demobilisation factor. However, it is clear from a conversation between Sean MacEoin and Dad on other tapes [40,41] that some of the senior officers in the army were interested in reviving the IRB "to further the national and cultural aspirations of the country", whatever this meant. It was apparent that Dad as minister of defence was not privy to these plans. Dad was probably a little naive in thinking the IRB was moribund at this juncture in the history of the State, although he was certainly correct in thinking that IRB influence in the army was of no significance.and that it had no further military aspirations. Nevertheless, he seemed a little embarrassed when he heard from MacEoin that Sean McMahon, the chief of staff of the Free State army, was the head of the IRB in 1923, and that Sean O'Muirthile, the quartermaster general, was its treasurer [41].

Tobin, Dalton and the other leaders of the mutiny had been part of the Collins group during the war of independence. I believe they resented having to serve with any other leader. Talking of their lack of discipline, Mulcahy said of Tobin and Dalton, continuing on tape [21,37]:

.... that even Collins, who didn't always require people to be disciplined around him, had pushed the two of them out of Dublin in the early stages of the Civil War to be out of his way.

In response to my question about O'Higgins's knowledge of the army and its problems during the civil war and to dad's secret meeting with de Valera in late September 1922, Dad said of O'Higgins (that):

.... he was blindly ignorant of the problem that my mind was up against and that the army command was up against.

Dad had been pressurised to meet de Valera in late September during the civil war with a view to a reconciliation. The priest who induced him to do so maintained that Dev was "a changed man." Dad met him reluctantly, with the approval of Eoin MacNeill, whom he consulted, and despite an earlier decision by the cabinet that no discussion was to take place with the irregular leadership without the cabinet's knowledge and approval. Dad's opening remarks can be summarised by his view that he didn't give a damn who ran the country as long as the government conformed to the democratic will of the people. Dev response was to say "some men are led by faith and some men are led by reason. Personally, I would tend to be led by reason, but as long as there are men of faith like Rory O'Connor taking the stand that he is taking, I am an humble soldier following after them". The meeting ended in less than two minutes. When the episode was later reported to the cabinet by Dad, O'Higgins was not pleased with dad's initiative.

The latter half of tape 136B [21] deals with my mother's story about Mrs Cosgrave's visit to her after dad's resignation from the ministry:

> Mother: ....when that was going on before the (Mutiny) enquiry, Maire was born at that time and I was up in my room in bed and Mrs Cosgrave described that he, her husband, had retired with illness. The doctor said he wasn't to go out. She came in to see me in a great (state) - I was in a bit of a state myself but I wasn't as bad as that about this whole thing. Dick came home one night and told me he was out of everything
>
> She(Mrs Cosgrave) said: '.... it's just the same with Willy (Cosgrave), he's there and O'Higgins wants him to resign.' He wants Cosgrave to resign, she told me, and that he was to take over the whole thing. She told me that, I remember that, she said he is a terrible man. I didn't know what to say to her, I had enough on my own mind. I don't remember what I said about Cosgrave, whether he had to stand down or else. She thought that time that Cosgrave was going to resign. She said you'd be afraid of this fellow.

This led to a prolonged conversation between Dad, mother and myself about O'Higgins and Cosgrave. My parents postulated that Cosgrave's removal and dad's resignation would confirm O'Higgins's ambitions to lead the Government. Dad talks about Kevin O'Higgins's ambitions, and his rather contemptuous attitude to Cosgrave [10]. He comments too about Cosgrave, his character and his rather sensitive nature.

Some days after Mrs Cosgrave's visit, my mother had an invitation from Mrs O'Higgins who invited her to tea to explain that her husband's opposition to Mulcahy was not personal [16]. Mrs O'Higgins explained that on occasions her husband protested when he was in the presence of people who for one reason or another criticised Mulcahy.

Dad discusses the adverse effect the Mutiny had on the fortunes of the Cumann na nGaedheal party:

> .... reducing the prestige of the government and leaving the direction force in the parliamentary party and in the government completely denuded of those people and names who stood for the Griffith approach and policy in relation to industrial development [42].

One might naturally think that the army mutiny and its aftermath, including Mulcahy's resignation from the ministry, might have left him with a feeling of frustration and bitterness. However, when I questioned him about the event and as I speculated about other outcomes which might have caused him less personal loss, he replied that it was only by the Grace of God that the compound problems faced by the Government from 1922 to 1924 ended as peacefully and as well as they did. His only expressed regret was that the Mutiny did irretrievable damage to the Government and to the Treaty supporters in general, and contributed to the failure of the Boundary Commission and to the near failure of the government in the first election of 1927. He may not have approved of the Government's treatment of the members of the army council in 1924, but I suspect that he understood the dilemma the demobilisation conflicts caused the government at the time. It is also likely that his resignation and the unfair dismissal of the army council members may have received the acquiescence of his cabinet and Dail colleagues because they may have been motivated by the need to maintain the stability of the pro-Treaty government.

Dad's views about the genesis and effects of the army mutiny are recorded [10,11,22,43] and his views are supported by Michael Tierney in his biography of MacNeill [44] when he writes:

> In the long run the episode of the so-called 'mutiny' did immense damage to the cause of the government. In November, (Joe) McGrath* and eight of his adherents resigned from the Dail,

* [McGrath had been a minister in the first Free State government and had been sympathetic to the mutineers. He resigned from the Dail in 1924 because of the dismissal of the mutineers from the army. He subsequently pursued a very successful career in the commercial world and was best known as the organiser, with Dick Duggan, of the Irish Sweepstakes which gave such great support to the Irish hospitals].

precipitating a series of by-elections which were described as 'a miniature general election'. Of the five seats contested, the government lost two, but the number of seats was less important than the general feeling of depression which the incident created. Thousands of ex-officers and ex-soldiers scattered up and down the country brought with them a message, no longer of revolution, but of vague disappointment and discontent. On the Treaty side of the division which the civil war had made permanent, courage and determination gave way too often to cynicism and disillusionment. The only beneficiary of the whole sad episode was de Valera.

Chapter 7

The Years 1924-1932

7.1 Political Wilderness

By resigning the ministry of defence, Dad apparently pre-empted Kevin O'Higgins's intention to demand his resignation. Compared to his recent prominent role in the military and political affairs of the new state, he was now suddenly precipitated into the political wilderness as a back bencher.

Despite his protests in parliament at the treatment of his senior officers, he received little public support from his political colleagues. Their attitude was perhaps understandable because of the need to preserve intact a united cabinet and a stable government at this critical post-civil war period. However, he received many private expressions of support, and, if one is to judge from the collection of letters in the UCD archives [1], there were many expressions of regret about his departure from the cabinet, and a genuine appreciation of his national record and his public spirited defence of his army colleagues.

Bishop Fogarty of the Clare diocese wrote:

> I write now, not so much to utter the deep sympathy I feel, but to express my admiration for the public spirit and most edifying and gallant patience with which you have met a situation and a set of circumstances that are surely hard to bear. It is like you and worthy of your distinguished past, and is sure to bring its reward sooner or later. I wish all others had the same public spirit. There is widespread sympathy with you personally and a fixed conviction that you will soon be back again in the government where you rendered such eminent services to Ireland.

In his reply to the Bishop he wrote "I feel confident that the line of action which I have taken in recent circumstances will be all for the best generally...." [1].

Another correspondent wrote:

> Please accept my sincere sympathy on the sorrow and sadness
> and hardship received through the scant courtesy - or total want
> of it - given you by our present government. You fully gave your
> work, your whole, your very life for Ireland. While you live you
> still will be a creditor no earthly power or government can
> repay. I feel there is still a greater future for you in Ireland's
> cause ....

His uncle John Slattery wrote of the pain the news caused him but also of the
delight and pride he and his family felt because of:

> .... the high standards of honour you have always maintained in
> your position. You may rely on it that the country will not be
> slow to remember and recognise who it was who saved the Free
> State, and upon whose honour and integrity they can always
> place their entire trust.

Many other tributes were along the same vein - his services to Ireland, his
defence of the army, the country's need for his continued services, his
integrity and lack of personal ambition, and his equanimity in the face of
adversity.

Eoin MacNeill, in his speech in the Dail after Mulcahy's resignation, had
this to say about him:

> If there is a man in this assembly whom I would like to call a
> friend, if there is a man whom I would be proud to call my
> friend, if there is a man whom I would hope in the future to call
> my friend, and who, I hope, will be my friend, it is the ex-
> minister for defence. There are few men in this assembly who
> know and are able to appreciate what this country owes to
> General Mulcahy. I doubt if but for General Mulcahy it would
> now be possible for us to be discussing the conduct of General
> Mulcahy. I remember when there was a price upon his head and
> we remember the extraordinary difficulty when he was covered
> with every obloquy that hostile minds could think of, and I do
> not think there is a man alive, and I think there are very few men

dead, to whom Ireland owes more than it owes to Deputy Richard Mulcahy, and I think the members removed from positions in the administration of the army as subordinates have also in their time deserved well of the country.

Mac Neill and Dad were very close in many matters, and had a lot in common in terms of political outlook and in relation to the Irish language and Irish culture. On several occasions during the war of independence and the civil war, when Dad was faced with difficult decisions, he sought the advice and support of MacNeill. He had the same admiration for MacNeill which he had for Griffith and Collins, although he considered that MacNeill lacked the political clout of some of the other ministers in the Sinn Fein and Free State cabinets [2]. He had a great capacity to ignore any faults or shortcomings in those whose views, actions and policies he approved of, not that I am suggesting that MacNeill had any such shortcomings. It was simply that when he had a commitment to a colleague, it was one of unadulterated loyalty [3-6]. He had sympathy for MacNeill because of his reluctant membership of the Boundary Commission. He felt that the appointment would inevitably lead to his political demise and that he accepted the appointment because a younger man in politics could ill afford to sacrifice himself in such an unenviable situation.

After 1924 my father drifted out of the mainstream of affairs, at least in his biographer's opinion and that of a few who reviewed the biography. He spent the months after his resignation preparing his submission to the army mutiny enquiry set up by the government. This proved to be an unsatisfactory affair, largely because of the terms of reference of the enquiry and because many of the crucial witnesses who were participants in the mutiny refused to testify. Like many similar government enquiries since, the setting up of the mutiny enquiry served mainly to defuse a critical situation at the time. In preparing his submission to the enquiry, my father had access to all his and the army's truce, civil war and post-civil war papers in Portobello Barracks. He removed them to his home at Lissenfield at the time and retained them afterwards. They now form an important part of his papers which are lodged in the archives of UCD.

He continued to attend the Dail during 1924 as a backbencher. Details of the 1924-1927 period of political isolation are described by Dad in his tape recordings. Although apparently outside the corridors of power during these years, he continued to support the government from the back benches and he continued to play an active role in the affairs of the Cumann na nGaedheal party, among whose members his prestige remained undiminished.

Dad confirms that, from the end of the civil war in April 1923 until the assassination of Kevin O'Higgins in August, 1927, he travelled throughout Dublin and the country freely and without protection [7]. During this time he was never molested or threatened by anybody (apart from the Irish in America) nor was he ever conscious of being at risk of any attempt on his life, despite receiving several anonymous letters with threats to his life.

> From the time I dropped the uniform after the civil war and went up for the 1923 election, even after that I went to every part of this country (where) I wanted to go unarmed and unattended and I never got a belt in the mouth.

In response to my question about O'Higgins's vulnerability, he said that "It was not what he did but by his disposition" that perhaps made him more vulnerable.

I find it quite extraordinary that the man who directed the civil war and who was most closely associated in the public mind with the draconian measures adopted by the Free State army in pursuing the Irregulars should have travelled the four corners of Ireland without any protection and without any consciousness of being vulnerable to the assassin's bullet. The residual bitterness following the civil war left many trigger-happy dissidents who must surely have thought it a moral duty to eliminate the architect of their defeat and a traitor to the Republic! After the O'Higgins' assassination, guards were provided for the members of the cabinet. From then until the mid-thirties his home, Lissenfield House, was guarded day and night, and Dad was accompanied by two guards wherever he went.

The guards were housed in a large galvanised hut under the old beech trees close to the avenue in our family home in Rathmines. This hut was built by the army in the early twenties to house the men who were charged with dad's protection. They were welcome company to us as children and we could take most liberties with them, but they wisely never allowed us to handle their Thompson submachine guns. Apart from our visits to their hut, they appeared to be a very unobtrusive group. During the civil war the house was attacked by the Irregulars but they were beaten off, with one intruder killed by the guards. As far as I know, no other attempt was ever made on dad's life.

Sometime later, perhaps in the mid 1930's, the guards were withdrawn and a police car staffed by two detectives was provided. Dad insisted that he needed no protection and he was obdurate in refusing to recognise their presence. He asked the department of justice to have the escort withdrawn, without success. I have the impression that we thought he treated the men rather badly, by deliberately dodging them on all occasions and by ignoring them as he passed them on the footpath on his way to the tram stop. It is difficult to understand his motives in treating these men in the way he did, but it was quite characteristic of him that, once having made a decision to act in a particular way, nothing in the world could change him. The police car was not permitted to enter the grounds of the house, and for several years the car remained parked out on the roadway, always manned by the two detectives. Dad may have been sensitive about the possible public perception that he was the recipient of the Fianna Fail government's patronage.

He describes on tape his two-week journey around Ireland in the Murchu shortly after his resignation [8,9]. He was a guest on board of the minister of fisheries, Fionan Lynch, who was, according Mulcahy, the only minister to support him in the cabinet at the time of the mutiny. The Murchu was the first naval and fishery protection vessel acquired by the new government.

Later in 1925 he represented the government at the Inter-Parliamentary Union Meeting in New York, accompanied by the chairman of the Dail, Michael Hayes and Thomas Johnson, the leader of the Labour Party [9,10]. Here he received the accolades of the pro-Treaty supporters but also the more vocal abuse and vituperation of the anti-Treaty Irish-Americans. He and his two colleagues were set upon and mobbed by an aggressive crowd of protesters when they disembarked from the liner at Hoboken Pier in New York. The detailed newspaper report states:

> As the baggage inspection was in progress, a group of men rushed at the General. One struck him in the face and another kicked him in the legs. The General was nearly swept off his feet.

His companion on the pier who was leading him was then felled by a blow to the jaw. The report goes on the say:

General Mulcahy was pummelled with fists and pelts (sic) with eggs and tomatoes. But he stood his ground until the arrival of the police. When General Mulcahy and his party started to leave through the gate they were showered with rotten eggs. One of his aides was struck on the eye by a stick hurled at him.

The placards carried by the protesters carried such slogans as "If Emmet had not been executed in 1803, Mulcahy would have executed him in 1923" and "Mulcahy murderer, Mulcahy perjurer, Mulcahy traitor"! The following resolution was passed at a meeting of the St. Brendan's Society in Boston "His hands are dripping with the blood of his former comrades, as an enemy of liberty and American ideas and principles". It is a reasonable question to ask if the influence of the Irish-Americans did more harm than good to Ireland and to our relations with our neighbouring island and with our brethren in the North.

He spent five weeks in the United States and Canada [11]. He was greatly impressed by the United States and its people, and by its President, Coolidge, and his regard for the United States was to last his lifetime. "I was never in a more cheerful and hospitable nation than this, which I consider the first ranking democracy on earth". On many occasions later in life he prophesied to me that the United States would play a major role in maintaining world peace and in creating a rational world society.

William T. Cosgrave, President of the Executive Council, The Irish Free State, 1922-1932

The year 1926 was spent largely in parliamentary and party work. Towards the end of the year, Dad asked Cosgrave if he would be reinstating him in the cabinet in the event of the government winning the election, and if the party should return to power. The election was due to take place in the Spring of 1927. He gives a detailed account on tape of his strategy from the moment in the autumn of 1926 when Cosgrave, in response to his enquiry, curtly dismissed the idea of re-appointing him, to his appointment as minister for local government and public health in the new cabinet in March 1927. His appointment was made by a reluctant Cosgrave who was obliged to respond to pressure from members of the Cumann na nGaedheal party [8,9,12-14].

On being refused by Cosgrave, he put his name forward for a forthcoming election to the Cumann na nGaedheal *Comhairle Ceanntar* (executive body) stating in his submission that he was doing so solely on the issue of his re-appointment to the cabinet. He was supported by a large majority of the party members, indicating considerable support by the rank and file of the party. Cosgrave apparently then yielded to pressure by some of his colleagues, including Kevin O'Higgins and Paddy Hogan, to avoid a serious division within the party.

Paddy Hogan informed Michael Hayes, who was chairman of the Dail from 1922 to 1932, that they regretted that they had forced him to resign at the time of the Mutiny [13]. The fact that O'Higgins supported the move to re-install Dad in the cabinet before this election makes this credible. Despite his rebuff and apparent lack of sympathy towards my father, Cosgrave was served with the greatest loyalty by him up to Cosgrave's retirement in 1944.

Dad describes on tape how the various differences which existed between himself and some of his political colleagues during these years, and the ensuing crises, did not materially affect his personal relations with them. Nor did he ever waver in his support of the government. It may be, however, that his implied withdrawal of support for the government after the approaching 1927 election, if he was not offered a cabinet post, was an added factor in influencing Cosgrave to accept his nomination. Whether or not he would have resigned from the party and withdrawn support from the government if he had not been included in the cabinet is a moot point. I very much doubt if he would have done so. He maintained that the failure to include him in the cabinet would have destabilised the government. I have little doubt he is correct in this view, bearing in mind the increasing difficulties facing Cosgrave after 1924, In justice to Cosgrave, Dad was offered a parliamentary secretary's appointment some time after his resignation in 1924, but this, Dad states, he "naturally" refused [9].

At the time he resigned from the cabinet, he had acquired a fourth child and was soon to have two more. He suffered the humiliation of having to borrow £100 from William Cosgrave about this time [15] and he received further financial support from some Cumann na nGaedheal colleagues who responded to an appeal from Michael Hayes on his behalf [9]. Michael Hayes was certainly dad's closest and most intimate friend. They frequently walked together, were constantly visiting each other's houses and shared godchildren. Their wives were on excellent nattering terms and were more vehement when sharing their husband's views about the malign influences which beset Ireland and its history since 1922. Hayes chaired the Dail from 1922-1932. He had been an assistant professor of French at UCD until 1922 when he was appointed to the faculty of Irish. He succeeded Prof. Cormac O'Cadhlaigh as professor of Irish at UCD in 1952.

It is a measure of dad's commitment to politics that he never thought of entering a profession or the business world, despite his chronic state of penury during the mid-twenties and when in opposition during the sixteen years of the Fianna Fail administration.

As his contributions to the Dail debates in the 1920s and his pre-election manifesto in 1927 will testify, he had a wide and eclectic interest in the affairs of the nation, including education, economics and industry, agriculture, the medical services, and Irish culture and the arts. Parliament to him was an institution for ordered debate and the achievement of a mature consensus about the affairs of the nation. Certain critics mention that he made little contribution to Irish affairs after 1924, apart from making long boring speeches.

Kevin O'Higgins Funeral, July 1927.
left to right: Ernest Blythe, Michael Hayes, Richard Mulcahy,
John Marcus O'Sullivan and Paddy Hogan.

His reputation for the short word and the short response, and his incisive and clear cut speech, which were a feature of his public image during the revolutionary period and his early years in politics, (except on the rare occasions when he gave a formal address in the Dail) was in striking contrast to his latter day wordiness, his convoluted thoughts, his frequent use of flamboyant metaphor, and his late preoccupation with the failures of de Valera and the Fianna Fail party. He was certainly capable of making long speeches during his later years in politics but this mattered little in a parliament where peace reigned and where matters of legislation were dealt with in circumstances which some of our latter days critics describe as boring. Nor did his 37 years in public life lack merit when one notes that he was a full-time parliamentarian among a host of part-time colleagues, and that he played an important role in establishing the traditions of our Irish Parliament. If his contributions to the Dail were boring to the reviewer, it was probably because during a long parliamentary career he concerned himself with subjects such as education, economics and other subjects which lacked the controversial and adversarial ingredients beloved of the media, and attention to which was the fruit of having achieved a peaceful democratic state.

After retirement he gave numerous talks to various organisations, and his tendency to talk at length and to indulge in interminable sentences caused me a little apprehension. One was at times anxious to know if he would ever complete some of his interminable sentences in a proper syntactical order because of his numerous parentheses and subordinate clauses. He spoke about Collins to the Donegal Mens' Association for two and one quarter hours in the early 1960s, but he apparently did so without provoking any adverse reaction and without causing the members any inconvenience, apart from missing the last bus home!

He would have considered that his full-time occupation as a parliamentarian from 1922 to 1961 was his single most important contribution to Ireland and its welfare, even if it contrasted in terms of notoriety and public recognition with his earlier military period. And despite his low and diminishing profile with historians and some newspaper correspondents, he continued to play an active and effective role in parliament and his party. Maurice Manning wrote about him on the 100th anniversary of his birth [16]:

Throughout Fine Gael's dismal years of opposition in the 1930s and 1940s the burden of work - much of it thankless - fell more and more on Mulcahy and it was no surprise that with the retirement of W.T. Cosgrave in 1944 he was the unanimous choice of the party as its new leader. He could hardly have taken over at a less hopeful time. Against this background the facts of Mulcahy's leadership are impressive. When he took over, Fine Gael had 30 seats. Ten years later it had 50.

In a comment on the hundreth anniversary of his birth [17], a correspondent had this to say:

> It was he, with his close friend Michael Hayes, who did most to establish the dignity and authority of Dail Eireann from 1923 until 1933. He gave the impression of having more respect for Dail Eireann than any other of its members and he used it to considerable effect during the long years of his membership.

There is little reference in his numerous tape recordings to his five years as minister for local government and public health from 1927 to 1932, but he left a large number of papers covering the period of his ministry which are now housed in the UCD archives [18,19]. This ministry provided him with the opportunity to enjoy his organisational and administrative skills, and to become familiar with the local administration of Irish affairs. It also afforded him an opportunity of advancing the public health services of the country. With his tidy and orderly mind, this position should have suited him admirably. He was apparently popular with his civil service colleagues and as usual became totally absorbed in the detailed work of the department. During this time he was elected a member of the Royal Irish Academy and of the Royal Institute of Public Health.

Included in the 1927-1932 ministry papers are numerous letters from supporters and others seeking his support for members of families and friends who were seeking jobs in the public services. His response to these letters almost invariably underlined his inability or unwillingness to help because of structures which had been put in place by the government to ensure that such appointments were to be made on merit and not through political influence. The Local and Civil Service Appointments Commissions were specifically set up by the *Cumann na nGaedheal* Government in 1926 to

Richard Mulcahy at his desk in the Department of
Local Government and Public Health, 1928.

ensure that there should be no element of jobbery in the making of public appointments. By being direct and blunt with seekers of his intervention he undoubtedly confirmed his reputation for integrity. However, the following letter noted in the archives was not likely to enhance dad's popularity with his supporters. It was in response to a letter he received from a supporter in Cork who wrote to Dad on behalf of a public health nurse seeking a job, claiming the support of the Bishop of Cork:

> No, the Bishop of Cork did not write to me .... and, in any case, it wouldn't be any use in this case. The appointment will be filled as a result of a selection committee examining all possible applicants, and their general experience and qualifications ...., without any marks for religion or changes of religion. Besides, too, there really is a ministerial function to be exercised and it could not be exercised by anyone telling people what nurses should be appointed, and what workmen, and what carpenters, and what engineers, and what doctors, etc. etc. So please ... [20].

Dad refers to the Appointments Commission elsewhere and emphasises that it must not discriminate, among other criteria, in matters of gender or of place or country of birth[21].

One of his greatest problems during his ministry was the collection of the local rates. Following the civil war, local administration had seriously broken down, particularly in relation to the collection of taxes and rates. Even as late as 1928, he had reason to complain to the rate collectors in Co. Leitrim that, of the total annual rates of £46,000 due from the county, just over £5,000 had been collected.

In the next paragraphs I refer to Cumann na nGaedheal's disastrous record as a political party during its ten years in office, and to the various factors which contributed to its disappointing electoral results during the 1920s and its downfall in 1932. It is often said that the failure of the party to give preference to its own supporters in public appointments was one factor and was to alienate many of those who originally backed the Treaty and the new government.

7.2   Cumann Na nGaedheal

Maryann Valiulis, in her paper *After the revolution: The formative years of Cumann na nGaedheal* [1], underlined the considerable stresses which existed within the Cumann na nGaedhael party from 1923-1927. Many of the party's members, who were still committed to the Treaty and were vehemently opposed to Dev, believed that the government, and particularly the cabinet, was failing to satisfy the more nationalistic aspirations of the revolutionary movement. The government, in strictly adhering to the spirit and the letter of the Treaty, was, according to the dissidents, maintaining the power and privileges of the wealthy Protestant minority, and was retaining the institutions of the British regime while neglecting the needs and energies of their own supporters who had fought for the freedom of Ireland and who had supported the Treaty.

My father, as one of the leaders of the party and the pro-Treaty group, and being outside the cabinet, was in a unique position to act as the honest broker between the two conflicting groups. On a few occasions he played a role in reconciling the differences between the government and the dissidents. Maryann's account of the difficulties which existed within the party up to 1926, and of the cabinet's conservative approach to party organisation and to its limited participation in formulating a national grass roots system of support, clearly outlines some reasons for the government's failure to maintain public support from 1927 onwards.

Her analysis of the evolution of Cumann na nGaedheal during the 1920s makes interesting reading and is based on the party's minute books and on the extensive papers in the Mulcahy collection. Maryann fails to mention the difficulties which were created for the government and the pro-Treaty party by the constant public opposition and sniping by the defeated republicans, whether it was sneering at the ministerial top hats, fraternising with British ministers, accusations of being traitors and West Britons, or shooting the odd policeman.

It was perhaps fortunate for those who supported the Treaty that the Cosgrave government did survive until 1932. It is surely ironic that, without the assassination of Kevin O'Higgins in July 1927, and the second election after his death which gave the government a more stable majority, the government might have been defeated at a much earlier date. Despite the fact that the Treaty was supported by more than 80% of the people in the 1922 election, the Cumann na nGaedheal party won only 47 out of 153 seats in the first election in June 1927. It continued in government because of support from other groups and the absence of the 44 Fianna fail deputies who had not yet entered the Dail.

However, the government only survived by the chairman's casting vote when Fianna Fail were forced by a new electoral act to enter the Dail in August 1927, after the O'Higgins death. Six of the Sinn Fein deputies refused to join Dev in entering the Dail. Otherwise the government would have been defeated in August 1927. After this near defeat and in the circumstances of the O'Higgins assassination Cosgrave called a second election. Cosgrave won 62 seats, enabling the government to survive another five years, although it was far from being a stable government during this period. In 1930 Cosgrave was defeated in the Dail and promptly resigned. He was forced to continue because de Valera refused to form a government at the time. By 1927 the government and Cumann na nGaedhael had lost many of their supporters to other parties, including Labour, the Farmers' party, the Nationalist League, a large number of independents, and even to Fianna Fail.

Dad talks at length about the inexorable decline and fall of the Cumann na nGaedheal government [2,3]. According to Dad, it was paying the price of the army mutiny and its political consequences, and of the government's neglect of the army after the mutiny, a situation which, he states, was compounded by the lack of interest and sympathy of the two ministers of defence who succeeded him, Hughes and Desmond Fitzgerald. He thought that Hughes, who replaced him as minister for defence shortly after his resignation, was particularly unsuitable for the post and had no qualifications for the position. He believed that Desmond FitzGerald who replaced Hughes (the latter was defeated in the first 1927 election) was out to "destroy the army" [4]. He describes the disillusionment of the army men and the many who supported the government during the difficult times of the civil war. The government had alienated itself not only from the army following the mutiny, but from the IRB spirit, the Irish language, and other symbols of the national movement [5].

The failed Boundary Commission was another factor at the basis of the party's decline. Dad reminds us that Michael Tierney, in his biography of MacNeill, attributes the Boundary Commission's failure to ambiguities in article 12 of the Treaty [6]. Perhaps, most of all, the cabinet's lack of sympathy for and cooperation with its own supporters in Cumann na nGaedheal was a factor in its decline.

Cumann na nGaedheal was also to lose the support of the Labour deputies because of the government's parsimony in dealing with the poorer members of the community, taking a shilling off the old age pensioners and, later, a shilling off the school teachers. The Labour leaders believed the government was more sympathetic to the rich and to the old establishment. This apparently was the principal reason the Labour party changed its allegiance to Fianna Fail in 1927.

Dad was critical of the party's organisation and policies for several other reasons. He regretted its failure to retain the title Sinn Fein and he believed it had alienated itself from the economic policies of Arthur Griffith. Dad makes no reference that the executions policy during the civil war and the part this and the prolonged war itself may have played in alienating some of the party's supporters. Despite the fact that he received a huge vote at the 1923 election immediately after the end of the civil war, confirming the electorate's approval of his role in bringing the war to a conclusion, the government did less well and, and even at this early date, was already showing significant signs of loss of support by the electorate in the 1923 election.

The party's defeat became inevitable in 1932 because of the effects of the worldwide depression and because of the alienation of the Labour Party. Most of all, the party lost support because of the cabinet's poor relations with the rank and file of its own party and because of its total neglect of organisation at constituency level at a time when Fianna Fail was setting up its efficient network of cumainns nationwide. The government may also have over-reacted to the O'Higgins' murder by setting up the military courts to try the residue of republican dissidents.

Dad had apparently been critical of the party because of its neglect of an efficient electoral machine [3] and particularly its failure to develop constituency organisations. Constituency organisation depended largely on the whim of the local TD and in general was patchy or nonexistent. Virtually all the Fine Gael TD's in 1944 were veterans of the early years of the state and had grossly neglected their constituencies. Compared to the well oiled Fianna Fail machine, the Fine Gael organisation, and its precursor, Cumann na nGaedheal, was clearly ineffective in most parts of the country. Cosgrave, O'Higgins and the general secretary of the party, Liam Burke, and a few other leaders of the party were opposed to involvement in local politics and in setting up branches in every part of the country as had been done so effectively and successfully by Fianna Fail. Fianna Fail also became involved in local politics in the early 1930s, which contributed enormously to its success as a national party.

Michael Hayes, the chairman of the Dail and the closest to Cosgrave, believed that Cosgrave was more interested in the country than the Cumann na nGaedheal party [7]. This view is supported by Cosgrave's anxiety to advance the democratic process by forcing the Fianna Fail deputies to enter the Dail, even though their entry was certain to be a serious threat to the survival of his government. It was also supported by other aspects of his tenure of office, including his insistence that the attorney general should be independent of government.

Indeed, the same concern for country rather than party may be said of the cabinet in general, and their primary commitment to country rather than party may be one reason for their increasing unpopularity during their tenure of office. It is said that a politician is somebody who looks forward to the next election, while a statesman is somebody who looks forward to the next generation. I have often wondered about the definition of a statesman.

My Random House dictionary defines a statesman as a man who is experienced in the art of government or who exhibits great wisdom and ability in affairs of government. My own definition implies integrity as well as wisdom and certainly Cosgrave deserves the title of statesman, as indeed do many of his colleagues in the first Cumann na nGaedheal government,

Maryann Valiulis, in her examination of the evolution of the Cumann na nGaedheal party during the 1923-1932 period [1,8] referred to the government's disdain for the ordinary workings of the organisation and its failure to appreciate the need to have strong grass roots support. She goes on the say:

> ....at a party meeting discussing an appeal which was to be made for funds, Richard Mulcahy, former minister for defence, suggested that President Cosgrave's name would be a more effective fund-raiser than that of Eoin MacNeill, president of the organisation and the proposed signatory on the circular. The indignant reply of Kevin O'Higgins testified to the type of disdain felt about this kind of activity. O'Higgins rejected Mulcahy's proposal and rather contemptuously added that he hoped that they had not yet reached the point where it was necessary for the President to appeal for funds.

Dad had other comments to make about the party's woes in the late 1920's. He regretted the departure from politics of his friend, Eoin MacNeill, following the Boundary Commission debacle [3]. He thought Joe McGrath's resignation in 1924, at the time of the mutiny, was a big loss to the government, despite the fact that McGrath supported the army mutineers and was opposed to Mulcahy. McGrath had an entrepreneurial spirit which was sadly lacking among the more conservative members of the cabinet. He was the successful founder of the Irish Hospitals' Sweepstakes in 1930 and became a well known figure in the commercial life of the country and as a supporter of many charities and lame ducks.

J.J. Walsh's defection from the party in 1927 was also a big loss because of his interest and pro-active outlook on economics, his practical disposition, his attributes as a good organiser, and his strong nationalist outlook (Mother described him as a Seán Lemass). Walsh's entrepreneurial attributes were recognised as early as November 1921 when the cabinet awarded him a grant

222

of £2,000 to assist in Ireland's participation in the Olympic Games in Paris. Dad believed he pulled out of the second election because of disillusionment with the cabinet's conservative economic policies and that he, Walsh, felt he could be better occupied elsewhere. Dad believed the rest of the cabinet, with the exception of Paddy McGilligan, had lost some of the spirit of nationalism engendered by the war of independence and the setting up of the first Dail.

Dad saw in O'Higgins, Blythe, Fitzgerald, John Marcus O'Sullivan, Hogan and to a lesser extent, Cosgrave, a group who evoked diminishing support in the country because of their reactionary economic policies and their gradual distancing from the economic, social and nationalistic policies of Griffith[3]. When Dad was critical of Liam Burke and his lack of interest in the grass roots elements of the party, John Marcus O'Sullivan, the minister for education, accused him of "being out after Burke." Despite this charge, both Burke and O'Sullivan were close friends of my father's at the time and remained so afterwards [3].

The 16 years in opposition from 1932 can also be attributed to organisational neglect. According to Denis Burke of Clonmel, Dad, as early as 1934, advocated involvement in local politics (Clonmel Nationalist, 28 November 1959) but clearly he was unable to bring about any great enthusiasm within the party for such a policy or for more active constituency involvement until he replaced Cosgrave as president in 1944. His first task as president was to insist on more constituency activity and to bring fresh talent into the ailing party.

During the twelve years of opposition before he assumed the presidency of the party in 1944, he may have had the right ideas about party organisation but he must have lacked the influence or energy to have his ideas accepted by Cosgrave and his colleagues. I expect that he did not push his views on the matter of constituency organisation because of his unwillingness to come into conflict with his front bench colleagues. However, from 1944 onwards the party assumed a much more active role, both at grass roots level in the constituencies and in opposition in parliament. The party's subsequent revival bears testimony to the success of this much neglected initiative.

7.3 The Irish Language

Perhaps Dad's most important contribution during the three year period 1924 to 1927, when he found himself in the political wilderness, was to chair the Gaeltacht Commission. This appointment was made despite the opposition of some of his colleagues in cabinet, including Ernest Blythe, minister for finance, who shared with him more than any other cabinet colleague (except Eoin MacNeill) a strong commitment to the revival of Irish. It was an unpaid appointment, but one which he accepted with enthusiasm because of his lifelong dedication to the Irish language and Irish culture. While he was in the cabinet he had already suggested a commission to investigate the extent and viability of the Gaeltacht. He also influenced the cabinet to set up a manuscript commission [1].

Dad was devoted to the language and spoke it as well as a native of the Gaeltacht. His first contact with Irish was during his later schooldays in Thurles, but the real inspiration came when he first went to Ballingeary, in the heart of the West Cork Gaeltacht. This was during his early career in the Post Office when he was stationed in Bantry in West Cork. He was then about 17 years of age. He became deeply involved in every aspect of Irish culture, and continued to study the language right up to his last years. His proficiency and great love of the Irish language is clearly apparent from the conversations he recorded on tapes and from the talks in Irish he gave to various groups and societies during his retirement. He spoke the language with an excellent *blás* or accent, and with an emphasis as if he savoured every word and phrase.

His love of the native Irish culture is apparent from his tape recordings. Learning Irish was to him much more than an academic exercise. It was part of immersing himself in the culture and traditions and history of the native Irish people. As he implies in the tapes, his university during these years was the hearth and homes of the local people of Ballingeary and of that beautiful part of West Cork which stretches from Ballingeary through Gougane Barra and Ceim an Aodha to Bantry and Glengarrif. It was not the precincts of the Irish College in Ballingeary nor any other academic institution.

His was the influence that directed us children to Irish-speaking primary and secondary schools. While he may have spoken Irish to us during his relatively short contacts with us as children, I cannot recall that he put great pressure on us to speak the language during the later years when we had finished our schooling. Despite his dedication to the language, his commitment to it, like his strong commitment to his religious and spiritual life, was a very private matter. He would be incapable of imposing pressure on others to adopt his enthusiasms or to follow his own inclinations in such matters.

Coláiste Mhuire, the first Irish-speaking secondary school in Ireland, was established by Ernest Blythe and my father in 1927. It was in Coláiste Mhuire that I and my brothers received our secondary education. The school was established under the direction of the Christian Brothers. This was the first Irish-speaking secondary school to be established in the State. Both Blythe, a Northern Protestant who was minister for finance in the Irish Free State government, and my father, who was minister for local government and public health, were excellent self-taught Irish speakers, and were enthusiastic about the revival of the Irish language.

It was characteristic of Dad, and perhaps an inevitable part of his wishful thinking, that he was confident that the Irish language would be successfully revived by the policies adopted by the Government in the early years of the state. Michael Tierney expressed pessimism about its revival in an article in *Studies* [2] in April 1926. Dad in a commentary on Tierney's review was critical of his pessimism [3], stating that it could be restored as the functional language of Ireland. He instanced Greece before the time of Aristotle, Finland after the Swedish hegenomy had ended, and the survival of French as the functional language of the French-Canadians.

That Dad was speaking more from the heart than the head in response to Tierney's measured assessment of the prospects of the revival of Irish is apparent from his reference to the revival of Greek during the fifth century B.C.:

> I wonder has Professor Tierney nothing to tell us as to how the Greek people brought their language from its folklore stage at the time of Herodotus to be, not more than a century later, in the time of Aristotle, a most perfect instrument of the highest human thought. Will he tell us that modern Irish gives less promise to-day than folk Greek gave five hundred years B.C.?

The Greeks of Herodotus of the fifth century B.C., unlike the Irish of the twentieth century, had not already available to them the ubiquitous, advanced and highly functional language of English.

Despite the influence of two prominent ministers who were devoted to the Irish language and its propagation, one wonders why the Irish language movement failed to bear fruit and why the Gaeltacht of the North, South and West has undergone slow and inexorable atrophy. Reasons are numerous and complex, and rational discussion on the subject, as is so frequent with matters of language and religion, can be easily impaired by emotion and prejudice. Irish could only be revived by stimulating an esteem and love for the language and its culture. It could not be revived by financial inducements, by the *deontas* and the cupidity induced by the *deontas*, nor by compulsion. Sadly, public policies copperfastened the indifference to the language of the great majority of the people and contributed to resentment and cynicism rather than the esteem which this beautiful language deserved.

Many of dad's political colleagues had a greater sense of realism about the prospects of revival, and many others were entirely indifferent to the language and cared little about its revival as a cultural or political factor in the Free State's future. By 1922 English had long become the functional language of Ireland in every aspect of life - economic, academic, professional, scientific, cultural, and social. Even ignoring Ireland's close ties with Britain and the United States, and the Irish diaspora in these and other English speaking countries, the rapid spread of the English language worldwide, particularly in science and economics, made it more likely that the revival of Irish as a functional language would be redundant. The 1916 Rising and subsequent political events could not easily or effectively reverse the trend towards an anglican culture among the people, particularly in our urban areas, and the heavy emigration to English-speaking countries during most of the last 75 years was an important disincentive.

The after-effects of the civil war were still evident in the late forties and early fifties when my father was minister for education. This was so at least among our politicians. To abolish compulsory Irish at that time would have been pragmatically correct but might have been politically disastrous, and would have caused the ultra-nationalistic Fianna Fail party to condemn my father as pro-British and anti-national. This would not happen in the 1990s but was part of realpolitik in the 1940s and 1950s.

For these and other reasons, it is not surprising that the Irish language revival policy of the last 75 years has not succeeded, at least in terms of its revival as a universally functional spoken language.

But the rot of compulsion, hypocrisy, cynicism and the *deontas* mentality may have had its early beginnings even before the civil war. The early Dail cabinets had a minister of Irish (Sceilg, an Irish speaker from Co. Kerry) and at least a notional department. It also had an assistant minister, paid £400 annually, £50 more than the assistant minister for defence and chief of staff! Yet despite 115 meetings of the cabinet between March 1919 to December 1921, there is scant mention of Irish and its minister. One of the rare references to Irish was to consider granting a sum of $25-50,000 to establish an Irish bookstore in New York and possibly in Chicago [4]. Whether the plan was implemented is not clear. I doubt it. Another was to award fishing associations who agreed to conduct their work in Irish a 20% grant on any loan they were to receive from the government [5]! On the same day the minister for Irish was asked to approach the Gaelic League to formulate a policy aimed at the revival of Irish. Otherwise the Irish language received no attention from the cabinet and one wonders what occupied the minister and his assistant who were both in fulltime positions, at least in terms of salary.

The question of general education policy after the foundation of the State and the more specific question of the Irish language policy in the schools are raised at a few points in the tapes [6]. It is stated by one of those whom Dad interviewed that Father Christie O'Flynn, of Passage East, Co Cork, a great Irish scholar and enthusiast whom Dad knew and greatly admired for his dedication to the language and Irish culture, having attended a government committee on the Irish education and language policy in 1922, came away disillusioned because he could foresee no change from the stultifying methods of education which prevailed during the British regime. Dad disagreed with Father O'Flynn's view that nothing would change, but, as happened so frequently during his declining years, Dad unfortunately provided no convincing reason to support the contrary view that much had changed, and he tended to obfuscate the question by making quite irrelevant and sometimes Delphic points in response to O'Flynn's comments.

He referred to the residual effects and political distractions of the civil war. As in the case of other national aspirations which might have evolved after the Treaty, the civil war and its consequences certainly destroyed much of the country's interest in the Irish language revival. The general cynicism which was the product of the civil war spilled over to the language. Parliament too can be blamed for the failure of the revival. Our political leaders were quick to impose compulsory Irish on an indifferent people, while they made little attempt to adopt the language as a functional part of legislative proceedings. Logically they should have made the ability to conduct business in Irish an essential qualification for every Dail and Senate candidate, having insisted that this condition operated in most public and educational appointments. It was surely a reflection on parliament that only a handful of members over the years of self rule could speak the language sufficiently well to use our native tongue in the proceedings of the Dail and Senate.

The great majority of both the Cumann na nGaedheal and Fianna Fail deputies cared little about the revival of Irish, whatever lip service they may have paid to the subject. Dad complains about the lack of sympathy for the language and the lack of cooperation shared by some of his ministerial colleagues in the Cumann na nGaedheal cabinet, more particularly John Marcus O'Sullivan who succeeded Eoin McNeill as minister for education in 1925, and who made little effort to solve some of dad's difficulties in maintaining Scoil Muire and Scoil Colmcille as Irish speaking primary schools [7]. The Irish language provided the emerging state with its most prolific source of cynicism and hypocrisy.

In 1963 Dad talks at length about the Department of Education as he found it on taking office in 1948 [8]. It took him six months to realise the nature of the malaise which he found there, a malaise which was aggravated by a six month strike by the teachers at the time:

> There was no sense of initiative, vision or power. No cerebration.
> The reason was that there had been no ministerial function in
> the Department for years and that Derrig was simply a blue
> bottle on a window there
>
> The Department did not believe in the policy they were operating
> for (compulsory) Irish and they had no idea of the attitude to the
> language of the native speakers in the Gaeltacht, where the
> language was in progressive decline. There was no policy for

primary or secondary education, and university education was neglected by both the Department and the universities themselves.

Thomas Derrig had been the Fianna Fail minister for education for the entire Fianna Fail administration from 1932 to 1948.

I asked Dad if he had confidence in the compulsory Irish policy. He answered "I hadn't but I was caught for a way out" [8].

And he added later:

> I often feel ashamed of myself to think I was in the Department of Education for two periods of office and I ask myself what did I do there?

Whatever about his failures as minister for education, he complained on several occasions that the then minister for finance, Paddy McGilligan, was not only parsimonious to a great degree in giving money to his department but was almost impossible to contact. McGilligan was frequently absent from meetings, usually for reasons of health, and I believe that he had an over protective wife who looked after him with consummate care. Her administrations were obviously effective for he lived to the reasonably advanced age of 90. The difficulties of making contact with him were probably an advantage for a finance minister who was probably perceived by his colleagues to possess a bottomless pit of money. Paddy Lynch, who was a confidante of Costello's during the first Inter-Party government, told me the the department for education was treated with little more than contempt by other ministers and departments. This might explain dad's financial problems as minister. Despite dad's frustrations with McGilligan, they and their wives always remained close friends, and Dad had a high opinion of McGilligan's abilities.

I do not think that even as early as 1948, when he first became minister for education, he showed any sense of innovativeness about the inert language revival. He was happy to accept the *status quo*. Compulsory Irish remained a sleeping dog, carefully watched over by the two parties which had broken on the Treaty, lest one should be accused of being less patriotic than the other. I expect that Dad, like his other political colleagues, did not wish to stir the dormant passions which can bedevil a language movement nor was he likely to welcome the political implications of confronting such a controversial issue. Even as early as 1948, he and his colleagues on both sides of the political divide must have known in their heart of hearts that the compulsory Irish policy was not succeeding and was not likely to succeed in the future. Dad's conservatism, most evident during his later years, was symptomatic of his civil service mentality and training. If a political mentality requires a sense of scrutiny of the *status quo* and a willingness to adopt new ideas and to accept the necessity of change, he was hardly suited to a political role, at least during his later years in parliament. The same could be said of his ageing political colleagues on both sides of the political divide.

Dad did, however, set up a council of education to advise the government on the function and curriculum of the primary schools. This decision was approved by the cabinet on the 21 March 1950. It reported to his successor in 1954 and its recommendations are summarised by Dr John Coolahan as follows:

> It called for no fundamental or radical changes though it did urge the inclusion of drawing, nature study and physical education as compulsory subjects, and it called for a more generous scheme of scholarships for pupil participation in secondary education [9].

Few of these recommendations were implemented. In 1954 the council undertook an appraisal of the secondary school curriculum and provided its report in 1960 which was published in 1962. "It identified the dominant purpose of the schools as the inculcation of religious ideals and values" [9]. It made some recommendations but had little effect on general education policy until Donough O'Malley introduced free secondary education in 1967. The 1960 report had observed that free secondary education was "untenable" and "Utopian" [10]. Politics is rightly described as the art of the possible but O'Malley was able to show that sometimes the impossible is possible, even in a highly conservative society.

The Irish language and the Gaelic culture formed the keystone of dad's sense of nationality. Although being proficient in Irish and establishing an Irish speaking household, his 35 years in parliament and his six years as

230

minister of education did not appear to encourage him to any more radical policies than those of our successive governments. He may have thought that current policies were succeeding. Whatever may have been his thoughts on the subject, I cannot ever recall any criticism by him of compulsory Irish nor of any other aspect of the language policy, nor can I recall his expounding any innovative ideas on the subject. Indeed it is remarkable how a patently unsuccessful language policy gave rise to so little public comment or concern over so many years. As far as the great majority of the Irish people were concerned, the aspirations about the revival of Irish ensured that apathy and hypocrisy remained alive and well. The entire Irish programme was an exercise in hypocrisy and cynicism, and largely succeeded in alienating the people.

My five siblings and myself were educated through the medium of Irish and Irish was generally the spoken language among us in our home when we were schoolchildren. Without exception, we ceased to speak Irish after going into third level education, and, as for myself, I had no opportunity to converse in the language during my six years in the university and medical school, and my 50 years in hospital practice, nor did I have any inclination to do so. Our experience, like that of every other child who was subjected to compulsory Irish in school, was predicted by Eoin MacNeill when he wrote:

> You might as well be putting wooden legs on hens as trying to
> restore Irish through the schools alone [11].

And yet it is ironic that it was MacNeill, as minister for education, who introduced compulsory Irish in the primary schools in 1924, and who made Irish a compulsory subject for the intermediate and leaving certificate examinations. There was some resistance to the Irish revival policy by such academics as Michael Tierney but I believe that, while a few ministers including Mulcahy, Blythe and perhaps MacNeill, sincerely believed in the programme, the real motives behind such an unsuccessful approach to the language's revival may have been as much the result of the bitter West Britain charges by the anti-treatyites as any profound attachment to the language and its culture.

The children of Ireland were subjected to compulsory Irish in the schools from the early years of the state. They were badly taught in most cases, certainly in terms of learning Irish as a spoken or functional language. Many

231

teachers were unfit to teach the language, either because of their ignorance of the tongue, or because of their training. Other teachers were simply cynical about the revival of Irish and about the utility of the revival programme. And when the children went home and into the outside world, they found that English was the only language spoken.

Although an excellent and self-taught Irish speaker, with a great devotion to Irish culture, Dad never attempted to influence others in matters of the language. It is with some sense of guilt that I recall that I never initiated a conversation in Irish with him, at least after my schooldays. He would have been pleased by my doing so.

Chapter 8

1932 and After: Opposition and the Inter-Party Government.

After his resignation from the ministry of defence in 1924, my father's public life and his full-time commitment to politics continued without interruption up to his retirement as president of Fine Gael in 1959. It is true that, in the public perception, his stature as a national leader was gradually overshadowed by events and by his successors. However, that is not to say that he did not continue to contribute his share to the advancement of the country. During the 37 years from 1924 to 1961 he was one of the most active and diligent parliamentarians in the Dail, and for two brief periods in the Senate. He devoted his time fully to the affairs of the legislature and to his own political party. In his fulltime capacity as a parliamentarian, he held many briefs and acted as a watchdog for his party in the Dail and the country. He was undemonstrative by nature, both in his public and private life, and was free of the techniques employed by politicians to attract public attention. Cant had no place in his mind and he had no interest in the "Bodenstown" strategies employed by his political opponents.

Later he became rather prolix and his vision of public affairs may have narrowed. He was described by one reviewer of the biography as being a dedicated, hardworking and a sincere politician but not a successful one. Another stated that he made long boring speeches, and certainly this was true of his later years. In his last few years his letters were such that on one occasion in commenting on one letter [1], I wrote

> It is a most perfect example of his tortuous, allusive, parenthetical, opaque, metaphorical and obscurantist writing which was a feature of his last years!

Eoghan Corry, writing in the *Irish Press* on the 26/6/1992, wrote:

> But it is a sobering thought that a general who won the admiration of friend and foe alike during the war had so little to offer the republic he helped found"

233

and in the Phoenix, 26 June 1992:

> Her book (that is, the Valiulis biography) concentrates almost
> entirely on the '20s, which is just as well as Dick's career was
> one of those which peaked early and dragged along rather
> boringly thereafter.

There is some truth in the statement that he made long, boring speeches,
particularly during his later years, but he was among one of the more active
and longest serving parliamentarians, and I would have thought that his use
of parliament was designed to advance and encourage the democratic process.
His failure to indulge in political and public histrionics is hardly a reason
for such dismissive views.

Another stated that, following his acknowledged contribution to the State up
to 1924, he failed to give any further worthwhile service It was certainly
true that he was an unsuccessful politician in terms of his personal fortunes
and as measured by political advancement and material acquisitions, but it
would be interesting to know what success really means in politics. I suspect
it would depend on whether one viewed politics as a career or a vocation. He
would have been satisfied that his own long contribution to parliament and
to the democratic process, unspectacular as it may have been in the
perception our present day media, was the type of success to which he would
consider it proper to aspire.

Dad remained in the Dail until 1961, with two short breaks in 1937 and
1943. He was defeated in both these two elections, but was fortunate that
both parliaments lasted only one year. He was returned in 1938 and 1944.
He retired from the Dublin North-East constituency in 1944, to take up
Gerry Ryan's seat in Tipperary, South Riding. Dublin North East was a three
seat constituency, with four "big guns" - Jim Larkin, the well-known labour
leader, Alfie Byrne, the long-standing lord mayor of Dublin, Oscar Traynor,
the Fianna Fail minister, and Richard Mulcahy. Dad, as leader of the Fine
Gael party in 1944 probably thought it more prudent to shift to a safe seat
in Tipperary South Riding. I recall the numbing shock in the household in
1937 when he first failed to be elected. A blanket of gloom settled on the
family and on many sympathisers. The only person who remained calm and
serene, at least externally, was the failed candidate himself.

The Fianna Fail electoral success in 1932 must have been a sore disappointment to Dad, his family and his colleagues in Cumann na nGaedheal. Fianna Fail's success in the 1933 election must have been a greater disappointment, particularly as Cumann na nGaedheal lost nine seats and Fianna Fail gained an overall majority. I recall the 1933 election because of the serious disturbances which occurred at the Cumann na nGaedheal public meetings, caused by Fianna Fail and IRA supporters. I recall being present at the large meeting where Dad and Mrs Collins O'Driscoll and other candidates were attempting to address the public at the Parnell Monument in O'Connell Street. The speakers could not be heard because of the continuous din of interruptions, and shortly after the meeting started, the platform was rushed, and the meeting broke up in disorder.

It was a recurring complaint among Cumann na nGaedheal supporters that the guards made little effort to control the mobs. These and earlier disorders, and the inability of the police to control the crowds, were largely responsible for the birth of the Blueshirt movement and its precursor, the Army Comrades Association. The ACA was first organised by some army officers in early 1932 to ensure that the new Fianna Fail government did not purge the army after its anticipated winning of the 1932 election. By 1933, it had adopted the function of protecting the democratic right to free speech which was perceived to be under serious threat when Cumann na nGaedheal platforms were being attacked by republican and Fianna Fail mobs [2].

Dad speaks about the setting up of the Blue Shirt movement [3]. Members of the ACA met about July 1933 at the Cumann na nGaedheal headquarters at 5 Parnell Square to decide on a uniform for their organisation. Blue or grey were considered but Dad was the only person present to favour grey. A subsequent convention attended by a large number of ACA members in the Hibernian Hotel on the 22 August 1933 was held to elect a successor to Dr Tom O'Higgins who had been head of the ACA but who was prevented from continuing because of his fulltime post as chief medical officer of Co. Meath. Both Mulcahy and O'Duffy were proposed but Dad refused to go forward. He said "I had no fancy for that particular type of thing at all".

On my questioning him about O'Duffy, Dad said that he was on good terms with him in the army, that he was an excellent organiser, and he was considered a "spectacular and colourful" figure. He added that O'Duffy was "a bit of a prima donna". When O'Duffy later replaced Cosgrave as head of the party and other parties, including the Farmers' Party, joined to form Fine Gael, O'Duffy became more bellicose and his tenure of leadership was short and terminated after the Blue Shirt organisation was banned by the government. Whatever about his merits as a senior officer of the army and as highly regarded head of the emerging police force, he proved a disaster as a political leader.

At no time during the turbulent days of the 1933 election did the Fianna Fail leaders condemn the disturbances and riots. I recall it as a disorderly and dangerous time when there were fears that the government might take draconian measures against the opposition. No doubt, however, the government was restrained by many factors, including the presence of the standing army and the fact that many important families, such as my mother's, the Ryans of Wexford, had strong supporters and political influence on both sides of the political divide.

In September 1933 de Valera caused astonishment in my family when he accused Dad in the Dail of travelling to Scotland to meet Lord Hailsham, allegedly seeking arms for the Blueshirts, the purpose being to destabilise the government and to end the economic war. There was general disbelief among dad's colleagues and indeed among all those who were aware of dad's commitment to our democratic institutions. Dad had been in Glasgow earlier in the summer with my mother holidaying with family friends, John and Ellie Keavey. John Keavey was a well known cattle dealer. Dad challenged Dev to repeat the accusation outside the Dail. Dev later withdrew the charge, blaming wrong information from an *Irish Press* reporter, and, if I recall correctly, the reporter was subsequently found guilty of malicious intent in court and received a short prison sentence.

Mike Cronin, in his *The Blueshirts and Irish Politics* [4] says "the issue was never concluded beyond de Valera blaming an *Irish Press* journalist for faulty information". Cronin goes on to say "the concept of the Blueshirts working with the British to overthrow Fianna Fail is an intriguing prospect ....". It may intrigue Mr Cronin but it is without any foundation.

Both innuendos by Cronin are preposterous, bearing in mind the total lack of evidence to support his speculations, and the reporter's guilt, confirmed in court. Such an act by my father, whose whole military and political career was devoted to preserving democracy, would hardly have been credible.

Cronin adverts to the point, beloved of revisionist writers, that "No records of any description were available to prove or dismiss the claim." Equally he states that Richard Mulcahy's son would neither deny nor confirm that his father met Hailsham in Glasgow. Neither my two brothers nor myself recollect making such a statement, the ambiguity of which leaves the issue in the air. My eldest brother was only thirteen years at the time, I was eleven.

Dad was active in the Blueshirts when it was led by Eoin O'Duffy, but his commitment to O'Duffy must have been short-lived. Dad was of course totally opposed to the fascist concept of a corporate state, like the rest of his colleagues in Fine Gael. However, there was a great feeling of respect and admiration among the Irish for Mussolini and the tremendous advances he had made in the Italian state and in the enhanced prestige of Italy during the 1930s. De Valera was one of many to express their admiration for Mussolini's successes [5] and the rejection of Mussolini's regime was largely retrospective and did not follow until Italy's entry into the war on the side of Germany.

Maryann, in the epilogue of the biography, states that, after 1924, Dad no longer occupied the centre stage in Irish affairs. Certainly his star began to wane as he occupied himself almost exclusively with party work and as he settled down to the life of an active parliamentarian. In particular, his role as one of the founders of the State was gradually forgotten as his own contemporaries began fading from the scene and as he became more involved in the mundane life of party organisation and routine parliamentary work. Although he remained president of Fine Gael from 1944 to 1959, his image faded further because of Jack Costello's tenure as Taoiseach in the two Inter-Party governments, and the perception that Costello was the de facto leader. I suspect that the circumstances of the relationship between Dad and Costello bears an analogy to the earlier relationship between Dad and Collins. Mulcahy was the de jure head but Costello was perceived to be the real leader. This circumstance did not bother Mulcahy in any way and indeed by his deference to Costello in his capacity as the leader of the government, he contributed to his own overshadowing.

About this time Aknefton, writing in the *Irish Times* (5 September 1953) about the leadership of Fine Gael:

.... so John Costello became Taoiseach. But Mulcahy is the power behind Fine Gael. This role of the Machiavelli behind the throne is nothing new to Richard Mulcahy. The same old story repeats itself time after time. Rory O'Connor, Michael Collins - these men and many others were celebrated in song and story; yet the chief of staff, the man who accepted military responsibility for the whole campaign against the Black-and-Tans - Richard Mulcahy. In this man you find cold, ruthless logic, a master mind, if you like, but not the popular appeal which will bring the mass of voters to the polls shouting 'Up, Mulcahy' as they would be prepared to shout 'Up, Dev.

I think the writer takes a rather oblique view of my father when he invests him with the attributes of the Prince, as Dev once described Machiavelli to Dad. I would think of Dad as being a backroom boy who had an unusual gift of organisation and a strong dedication to achieving his goals, but who lacked the vanity which can only be satisfied by the approbation of others. I suspect that he was too self-effacing to be a clone of Machiavelli.

While he was a dedicated worker for Cumann na nGaedheal and its successor, Fine Gael, and its principal watchdog in parliament during long years of opposition, he failed to create an impact in the country as a political innovator or as a political controversialist. His six years in the ministry of education (1948-51;1954-57) during which he buried himself in the work of the department further removed him from the public eye. Nor was he by temperament a person born with the mantle of leadership - he lacked the personal ambition for power, and he lacked the mystique and the detachment from the common man which attracts the loyalty, admiration and adherence of others - but when he was thrust into a leadership role, as he was from 1918 to 1924, he did not shirk the responsibilities of his office, Any success he had as a leader was based almost entirely on his organisational ability, on his diplomacy in dealing with difficult situations and colleagues, and on his dedication to the ideals of his own political creed.

During the war Dad represented the Fine Gael party on the National Defence Conference, a body set up to advise the government about general wartime policy. Fine Gael's request to have a national government at the beginning of the war was refused by de Valera, but the Conference was established as an alternative. Dad attended meetings regularly but was totally disenchanted by its proceedings, claiming that Dev only paid lip service to its deliberations and recommendations. Just as he did during the Treaty days, Dev kept things close to his chest. Nonetheless, Dad did appear on the same platform as Dev and his ministers during the recruiting campaign in the early years of the war.

Dad had been leader of Fine Gael since 1944 and had seen his party recover during his first ten years as leader from a perilous state of decline with only thirty seats and a general state of demoralisation to fifty seats at the 1954 election. He led the party into a new spirit of enthusiasm and confidence, inspired by a fresh influx of post civil war youth and talent.

He retained the leadership of the Fine Gael party during the two Inter-Party governments of 1948-1951 and 1954-1957 although the perception of his leadership role must have been blurred by Costello's appointment as Taoiseach on both occasions, and by Costello continuing as leader of the opposition from 1951-1954 and 1957-1959. Dad's presidency of Fine Gael continued from 1944 until he retired in 1959, nominating James Dillon as his successor. He apparently preferred Costello as his successor, but Costello refused to take the presidency in a full time capacity. This caused Dad to nominate Dillon and to say, rather harshly, about his close friend Costello that he had "renaged on his leadership" [6].

In his letter of the 26 October 1959 refusing the leadership of the party, Costello finished with a warm tribute to Dad:

> Your selfless and unselfish devotion, indomitable courage, and tireless energy have ever been an inspiration to me, and sustained us all in the work that we were doing, and in the conviction that we were working not merely for party but for Ireland. Not only have you never looked for reward or thanks - you never even thought of it. If your recompense is not here it will be hereafter [7].

And T.J. O'Farrell, writing at the time of his retirement, finished by saying:

> I admired your very quiet, unassuming demeanour for a man with such a national record. That has been your attitude ever since in a period of national stress and storm and peril. You are one of those who helped to build this state at the same time as you

defended it, in circumstances that were at times as fantastic as they were baffling and perilous. You have made history that will last long after you and I have passed to other realms. Thanks for what you have done (7).

Stephen Barrett, writing from Cork

I would like you to know that many people share my personal conviction that your time in public life has done more for the country than almost any living being (7).

Before his resignation from the presidency of Fine Gael in 1959, he fought a vigorous battle against de Valera's proposal to abolish proportional representation and to create single seat constituencies without a transferable vote. He saw Dev's proposal as a move to perpetuate the hegemony of the Fianna Fail party and as a threat to our democratic system. His other colleagues in Fine Gael were equally committed to resisting the move, as well as all other political parties except for Fianna Fail. Despite objections by Fine Gael and the other opposition parties, the government insisted on holding the necessary referendum on the same day as Dev was opposing Sean MacEoin for the presidency. Dev was elected fairly comfortably but the opposition parties were vindicated when the proposal to abolish PR was defeated equally comfortably. During the entire campaign leading up to the referendum Dad was absorbed in opposing his old foe, Dev.

Maryann refers in the epilogue of the biography to dad's problems when he took over the leadership of Fine Gael. Apart from himself, who had always been a regular attender at the Dail, where he was the party's watchdog for many years, and who was the only member of his party to devote his full time to political work, attendances by his colleagues in 1944 were only sporadic. The poor level of political participation was symptomatic of a demoralised and flagging political party and opposition. Support for the party countrywide was gradually waning and there was talk of the party's early demise.

His worries were aggravated by his failure to get candidates to stand for four of the five by-elections in December 1945, and for one later by-election. Fine Gael won none of the ten bye-elections during the 1944-1947 period. This was the time which brought Clann na Poblachta into prominence. Dad's worries were further aggravated at this time when Liam Cosgrave, the son of

William Cosgrave, who was elected to the Dail in 1943, had announced his intention to resign from the party. Liam was one of the few young post-civil war deputies in the party and was highly thought of as a promising future politician, an excellent constituency worker, and a potential future leader. By attending carefully to his constituency of Dun Laoghaire/Rathdown, Cosgrave was one of the few members of the party to realise the importance of grass roots support. His constituency work was reflected by the strong support which he received in successive elections.

Dad believed that his resignation would have a disastrous effect on the party's image. Fortunately, despite Cosgrave's natural misgivings about the party's future, he was induced to remain. He was eventually to be parliamentary secretary to the Taoiseach in the first Inter-Party government and minister for external affairs in the second. He was appointed head of the party after Dillon resigned and was Taoiseach in the 1973-1977 coalition government.

Dad had always favoured a more active political machine and much better attention to constituency organisation, along the lines of Fianna Fail's policies. As soon as he took over the leadership of Fine Gael, he threw himself into the task of restoring the fortunes of the party by building a more effective political machine, through more active participation by the deputies in the Dail and by mobilising more active constituency support throughout the country. After the 1943 election when Fine Gael had lost a further ten seats and was down to 30 seats, it was widely believed that the party was in the last throes of decline. However, the 1948 election marked the turning point of the party's fortunes. Although the number of elected TD's remained pitifully small with an increase of one member only, at least the former drift was reversed and, most important, there were seven new, young and ambitious TD's elected who promised to reinvigorate party

I and my family can recall Dad's strenuous and dedicated work to restore the fortunes of the party during the first four years of his presidency. Without a car, he travelled the four corners of Ireland on an autocycle - a heavy bicycle with a 100cc engine to propel the front wheel. He carried two heavy leather panniers on the back carrier, and a heavy leather coat was to protect him from the elements. He had stated to his party members that he was available to travel to any constituency in the country and was thus almost always away at weekends. As leader of the party, he did not have the use of a car until the start of the general election campaign in 1948.

Maryann gives him full credit for reviving the fortunes of the party through his dedicated organisational work, the constant pressure and encouragement he exerted on his colleagues to be more active and visible in opposition and in their constituencies, and his seminal role in forming the two Inter-Party governments of 1948 and 1954. Fine Gael was never a party to uphold a hall of heroes but his colleagues in the 1940s and 1950s would certainly acknowledge the important part he played in restoring the fortunes of his party and as a family we were well aware of his unique contribution.

Prof. John Murphy, in his review of the Mulcahy biography [8], states that Maryann is too generous in giving him the credit for the revival of Fine Gael's fortunes in the 1950s. While acknowledging the important fillip to the party provided by participation in the Inter-Party government, an institution which was his brainchild, I know no other factor which may have contributed to the turnaround, apart from his tireless encouragement and emphasis on the importance of constituency work during his first four years as president.of his party. In his Thomas Davis lecture about the party system 1945-1951, Murphy makes no reference to Dad, either in relation to the revival of Fine Gael's fortunes or to the formation of the first Inter-Party government.

The Inter-Party Governments

Before the 1948 election, while I was still in London, I recall writing to him when I became aware of his proposal to organise an alternative government to Fianna Fail. The successful formation of a coalition required the participation of five parties and of some of the independents. It seemed an impossible task and I was not slow to say so in my letter, particularly in view of the fact that Fianna Fail had substantially more than twice as many deputies as his party. I did not think that anybody took Dad seriously when he advanced such an unlikely proposal and I believe that included most if not all members of his own party. The success of his plan and the success of the first Inter-Party government, made up as it was of so many diverse groups and rugged individualists, must surely be one of the most extraordinary events in the parliamentary life of this country.

The thrust of Mulcahy's proposal was based on his desire to get rid of the Fianna Fail government which had been in power for sixteen years. He was not impelled by personal ambition. That his desire to get Fianna Fail out

242

transcended any sense of personal ambition must surely be confirmed by his willingness to support John Costello as the new head of government. Before the election he spoke about the need for representative government, not strong government as advocated by the Fianna Fail party.

Leaving Leinster House after the election of the first
Inter-Party Government - February 1948.
left to right: Peader Doyle - Lord Mayor; Richard Mulcahy;
Jack Costello; Sean Collins and Dan Morrissey.

Immediately after the election results were announced he described the coalition concept which he was advocating as an experiment in democracy, and after the Inter-Party government was formed the editor of the *Irish Independent* (19 November 1948) used this phrase to welcome the new administration.

He was a great admirer and loyal colleague of Collins and never resented Collins's public reputation nor his frequent incursions into the domain of the chief of staff. Nor, having a similar close relationship and admiration for

Costello (which Costello reciprocated), did he resent Costello's rise to prominence in 1948 when he became the head of the Inter-Party government and subsequently remained leader of the opposition when out of power until Dillon took over the presidency of the party in 1959. In the first case he was satisfied that Collins was playing a unique part in the military and political fields in the fight against the British. In the second case, Costello's participation was a major factor in keeping together so many disparate groups and individuals in the two Inter-Party governments, and in excluding Fianna Fail and de Valera from office. He believed Costello would make an excellent compromise choice. I have often thought that dad's fundamental attribute was to be of service. Perhaps he needed a leader to fulfil his devotion to service and his sense of loyalty to the institutions he served.

His anxiety was to smooth the path of diplomacy in attracting the various individuals and parties to cooperate in forming the new government. Whether he had an ambition to be Taoiseach or not, I believe that he was happier in the role of a backroom boy in the department of education. His interest in education impelled him to ask for this position in the cabinet and not for one of the more prestigious ministries which he was offered by Costello.

The view that Sean MacBride* would not have Dick Mulcahy as Taoiseach still persists. I have challenged some of the historians who expressed this view to provide documentary evidence in its support. None has been forthcoming. His main reason for standing down as Taoiseach was William Norton's suggestion that, with such a disparate group of parties and people involved, and with dad's prominent role in leading the army in the civil war, it would be best to chose a Taoiseach who was not a leader of a party and who would be compatible with the different ideologies and political views of the participants. At the meeting where Norton made this proposal Dad said that he expected as head

* [Sean McBride, the son of John McBride, the executed 1916 leader, opposed the Treaty and was chief of staff of the IRA as late as 1938 when he resigned from the organisation because of the IRA's bombing campaign in Britain. He founded the Clann na Poblachta party in 1946 and was minister for external affairs in the first Inter-Party government. He subsequently was active in the Amnesty organisation and was awarded the Nobel and Lenin peace prizes for his subsequent dedication to international human rights. There was surely a certain irony in these awards in the light of his undemocratic political stance in Ireland during the first 16 years after the acceptance of the Treaty].

244

of the largest party to be Taoiseach but he added "Well, if I am standing in the way, I'll stand down and you can have anybody else you like".

These circumstances are confirmed by Jack Costello in his valedictory address on RTE in 1961 [9-11]. Apparently the Fine Gael Senator, Harold Douglas, approached Costello on behalf of the various parties. Jack Costello, who was on the Fine Gael front bench, received the full support of all parties and the independents, and was either suggested or enthusiastically supported by my father. He was a close friend and colleague of dad's, and a leading barrister. He was also a professional colleague of MacBride's and stated by Costello to be on friendly terms with him. It is possible that MacBride had influenced Norton in suggesting Costello, although, to the best of my knowledge, there is no documentary evidence to support this suggestion. Costello accepted the position with great reluctance as initially he thought that Mulcahy should have been Taoiseach. Costello was finally induced to accept the nomination by his legal colleague and friend, Arthur Cox.

At no time did Dad speak to us about leading the government, or at least he never expressed such an ambition. Any effort to actively promote himself would have been uncharacteristic of him, particularly as he was aware of the fragile political structure which he was proposing. Indeed, I am of the opinion that Dad may have been relieved that he was not faced with the responsibility of leading such a disparate group.

In later years Dad was critical of certain aspects of Costello's role as Taoiseach of the two Inter-Party governments. He believed that Costello was greatly influenced by a small coterie of friends and acquaintances who were outside the party and outside parliament. Dad describes him as having "a hard crust of intellectualism around him". One member of this group was Alexis Fitzgerald, Costello's son-in-law and a well known solicitor. Another was Patrick Lynch, an economist and lecturer at University College, Dublin, and an ex-civil servant, who was highly thought of by Dad and other Fine Gael leaders. Fitzgerald and Lynch were the forerunners of the spin doctors who were to become such prominent non-civil service ministerial advisors in recent times. Dad believed that this group weakened Costello's contact with his cabinet members [12] and that his closest ministerial colleagues were William Norton, who was Tanaiste, and James Dillon, who was Minister for Agriculture. Costello states that he often consulted Norton when faced with problems, and he had apparently always been on very friendly terms with him (10,11).

He believed that Costello was not sufficiently aware of the activities of the various government departments, a not surprising fact in view of Costello's reluctance to accept the position of Taoiseach and his trust in such senior colleagues as Mulcahy, Dillon, McGilligan, and Norton. It is also likely that he would have been a little inhibited in adopting a hands-on approach to ministerial colleagues who belonged to political parties other than his own. Dad speaks about his relations with Costello at the time of the Inter-Party governments, and "Costello's remoteness from his ministers." (12). Dad's remoteness in the department of education was even more remarkable. In the same tape he describes his reaction to Costello's declaration of a republic in Canada in 1949.

At this juncture, it might be worth referring to some of the political events which dominated the first Inter-Party government of 1948-1951 of which Dad was the architect. Controversy still exists about the manner in which Jack Costello announced the intention of his government to rescind the External Relations Act and to declare a twenty six county republic - "to take the gun out of Irish politics". Controversy also exists about the wisdom of the constitutional change. Dad discusses Costello's declaration of the republic in Canada at length on tape (13), where he is defensive of him.

It has been suggested that Costello made the decision in Canada on the spur of the moment and in response to some slight he received from the Governor General or the authorities there. Costello denied this and implied that the decision to declare a republic had already been made with the knowledge of his cabinet colleagues. On Sunday morning, the day the subject was first mentioned in the newspapers, I was breakfasting with my father. *The Sunday Independent* (5 September 1948) arrived with front page banner headlines announcing the proposed constitutional change. Although my father said little at the time, it was clear that Costello's statement came as a surprise to him. He intimated that he had no knowledge of its being discussed in cabinet and the announcement in Canada was unexpected (12).

In fact the first mention of the repeal of the External Relations Act at cabinet level was on the 11 October 1948 (14) after Costello had returned from the United States and Canada. Dad would have been too loyal to Costello

246

and too protective of the Inter-Party Government to show any disagreement but I often wonder what he really thought of the wisdom of the proposal when one recalls that only four years earlier, in 1944 when he became the President of Fine Gael, he announced as part of his party's policy his intention to remain within the British Commonwealth. The text of Costello's report to the cabinet on the 11 October [14] was as follows:

> The Taoiseach reported on his recent visit to Canada and the United States of America and gave an account of discussions he had with the various people whom he had met and of the addresses and interviews he had given during the course of his journey through the two countries. The action taken by the Taoiseach during his visit to Canada and the United States of America was approved.

This minute was followed by a further note:

> Repeal of Executive Authority (External Relations) Act 1936. Communication from British Government. The Taoiseach brought to the notice of the government a communication which was handed to him by the British representative in Dublin on the 7 October 1948. on the subject of the proposed repeal of the Executive Authority (External Relations) Act 1936. A copy of the communication appears in the annexed schedule A. A reply in the terms of the annexed schedule B to be handed to the British representative by the minister for external affairs was approved.

Before Costello's visit to America, it was decided at the cabinet meeting of the 19 August 1948 [15] not to accept an invitation to attend a forthcoming Commonwealth Conference in London "as a member of the Commonwealth". It was, however, decided to attend "subject to Ireland's position in relation to the British Commonwealth of Nations being made clear...." This decision may have arisen because of conversations Costello claims were taking place with individual cabinet colleagues about the repeal of the External Relations Act 1936. The request to attend as an observer rather than as a committed member of the Commonwealth was refused by the British on the grounds that there was no precedent for such a special category of membership [16]. The cabinet's proposal seemed an "Irish" solution to the dilemma!

Subsequent to Costello's report of his visit to America, there are several references in the cabinet minutes to the negotiations which were conducted with the British which led to an amicable settlement of relations between the two countries [17-19]. The one contentious issue which was not resolved was the British guarantee to the North of Ireland that its relations with Britain would not change without the agreement of the majority of its inhabitants. This led to a strong note of protest from the Irish government and an outburst by Costello which hardly seemed justified in view of the fact that implicit in the British guarantee was that the North's status was not deemed to be permanent [20]. Subsequently, the cabinet sent a long aide-memoir objecting to the North of Ireland aspects of the "Ireland Bill" presented to the House of Commons as a result of the repeal of the External Relations Act [21].

Dad mentions "forces" behind the declaration of the Republic, where it is implied that it may have been based on legalistic motives, possibly enhanced by irritation, rather than by ones of nationalism [22]. My father did say to me at some juncture that, as a constitutional lawyer, Costello was unhappy with the anomalous relationship between Ireland (or Eire as it was then called) and the United Kingdom and the Commonwealth which existed since the 1936 External Relations Act and that he was anxious to put the relationship on a more rational basis. He never suggested to me, or to anybody else to the best of my knowledge, that McBride was responsible for the decision nor is there evidence as far as I am aware that MacBride had any hand in influencing Costello. Dad's only reference to McBride was that "he was a weak person." [23].

F.S.L. Lyons, in a Thomas Davis lecture on Radio Eireann, declared unequivocally that the move to declare a republic had been decided by the cabinet before Costello's visit to Canada, although he adds that some of the ministers were unable to recall the discussion [13]. Jack Costello had a valedictory interview with David Thormley on RTE 1 at the time of his retirement from politics in the early 1960s [9-11]. This interview presents Costello's account of the two Inter-Party governments, of the Browne affair and of the declaration of the republic.

I believe that the most credible account of the declaration of the republic was given by Jack Costello himself during this interview. and that he makes a good case for the wisdom of the constitutional change. He said it was utter nonsense that he had made the declaration in Canada in a temper in response to the slights he received from the Canadians. He denied that McBride had ever spoken to him about the matter but that both James Dillon and William Norton had recommended the repeal of the External Relations Act long before the change was announced. He stated categorically that the proposal had been discussed in cabinet and that when the subject was broached by Norton in the Dail, de Valera replied "if you do it you will get no opposition from me". He was not too clear if the decision by the cabinet was recorded in the minutes and added that the minutes were rather casually kept at those days. In fact, the minutes of the two Inter-Party governments seem to me to be quite comprehensive and detailed. I expect that Costello is not quite correct that the subject was formally discussed in cabinet but it may have been discussed informally with individuals at the time of cabinet meetings.

Costello was conscious of the anomalous situation created by the External Relations Act in Ireland's relationship with the Commonwealth and other countries and, above all, he believed that a republican constitution would eliminate for ever the continuing sore of violence by republican dissidents. It would take the gun out of Irish politics. Finally, he was anxious that the government should be seen to be the proposer of the constitutional change. He feared that some independent member might take the initiative in the matter and that such a circumstance would be a serious embarrassment to his government.

There clearly was some discussion about the proposal with his colleagues during the first year of the Inter-Party government   The declaration may have been precipitated prematurely by the anger Costello must have felt at two unfortunate transgressions of protocol, one when the promised toast to the President of Ireland was not proposed at the banquet given to him by Lord Alexander, the Governor-General of Canada, the other when the symbol of Ulster Unionism, *Roaring Meg*, was placed before him at the banquet table. However, F.S.L Lyons maintained that Costello decided to announce the change in Canada, two days after the government's intentions were leaked by the Sunday Independent. Paddy Lynch accompanied Costello on his visit and this was also his opinion of the events [24]. Lynch was convinced that the leak emanated from some person who was close to Costello, such as James Dillon, but this assertion was apparently strenuously denied by the then editor of the *Sunday Independent*, Hector Legge. Mr Legge however refused to divulge the source of his information.

According to Lynch, both he and John Hearne, the Irish High Commissioner to Canada, advised Costello not to make the announcement during his visit, and the same advice, according to Lynch, was proferred by Sean MacBride who was minister for external affairs and who telephoned Costello after he had read the Sunday Independent announcement. Why Costello disregarded this advice is not clear. Dad's surprise at the announcement in Canada was confirmed by his remark to Paddy Lynch at the liner's terminal in Cobh, where Dad had gone to greet Costello on his return to Ireland, "The Taoiseach must have been drinking some heady wine in Canada".

In a personal communication from Deirdre McMahon, she tells me that in her researches in the Public Record Office in London (PRO DO 130/93), she found the following extract:

> Lord Rugby (UK Representative in Eire) to Sir Eric Machtig (Permanent Secretary, Commonwealth Relations Office) 28 October 1948: Costello's action 'looks completely illogical against the background of Irish politics. I wonder very much what General Mulcahy is thinking. I do not believe that he would have taken this action because, as Mr MacEntee points out, if this is the Fine Gael doctrine the Civil War was quite unjustifiable.'

Lord Rugby was referring to a speech by MacEntee which was reported in the *Irish Times* on the 27 October 1948.

To those who knew him less well, Costello could appear a rather humourless and gruff person. Urbanity was hardly part of his personality. He could be rather rigid in his opinions and the stances he might take. Although a man of few words to the casual observer, he could respond vigorously and trenchantly to criticism or confrontations by an opponent as is clear from his valedictory interview on RTE at the time of his retirement. He, with Cecil Lavery, was the outstanding member of the bar in the 1940s and 1950s. He was a brilliant advocate and had the enviable reputation as a lawyer of believing implicitly in his client's case, no matter what the circumstances were, and of being totally committed to achieving a successful outcome, however unlikely the prospects of success might be. It used be said that his professional fees were so modest that other less successful barristers found it difficult to make a living. This situation was to change and the first to bring about a real increase in legal fees was said to be Billy Fitzgerald, another successful lawyer and very much junior to Costello.

Jack Costello first entered public life when he was appointed assistant to Hugh Kennedy in 1922. Hugh Kennedy was the law officer attached to the Provisional Government and attorney general to the first Free State government. Costello became attorney general in 1926 when Kennedy resigned and he remained in this position until the change of government in 1932. He reminds us in his RTE interview that Cosgrave and O'Higgins insisted that the attorney general should not be a member of the Dail and that the position was non-political and designed to give independent advice to the government. Presumably the attorney general's independence prevails since that time.

He entered the Dail after the 1933 election, taking the seat in the Co. Dublin constituency of Thomas Finlay who had died. In later years he represented the Dublin south-east constituency until his retirement in 1961. Whilst he was scarcely the best organised constituency man, and therefore clearly in the Fine Gael tradition, he was popular and highly regarded by his largely middle-class constituents. He had no difficulty in being re-elected at successive elections.

I recall being asked by my father if I would accompany Costello to Moville in Co. Donegal one afternoon where he was to address the local electors on the occasion of the "Flatfoot Platypus" by-election, the first by-election after the formation of the Inter-Party government, and therefore a vital test for the new government because of its slim and fragile majority in parliament. The Fianna Fail opposition used the title to deride the makeshift coalition which was in power. I was apparently to provide Costello with company on the long and tedious car journey. I might have been of help if there had been a medical emergency but his monosyllabic responses to my efforts at conversation, if providing conversation was the motive behind my father's request, must have been as embarrassing to him as it was to me.

It proved to be an appallingly wet evening with a continuous downpour. Driving must have been very difficult and sometime after we had crossed the Cavan/Fermanagh border the car came to an involuntary stop because of serious flooding on the road. At this stage we were being followed at a discrete distance by a Royal Ulster Constabulary car. We soon found wading policemen surrounding the car and reassuring us that we would be rescued promptly. And so after a few minutes a large vehicle arrived, we were rescued without mishap and proceeded on our journey in another vehicle. The police acted with courtesy and efficiency, as one might expect. I describe the incident because I was astonished by the curt and very gruff way Costello responded to the assistance of the police, as if they were the embodiment of all his prejudices about the North and partition.

The other event requiring comment was Noel Browne's proposal to introduce a free mother and child scheme. Noel Browne was one of the bright jewels of the new administration. He achieved considerable public support and approbation for his energetic public health measures, particularly in controlling the tuberculosis epidemic. He also proposed a free mother and child health scheme which had much to commend it but which, as a measure of social progress, might be easily perceived as being ahead of its time, particularly in such a conservative community as predominately Roman Catholic Ireland. Dad discusses this affair in some detail on tape [13].

The scheme was greeted with dismay and provoked violent opposition among the medical profession and some members of the Catholic Hierarchy. It was inevitable that the cabinet, made up of mostly conservative members chosen from and representing a conservative electorate, would yield to the widespread pressure from the reactionary groups. Browne was asked to modify or to withdraw his free scheme. He refused to do so, and after much misunderstanding between himself and the bishops and increasing disagreement with his cabinet colleagues, he was asked to resign by the leader of his party, Sean MacBride. Whether his discussions with his colleagues were at a person to person level or at a cabinet level is difficult to say. According to Dad he was not aware of any cabinet discussions on the subject of the Mother and Child Scheme.

The Health Bill 1949 was first mentioned in the cabinet minutes on the 4 November 1949 [25] when it was approved for circulation to the Dail. It was next mentioned at the cabinet meeting of 14 November 1950 [26] when a new section was approved of but there was no mention of the details of this change or addition The next and last mention of the scheme, now entitled the Mother and Child Health Service, was on the 6 April 1951 [27]. Browne was present at this meeting but resigned immediately afterwards. The text of the minute is as follows:

Following consideration of a letter dated 4/4/1951 to the Taoiseach from his Grace, the Archbishop of Dublin, Primate of Ireland, on behalf of the Catholic Hierarchy of Ireland, intimating that the particular scheme called the Mother and Child Health Service proposed by the minister for health is opposed to Catholic teaching, it was decided

(I)   that the scheme referred to should not be further pursued.

(II) that in the light of the government's conviction that mothers and children should not be deprived of the best available health care by reason of insufficient means, a scheme or schemes for a mother and child health service should, as soon as possible, be prepared and undertaken which would: (a) provide the best modern facilities for those whose family wage or income does not permit them to obtain, of themselves, the health care that is necessary of mothers and children; and (b) be in conformity with Catholic social teaching; and

(III) that consideration should be given to the question whether any amendments of the Health Act, 1947, additional to those proposed in the Health Bill, 1950, are necessary and desirable and, if so, that proposals for such amendments should be submitted to the government.

What are we to conclude from the statement by the cabinet? Firstly that Browne resigned because he would not accept a means test for those availing of the scheme. Secondly, that the cabinet was reasonable in its decision to modify the Bill in the light of the Hierarchy and the medical profession's opposition. Thirdly that the Hierarchy's opposition was based on fatuous grounds, at least to those in judgement fifty years later, and, fourthly, that the medical profession opposed Browne's scheme because doctors feared loss of private practice.

Browne's scheme might have been perceived as being ahead of its time by a conservative public, medical profession and the Church. But it was certainly less radical than the National Health Service introduced in Britain the year before. As I recall the event, the main thrust of opposition came from the medical profession, and particularly from the Irish Medical Association, and the consultants. The latter included my own senior colleagues at St. Vincent's Hospital, Bob O'Connell and the Fitzgerald brothers, Paddy and Oliver, brothers of Alexis who was one of Costello's closest advisors. Many of the consultants in Dublin had close social and professional relations with the members of the inter-party cabinet, including my father. I recall the strenuous lobbying of the members of the cabinet, particularly by O'Connell who was as energetic as he was politically minded, and who was a very prominent member of the Irish Medical Association. I believe that if the medical profession had not opposed Browne's scheme, the cabinet and the Church might not have intervened.

The Browne affair was followed two months later by the dissolution of the Inter-Party Government after three years of office. It had too small a majority to continue without the support of Noel Browne and the one or two deputies who supported him, as well as a few independents who were disenchanted with the government's economic policies.

The end of the three year administration of the first Inter-Party government is generally attributed to Noel Browne's intransigence in relation to the Mother and Child Scheme, and to his resignation and that of one or two supporters. However, Patrick Lynch, who was close to Jack Costello and who was aware of the affairs of the cabinet and its members, has stated in a conversation with me that, while the failure of the cabinet to accept Browne's scheme was a dominant factor in the failure of the government, its early demise was inevitable because of increasing tensions within the Clann na Poblachta party and particularly between Browne and Sean MacBride. Their differences were based on personal rather than political matters according to Lynch. The government was also under increasing pressure because of serious inflationary and economic problems.

Browne's scheme failed because it was before its time, at least in the sense that it provoked the opposition of an influential and reactionary medical profession. Throughout his political career he failed to learn two of the fundamental attributes of a successful and effective politician - that politics is the art of the possible and that the best should not be the enemy of the good. His subsequent political career was unsuccessful because he never had the capacity to understand these precepts or to compromise in matters of practice or principle. Only a very uncompromising character would destroy what was a progressive piece of health legislation on the grounds of a means test. I often wondered if, like some of his patients, he was not a little paranoid. He certainly could be and was bitter in a personal way about some of his colleagues. He was not able to compromise on many issues which required consensus, and he was happy to receive all the accolades in relation to the control of the tuberculosis epidemic although the campaign against tuberculosis had been launched initially by his predecessor in the ministry of health, Dr Jim Ryan of Fianna Fail. And fundamental advances in the treatment of tuberculosis had coincided with Dr Browne's arrival on the scene.

There was much confusion about the Browne debacle and the resultant demise of the first Inter-Party Government because of different accounts of the proceedings leading up to Browne's resignation. Although a number of senior cabinet ministers did try to influence Browne during the negotiations about the Mother and Child scheme, some blame must at least in part be attributed to members of the Cabinet, and particularly to the senior and more experienced members. Costello appears to have imposed little ministerial accountability on his colleagues, and clearly this must have been so in the case of the Browne episode.

In my father's case he had characteristically buried himself so thoroughly in the detailed running of the department of education that he must have had little awareness of the wider political aspects of government. Maryann Valiulis in her biography refers to his total and meticulous dedication to whatever responsibility and work he undertook. She noted this aspect of his personality and underlined the advantages and disadvantages of such an attribute. As chief of staff, charged with organising a revolutionary army and subsequently a peacetime force, this trait proved of inestimable value, but as the senior member of the Inter-Party cabinet, his remoteness in the department of education must have contributed at least some part to the final dissolution of his government.

I cannot believe that even such a rugged individualist and political loner as Noel Browne could not have been influenced to modify his ambitions by more experienced colleagues, particularly if better ministerial accountability had prevailed, and if he had not had such an unsatisfactory relationship with his own political leader. He also appears to have had little insight into the motives of his professional colleagues who feared any changes in the health services which might threaten their livelihood. Costello, in discussing the episode in the Dail after Browne's resignation, stated that Browne was incapable of taking advice and was impervious to reason or argument. Although the episode is described in some detail in Brian Maye's *Fine Gael - 1923-1987* [28] the story is confused by the varying accounts of what transpired between Browne and the bishops, and between him and his ministerial colleagues during the development of the crisis.

It is evident that the first Inter-Party Government had some considerable successes, despite the Browne episode and its serious post-war economic difficulties. It broke the hegemony of the Fianna Fail party and established for the first time the role of coalition government which has in more recent times been the rule rather than the exception in Irish political life. It survived for more than three years, despite the gloomy predictions of those who thought coalition governments were not a viable alternative to single party control. Thus, it confirmed the cohesive effect of power in keeping people and parties with different ideologies together. Its formation was also to lead ultimately to the realisation that, because of the trivial differences between our political parties in terms of policies and ideologies, it matters little what party or combination of parties are in government in Ireland.

After the repeal of the External Relations Act the government extracted important concessions from the United Kingdom which left the relations between the two countries little different from those which existed within the Commonwealth. It achieved much with land reform and drainage, and with Dillon's* "one more cow, one more sow, and one more acre under the plough" campaign. It began the long and ultimately successful process of post-war economic development. It established the IDA, and an independent Central Statistics Office, detached from the Department of Industry and Commerce, which has since provided comprehensive national, demographic and economic data essential to the function of a modern state. Dad, according to Paddy Lynch, pushed the concept of an independent statistics office and recommended Roy Geary as its director. Geary was to prove a brilliant success as the first head of the CSO and the CSO continues to give an excellent service to the government and the community.

* [James Dillon was originally a founder of the National Centre Party which joined Cumann na nGaedheal in 1933 to form the Fine Gael Party. He resigned from Fine Gael in 1939 because of disagreement about neutrality but joined the two Inter-Party governments as minister for agriculture. He rejoined Fine Gael in 1951 and succeeded Mulcahy as president of the party from 1959 to 1965].

Cooperation with the North was first initiated by the Inter-Party government in relation to the Foyle Fisheries, the Erne hydroelectric scheme, and the Irish transport system when the latter was overhauled and rationalised. However, the break with the Commonwealth cannot have furthered reconciliation with the North.

I cannot recall speaking in any great depth with Dad about the Northern situation and the possible reunification of Ireland. I suspect he would have approved of the late John Kelly's views on the subject, which, in a nutshell, stated that reunification is entirely dependent on the wishes of a Northern majority, that now and in the foreseeable future the majority will remain committed to Britain, and that a change to a united Ireland or a federal country can only be achieved by making the South more attractive than the British option. The Good Friday Agreement of 1998 would no doubt have been seen by him as another step towards the unity and freedom of the country. It was in this belief that I attended the Sinn Fein Ard Fheis of the 10 May 1998 as a visitor and told Gerry Adams that I was representing my father who would greatly approve of Sinn Fein's endorsement of the agreement as a further stepping stone following the first step, the ratification of the Treaty in 1922. After the declaration of the Republic of Ireland, Britain gave formal assurances to the North that its relationship with the Britain would not change without the consent of the Northern people. Costello reacted to the British step by stating "we would hit Britain in her pride and purse" but realistically there was little he could do. However, he started the Anti-Partition League, and thus began a national and international campaign to publicise the injustices of partition, which lasted for a few years but which gradually petered out because of the indifference of the Irish diaspora and the ignorance of the rest of the world. Costello was supported by the opposition, including de Valera. I have no record of my father's attitude to the League and its objectives. I suspect that he was too occupied in the department of education to give it much thought.

The Anti-Partition campaign did nothing but further antagonise the Northern majority and widen the gap between them and the rest of their countrymen. It was worse than futile and this was stated by Dad in later years [29]. Whether Dad thought it futile at the time is not clear. It merely entrenched the northern loyalist intransigence and had no effect on international opinion nor could the Americans, Australians or any other world community, however powerful the Irish diaspora in their midst, have affected the position. As one speaker said, preaching against partition was like preaching against sin.

The great hope for a lasting solution to the northern question lies in the present closer cooperation at economic, social, cultural and sporting levels between the two parts of the island. And, of course, it would greatly solve the Northern problem if sectarian education were abolished at the primary and secondary levels there. It has taken us more than seventy years since the Treaty to realise that the only realistic approach to a real reconciliation and to a more cohesive answer to Ireland's problems is cooperation and mutual understanding between the two communities. Fundamental to the whole question is the fact that the North's economic, social and environmental problems are akin to those of the South rather than to those of Britain, and that, whatever the Unionists may say, they will always be marginalised as long as they are controlled from Westminster.

Fine Gael won 50 seats in the 1954 election and was able to form the second Inter-Party Government with only two other parties, Labour and Clann na Talmhan. Jack Costello was again elected Taoiseach but it seems to me that the reason my father was not elected Taoiseach in the first Inter-Party was no longer relevant in the second, particularly as Fine Gael now had a substantially larger number of deputies in the Dail. It is also difficult to understand why Costello continued after the two Inter-Party governments as leader of the opposition.

Unfortunately I cannot recall discussing these anomalies with Dad. I would strongly suspect that Dad may have been responsible for maintaining the leadership *status quo*, perhaps because he was not encouraged by his colleagues to claim the right of leadership or, more likely, because he was unwilling to seek the post. If he had any regrets, they were never expressed to his family nor I expect to anyone else. According to Liam Cosgrave and Tom O'Higgins, with whom I discussed this point, the question of dad replacing Costello as leader of the opposition and Taoiseach was never mentioned and probably never arose, nor did either of these two prominent Fine Gael members of the 1948-1951 Dail think that dad would have agreed to such an arrangement.

This second coalition had a majority in the Dail and was clearly in a stronger position than the previous Inter-Party government, depending as it did on five parties and a few independents. The prospects augured well for the new government but, unfortunately for these prospects, it was faced with a major economic recession which was worldwide. The recession was caused in Ireland by serious balance of payment problems, leading to public expenditure cuts, increasing unemployment and heavy emigration. Despite setting up structures to restore the country's economy, which were to pay dividends in later years, the government, yielding to increasing pressure and criticism, and about to face a no confidence vote in the Dail, resigned in 1957 and went into opposition after the election. Fine Gael was to face another sixteen years in opposition before the next coalition government would be formed in 1973, led by Liam Cosgrave.

Dad returned to his position as minister for education in the second Inter-Party government, while remaining president of Fine Gael. The 50 seats won by Fine Gael in the 1954 election was a measure of how successful he was in reorganising the party and in proposing the concept of the first Inter-Party government. However, he must have been greatly disappointed in 1957 when the party was again reduced to forty seats. His tenure of the ministry during 1948-1951 and 1954-1957 removed him entirely from his organisational role in Fine Gael, which probably accounted in part at least for the deterioration in the party's fortunes in the 1957 election.

David McCullagh has recently published a detailed account of the first Inter-Party government [30].

Chapter 9

Later Years and Last Days

During dad's years in parliament he was not given to much political talk and certainly not to much reminiscing about the past. His later preoccupation with Dev's influence in provoking the civil war lay dormant. However, after his retirement and as he become more occupied with his papers, he became greatly absorbed by the history of the foundation of the State and by his own experiences during these early years. While he was active in parliament and in the Fine Gael party, he had an exceptional capacity to be totally absorbed in his work. This exceptional absorption in his day-to-day work was particularly evident when he was minister for education in the two Inter-Party governments. It left him with little time to be concerned with wider political issues. This trait was certainly a factor which contributed to the decline of his public image and to his description by a reviewer as a forgotten hero.

There were occasions when he appeared to be motivated by an unusual degree of stubborness. Some years before his death a monument was erected on the road to Slane near Ashbourne where the successful action against the RIC had taken place in 1916. Dad was acknowledged by the survivors of the action to have been the brains behind the successful assault on the police column, and their ultimate defeat and capture. The unveiling was performed by his brother-in-law, Sean T. O'Kelly, the President of Ireland. Dad refused to be present. I cannot recall the reason for his refusal but I feel certain he was impelled to do so because he had little respect for Sean T. as a man and none as an activist during the war of independence. He never forgave him his anti-Treaty stance, and his strong prejudice against de Valera and the Fianna Fail party would inevitably include Sean T. I would suspect that he could not bear to be seen to be patronised on such an occasion by a man he deemed to be a political lightweight. Nonetheless, it was surely very odd that the person whose widely acknowledged military reputation was initially based on his leadership and inspiration at Ashbourne in 1916 refused to be present at this important commemoration. What must the other survivors who were present, and who had such regard for Mulcahy, have thought of his unexplained absence?

During the war of independence, Truce and pre-civil war period, he and Collins were equally acknowledged as the leaders of the army and as the inspiration behind the Irish resistance to the British military and police. During the eighteen months from Collins' death in August 1922 to the army mutiny in March 1924, Dad alone symbolised the leadership of the emerging peacetime Free State army. Despite his political appointment as minister of defence in January 1922, a position he held up to the mutiny, he was widely thought of as an "army man", and as such widely admired by his supporters and respected if not feared by his opponents. Yet, despite his dedication to the advancement of the army as a highly professional peacetime force, well recounted in the biography, and despite his palpable pride in its role in building a democratic state, he never allowed himself to be associated with the army or to be seen to have any connection with the force from the day he resigned as minister of defence in March 1924. His complete break from the army. and his distancing himself from its image and its progress, must be one reason why his political and military reputation acquired at the time of the foundation of the state was eroded by the passage of time and the earlier biographies of many of his colleagues.

His post-mutiny attitude to the army was not an expression of loss of interest or loss of pride in its achievements. Mother remained chairman of the army benevolent fund for many years and was obviously encouraged to do so by Dad. I would put forward two reasons as likely to account for his reaction, although I must admit that my views are somewhat speculative, for it was difficult to question him on his personal motives. He tended to be totally absorbed in his current activities, to the exclusion of all other matters, a feature of his personality which I have already underlined. His future lay in politics, not the army, according to his own perception, and he threw himself into the life of the Dail, his party and the task of chairing the Gaeltacht Commission and of writing its full report.

He may have wished to leave the army's future development and evolution to those who took over from the army council, the members of whom had been sacked by the Government at the time of the mutiny. I think that this was the chief reason he distanced himself from the army. He was certainly the type who would be sensitive to accusations of interfering in areas not his concern. I cannot recall if I have ever discussed his post-mutiny attitude to the army with him. It is unlikely he would have gone into his reasons, and certainly not in the years before his retirement. His answer would certainly be brief and he would probably close the conversation with a remark like "Hadn't I enough things to do without meddling into other people's business." One need look no further than the papers and tapes in the university archives to appreciate his lifetime pride in the army and in its non-political record.

On another occasion, perhaps in the early sixties, he was invited by Sean MacEntee, then a minister in the Fianna Fail administration, to join an all party committee to decide on certain aspects of the design of the Garden of Remembrance which was to be located in Parnell Square. Dad mentions the invitation in a conversation with an old colleague and gives the most tortuous and incomprehensible reason for his refusal to accept what was a perfectly ecumenical gesture [1]. As far as one can glean from his remarks, his refusal was linked to his strong prejudice against MacEntee and his party.

Why was his military contribution to the foundation of the new state and his subsequent political career largely forgotten by subsequent generations? Valiulis attributes it partly to the harsh decisions he made during the civil war but if, through his conduct of the civil war, he acquired many enemies, he also acquired at least as many devoted friends and admirers who appreciated his efforts to defend the democratic constitution of the country.

His neglect was, I believe, largely the product of his own personality combined with his survival to old age. During his active years up to his retirement on 1961, he was reluctant to speak of past events, except perhaps in private and in response to the questions of family members and friends. His constant theme when discussions arose about the revolutionary period, and particularly the civil war, was "Haven't we enough to do with the country in the state it is, without worrying about what happened in the past." He would never comment publicly on matters which he would perceive to be historically inaccurate, particularly when they applied to himself. One example of his determination to avoid unnecessary controversy was his refusal to review Beaslai's biography *Michael Collins and the Making of a New Ireland.* [2] although during his retirement he was able to dictate a 460 page critique of the book which is replete with comments disagreeing with the author's facts, interpretations and omissions. His response to the publication of the Beaslai book, when invited to review it by the publisher, was characteristic of his unwillingness to get involved in what he perceived to be harmful controversy at the time.

He contributed to the eclipse of his reputation for other reasons too. While he gave numerous interviews to media representatives, historians and students of history during his retirement, he was a difficult and at times cantankerous interviewee, particularly during his declining years. He cannot have evoked the sympathy and understanding of some of his correspondents. He was also unpredictable in his response to invitations to attend functions which bore directly on his own career, and which at times concerned him as the principal figure.

He was a self-effacing person who lived to a good age. Most of his contemporaries who were aware of his military and political contribution to the founding of the state, and who held him in high regard, predeceased him. In his last few years he showed the subtle signs of intellectual deterioration which affected his judgment and which distorted his opinions, and thus the views of his critics who judged him more by the writings of his declining days, rather than by his earlier work.

These are some of the reasons that led to the decline in dad's reputation and which compelled Maryann Valiulis to describe him as the forgotten hero. I feel sure that his real contribution to Irish history will be acknowledged eventually, not through my efforts, but through the publication of Maryann Valiulis's biography, and perhaps more effectively by the good fortune that he left behind him such a complete and remarkable collection of war of independence, Truce, civil war and Cumann na nGaedheal papers. His integrity and his high standards of service were reflected in the careers of his other siblings and were a feature of many middle-class Catholic families emerging with strong Victorian ideals. His Quaker background may also have been a factor.

I ponder at times about dad's concept of nationalism. Michael Tierney, in his biography *Eoin MacNeill, Scholar and Man of Action, 1867-1945* [3] writes in detail about the conflict between nationalism as applied to the state and nationalism as applied to culture and race. He writes convincingly about the divide between those whose national aspirations were based on the preservation of the Irish language and the Celtic culture, and who were largely associated with the Gaelic League at the turn of the century, and those nationalists who were committed to the formation of an independent state, with little commitment or even opposition to the ancient Gaelic culture or language. I had not thought along these lines until I had read Michael Tierney.

It was quite clear that dad's concept of nationalism was based on the preservation of the Irish language and the Gaelic tradition, but I expect that he, like many others who thought that language and tradition were of crucial importance, saw their form of nationalism as an effective means of eventually achieving independence. His concept of nationalism as applied to the state was a pragmatic one, and he would have been happy to remain part of the British Commonwealth as long as we were free to counteract the pervading anglicisation of Irish society. Dad was close to MacNeill in many ways, in thought and action, and, as MacNeill was described by Tierney, he was "a traditionalist who saw that the essence of a nation was its history, not its aspiration to or achievement of statehood".

Father Desmond McCarthy of Bray, Co Wicklow, wrote to my cousin, the Rev Richard Mulcahy on the 18/10/1992 after he had read Maryann's biography. He was an old friend and admirer of Dad's, and was familiar with the literature of the revolutionary period. He thought that the biography was the most accurate account of the civil war and of the circumstances surrounding the foundation of the Irish Free State which he had read. Father McCarthy also had this to say about the biography:

> You asked me what I had thought of *Portrait of a Revolutionary - General Richard Mulcahy.* I found it a very informative work. To my mind its account of the Civil War and of the setting up of the Free State is the best yet published - and I have read many books treating of that period.

> There was one aspect of the work in which I was disappointed. The public figure of Richard Mulcahy is excellently presented but, to my mind, the man himself, his affability, his graciousness, his thought for others, his sense of humour would seem to have been passed over. The book did not deal with the Dick Mulcahy I knew. I met a public figure not a person in *Portrait of a Revolutionary.*

On 1 December 1922, during the civil war, a newspaper article referred to Dad's response to a special correspondent from the Press Association who asked him if he would care to give any reassuring message to the people of the ability of the army to deal with any outbreak. Dad replied that the people would not be more assured of the effectiveness and ability of the officers and the men of the army by his speaking of it. He went on to say "Our most effective work has always been done with our mouths shut!" [4]. It is easy to understand why Dad acquired the public reputation referred to by Father McCarthy!

All Mulcahy's intimates would agree with Father McCarthy's analysis of his private persona. In the house he was affable and easy-going, and fitted well into the rather casual and informal family scene. He attended seven o'clock mass every morning, was a sparing eater of simple food, was a keen walker, did not smoke and drank very lightly and then only on formal occasions. Apart from the mild asceticism which he practised in his daily life, he showed none of the rigidity and social reserve which made him an object of respect if not fear by his army colleagues who were not intimate with him.

However, neither I nor my brothers or sisters were too concerned about the omission of the more personal aspects of dad's personality or family life from the biography. The biography fulfilled an important purpose and satisfied our best hopes, which were to record the particular role Dad played in organising and directing an army, both in military and ethical terms, which would successfully stand up to British aggression, which would not alienate the local population, and which would play its role in establishing a free and democratically elected parliament.

Opinions can differ widely about people. A Mr Boilbester, a journalist in the *Irish Times* in the late 1920s, refers to Ernest Blythe and Mulcahy in a letter to Lady Lavery, quoted in her biography [5].

> Blythe and his cultural alter-ego (Richard) Mulcahy are sour faced Puritans with all the zeal of that type and all its fanatical obstinacy. Blythe is a Lisburn Presbyterian. Mulcahy's grandparents are Quakers. Both he and Blythe are rabid teetotallers. So there you have the Free Staters' woes in a sentence. They are the sea green incorruptibles who will not be satisfied until the British connection - which bred both of them - has been snapped and until the jabber of the Gaeltacht echoes through a de-Anglicised countryside. Blythe and Mulcahy the Orange convert and the soldier saint as poor Kevin O'Higgins used to call them ....

Padraig Colum, in his biography of Griffith [6] says of Dad, comparing him to Sean MacEoin:

> He was a soldier of a different type, austere and intellectual, the presentment of a military monk. 'Every word,' writes an observer (in *Free State or Republic?* by Padraic de Burca and John F Boyle [7] Dublin: the Talbot Press), noting him at a later session, 'came slowly and earnestly, almost softly from the thin lips, the sharp jaws, with the thoughtful eyes above, and the meditative brow shadowing the whole countenance'.

Whatever about being a soldier saint, he was never a person to show the intolerance and the puritanical zeal attributed to him by Mr Boilbester. I expect that the latter's views were based on hearsay from casual acquaintances of my father.

Dad seconded the proposal in the Dail that de Valera be elected President of the Republic in August 1921. A newspaper report of the proceedings went as follows:

> On the heels of Mr MacEoin, seconding his resolution, came the second phrase maker and recaller of the past, Richard Mulcahy. I looked at him with surprise. Was this the redoubtable Mulcahy, "Chief of Staff", the planner far more than Michael Collins ever was on ambushes and raids, organiser of the flying columns. A little man in a blue coat, much too large for him, looking vaguely as if he had something to do with horses, and vaguely as if he had something to do with ideas. Well, the little man, with clear brow and fullish lips, was soon speaking and his words were the only real trial of the day. Downcast, looking at no one, his gaze deep in the realm of history, he began to speak of the threshold of Irish history, and heaven knows how far back that can have been, when 'The hosts of Connaught marshalled themselves against Ulster, when Ulster's leader, Cuchulann, was overcome by sickness and ' he hesitated for a moment 'by magic and how the youths of Ulster were summoned and held the ford and saved the land' [8].

Last Days

My father had been always been in good health and lived to his 86th year. His habits conformed to the best principles of modern health promotion. He was mildly austere in his habits. He was a frugal eater, and a lover of plain simple food, unadulterated by the garnishings which have become a feature of our modern cuisine. He drank little alcohol, and then only in later life. He made an unsuccessful attempt to adopt the habit of cigarette smoking in the late 1930s. He was a regular and brisk walker, and led a very regular life. He was an excellent sleeper, and, unfortunately for my mother, a heavy resonant snorer. No circumstance in his life, however pressing or urgent, appeared to affect his sleep pattern. He was slim, of medium height (67 inches), and athletic in build, although he became a little heavier during his retirement. At no time could he be described as corpulent. There is an extensive file in the archives which contains his collection of publications confirming his interest in healthy living and physical fitness [8].

Frank Holland questions Dad about his good health and his longevity, and gets the answer - hard work, early rising, walking [9]. Both Holland and he attribute their good health to not smoking and not drinking alcohol! Even to the most obsessive health-promoting professional of the 1990s they would be perceived as paragons!

In his last few years his vision deteriorated and he was almost blind at the end of his days. He found it difficult to reconcile himself to his loss of vision. His chronic anxiety about his sight was aggravated by his doctor's failure to counsel him properly about the reality of his age and its inevitable consequences on his vital functions. It was not surprising that his regular and frequent visits to his eye specialist, with the perception that something could still be done to improve his sight, engendered a false hope of recovery [10].

In June 1971 he complained of indigestion. He was admitted to the Pembroke Nursing Home where a diagnosis of a large fungating stomach cancer was confirmed by X-ray, a condition which had then, and still has, a very poor long-term outlook. Despite its prognostic implications, most surgeons would advise operation, perhaps to confirm the diagnosis or, more likely, to prevent the distressing end they would envisage if the tumour were left in situ. I had had twelve years experience until 1964 attending terminal cancer patients at Our Lady's Hospice for the Dying at Harold's Cross. Most of the patients whom I encountered there had not been submitted to surgery, and the current chemotherapy regimes had not yet emerged. Many had cancer of the gastro-intestinal tract, including the gullet, stomach and large bowel. The spectre of increasing and intolerable pain and a distressing end may have been in my mind at some stage in my earlier career but was seldom or never encountered by me during my twelve years attending these patients; and this was before the era of total pain control and analgesia had become the rule in these institutions. We did however, relieve our patients anxiety, pain and distress with the traditional Brompton Mixture which contained opium and codeine among other pain relieving and sedative preparations.

The great majority of terminal cancer patients sink slowly into oblivion, their cognitive and perceptive functions sinking at the same time as their bodies wither and die. Many surgeons still operate on tumours with a clearly defined hopeless prognosis and will do so to prevent a distressing termination to the patient's illness. Unfortunately they may be unaware of the natural course of things when cancer is allowed to proceed without intervention and without great distress to its end, particularly as nowadays we possess excellent methods of pain control and palliation, and much improved counselling for patients and their families.

I would much prefer to die in the company of my family and friends, and in the familiar surroundings of my home, than to die in the impersonal clinical surroundings of the hospital or nursing home. It is wrong to submit the dying patient to the indignity and discomfort of the many high technology interventions which are too often inappropriately used in patients without hope of cure. Keeping such patients in hospital may also engender hopes that only serve to prolong anxiety and, most of all, that prevent the patient and family becoming reconciled to the realities of the situation. Most of all, the most important event in the life of a family, the death of a loved one, should if at all possible take place in the home, or at least in an institution, such as Our Lady's Hospice, which has the expertise and tradition of looking after the dying and not denying its inevitability.

In my father's case, I refused the offer of surgery and took him back to his home in Temple Villas. He was not aware of his condition. I do not think he ever contemplated an early death. He returned to his papers, his newspaper reading, his long and prolix discussions with his many visitors. By now, although still able to look after himself and his personal hygiene, and while still perfectly aware of his surroundings and his family, his physical and mental faculties began to deteriorate. In early November he retired to bed for the last time. At this juncture all his personal needs were attended to by Maggie whose devotion to him greatly exceeded the bounds of duty.

With his physical deterioration, he gradually became more detached from his surroundings although he had lucid moments up to a week before his death. We employed two nurses for the last six weeks of his life. I cannot speak too highly of their devoted service to him and my admiration of their professional commitment was confirmed when, on the day he died when I arrived at his bedside. I found both of them kneeling and praying and weeping at his bedside. He died in perfect peace and tranquillity in the presence of his wife, children and his devoted housekeeper and friend, Maggie. It was a sad but supremely happy and fulfilling event in the life of our family.

Dad died on the 16th of December, 1971. His death was marked by widespread press coverage and by a moving military funeral, attended by, among many others, his old foe Eamon de Valera. For a few days he was no longer the forgotten hero as his distant military exploits were remembered and as his more recent and more pedestrian political career was recalled. I did a long tape recording encapsulating some of my immediate reminiscences of him [11].

There were tributes paid to him after his death.

From Eoin Coyle:

This was he/ all men-at-arms should wish to be [12].

Ulick O'Connor, referring to dad's speech over Collins's grave:

.... which to my mind stands with Emmet and Pearse as one of the great pieces of valedictory oratory [13].

John Cusack, writing after dad's death said "*History will record him as one of the Greats of all time.*" [14].

One old friend wrote to me after his death

> .... he walked across the pages of history, leaving indelible
> prints .... his utter indifference to his own fate, as a man of
> destiny, and his utter dedication towards us, for the right to
> decide our destiny through the ballot box [15].

Professor John Murphy in his review of the Valiulis biography[16] described
Dad as a hero to his family. This was quite true. He was greatly admired and
respected, particularly by his brothers and sisters and by his more intimate
friends. He was also greatly admired by his children but perhaps our
appreciation of his qualities was something that came with maturity and
with a more adult relationship. His sister Nell, Sister Angela, was
particularly close to him and maintained a regular correspondence with him
during his lifetime. Angela kept all his correspondence but towards the end
of her life she confessed that she had destroyed the letters, believing that
the pleasure she received from reading and re-reading them was such that
she thought it might be the occasion of sin!

My attitude to my father could be described as admiration compounded by
curiosity. My admiration was not only based on his idealism, but also on his
apparent complete lack of personal ambition and acquisitiveness. Nothing
he ever did appeared to be motivated by self interest. His career testifies to
his commitment to the cause of Ireland. When personal gain or self interest
conflicted with the interest of his party or the state, he would scarcely give
a thought to himself. His support and encouragement of Collins during the
war of independence and the Truce, his increasing admiration rather than
resentment of Collins as the latter's military and political reputation
soared, his toleration of the rebuffs of Cathal Brugha during the Truce, and
other difficulties encountered during the Truce and the civil war periods,
and his resignation from the ministry in 1924 were all important in the
evolution of the army and the successful formation of a peacetime force. His
continued loyalty to and support of William Cosgrave and his party after the
mutiny, his full-time attention to party and to parliament to the exclusion
of any other gainful employment, his years of organisational work on behalf
of Cumann na nGaedheal and Fine Gael, his decision to accept the ministry
of education in 1948 and 1954, his relinquishing the position of Taoiseach
in the two Inter Party governments, and his support of John Costello, all
testify to a stable and mature political outlook and a personality of unusual

idealism and self-abnegation. He was resolute in his devotion to party and to parliament.

He seemed to possess a sense of detachment which allowed him to accept without resentment or concern whatever might befall him, particularly any circumstance which he was unable to influence or control. He slept soundly whatever crisis was at hand and I never heard him complain about any aspect of his life, apart from his criticism of those whom he perceived to be opposed to the welfare of Ireland and its people.

In private life, he was frugal and simple in his tastes, and limited in his demands and needs. He applied the same discipline in his personal lifestyle as he expected among his troops. If he expected his soldiers to get up early to greet the sun, he set them a good example. While he may not have scorned such attention, he certainly did not seek publicity and notoriety, and, although he might respond to unjust criticism, he never expressed regrets about his actions in defence of the army and of the state. He abhorred criticism of others of a gossipy nature and we were always careful not to evoke his anger in this regard.

I was aware that his public persona conveyed the impression of sterness, discipline and asceticism - O'Higgins's soldier saint - but we need to be reminded that in private life he was very different. Father McCarthy had to remind Maryann Valiulis, after reading the biography, about his private profile, his affability, his graciousness, his thought for others and his sense of humour.

As I advanced in years and my relationship with Dad matured, I realised he was a most unusual person in terms of his devotion to Ireland, its traditions and its culture, and his own lack of personal ambition. I was therefore determined to write about him as objectively as possible. I had enough insight to realise that I could only portray a true picture of him by the strictest candour and objectivity. I hope I have succeeded in this endeavour.

It was because of his unusual career and his idealism that I felt that we owed it to his memory and to posterity to add more details of his personal and family life to those recorded in Maryann's biography and to have him occupy his rightful place in the history of the country he loved. I like to think I would have exerted the same energy to have his role in history recorded if he had not been my father but somebody else about whom I had the same knowledge and admiration.

Chapter 10

Min and the Ryan Family.

It would be difficult to give a balanced account of my father's career during the period from 1919, when he married, to his death in 1971 without mentioning my mother and my mother's people. She was Mary Josephine Ryan, known as Min to her family and her intimates. Mother was one of the large family of Ryans of Tomcoole in County Wexford, a family which played a prominent part in the war of independence and subsequently in the civil war and the future political life of Ireland. It was a family which, like many other families in Ireland, was bitterly divided on the Treaty issue.

A conversation is recorded between my mother and father and a reporter from RTE who was preparing a programme for the fiftieth anniversary of the Rising [1,2]. It deals with mother's experience during the week of the Rising, before she had met my father. This was followed by a general talk about Easter week. It gives a good insight into the circumstances of the week as seen by mother. Her description brings out the more mundane aspects of the week and adds little to the more romantic impressions which seem to gain in retrospect. She and her younger sister Phyllis were members of Cumann na mBan. They acted as messengers during the Rising and were able to move around the city freely and visit the GPO daily up to and including the Thursday of Easter week. Apparently few shots were fired from the GPO until that day.

Her account is wholly lacking in dramatic emphasis or hyperbole. She describes her meetings with the various leaders in the Post Office, including a conversation with Tom Clarke who believed that they would be criticised for their action and who was therefore anxious that she and her sister should understand the three reasons why they had decided to organise the Rising.

Clarke said that an armed rising was necessary if Ireland was to achieve freedom from the British and that it was best that this should take place before the end of the war. Such an action would provide an opportunity during the post-war settlement to achieve independence in view of the allied commitment to the freedom of small nations.

275

The Ryan Family, Tomcoole, c. 1910.
Back row (left to right): Jim, Chris, Jack ,Kate, Mick, Nell, Min.
Front row: Liz, Father Martin, Elizabeth Ryan, John Ryan, Joanna (Mother Stanislaus), Aunt Jane.
Seated: Agnes and Phyllis.

Secondly, such an action was necessary to shake the Irish out of the apathy and complacency they showed to nationhood. Thirdly, he believed that the Volunteers could not continue to drill for ever nor would they continue to be active or effective without a more positive approach to counter British domination.

She talks about O'Rahilly's chivalry in dealing with the captured British officers and she refers to the euphoria which was evident among the Post Office occupants [3,4]. Dad intervened in her talk to say that most people who participated in the Rising did so by chance and that the action was almost entirely without a plan. In another place he said that while it was an obvious military failure, it could not have been more successful politically even if the arms had been landed in Kerry and if the fighting had taken place nationwide.

Mother had a particular involvement in the Rising because of her membership of Cumann na mBan and her close association with Sean McDermott. Sean was a handsome person who was afflicted by a limp, the result of poliomyelitis. He was a signatory to the Proclamation of the Republic and was executed by the British after the Rising. He had been the main organiser of the Rising through his full-time employment as secretary of the IRB and was known and loved throughout the country. He was a close associate of Denis McCullough who had been elected President of the IRB after his release from gaol in November 1915, but who was not brought into the confidence of the leaders in 1916. Sean McDermott, or MacDiarmada (1883-1916) and mother were very close and almost certainly intended to marry.

A short biographical note was written by the Very Rev Charles J. Travers about McDermott on the occasion of the fiftieth anniversary of his execution [5]. Sean's last letter reproduced in his biography and written to his brothers and sisters from his cell in Kilmainham before his execution, contains a reference to mother as follows:

> If I think of any other things to say I will tell them to Miss Ryan, who in all probability, had I lived, would have been my wife.

Mother published an article about McDermott, where she described her visit with her sister Phyllis to him in his cell in the early hours of the morning just before his execution [6]. It is a matter-of-fact but moving account of his composure, his concern for those he was leaving behind, and his calm acceptance of his forthcoming death. She wrote:

> At four o'clock on that Friday morning when the shooting party had done their work, a gentle rain began to fall. I remember feeling that at last there was some harmony in Nature. These were assuredly the tears of my Dark Rosaleen over one of her most beloved sons.

Mother was one of the messengers sent urgently by Eoin MacNeill to call off the Rising on Easter Saturday. She travelled that day to Wexford to meet the local Volunteers to inform them of MacNeill's orders [7]. After the Rising she travelled in July 1916 to the United States on the instructions of the executive of Cumann na mBan with a message for John Devoy and a report about the Rising [8]. Apparently, because of strict censorship by the British, virtually no information about the Rising reached Devoy and the Irish-Americans. There appears to be no record of the contents of the communication she carried to Devoy nor does she mention her meeting with Devoy. She probably gave him a first hand account of the Rising and its sequelae.

Mother had not met her future husband at the time of the Rising but must have done so shortly after he had returned from Frongoch at the end of 1916. They were married in June 1919, some months before the active phase of the war of independence commenced.

In a conversation between Rosemarie Mulcahy, my brother Sean's wife, and mother, Rosemarie questions her about her family and her early life in Wexford [9]. Mother is old at this time. I do not have the date of the recording but while she is slow in remembering names and events, she is quite clear in her recall of her early life. She gives an interesting account of her childhood in Wexford and her time in Dublin before and during the revolution, and before and after her marriage to Richard Mulcahy. This and another conversation [10] give a useful account of the Ryan family. A number of her siblings strenuously opposed the Treaty, thus creating a serious and bitter division within the Ryan family.

278

She was the sixth in a family of twelve and the fourth eldest daughter. She complained that being in the middle of a large family, she had none of the advantages of the older children nor any of the younger. She was apparently a more independent spirit for this reason and describes herself as a pusher who wanted always to be in the centre of things.

The Ryans were a highly gregarious and political family who, because of their prominence in the political life of Wexford and the country, acquired the sobriquet of the Ryanocracy. The women in particular were a pragmatic lot, great talkers and always full of plans for their families and for any other undertakings that interested them.

Tomcoole, the Ryan home in Wexford.

All twelve received a secondary education and eleven went on to tertiary level, either at the old Catholic University, at University College Dublin, or, in the case of Jack and Martin, at the Maynooth Seminary. The Ryan family shared the same hunger for education that was evident in the emerging Catholic rural and middle class population at the end of the nineteenth and early twentieth century. The anxiety to provide an education was as evident in the case of the girls as well as the boys. Unlike the Ryans, my father's parents provided a university education for their five daughters but did not do so for their three sons.

Both families must have made great sacrifices to provide tertiary education for their numerous children. It was perhaps somewhat easier for John Ryan, with his many acres, but nevertheless the Ryan family was dependent on a few priest relatives to assist them during the long years before the children became independent of their parents. I have a photo in my possession of a Father James Ryan PP who was a brother of my maternal grandfather. Father Ryan was apparently the source of constant financial assistance which made it easier for them all to go to university and to finishing school. When Father James retired from his parish he went to live in Tomcoole where he remained until his death.

It was surely a remarkable sign of the thrust of the emerging Catholic population that her father, with tenure of 150 acres of land in Wexford at the time she was born, could send seven of his eight girls and his four boys to be trained for the professions of teaching, the Church, medicine and agriculture. I suspect that no subsidies were then available to help. They depended on parental sacrifice, prudent living and the support of the older sisters, Kate and Joanna, who provided lodging and support in Dublin to their younger siblings. The family received considerable support from two uncles who were priests in the diocese of Ferns. Apart from being a source of pocket money for the children, they provided support for their subsequent university education. Credit must also be given to the authorities at the time who provided free tertiary education at the newly established National University. It was inevitable that Britain would lose political control of Ireland once secondary and tertiary education was made available to the masses.

The early favourable attitude of the Ryan family to the terms of the Treaty agreement and its subsequent rejection by some of them is the subject of a conversation between Dad, mother and myself [11,12]. The conversation includes a valuable sharing of views about aspects of the post-Treaty split. We continue the discussion about the divisive effect of the Treaty on the family followed by the later reconciliation and the factors which brought the reconciliation about [10].

Wexford was one of the inactive counties during the war of independence and Dad refers to some correspondence he had with the Wexford brigade commander which underlines the futility of GHQ's efforts to activate the Volunteers there [10]. The contrast with their activity during the civil war was not lost on my parents nor did they think much of the Ryan siblings who were so vocal in support of the Republic afterwards. Their opinion of the anti-Treaty Ryans was further diminished by the fact, recounted by mother, that they had initially greeted the Treaty terms with enthusiasm but had been influenced against it by Sean T. O'Kelly.

Sean T. O'Kelly, longstanding member of Fianna Fail cabinet 1932-1945; President of Ireland 1945-1959

The divisions created by the Treaty and the subsequent civil war caused a deep and bitter division within the Ryan family and their in-laws, as happened in so many other Irish families, but happily a gradual rapprochement occurred during the late twenties, despite dad's prominent part in leading the Free State forces during the War. All evidence of bitterness and recrimination had gone by the time we children had reached early adult life. The rapprochement must be attributed to the good sense and spirit of reconciliation shown by the members of the Ryan family and their spouses. I recall my father's response to any remark we might make about the civil war or indeed to any contentious aspect of recent Irish history. With uncharacteristic impatience and irritation he would say "Haven't you something better to talk about than things that are better forgotten".

My sister Elisabet, in response to my remark that, despite the serious division in the family on the Treaty issue, there was a surprisingly early reconciliation, said that the women could not bear to be deprived of "the opportunity of having a good talk." I suspect that their brother Father Martin's death in 1929, six years after the end of the civil war and their mother's death in 1930, and the attendance of all the family at the funerals, must also have played a part in their post-Treaty reconciliation.

The Ryans of Tomcoole had a mixed farm which was worked by four or five men and which was supervised in the early years by my grandfather John Ryan. He was a quiet, gentle person who spent his time walking the farm and whose principal task seems to have been to bring in the cabbage and potatoes for dinner every day. Her mother was a busy and practical person who had little time to spare from her duties in looking after the house and the 12 children. She was assisted in the house by her mother and her mother's sister, both of whom lived with the family. Mother describes how the grandmother and grand aunt were of such important help in the domestic scene, particularly in caring for the younger children, and how they were treated with great consideration by everybody.

The children first attended the local national school. Their leisure time and holidays were spent at home. Toys or dolls were unknown and their leisure activities were almost entirely in the open air, mostly playing at farming in their earlier years. In later years conversation among themselves and with the many visitors and relatives who arrived in the house occupied their leisure hours. The women, unlike their rather taciturn brothers, were great talkers and inveterate planners when they came together in later years.

Virtually all the food eaten in the house was homegrown. There appears to have been a heavy emphasis on home cured pork and bacon, and on potatoes and cabbage. Other vegetables were rarely if ever eaten. Butter, milk and buttermilk were also home produced, and, apart from tea and sugar, little food was imported into the house. There was obviously a great emphasis on hearty eating.

No alcohol was drunk or available in the house but her father always had a few glasses of whiskey after the monthly cattle market in Taghmon, the neighbouring marketing town. She describes him as returning home on each occasion in an uncharacteristic merry mood, slightly tipsy, and being greeted impatiently and with considerable irritation by his wife. I cannot recall any tobacco being taken in the household.

The Ryan family was non-political until the turn of the century. A new sense of nationalism was re-awakened in Ireland and particularly in Wexford on the occasion of the hundreth anniversary of the 1798 rebellion. Mother's eldest brother Martin who was in Maynooth at this time and later joined the Ferns diocese became very interested in the Gaelic League and in the Sinn Fein movement. His many visits to their home in Tomcoole were spent talking about his new interest in nationalism. His influence was further enhanced by Sean T.O'Kelly, who became a friend of Mary Kate and was subsequently to marry her in 1918.

Sean T. was a Sinn Fein councillor on Dublin Corporation and was a constant visitor to Tomcoole in the early days of the century. The family considered him charming, generous, and a real gentleman, and he appeared to be a property owner and well-off compared to their many other associates. He too was an ardent nationalist and was an early supporter of Arthur Griffith and the Sinn Fein movement. While the older Ryan sisters were attending university, they met him frequently in Dublin where he held an "at home" every Wednesday afternoon. The family became more politicised after the 1798 centenary celebrations, and many of them were to become prominent in the forthcoming national movement. Their political sentiments were certainly enhanced during their university years in Dublin.

Mother's family lived in Tomcoole, a townland close to the village of Taghmon about seven miles west of Wexford town on the New Ross road. She and her sisters, Kit, Agnes, Phyllis, and Nell were closely associated with the national movement through their membership of Cumann na mBan and through their contact with some of the leaders of the 1916 uprising, and subsequently with the leaders of Sinn Fein and the Volunteers. Jim was a member of the first Dail and remained in parliament until his retirement in 1965.

The twelve Ryan children were born and reared at the family farm. They can be traced back to their great-great-grandfather, John Ryan, who was born in 1745. Their father, also John (1844-1921), married Eliza Sutton (1848-1930). By the early years of the century John Ryan had added more land to the Tomcoole farm, which he acquired as gifts from relatives or purchases from other farmers.

The Ryan children were as follows:

Joanna (1877)   Kate (1878)   Lizzie (1880)   Nelly (1881)
Martin (1883)   Min (1884)   Mike (1886)   Jack (1887)
Agnes (1888)   Chris (1890)   Jim (1892)   Phyllis (1895)

Joanna, the eldest, joined the Loreto order, adopted the religious name of Stanislaus and acquired a great reputation as a teacher. She was popular as a tutor among the students of University College which was beside her convent at St. Stephen's Green. She adopted a neutral attitude to the Treaty and was seen by us younger generation as a lynch-pin holding the family

283

together during the divisions which occurred afterwards. Isolated as she may have been in her community, she may have been a little naive in her political attitudes. On the Thursday of Easter Week, she said to my mother who had called on her "Tell Mr Pearse to stop it now. They've done enough. They should stop it now!" (13).

Mary Kate (Kit) was a brilliant student. Having finished at the Catholic University, she went to Cambridge where she got a double first in her degree there. At the time of her death she was lecturer in French at University College, Dublin. Joanna and she were the two who, when domiciled in Dublin afterwards, looked after and guided their younger siblings who joined them for their university education.

After graduation, Kit took her younger sisters under her wing during their undergraduate years. She married Sean T. O'Kelly in 1918. He represented the Dail at the peace negotiations in Paris in 1919 where he was seeking international support for Irish independence and he remained there until the ratification of the Treaty as a representative of the Dail. He was a member of the Dail from its inception in 1919 until his appointment as President of Ireland in 1945. He was vice president, Tanaiste and a member of the cabinet of the Fianna Fail administrations from 1932 to 1944. He opposed the Treaty. According to Jennie Wyse Power, who was in Germany with Kit at the time of the Treaty signing, Kit was delighted with the news of the Treaty, but must have been subsequently influenced by her husband to oppose it. During the civil war Kit wrote to my mother advising her to leave her husband because of his stance on the Treaty. Sean T. relates his story up to 1916 to Proinsias O'Conluain in *Scéal a Bheatha a insint ag Seán T. O' Ceallaigh*. (14).

Kit died from rheumatic heart disease in 1934 at the age of 56. She died in Baden Baden three months after she had been sent there by an eminent physician, apparently on the grounds that it was essential for her recovery. I recalled visiting her shortly before her departure for Germany. She was then confined to a wheelchair and had severe dropsy which in later years I was to learn was a semi-terminal sign of advanced rheumatic heart disease. In going to Germany she was separated from her husband and her sisters and extended family. Sean T. was vice-president of the Executive Council of the Fianna Fail government at the time and I believe was unable to visit her on more than two or three occasions. It must have been a sad and lonely three months for Kit and her family. Her sad end is a reminder of how inconsiderate doctors can be. Her eminent physician was either crassly ignorant of the prognosis of advanced rheumatic heart disease or totally insensitive to the emotional needs and support required for dying patients and their loved ones. Sean T. subsequently married Phyllis, the youngest of the Ryans.

Liz was the housekeeper in Tomcoole. I suspect she kept her opinion about the Treaty to herself but she was too dominated by her sister Nell to show her any disloyalty. She was a quiet person who might have been thought almost servile when Nell was around. I never heard her express any political or controversial view. I guess that she was an intelligent and educated person but she was obviously happy to stay in the background and to let Nell provide the *vis a tergo* of the household. She seemed to be content to live under the powerful matriarchy of her spinster sister, if this is not a contradiction in terms!

Nell came into prominence after the Treaty was ratified when, with her sisters Kit and Phyllis, and her brother Jim, she opposed the Treaty and was subsequently a very active supporter of the Fianna Fail party. Nell remained in Tomcoole with Jack and Liz. She was unmarried. She played an active political role as a Wexford county councillor. I had the impression that she was the most passionate of the anti-Treaty members of the family. I recall driving her and my mother home from Wexford on one occasion in the 1950s. Nell unselfconsciously spoke about the virtues of her political party and its leader at one stage of the journey. My mother, who was nothing if not outspoken, showed remarkable and unexpected tolerance to Nell's lack of tact by keeping her mouth shut! I was concentrating on my driving!

Despite Nell's trenchant views opposing the Treaty, and her tendency to dominate the family scene, she was described as a most generous and unselfish person by her niece, Betty Glavey, nee Ryan, and was a constant source of help to her numerous Ryan nieces and nephews who lived in the neighbouring farm. I expect, however, that she may have intimidated their mother, Molly, whom I recall as being a particularly gentle soul.

Nell was imprisoned during the civil war and promptly went on hunger strike. She had been acting as a despatch rider on behalf of the Irregulars. Mother relates how she received many appeals from her family to have Dad agree to her release, but, as one might anticipate, he was obdurate in his refusal to be influenced. She also received appeals about a young Wexford man, a distant cousin, who was imprisoned and who was about to be executed but she explained that she was powerless to influence her husband. If I had been around at the time, I too could have advised that they were wasting their breath.

Martin became a priest and served in the diocese of Ferns until his early death in 1929 from blood poisoning contracted from an infected chilblain on the ear. There was some compensation in that the tragedy of his early death may have helped to bring about a family reconciliation following the Treaty. Martin had a distinguished career as a seminarian. He earned a doctorate in theology and was a professor in St. Peter's College and Seminary in Wexford. However, the Bishop of Ferns at that time disapproved of Martin's nationalistic views and, according to Betty Ryan, he was relieved of his professorial duties and appointed curate to Poulfur, the poorest parish in the diocese.

Jack retired from the seminary at Maynooth because of incipient blindness. He took over the management of the farm at Tomcoole. Despite his disability he ran a model farm with Nell's assistance. He was wonderful company for us youngsters when we stayed on our holidays in Tomcoole in the 1930s because of his eclectic interests, his prodigious memory and his unpatronising approach to young people. He was the salt of the earth and it must have been distressing to him, as it was to many other people, that the wonderful achievements which lead to a settlement of our age-long dispute with Britain should have ended so tragically for his family and for the country as a whole.

Michael remained in Wexford and farmed land contiguous to Tomcoole, firstly at Colteen and later at Old Boley. The two brothers shared about 600 acres by the early 1930s. By any standards this had become a large holding as they and their father acquired more land through bequests and acquisitions.

Jack and Michael may have been less extreme than their sisters in their attitude to the Treaty although they would naturally be careful not to disagree with Nell. She might have made life difficult for the two men if they had shown any lack of commitment to the party and the cause. They were both quiet, easygoing men and very tolerant of their sister Nell's energetic republicanism. Michael, who managed the farm at Coolteen, and his wife, spent a few days of their honeymoon during the height of the civil war at Lissenfield with my parents. Nell was in prison and on hunger strike at this time. Michael's wife, Molly, was a very tolerant woman, although I expect that she too would have the good sense to humour Nell by agreeing with all her trenchant views.

Michael used walk over to Tomcoole every evening at nine o'clock to visit Jack. He was a tall man and had strikingly big hands like his brother Jack. He would come stooped and quietly into the living room, hang his cap on the butt end of the high curtain rail inside the door, utter a grunt of greeting to nobody in particular, sit down on his appointed chair and remain until the rosary was about to commence. He and Jack would conduct a very desultary conversation, apparently about current farming affairs. The conversation was conducted in occasional low pitched grunts which were quite incomprehensible to us city lads. That they understood each other was evident from the occasional nod of the head and slow measured reply. That they were conversing in English was obvious to us because we could detect the odd English word if we listened carefully.

Michael died at the age of 63 from heart failure and Molly at 54 from a coronary attack. When I attended Molly's funeral I remarked to a stranger beside me at the cemetery that Molly's sudden death at an early age was both unexpected and tragic for her large family of 12, with several children still under the age of ten. The stranger replied "Sure, she had the Shortall heart". On further enquiry I learnt that she had one sister and nine brothers. All the brothers died suddenly and at a young age. The Shortall heart might have been attributed at the time to Divine intervention. Nowadays we would check their blood cholesterol levels and seek other risk factors for coronary disease and we would almost certainly have prevented such a family tragedy.

Agnes was married to Denis McCullough who had been president of the IRB until shortly before the 1916 Rising. McCullough, with Bulmer Hobson. played the major role in rekindling the nationalist movement in the North. Introduced into the IRB by his veteran nationalist father, McCullough found the national movement and its adherents in Belfast to be lacking in any spirit of activism or separatism, and was greatly disillusioned by the apathy there. With Hobson, who was a Quaker with a nationalist background, he established the Dungannon Clubs in 1905 with the object of restoring the 1782 constitution in Ireland and with policies which were not dissimilar in many ways to those of Griffith in Dublin. However, as happened so often among nationalists in Ireland, the Dungannon Clubs, and Hobson in particular, differed at times with Griffith on some aspects of political ideology, although McCullough in later years played down the differences between the two parties. Others who joined the Dungannon Clubs were the writer and poet, Padraic Colum, Dr. Patrick McCartan, P.S. O'Hegarty and George Gavan Duffy. There is an account of the Dungannon Clubs and the early days of Sinn Fein in *Arthur Griffith and non-violent Sinn Fein* by Richard P. Davis [15]

Denis McCullough.
Co-founder of the
nationalist Dungannon
Clubs in the North and
President of the IRB
before the Rising

McCullough was closely associated with Sean McDermott and was responsible with Hobson, Tom Clarke and Sean McDermott for the reorganisation and "cleansing" of the IRB before the 1916 Rising [16]. Nevertheless, he was not informed of the plans for the Rising, perhaps because he was somewhat isolated in Belfast or because McDermott and his colleagues thought he was not radical enough to support such an adventure. Nonetheless, at the time of the Rising he commanded the Belfast Volunteers and led a group of 132 men from Belfast to Coalisland with the object of joining up with the Connaught volunteers. They eventually disbanded there after the MacNeill countermanding order was conveyed to them. McCullough was imprisoned in Knutsford and Frongoch afterwards and had spent several subsequent terms in prison during the war of independence. Admissions and discharges from prison were so frequent for activists such as he that the time was dubbed the 'cat and mouse' period. As a nationalist and an active person in the Volunteers and in nationalist politics, he was working in a particularly hostile ambience in Belfast during and after the Rising.

It was he and Bulmer Hobson who, with Griffith, first lit the embers of Dad's nationalism when he read their writings during his early days in the post office in Bantry. McCullough's father was a publican in Belfast. Denis established a music shop in Belfast in 1909, having been trained as a piano tuner. His shop was burned out during the pogram there in 1920. He then moved his business to Dublin. McCullough was one of the few nationalists to play a prominent, progressive and successful role in developing the country's commercial life in the early years of the new state. He was a Cumann na nGaedheal deputy in the Dail from 1924 to 1927, and then retired from politics at a time when his business was expanding. He and his wife remained close friends of my parents during their lifetime and he was my godfather.

McCullough was a prudent but generous godfather. I don't think he ever forgot my birthday, at least up to my twenty first. The twenty first however proved to be a rather embarrassing occasion. He sent for me on the 13 July, 1943, and presented me with a five pound note, a considerable sum and a generous gift at that time and most welcome to an impecunious student. He complimented me on my four year record in the university, emphasising in particular his belief that I gave excellent example to his two boys by not smoking and drinking. His two boys, Mairtin and Donncha, were younger than I and had followed me into the College and into the rowing club. In fact, I was drinking and smoking by this time, but I had concealed the fact from my parents and the older generation. Nor did I think it an opportune moment to confess my frailties to my godfather. Naturally, I did not wish to upset him and, most of all, I did not wish to jeopardise the financial arrangement he had made.

I was greatly comforted by the sudden improvement in my finances, and, in this moment of gratitude and elation, I invited my two boat club friends, Des Hogan and Kapo O'Sullivan, to join me next morning in Davy Byrne's for a pint. Not being regatta time and not being in training, we were free to enjoy a smoke and a few drinks. We were comfortably ensconced with our cigarettes and pints in the snug at the back of Davy Byrne's, with its discrete entrance from the adjoining lane, when the door opened and in came M.W. O'Reilly, the chief executive of the New Ireland Assurance, followed by the chairman of the board of directors, Denis McCullough! My poor godfather was struck dumb. He stared unbelievably at me and the fresh pint in my hand. He stood transfixed for what seemed an interminable time and, after a strangled and disapproving grunt, followed slowly after MW into the front lounge of the pub. We stayed in situ, even if it was for me only a question of drowning my sorrows. I had a bizarre notion for a while that he might demand his money back.

Surgeon Michael O'Malley,
Professor of Surgery at
University College, Galway.

At first I thought his state of shock and dismay was caused by the sudden revelation that, rather than being the paragon he thought, I appeared to be well on the road to ruin. However, later and on more mature reflection, I realised that his upset may have been at least partly caused by his having to take his morning drink in the main bar where he would certainly be seen by his employees from the nearby New Ireland offices. He was a man who, at least in social matters, liked to keep a low profile. Although prudent in his habits, and concerned always about his reputation of middle-class sobriety and respectability, he enjoyed his occasional glass of whiskey and was one of the few who was offered a ball of malt during visits to my home.

Chris Ryan qualified as a teacher in University College, and taught in Ireland and abroad. She married Michael O'Malley, a surgeon in Galway. He was well known and greatly respected throughout Galway and the West. He was the second youngest of a family of fourteen, reared on a farm in Western Connemara, one of the most disadvantaged areas in Ireland. He had a brilliant academic as well professional career. He played a major role in the development of the medical services of Co. Galway after the foundation of the State. The memoirs of his life and medical career in Co. Galway are currently being published by his daughter, Sheila Mulloy. Chris lived for some years after her husband died. She moved to Dublin to be with her children and grandchildren.

Dr. Jim Ryan. Member of
all Fianna Fail cabinets
from 1932-1965

Jim also opposed the Treaty, while Agnes, Chris and mother were committed, like their husbands, to its acceptance. Jim became a doctor in 1917. While still a medical student, he was present in the Post Office during the Easter Rising. Like many other 1916 men he was imprisoned in Frongach. He was elected to the first Dail as a deputy for Wexford and remained in parliament until his retirement in 1965. After qualifying in 1917, he went into medical practice in Wexford where he was immediately successful but he returned to Dublin in 1920 to continue his practice and to act as medical advisor to the New Ireland Assurance. He was a co-founder of this first Irish assurance company with his brother in law, Denis McCullough, and others.

In opposing the Treaty, Jim spent a period in prison during the civil war. Why he was imprisoned is not clear. Perhaps he had made seditious speeches during the civil war. He was a founder member of the Fianna Fail party in 1926 and he served as minister for agriculture in all the Fianna Fail administrations from 1932 to 1965. Like Jack and Michael, he was solidly built, avuncular and rather taciturn and quiet-spoken. I think the relationship between him and my father was reasonably friendly but hardly cordial. He must have been a great source of comfort and support to his political leader, de Valera, through his long and loyal commitment to Fianna Fail. He also was wise enough to perceive that medicine and politics are incompatible professions, and the rest of his days were devoted to parliament and to his political party.

He married Mairín Cregan from Killorglin in Co. Kerry. As children we used visit or stay at their home in Delgany, Co. Wicklow. She wrote several popular books for children and she appeared to us youngsters as being more academic than her sisters-in-law and certainly less involved in their rumbustious domestic and social activities

Phyllis was the youngest child. She qualified as a biochemist at University College and set up as a public analyst in Dawson Street in Dublin. Her business was successful. She married Sean T. O'Kelly some years after his first wife, Kit, had died. She continued her work as a public analyst, but retired in 1944 when her husband was elected President of Ireland. She survived him by some years and died at an advanced age. I used to visit her regularly if somewhat infrequently in Ailesbury Drive during her widowhood.

I questioned her on one occasion about certain aspects of the foundation of the State and I was struck by her poor factual and historical insight into the period. Like my own mother, her views were obviously conditioned by her husband's but she would have been unable to discuss any specific event or

Mary Josephine "Min" Mulcahy, née Ryan - 1926

question with any authority. Personalities were prominent in conditioning the views of the women in relation to the civil war. I was particularly interested in her view of Collins whom she used meet when Collins called regularly on Dad at 19 Ranelagh Road during the war of independence. Like my mother, she was a little circumspect about him but passed off the question by saying something along the lines "Ah, he was a rough sort of fellow, who wouldn't take much notice of somebody like myself." I felt that she had nothing complimentary to say about him. Of course, the members of her generation who opposed the Treaty would give little credit to Collins and his contribution to the nationalist cause. It is only in recent years that those brought up in the anti-Treaty tradition have accepted Collins's seminal part in achieving Irish freedom from British hegenomy although a few of those I have met try to comfort themselves by suggesting that he may have been killed by his own men!

Phyllis became the guardian of the young Ryan family in Wexford after their parents' untimely deaths. She spent much of her time and energies helping and advising the younger children. Despite this commitment to the family, and because of other misfortunes, the 600 acres of land which were farmed by the Ryans were eventually sold as the boys to whom they had been bequeathed pursued other careers. To those of us who had been so proud of the Ryan dynasty, and who had such a feeling for the ancestral home in Tomcoole, the eventual sale of the house and all its contents and memorabilia of previous generations was a profound loss and a palpable shock to our pride in the family's heritage.

Mother studied French, German, and English in the Royal University in Dublin, where she was amongst the last students to attend that historic institution. She subsequently went to London University for one year to do a postgraduate diploma in education. While in London she established a branch of Cumann na mBan in the university. She then taught English in Germany for two years followed by a further four years teaching in London. Most of her sisters spent a few years teaching English in France or Germany after graduation. Whilst abroad they had an unusual method of communication. A writing book or large jotter was used and circulated from one sister to another in which each in turn contributed a letter. The manuscript did the grand rounds of Europe and was an excellent means of keeping the family in touch. I have a copy of one of these in my mother's papers.

She maintained a close tie with the Irish nationalist diaspora during her stay in London. She returned to Ireland after the Great War had started and taught German in the newly established technical school in Rathmines. In the few years before she married in June 1919 she lived with her sister Kit at 19 Ranelagh Road. This was also the home of the younger members of the family, Jim, Phyllis and Chris during their university years, and of others from time to time.

She had met Sean McDermott before going to London and they renewed their acquaintance after her return. They remained as close friends up to the time of his execution in May 1916. They expected that they would eventually get married but the courtship was a good deal less intimate than we might be accustomed to nowadays. Mother, in her tape recording, stated that they only kissed once! A kiss then must have had the same binding significance as consummation to-day.

Mother was an intelligent and practical woman and very popular with her many nephews and nieces and other young friends. I would not have classified her as an intellectual. That is not to say that she lacked the ability or talents to be an intellectual, but the circumstances of the times, particularly her large family and many domestic commitments from the time of her marriage, left little time to follow intellectual pursuits. It is also difficult for those just emerging from the circumstances and the relative academic isolation of a rural community to become part of an intellectual society, at least until they find themselves in a more favourable material and academic milieu. While she had no great love for domestic chores, she was a very practical organiser of the house and family and her role appeared to me to be more management than domestic.

She had a most practical disposition. Like all her sisters, she was happiest when she was planning. When they met together they were full of ideas and notions for themselves, their husbands, and their children. Their role in life was largely concerned with domestic and family matters and I am sure that many women to-day would disapprove of their lack of independence from their husbands and their children. Nonetheless, they were a closely integrated and stable family group who did not perceive that they had anything but an important role to play in family and social affairs. It is not at all surprising that they closed their ranks soon after the bitter divisions of the civil war and here they were encouraged by the spirit of reconciliation which was shown by their husbands. Hence, none of the bitterness of the civil war was transmitted to the next generation and none of the many cousins and relations were affected by the tragedy of the divisions which marred the early years of the State.

She was obviously a very attractive young woman with a strong interest in current affairs although, like her sisters, probably not with a great insight into the subtleties of politics and the struggle for national independence. She could be quite impatient at times and, while I can never recall her losing control of herself, she could be irritable with our shortcomings and with the minor frustrations which were part of the domestic scene. The brilliantine stains left by her guests on the drawing room armchairs were a constant source of annoyance, as were the hurried fitting of shoes without a shoehorn, the regular raids on our orchard, and the many other problems inseparable from the rearing of a family and of making ends meet.

She was at her best at family and social gatherings. At our annual Christmas dinners, to which relations and some close family friends were invited, she could be the life and soul of the party. She invariably made an after dinner speech at this function which was made all the more diverting and amusing by her susceptibility to an unaccustomed glass or two of wine.

She could be particularly irritable with me when I was roped in as her partner for a game of Bridge. I had the unfortunate tendency on these occasions to start yawning, a habit which I was not particularly prone to under normal circumstances, but which became uncontrollable at the Bridge table. I did everything in my power to suppress the habit but without great success. I tried a variety of strategies to conceal the yawn, such as rubbing my hands slowly over my lips, cheeks and nose as if in deep thought about the next card to play but I seldom succeeded in deceiving her. Our games never actually broke up in disorder, but I was left in no doubt about her disapproval of my apparent boredom. I was inclined to attribute yawning to a more acceptable cause such as a response to the intellectual challenge provided by the subtleties of the game, but none of my rationalisations would convince her that it was not the result of boredom. She could be irritable with Dad too at times when he partnered her. He had a tendency to jump into a major contract or a slam in a spirit of euphoric optimism and with a paucity of the necessary honour cards.

I cannot recall if she was a good Bridge player. I would doubt it. He certainly was not, mainly because of his chronically exaggerated idea of the value of his cards and his tendency to underestimate the holdings of his opponents. Nevertheless, Bridge was a popular pastime at home, particularly as we children reached the age to participate. First it was Auction Bridge then Contract, with Culbertson as the great Guru, and with victims like myself in constant demand as a fourth.

In a further discussion with my father and myself, mother describes her life in Dublin from the time of her marriage to the chief of staff in June 1919 to the ratification of the Treaty [14]. Life was uneventful enough until her husband was obliged to go "on the run" from the end of 1919 to the Truce in July 1921. During these 18 months he was a fugitive from the Black and Tans and the Auxiliaries and had several fortunate escapes, some of which I have described elsewhere. It must have been an anxious time for her but his preoccupation with the war did not prevent her from bearing him two children before the war ended in July 1921.

On several occasions she was disturbed by raids carried out by the Auxiliaries and the Black and Tans and probably more than once her flat was thrown into turmoil. She talks about dad's numerous and fortunate escapes from the British. She described some of the Auxiliaries, who were drawn from the officer class, as nice, grand fellows who even admired her new baby, but the Black and Tans, who were of a different class, were obviously a rougher and tougher lot. All became the object of her sharp tongue as she reminded them that they were pursuing poets and educated men who were perfectly in the right to seek the freedom of their country.

After her marriage, she lived in a flat in Oakley House in Ranelagh, which had been the first site of Patrick Pearse's school, St. Enda's, and which was then the property of Pearse's mother. After one particular raid, my mother was walking along Oakley Road when she met Mrs Pearse. She was both surprised and distressed when Mrs Pearse asked her to leave the flat because of the frequent raids and the damage which was being caused to her property. Mother asked her, speaking of Dad, "who would take in a man like that, if you didn't?" [17].

It was a difficult time for mother with her husband paying fleeting and hazardous visits, and with the effects of the curfew. Her first child was born

296

during the night but it was not possible to reach the doctor until the next morning. A nurse who was attending her sister-in-law, Maureen Ryan, in the same house and who had her first baby the day before, effected a successful delivery.

The disturbances in Dublin obliged her to move to Belfast for a few months in September 1920 where she stayed with her sister, Agnes, who was married to Denis McCullough. Agnes had two infants at the time. Being the "cat and mouse" period, her husband was only infrequently at home. Later my parents moved to 19 Ranelagh Road, which had been occupied by her sister Kate and her husband Sean T. O'Kelly. The O'Kellys eventually moved to more upmarket quarters at St Stephen's Green South and must have rented the house then to Dad. It was here, and earlier in Oakley Road, that Dad used meet Collins regularly during the last year of the war, and it was here that the Ryan sisters formed their opinion of Collins. My parents remained at 19 Ranelagh Road until they moved to Lissenfield House, attached to Portobello Barracks, at the time of Collins's death. 19, Ranelagh Road was unoccupied for a few years up to 1992 and was at the point of becoming derelict, I passed it every day on the way to my clinic and once thought of buying the property. However, I wisely decided to forego this further addition and complication to a busy life. The house was restored in 1992 and is now again occupied.

After dad's death, mother went to live with Maggie, another Wexford woman, in the garden flat of my brother Sean's house at Leeson Park. She remained there until a few days before her death at the age of 92 at Easter 1977. Maggie was her devoted friend, companion and nurse during these last years. During the last year or two of her life the clarity of her mind and the integrity of her personality began to deteriorate while her good physical health remained. She eventually required other attendants to lighten the load on Maggie's physical and emotional reserves. Eventually, because of her mental breakdown and her deteriorating physical health, she was admitted to Our Lady's Hospice where she died a few days later. Her death was a lonelier one than my father's, not because she died in the Hospice but because, following father's death, the parental home was no longer there to act as the focal point it had always been. Also the prolonged and gradual personality change which mother experienced, which is so particularly and distressingly evident in those with Alzeimer's disease, inevitably affected our impressions of her earlier attributes and personality.

I spent several summer holidays in Tomcoole during the late thirties, where I was accompanied by my brother Padraig, and by cousins of our own age from the McCullough, O'Malley and Ryan families. These were quiet, unsophisticated times but nonetheless most enjoyable. We were completely oblivious of the bitter divisions which affected our parents. The summer days were mostly spent listening to the test matches on an old wireless in the living room of the house, keeping careful records of every run and the fall of every wicket. We spent the warm days in the summer house close to the monkey puzzle tree playing Monopoly and cards. We wandered about the farm a bit but I cannot recall that we took any interest in the activities around us. We certainly never lent a hand with the farm work. We interrupted the day every now and then to cycle into the neighbouring village of Taghmon to buy chocolate and lemonade. We were enabled to indulge in this unaccustomed extravagance by virtue of the regular visits of the parish priest of Barntown, Father Paddy Brown, who was a great friend of the Ryans and who invariably parted with a half-crown to our group. He was popular for this reason and also because he used drive poor Nell to distraction by making snide remarks about de Valera and the Fianna Fail party. His remarks were invariably supported by Jack who would aggravate the situation by saying nothing but quietly nodding his head in approval.

At night we again played cards - poker or pontoon (*vingt et un*) among ourselves, or twenty-five or forty-five with the older generation. Our interest in cards may have been partly determined by the genes on the distaff side for the older Ryan generation were devoted to card games and in earlier years used have a house full of visitors and neighbours playing non-stop during the night and during the weekends,

The evenings finished with the rosary, led by Nell who would finish each Our Father and Hail Mary prematurely with a diminuendo rush of elided and incomprehensible words. This phenomenon was welcomed by us because it considerably shortened the whole exercise but it could lead to embarrassing and uncontrollable bouts of laughter among her nephews which was difficult to control even with a handkerchief stuffed in the mouth. Nell was apparently so absorbed in the spiritual exercise that she did not appear to notice our behaviour. Some nights we were disappointed when she launched into a prolonged litany to our Lady.

A glass of milk and a biscuit were routine before retiring and I still recall the quietness of these still warm summer nights while in bed when silence, almost audible, was only interrupted by the distant call of the corncrake.

In later years, after I had qualified as a doctor and became interested in epidemiology and the causes of heart disease, stroke and high blood pressure, I recalled the eating habits which prevailed in Tomcoole. We ate well and were encouraged to do so by our aunts Liz and Nell, whose constant precept at the table was "eat up"! We seemed to eat great quantities of meat, and particularly home cured bacon - fried bacon for breakfast, boiled bacon for dinner at midday, and cold bacon for supper. It was salty and delicious, but in retrospect it would not have been approved by latter day health conscious nutritionists. It was probably a disastrous diet because of its high salt content, the likely cause of high blood pressure and stroke which were so common among the Irish people at that time.

Most of my mother's siblings who left Wexford and emigrated to an urban environment lived to a good age - my mother died in her ninety second year - but the siblings who remained in Wexford died at a somewhat earlier age, possibly as a result of their high intake of salt and fat. Excluding Martin, who died from blood poisoning at the age of 46, Kit, who died from rheumatic heart disease at the age of 56, and Joanna who died from pernicious anaemia at the age of 70, the four Wexford siblings died at an average age of 74 years while the six who lived away from the family home died at an average age of 85. The Wexford siblings, who died from strokes, almost certainly caused by cerebral haemorrhage, neither smoked cigarettes nor drank alcohol, so these habits, so important as public health problems to-day, cannot be blamed for their earlier demise.

Dad tells how, when he visited Tomcoole shortly after the reconciliation, Jack suggested to him that he should write his memoirs. Nell, who was present, gave a short and reluctant grunt of assent. Dad's answer must have reassured her, for he gave a long and eloquent riposte which left them in no doubt about his contempt for history, or at least the history which was being written about the revolutionary period. He was nothing if not diplomatic and may have been aware of Nell's political sensitivity when he responded to the suggestion.

On another occasion during the civil war, Dad was travelling in an armoured car, or in some type of military vehicle, between Wexford and New Ross. The car broke down just outside the gates of Tomcoole and Coolteen, the two contiguous Ryan farms. While the car was being repaired he decided to visit Michael and Molly in Coolteen. Nell was in prison at the time so he must have felt more secure during his visit. He was in full military regalia. Molly reported later that she received a terrible shock at the sight of this military figure and that her first thought was that he had come to arrest her husband, Michael. I have never heard whether they told Nell about their unexpected visitor.

Chapter Eleven

The Family at Lissenfield

My parents were married in June 1919 before the military struggle against the British had become a widespread campaign. Isolated incidents had occurred before this time, all of a spontaneous nature and initiated by local groups, mostly in response to provocation by the British. Although father had been chief of staff of the Volunteers since March 1918, his military role was not recognised by the British nor was he a fugitive from the authorities. Maryann Valiulis deals in some detail in the biography with this stage in his military career which was characterised by a policy of waiting and seeing rather than aggression, and which was an important phase in the evolution of the volunteers in the context of organisation and consolidation as well as policy.

After their marriage my parents cycled to Glendalough where they spent their four-day honeymoon. I have in my collection a full set of postcards which they bought as a memento of the occasion, showing line drawings of the rugged scenery and of the remains of the great monastic settlement there. Theirs was a very happy marriage. In family he was a person with an equable temperament and unusual gentleness, particularly with my mother and my three sisters. My mother must have been devoted to him. I cannot recall her ever expressing any details to me about their relationship except on one occasion in her later years when she confessed that he was a very passionate man. Whether his passionate nature was in any way related to the arrival of six children between 1920 and 1927, and to one or two subsequent unsuccessful pregnancies, I cannot say but he certainly was quick to mollify her in the most gentle and most persuasive way on those occasions when she became irritated or annoyed, as she was prone to do. "Now, Min, is it worth getting upset about such a small matter" he would say, touching her shoulder or holding her hand.

Mother must have been a very good wife to him and I suspect she responded to his passionate nature. She must have lived many anxious moments from 1919 to 1924 and even later, saddled with a young family, partly estranged from her own sisters, and aware of her husband's vulnerability to capture by the British or, later, to the assassin's bullet. Shortly after their marriage, in

October or November 1919, Dad became one of the most wanted men by the
British. At that time she could hardly envisage or hope that he would
continue to lead a charmed life for the twenty months from then to the Truce
in July 1921. She must also have shared all the frustrations and anxieties
he was subjected to in his task of trying to please everybody as head of the
army during the Anglo-Irish war, the Truce, the immediate post-Treaty
period, the civil war and its aftermath of demobilisation, of mutiny, of
political divisions and of severe economic recession.

Richard Mulcahy with his wife, "Min" at Lissenfield, 1922.

I was born on the 13 July, 1922 while my parents lived in Ranelagh Road but
in August 1922, immediately after Collins' death, they moved to Lissenfield
House in Rathmines, apparently for security reasons. Lissenfield, being

contiguous to Portobello Barracks, was an ideal residence for my father during the civil war. Both he and Collins had set up their offices and GHQ in Portobello, so that, after moving to Lissenfield, he simply crossed the five acre military field from the house.to get to the barracks.

Dad continued to live in Lissenfield after Fianna Fail's election to office in 1932. It was a large rambling house of considerable character which was in its own grounds of about two and a half acres contiguous to Portobello Barracks, and facing the great copper dome of the Church of Our Lady Refuge of Sinners. It was a two storey house with a tower containing an attic, but its ten to twelve rooms and many cubby holes had been constructed at four different levels, the result of a number of additions to the building since it was first built, apparently as a farm house, as early as the end of the 18th century. The front block of the house contained the drawing room on the ground floor and the master bedroom where my parents slept on the first floor, and the tower section. This part of the house was designed by or in the style of John Nash who was a celebrated architect at the beginning of the nineteenth century and who was obviously influenced by the Italian school of architecture. The rest of the house was undistinguished, at least from the architectural point of view.

I have somewhere in my Lissenfield file a note about the house which was published in *An Cosantóir*, the Irish Army magazine. Before the house was leased to my father in 1922, it had been part of Portobello Barracks and was generally occupied by the officer commanding the barracks, or by some other senior officer, such as the army surgeon. It had also been occupied by various families from time to time and there is a record of occupancy by the well known Wexford family, the Adye Currans, in the mid-19th century.

I have a large file containing the correspondence between my father and the office of public works concerning Lissenfield. It was leased to him for seventy five pounds a year, and apparently this remained the consideration during the forty four years the house was occupied by my parents between 1922 and 1966 when I acquired a 150 year lease from the department of finance. The OPW undertook to look after the maintenance and repair of the house initially but sometime in the 1930s a new agreement was made fixing the rent but requiring the parents to take responsibility for the maintenance work. Rent-wise this may have been advantageous but maintenance became an increasing headache as costs rose and as the fabric and fittings of the old house deteriorated. Without the goodwill and the patience of the OPW officials, who were on a few occasions persuaded to spend the taxpayers' money on the house, and without the goodwill of my brother Padraig's friend, Chris Jones of the Jones Group, and of a few other contractors, the old place would almost certainly fallen down over our heads.

Mother with Padraig, 1921.

When I took over Lissenfield in 1966, I built an extension at the rear to improve the kitchen facilities and to update the existing bathroom and add another on the ground floor. The kitchen was re-equipped and a modern food storage and deep freeze facility was added in the new kitchen extension. I carried out minor alterations elsewhere, had the interior and pebble dashed exterior painted, added central heating and double glazing, and built book presses and extensive fitted wardrobes and cupboards. I had the rubble wall between Lissenfield and St. Mary's School repaired and a lot of external repair and stone work done on the rambling outhouses, many of which were semi-derelict. There was a large and commodious "loft" above the garage in the cobble stoned yard which I had refloored and refurbished, and I added a large weather vane above the entrance. This loft was regularly used by our children as a playroom while they were growing up, and it was mainly there that one got the first inkling of their leisure interests and initiatives and of their later personalities and avocations.

Looking back on the whole Lissenfield project, I must have been mentally deranged to have undertaken such a task, particularly as, unlike my father's circumstances, I did not delegate the work to my wife. I failed to recognise that Lissenfield was an old house, structurally defective in many ways when

I moved in with my family. By the early eighties it was apparent that it needed a new roof, new window frames, a new plumbing and sewage system, new gutters and down pipes, apart from routine maintenance work, such as painting and decorating. The cost of fully restoring the house had by then become prohibitive, so after some years of negotiations and many vicissitudes, it was eventually disposed of to builders in 1988.

When the sale was eventually arranged, at an advantageous price, there was a momentary and alarming hiccough, when An Taisce recommended that a preservation order should be put on the building because of its John Nash exterior, a feature which was confined to the front facade of the house and then only to one wing. However, I asked Maurice Craig to offer an opinion about the validity of the claim. He was the most distinguished architectural historian of Dublin at that time. He considered the house to be of little architectural value and the Bord Pleanala showed little interest in its preservation.

If my financial circumstances had been more fortunate, I might have left the house to the city or the nation as a military museum and as a memento of my father's role in the formation of Ireland's peacetime army. Unfortunately, my marriage separation in 1974 obliged me to sell the property nor do I think that the public authorities might have welcomed the financial implications of restoring and maintaining the property.

The atmosphere of the house when we were young was essentially practical, busy, unsophisticated and informal. We were not an overtly affectionate and touching family. I cannot recall that I ever kissed my mother until later in life when I had left home and became conscious of the normal adult conventions. There was absolutely no element of puritanism in our upbringing and although religion played an important but intellectually limiting part in the family, it was more part of our cultural heritage rather than a conscious source of personal commitment or of spirituality. There was still the residue of Victorian prudery to be recalled so that the subject of sex and of our more intimate personal behaviour was never discussed and indeed seldom in our minds.

I expect that the omission of sex and sexuality in the background of our lives accounted for the absence of kissing and those other common tactile manifestations of family affection. It comes therefore as no surprise to be told that at no time were we informed of the mysteries of sex and of procreation. My knowledge of these subjects was only slowly and belatedly acquired, by what means I cannot remember. I did not have the advantage of learning from my peers at school, as most Irish boys did, because of the limitations of Irish which was the spoken language of my six years of secondary education and which lacked, for us at least, the vocabulary necessary to delve into such an arcane subject. I am not sure that the young people of to-day would understand or even condone my innocence.

It is not surprising in the light of our family's remoteness from a consciousness of matters sexual, and the inhibiting ambience of the Catholic middle-class society of the time, that my own sexual development was grossly retarded in terms of emotional fulfillment and intimate contact with others, although my physical development was not in any way delayed or impaired. I recall that, during an hour long interview Cardinal Griffen had with Richard Dimbleby, probably during the fifties, he was asked if he ever thought about sex. After a pause, the cardinal replied "I have an enormous curiosity about it". I too for far too long had an enormous curiosity about sex.

Mother and father were religious during their entire lives, at least in terms of observance. Dad attended seven o'clock mass every morning. A brisk walk down the avenue, across the road to the Church of Our Lady Refuge of Sinners, then back to the bright, airy dining room to be served his breakfast. Mother would attend the later mass at ten o'clock. Added to his daily mass, Dad enjoyed the particularly devotional ceremony of Benediction. He was never happier than when he isolated himself from the world at weekend retreats at the Jesuit houses of Milltown and Rathfarnham. These retreats were for him a great spiritual catharsis. Yet his religious commitments and observances were private matters and he usually attended church on his own, although he did attend mass on Sundays with his wife. Like his siblings, his spirituality was quiet and serene and never obtruded on others, even his own family. I envied him his gift of faith.

In a conversation he recorded with an unidentified person, the latter claimed that Irishmen were "throwing away their rosary beads"[1]. Dad, contradicting him, said that he thought that Irishmen were as devoted as ever to their religious heritage. "There was still great goodness in the Irish". I think he was speaking more from the heart than the head, although the drift from religious observance was certainly less evident in the 1960s when he recorded this opinion than it is to-day. During his declining years, when he was doing his recordings, he was liable to indulge in flights of political, philosophical and religious thought about Ireland and Irish nationalism. In particular, he underlined the crucial role of the religious orders during the nineteenth and twentieth centuries in reviving Irish culture and nationalism [2], and of course in providing secondary education for the emerging Catholic population.

The Mulcahy children with cousins at Lissenfield, c. 1936.
left to right: Padraig, Neilli, Mairtin McCullough, Sean, Elisabet,
Domhnall McCullough, Risteárd, Maire.

I can recall at home no talk about scripture or the more academic aspects of religion. We were only concerned with the observance of our faith rather than with its spiritual and philosophical aspects. The practice of our faith was a routine, almost reflex, part of our daily lives, just as washing ourselves in the morning or eating our dinner. I suspect that this was true of many of the emerging middle-class Catholic families in Ireland at the time.

The basis of our religious commitments was secular rather than spiritual, which may account for my eventual disillusionment about Catholicism and that of a few of my siblings and most of my parents' grandchildren. I am satisfied that my own negative attitude to the Church is based on its secular imperatives and on its illiberal constraints on human behaviour which have no relation to spirituality or to the welfare of humanity. In these more rational and scientific times, a spiritual component still remains an essential part of the human dimension but those apparently conflicting elements cannot be reconciled by the current philosophy and precepts of the Roman Catholic Church and its head, Pope John II.

While some of my own siblings appear to maintain the same devotion to the Church and continue their parents' overt commitment to its observances, I have long ago rejected the belief that our Church is the only true and valid earthly manifestation of God's will. I cannot believe that God would confer such an unfair advantage on a minority of His subjects. I am satisfied that Roman Catholicism is and was an important vehicle for the propagation of the Christian virtues and to support our spiritual needs, and that the Church played an important role in preserving the Irish identity over the centuries of British domination. However, it is only one worldly vehicle of spiritual enhancement and cannot claim any special privilege over other faiths.

As a youth, my religious commitment was largely a cultural one, conforming to the family and social background. During my childhood and in my youth I accepted the concept of sin and of its implications in relation to the next world, and obviously also accepted the concept of another life to follow. The change came during my stay in London in the late forties. From being a regular if somewhat reluctant adherent to the sacramental demands of the Church, and being grossly inhibited in matters sensual and sexual, I gradually ceased to attend to my formal religious duties, while, at the same time, my inhibitions in the areas of sex, love and human relations, and my sense of guilt about my body and its functions, slowly receded. With my belated maturity I was to become a sensualist with a compelling dependence on the physical aspect in the expression of human love and with an attachment to the writings of Marcus Aurelius and the secular philosophy of the Stoics.

At the same time, the spiritual dimension of my life has been enhanced rather than diminished, and the Christian virtues of respect and toleration and love for our neighbours, such as they were in my case, have not been adversely affected. By using the term sensualist, I am not only referring to the pride and pleasure I enjoy because of my healthy body, and to my determination to protect it in the manner my Creator would approve of, but I have become more concerned about my immediate surroundings, and about all aspects of Creation. It is one of my criticisms of the Christian Churches that if they must adopt a secular role they should at least show more concern for the welfare of God's Creation including the physical and psychological well-being of His subjects, and, equally, the wellbeing of the planet.

I suppose strictly speaking I should be described as an atheist, at least in the sense that I do not believe in God as an entity, and certainly not as an entity in the image of Man. Perhaps I am a pantheist in believing that God may be part of all things but does not have a separate existence. I find it impossible to accept the basis of religious belief where a dichotomy is proposed between the material or secular life, and the non-secular as conceived by the existence of the soul and of an after life. Such beliefs are inconsistent with the lack of evidence available to us.

It is quite understandable that from the beginning of time Man must have found it difficult to accept that one is born into the world only to live and then die and to be condemned to eternal non-existence. It seems so pointless and what better means of rationalising our existence and of counteracting our fear of death than by accepting the prospect of an after life, however improbable the likelihood should be. From the beginning of time it was inevitable that we would invent religion and the concept of an after life, without realising that the permanancy of our genes may be sufficient reason for our own transient existence on earth.

I do not believe in God or in another existence outside the material world. However, I am prepared to believe in the state of Godliness as a state of human perfection based on full knowledge and understanding. The Stoics secularised their spiritual ideas on the basis of virtue, without demanding an acceptance of beliefs which are outside human understanding. Their philosophy at the same time included all the christian virtues and indeed their influence was the precursor christian morality. The Stoic philosophy is the one closest to satisfying my intellect and my instincts. Human perfection is based on the practice of virtue which advocates striving after wisdom and the proper conduct of man. It is the concept of human virtue combined with human intelligence which may hold the key to full knowledge and understanding, to the state of Godliness.

Faith may be a comfort to those who believe in another life, and long may it continue to reassure the believers. However, I am happy to know that, when my life is over, I shall have made my contribution, good or bad, to the world through my short existence and my perpetuation of the genetic pool which ensures that man may sometime reach a state of Godliness. Our immortality lies in our genes, not in ourselves.

Whatever about her failings in the spheres of cooking and domestic chores, my mother was an outstanding manager of the house and family. Except for the years 1927 to 1932, when Dad was minister for local government and public health, she must always have been pulling the devil by the tail. Dad apparently showed no inclination at any time to improve his material or financial state and to undertake any gainful employment, over and above his political and parliamentary duties. He relied for his income on his salary as a member of the Dail and on a military pension. I cannot say if he received any remuneration from the political party to which he devoted his full time energies and talents. If he did, it must have been a pittance. I know that in the late 1930s his total annual income was £650, made up of his Dail salary and his pension.

There is no doubt that our parents received great support from many friends, and I know that some of their financial crises were solved by loans from relatives and by one or two organised subscriptions by friends, colleagues and admirers of both my father and mother

It was against this background of financial stringency that mother was obliged to budget for her family of six children, for the open door policy of hospitality which brought streams of visitors, young and old, to our house, for a staff of cook and governess (*Máistreás Cónaithe*) and, in the early years, an assistant cook or parlour maid, for a gardener and no doubt for Dad's pocket money. She managed largely by prudence in spending but mainly by exploiting the resources of our two and a half acres to the full. She established a large vegetable garden, cared for and expanded an orchard of apple, pear and plum trees, covered the extensive rubble walls of the garden with loganberries, had a poultry farm of one hundred hens or more, a half dozen or more noisy ducks, and one and sometimes two milking cows in the military field behind the house and in the field facing the house beside the avenue. Virtually all our needs were provided by this mini-farm, apart from such staple items as meat, sugar, tea, and flour for baking. All this within one mile of Grafton Street.

The orchard was a continuous source of irritation to my mother. About twenty fertile apple and pear trees were situated at the back of the house, contiguous to Blackberry Lane on the north boundary and the military field on the west side. Raids by local boys from the lane and the soldiery from the field were not infrequent, and caused mother to protest at times to the police and to the military. The military responded by building a massive barbed wire structure on the army side which would do credit to Fort Knox or the Maginot Line, and the ten foot wall on the north side had a superstructure of wire and steel supports. But, impenetrable as these obstacles seemed, nothing was really effective against the inroads of the predators. Nowadays, of course, apples and pears seem to have little interest for young people, who are much too sophisticated to be satisfied with such simple fare. The family income was supplemented by the sale of eggs to various neighbouring houses and by the sale of milk to our cousins, the McCulloughs.

Until the late 1930s Jimmy Donnelly, who occupied the gate lodge and worked as a labourer in Portobello Barracks, managed the cows and performed other farm and maintenance work. In later years, after Jimmy's retirement to a cottage in Harold's Cross, Ned came with his family and was occupied full-time with Lissenfield management. No doubt mother's upbringing on a farm in Co.Wexford prepared her for these enterprises.

Mother's commercial activities were not without their adverse effects on my older brother Padraig and myself. We were obliged to take turns every evening to carry a can containing two or three pints of milk to our McCullough cousins' house in Leeson Park, about one mile distant. This task was generally carried out on a bicycle and I well remember the rather precarious journey on the old bike with the galvanised can full of milk hanging from the handlebars. We particularly resented being burdened with this task when, as often happened, the McCullough boys were in Lissenfield enjoying the use of our tennis court. However, the milk chore was nothing compared to other tasks, such as the occasion when I had to accompany Ned, our gardener, to drive a cow whose milk had run dry through the city to the north city cattle market to be sold. At one stage the animal stopped in Grafton Street to defaecate outside Bewley's restaurant, causing me considerable embarrassment. My brother, Sean, tells me that he had the same experience of leading a cow to the market but he was spared the Grafton Street episode and is thus left without the same psychological scarring!

Lissenfield House, Rathmines, 1926.

Family expenses must have been small in those days. Staff was glad of employment at salaries as low as ten shillings a week. Living with a family such as ours and becoming a member of the household, with secure employment as well as board and lodgings, at a time of great unemployment and poverty, was more important to them than matters of material gain or personal acquisitions. In fact, my memory of the thirties, both in my home and during my long summer sojourns with families in the Dingle Peninsula, reminds me that the acquisitiveness and materialistic preoccupations which are so evident and so destructive in to-day's society, both at a personal and sectional level, appeared to have had little place in the minds of people then. Those born well after the end of the World War have no idea of the frugality of our lives in the pre-war and immediate post-war years. Even the privileged middle classes led frugal lives although I have no reason to believe that we were any less happy then than we are now.

We children were carefree enough during the twenties and thirties, and naturally shared none of the cares and anxieties of our parents. We later became aware that mother was constantly beset by financial problems. There were always outstanding bills from the grocer, butcher and other suppliers, all paid by careful instalments decided during her monthly assessment of the financial situation. Dad must have been a trial to my mother who was constantly occupied with the problem of making ends meet on his exiguous income. He seemed oblivious of such mundane matters, at least if one is to judge by his dedication to a financially unproductive career. However, I do not want to give the impression that Dad was anything but a good family man.

Despite his total commitment to his military, parliamentary and party work over the years, Dad was always happy and relaxed in the domestic scene. He was not in any way a domineering or obtrusive person in the household and in particular he was affectionate and gentle with mother and the girls. His relationship with the three boys was a rather typical impersonal one, common to most Irish families, I would think, but our relationship with him matured as we grew older and particularly after we had left home to live our own independent lives. He had little concern with household matters nor was he concerned in any way with the garden or the "farm". However, I do recall that his was the job to prune the roses in the spring and to look after the electric fuses and the maintenance of our rather primitive electrical system.

Some time ago I asked my sister, Elisabet Berney, to write a few lines about her impression of him as a father.

> A very gregarious and fun loving person with people he liked - still a rather private man who got great happiness from his daily mass. Like many fathers of that time (he) was not very effusive in his affections and love - he really had very little time to spend with us when we were very young. Nonetheless, he was always delighted to be with us and in later years when he had more time he really loved having us around.

> He had a great way with his grandchildren and all the friends we had coming to Lissenfield over the years. He was a great favourite with all our college friends -they all thought mother and father were remarkable parents! Some still refer to him as Uncle Dick. When we were growing up he could not bear the family arguing and any discussion of a political nature was forbidden. Idle talk about people or anything personal used to really vex him.

> Whenever we had a problem he could not do enough to help. He used to say 'write all particulars down and I will see what I can do'. He was a really modest man in a lot of ways. I would say that there are very few people who are or were so considerate to all staff over the years, whether it was the staff in Lissenfield or elsewhere.

Dad's needs were modest and he was easily satisfied in matters of food, clothing and service. He was most conservative in his eating tastes. Boiled eggs, rice pudding, apple tart were among his favourites. His favourite restorative was hot milk and onion. On the only occasion that he was dragged to the continent on holiday by my mother, they were staying at an hotel in Dinard. He apparently disliked the French cuisine and puzzled and amused the waiters by constantly asking for du lait chaud et onions!

He was at all times most courteous and considerate of the domestic staff and had a particularly warm appreciation of and affection for our housekeeper, Maggie, and her role in the household from the time of her arrival from Wexford in 1945. He also enjoyed conversing in Irish with the girls from the Gaeltacht whom my mother regularly employed during the early years of the family. While he was not an intellectual person in the academic sense, he was an excellent self-taught Irish speaker and enjoyed enormously to speak the language with others who were proficient in the tongue. He was familiar with the French language, which he continued to read and to learn during his lifetime, although I can never recall hearing him take part in French conversation.

He was a regular and eclectic reader, mainly of books about Irish history, politics, economics, demography, philosophy, religion and works on self-improvement, memory and self-discipline but not, to my recollection, of novels, fiction and general literature. He had a large library of books in Irish which he continued to read during his lifetime with the object, I believe, of maintaining his knowledge and his fluency of the language. I subsequently presented his library of Irish language books to the Opus Dei students' residence in Galway after his death.

Mother with her chicks.

314

Mother rarely read a book. When I mentioned this to my sister, Elisabet, she replied that none of the Ryan sisters read - they were too busy talking! Mother was a dedicated newspaper reader but showed no interest in academic or artistic affairs. This may seem surprising in view of her earlier career as a teacher of English in Germany and her later position in the vocational schools in Dublin. However, she came from a farming family in Wexford and from a background where intellectual pursuits had no place in an ambience devoted to conversation, politics and work. As a family, I do not think there was a great tradition of reading in our own home although I do recall when, at the age of fifteen, when I was confined to the home for twelve weeks with an injured leg, I discovered the Irish folklore stories of Padraic Colum, James Stephens, and Standish O'Grady which I read avidly and in a burst of enthusiasm. A few years later I had become a regular reader, reading voraciously those newly discovered authors, Somerset Maugham, Evelyn Waugh, Graham Greene, Thomas Mann, and E.M. Forster.

Like my mother, Dad was a prodigious newspaper reader. He accumulated a huge collection of newspaper cuttings during his active political life and after he had retired. They were tied up in bundles and stored in the garage in Temple Villas, where they had gone to live in 1966. The cuttings filled a large skip when they were eventually disposed of after his death. I had always felt that he spent too much time reading the newspapers but I expect it was necessary for an active politician to be familiar with current affairs. However, I am sure he could have been equally aware of events if he had left much of the reading to the staff of his political party. I have a certain resentment about time spent reading papers because of their ephemeral contents, a resentment I may have acquired in those earlier years when I noted my father and mother's devotion to the habit. Thus by 1998 I rarely more than glanced at a newspaper and have taken few Sunday papers in recent years. My newspaper reading is now limited to buying and glancing at the Irish Times three or four times a week.

Like other educated people of his generation, he remembered many of the poems and excerpts from Shakespeare he had learnt at school. He would recite them with gusto during the gatherings of family friends and relations at Lissenfield. Except on social occasions and in the presence of company at home, he was constantly active in his study, preparing for his parliamentary work, sifting the newspapers, reading Irish to enjoy the language and to extend his vocabulary and his knowledge of *sean fhocla*, the vast number of adages and sayings which are a feature of our native tongue. He never seemed to have an idle moment nor did he ever seem to spend any length of time with us children. While his contact with us was warm, it was not his role to entertain or instruct us. This he left to the household staff and, less often, to my mother, although she too seemed to be always busy and was little involved with our education or entertainment.

Dad was in charge of the pianola which was a popular source of music before we had acquired a wireless in the early thirties and a radiogram in the late thirties. I recall the pianola during the early dances which my parents organised but how one could dance to this medium seems extraordinary to me. We had dozens of large cylinders which churned out piano renderings of Wagner, Beethoven, Strauss and other classical composers. The rolls of paper which surrounded the cylinders were perforated and the music was produced by a bellows action created by two pedals. I can recall no records of music suitable for the foxtrot, slow waltz or tango which were the popular dances at the time, although this form of dancing was made available when we acquired a radiogram and 78 records in the late 1930s. I expect the pianola provided music for the old waltz which was also popular at home but which, within the confines of our drawingroom, must have been the equivalent of one of the contact sports. The pianola was a German Steck which was bought in the early twenties from McCulloughs, the music shop in Dawson Street, owned by my uncle-in-law and godfather, Denis McCullough.

Later in the 1930s dance music was provided by a close friend of the family, Jock Harbison. I have a note about Jock written by my sister Neilli at the time of his premature death. Jock became part of the family and virtually lived in the house, without ever eating or sleeping there. He lived with his widowed mother and sister in Belgrave Square, less than half a mile from Lissenfield. His father had been a Nationalist MP for Tyrone and the family came from Cookstown. His father was elected to parliament in 1918 but, as a member of the Irish Parliamentary Party, he refused the invitation to attend the first Dail. He must have retired from politics before the 1921 election, which the Irish Parliamentary Party did not contest.

Jock was a gifted pianist, particularly at ad libbing, and he monopolised our piano during his long association with the family. The pianola was relegated to the past, although it is still intact with its large rolls of perforated paper in my brother Padraig's house. It was bequeathed to him at the time of Dad's death.

Jock was bouncy and good humoured. He had little interest in our more rugged outdoor activities of cycling, hurling and tennis. He became an engineer, qualifying in UCD, and subsequently became the head of a large consulting engineering firm. He was married to Eleanor, a well known artist and he died in his late fifties. We first met him when he joined the boy scouts. He became the leader of the Eagle Patrol, one of the four patrols in our troop in Rathmines.

Poor Jock died from cancer. I had the unenviable task of informing him of the diagnosis and of being obliged to say as diplomatically as possible that the outlook was far from good. I did so to ensure that he should have his affairs in order for the sake of his family. After a long and tortuous explanation of his medical problems and the ultimate prognosis, during which I thought I had reasonably enlightened him about the outlook, he said to me "But I'll be alright, won't I?". His eldest boy had just been capped for Ireland in the forthcoming rugby international. His pride in the boy and his anticipation of his appearance in Lansdowne Road blinded him to the grim realities of fate.

Unlike Jock, none of us six children became proficient at playing a musical instrument. We all received piano lessons and had to sit examinations at the Royal Academy of Music which was then in Westland Row. It seems to have been the rule in the thirties among middle class families in Dublin to have piano lessons provided for children, either at home if there was a piano in the house, or in one of the various academies which existed that time in the city. I had some of my lessons at the Reid School of Music in Harcourt Street and others at home. I remember the lady who used visit us to teach music in Lissenfield. I recall a rather large, old and formidable woman whose visits used cause me a certain trepidation, and occasionally pain, when the pencil was applied to my fingers as a corrective measure. I remember the boring scales and arpeggios and, perhaps most tedious of all, having to hold my hands over the keys in a most abnormal and unphysiological posture, with the fingers flexed at right angles at the metacarpophalyngeal joints(the proximal set of knuckles to the uninitiated). Rather than fondling the keys, I hovered over them like a bird of prey.

It is no wonder that none of my siblings nor myself learnt to play the piano. The formal and academic approach to teaching, the emphasis on scales and arpeggios, and on the correct techniques, could not hope to succeed. We might have been more responsive if there had been an emphasis on music appreciation and the fun which can be derived from learning to play a musical instrument, particularly if we had more group involvement. Even if we had started by playing simple tunes such as "Can You Wash My Daddy's Shirt" of "Home, Home on the Range", our interest might then have carried us along to a more serious and progressive approach to learning.

Mother had no interest in music. Dad considered music an important factor in the country's culture and education, as was apparent from his early launching of the Army School of Music, and his encouragement of music in the schools when he was minister for education. However, he played no instrument and as far as I know he had little time or inclination to attend concerts or musical recitals. In later years my parents became patrons of the Dublin Grand Opera Society and they enjoyed the biennial opera season in Dublin. The lack of parental example and commitment makes it difficult for children to show an interest in music or an aptitude for its expression.

When my children were young they frequently complained, as most children do, that they had nothing to do during their leisure hours. This was when television and radio were freely available, and when the increasing mobility of the population allowed them many distractions outside the house. In the thirties, such distractions were denied to us. We were more confined to the house and its environs, and yet we always seemed to be occupied. Perhaps we were more innovative in terms of self-amusement. Cards, Monopoly, chess, draughts and puzzles would keep us busy indoors. I had my Meccano and electric trains, while outside we played hurling and tennis and various contrived ball games.

There was a certain security in being confined to our house and grounds, and to the local Rathmines area. There was not the same obsession with "news" and with public affairs, and virtually no consciousness of events outside the country. The rare murder created a seven day wonder, and newspapers were not yet read by the masses. However we may strive for wealth or acquisitions, there is no evidence that they make us any happier. I also believe that the preoccupation with national and international news, which is a feature of to-day's society, adds nothing to our quality of life. Newspaper reading has become a feature of our latter-day obsession with affairs outside our own personal lives.

The 1930s and 1940s were so different from our current way of life that I wonder whether the contrast could not be at least in part generated by one's changing outlook and reactions with the advance of age. Things were indeed very different, at least in the material sense, but I cannot say that the affluence and acquisitiveness of our modern life has meant any improvement in quality of life, at least in terms of human happiness. Rathmines was not only our parish. It was to some extent the limits of our world. There was a close contact between the people of the parish, meeting as they did so often on the street, in the church and in the tramcar. My parents were held in great esteem by the neighbours and our neighbourliness meant a greater awareness of other peoples problems and misfortunes.

Padraig and myself were active members of the 20th Troop of the Catholic Boy Scouts. We met weekly in a small upstairs garret in Richmond Hill, close to our front gate. This brought us into close contact with the boys of other families and whatever class divisions existed within the parish, none existed among the boy scouts. As I recall it, class distinctions depended on one's occupation, but despite variations in affluence and therefore in one's standing amongst one's neighbours, there was a natural mutual respect and courtesy amongst the people. Our interest in scouting brought us camping in the Dublin hills at weekends and as far away as Kilrane in County Wexford for summer camp. I have no doubt that scouting knocked some of the grand ideas out of our heads which might have been generated by our relatively privileged standing in the community.

I look back on our days in the scouts with nostalgia. The Catholic Boy Scouts of Ireland was a strictly sectarian organisation, unlike the older and international Baden Powell scouts. Their's was a non-sectarian organisation although in Ireland it was more associated with the other religious denominations. Happily, as I write this and just after the Good Friday agreement of 1998, the two scout organisations are meeting to consider coming together as one organisation.

My years in the scouts taught me many important things about life and social integration which must have stood to me in later life. It taught the necessity and value of occasional hardship and for me it stimulated a lifetime interest in astronomy, the countryside and trees. It taught the satisfaction to be derived from service to others. There were probably about thirty boys in our troop. They came from all classes within the Rathmines community. While there was little demarcation of classes in our suburb among the Catholic families, there were obvious differences in their affluence, from those who were virtually destitute to those who were comfortably off, at least in the sense that they had enough to provide themselves with all the necessities of life as perceived in these relatively frugal times. Social and economic differences between our families had no impact whatever on us nor were our parents conscious of any anomalies in the situation.

Class consciousness was, nevertheless, a potent factor in the social life of Dublin at that time. It was always thought to be a tradition introduced by British culture and the Anglo Irish community. No doubt, at that time at least, it was a feature of many stable societies where wide differences of affluence and privilege existed among the people and where a whiff of modern egalitarianism had not yet emerged. In Ireland in the 1930s, class consciousness or snobbery as it was widely called was an attribute of the more affluent Protestant and the emerging wealthier "Castle Catholic" communities, mostly living in the outer suburbs of South and South East Dublin. We had many Protestants still in Rathmines in the twenties and thirties, but, like many of the Catholics there, they were members of the lower middle-classes, to use a Victorian phrase - the minor officials, civil servants, teachers and clerks - while the poorer parts of the suburb housed the artisan, the labourer, the unemployed and the other less privileged members of society.

The better off Catholics in Rathmines were mostly first or, at the most, second generation families who had come to Dublin from the country and who had not yet acquired the urban tendency to form special cliques, which is essentially the basis of class consciousness. Those of us who lived in Rathmines were not conscious of any great class distinction although, because my family lived in a large commodious detached residence in extensive grounds in the very heart of the community, and because of my father's national record and his unique military and political reputation, we were treated with special respect by our neighbours, as if my father were the local squire. However, we were only too conscious of the class consciousness which existed elsewhere in the city, and I recall being quite intimidated as a child and adolescent by the superior postures and the attitude of disdain which I detected, or thought I detected, among the children of Protestant and Catholic families who lived in Donnybrook and Ballsbridge, who had been educated in the more prestigious private day and boarding schools and, who were members of the elitist tennis clubs.

I recall two occasions when I wept in public as a boy scout. Shortly after I became a patrol leader, our senior patrol leader, an exemplary character by the name of McKenzie, was elevated to assistant scout mastership. The vacancy had to be filled by one of the four patrol leaders. Padraig, my older brother, was the senior of the four but for some odd reason the scout master, another excellent person called Frank Thackaberry, decided that he would leave the appointment to the four patrol leaders to be decided by secret ballot. The obvious choice was my brother Padraig because of his seniority. For us it was an early experiment in democracy. None of us wished to support Sean Coughlan, one member of the quadrumvirate. I voted for Padraig but unfortunately everything then went terribly wrong. Apparently in an effort to keep Coughlan out, the other two voted for me with some idea in the back of their minds that a wasted vote would solve their particular dilemma. Coughlan also voted for me, perhaps to keep Padraig out. When the result was announced I broke down completely, being perfectly aware that I was unfit for the job in terms of seniority and maturity. We had obviously failed in our first essay into the working of the democratic process. Eventually reason prevailed and Padraig was appointed, either at my suggestion or by agreement. Apart from his seniority, Padraig was the obvious choice. He was a most devoted scout and certainly was more consistent in his attendances at meetings, hikes and camps than the rest of us.

Padraig's total commitment to scouting was reflected afterwards in his similar commitment to the local defence forces during the war and subsequently to his lifetime loyalty to his golf club, Milltown, where he was Captain in 1964 and President from 1972 to 1975. He shared some of his father's qualities, particularly his unobtrusive but total commitment to his work and his leisure interests, and his organisational gifts. He was the founder of a quantity surveying firm in Dublin which was to prosper. I have little doubt that dad's organisational qualities have been passed on in great measure to his six children and indeed, if I am to judge by their success, by many of his grandchildren, nor can my mother's genes be entirely ignored in this equation.

On another occasion, I was one of four scouts who did the the Irish dance, the *Walls of Limerick*, at the annual scouts concert at the Gaiety Theatre. We were much younger then. We were trained to perfection but the stage manager insisted on our having a prompter for the big occasion.

Unfortunately his training left something to be desired. He gave us the wrong prompt early in the act, the dance fell to pieces and I started to bawl on the stage until I was removed by a sympathetic stage hand. Fortunately the embarrassment of these occasions fades with time.

In the early and mid-thirties there existed a mild form of apartheid among the six children in Lissenfield. Padraig, Elisabet and myself were clearly identified as "the big ones' while Maire, Neilli and Sean were "the little ones". This despite the fact that there were only 20 months between Maire and myself. We big ones did not actually treat the others with contempt but our approach to them was certainly patronising, and they were in no doubt about the priorities we claimed. Sean in particular seemed to have the worst of things when he was young. I recall him as a rather shadowy waif but he established an earlier independence from the family and the home than the rest of us. He also matured as a more urbane, charismatic and artistic character than Padraig and myself, and eventually became a well known personality in engineering and architectural circles in Ireland and abroad. He was more active in the social life of the city than I, so that in social circles at least I was often referred as Sean's brother. In more recent times I am better known as Richard's father, having originally being identified as Dick Mulcahy's son!

Sean's wife, Rosemarie, is a self-educated person who started her career as a model at the age of sixteen. She became a distinguished art historian among other attributes, and made important contributions to the interpretation and understanding of classical Spanish painting and the history of Spanish art. She became an accomplished linguist and with Sean travelled a lot. They were both well known in the world of art and architecture in Ireland and abroad.

As I recall the late twenties and the thirties, our daily contact at home was mainly with our governess, and the kitchen and outdoor staff. During the day we mostly occupied the "nursery" at the rear of the house where we ate, played and studied, and much time was spent in the cobble-stoned yard and the spacious garden and fields. At first mother and father were shadowy figures in the background, but their existence nevertheless dominated our lives, even if only because everywhere we went and to everyone we met, we were "Dick Mulcahy's children". In the 1930s he still retained much of his military and political reputation among the public and was greatly admired by many, while those who opposed him in the Treaty and who were aware of the draconian reputation he acquired during the civil war, had perhaps learned to treat him with more respect and less with hostility and fear.

The most prominent person at home in my early life was our *Máistreás*. Starting in the late twenties and continuing into the mid or late thirties, we had a native Irish speaker from Connemara, Donegal, or the Gaeltacht in West Kerry (*Corcha Dhuibhne*) in charge of our upbringing and education. Each girl arrived at about the age of 16 years, spent two or three years in the household, and was then sent by mother to train as a nurse, teacher or domestic economy instructress. Their function was to take charge of the children and principally, in response to dad's wishes, to introduce and maintain Irish as the spoken language of the household. All these girls became close friends of our family, as did their families in the Gaeltacht, among whom we children spent our summer holidays from about 1928 to 1935.

In the following paragraphs I have described my visits to the two homes in Corcha Dhuibhne, the Dingle Peninsula, where we came into close contact with the still unspoiled lifestyle and culture of the native Irish.

My earliest comprehensive memory as a child was our first visit to the Kerry Gaeltacht at Ballyferriter on the Dingle peninsula. The year was probably 1929. Dad was a minister at the time. I was accompanied by my older brother and sister, and probably by my second sister Maire. We were in the charge of our Irish speaking governess, whose first name was probably Maire and whose surname was Lovett. We were to spend the summer holidays there and to learn to speak Irish. Irish was then the functional language of the people of the distal part of the Dingle peninsula. Among some of the older generation, it was their only language.

The Lovetts had a forge about half a mile from Ballyferriter on a fork on the road leading to Dingle, and under the shadow of Brandon, Ireland's third highest mountain. I well remember the excitement of the forge, with the open furnace, with sparks flying and the red hot metal being hammered into shape by the brawny, sweating Lovett boys.

We travelled from Dublin to Tralee in a specially reserved compartment on the train. At Tralee we were greeted by the station master and brought to his house for tea, before we caught the next train to Dingle. It must have been a fairly leisurely affair because he arranged to delay the departure of the Dingle train by a half hour or more. These privileges were no doubt granted because of my father's reputation and his position as minister for local government and public health, Fragments of the journey from Tralee to Dingle on the narrow gauge railway still linger in my mind. The slow and wheezy crawl up towards the spine of the peninsula's mountain range, with wayside stops at houses and roadways to deliver parcels and other minor domestic articles, was followed by the rapid decline on the southern side of the peninsula when the train appeared to be out of control as it freewheeled down the steep slope into the Dingle terminus.

This visit to Ballyferriter was the first of many annual summer holidays on the Dingle peninsula. Our first two or three visits were with the Lovetts, but later we stayed on the southern side of the peninsula at Baile Mor, a hamlet of about six houses three miles from Dingle on the road to Ventry and Slea Head. During the first year or two I was accompanied by a few of my siblings, but my last few years up to 1936 were spent on my own. We were accompanied by our governess Rita Clery at her family home in Baile Mor.

The Clery family lived in one of three two storey houses overlooking a small creek or harbour in Ventry bay. The creek was called *an Cúsheen*. The houses and the the harbour were built at the end of the nineteenth century, probably as part of the rural relief schemes following the Famine. The house was a great improvement on the traditional cottages or cabins which were still a common feature of the Irish countryside at that time. There was a central door, a window on each side, and three windows on the first floor. The roof was slated, unlike the thatch which was still widespread in these parts.

The door led into the kitchen/living room, and on the right hand side was a smaller *seomra*, the equivalent of a drawing room. It was spotlessly clean, and, in my many visits to the Clery house, I rarely entered the *seomra* and I never saw it in use except on one occasion when my parents arrived and were entertained to tea. The room contained a variety of bric-a-brac which must have accumulated over the years. There was a table and a few chairs which, compared to the *súgán* chairs and rude furniture in the rest of the house, could be described as elegant. The *súgán* chairs were made of robust rough timber with seats of strong hessian. They may be collectors' pieces now for all I know. The Irish word *súgán* had an accent on both vowels, and was therefore pronounced "*soogawn*". The dresser in the *seomra* housed the

324

family heirlooms of china cups, plates and saucers, and of various ornamental figures in delph and pewter which must have been brought as gifts by visitors from Dublin, Cork or further afield from England or the United States. They were the only signs of acquisitivness in the family. A few pictures adorned the walls, including portraits of Pope Pius X1 and a faded one of Gladstone.

The kitchen had a stone floor and a wide hearth with all the accoutrements to hang the pots and other utensils for the preparation of meals. Turf or peat from the local bogs and hills was the only fuel and the live embers were always there in the early morning to rekindle the fire. Like all the houses in the west, the lingering smell of turf was never absent. Almost the entire domestic, social and personal life of the house took place in the kitchen. The weekly wash was conducted there or in the scullery or dairy at the back of the house, and toilet needs were dealt with in an outside privy or, in the case of the older males, in a closeby field. Everything went back to nature.

The little harbour was tidal and had two well constructed quays. The Clery boys were the sole fishermen in the area. The larger and best constructed quay was never used by them, almost certainly because it was too high above the tide to accommodate the curraghs. These were the only boats in use and they were clearly the most suitable craft for the lobster and other inshore fishing.

When I first went to the Clery household there were still four children in residence with their father and mother. The others, including Rita, had left home for Dublin or had gone abroad to join relatives. The Clery "diaspora" apparently was confined to Boston in the United States. The two boys remaining in the house, Míchéal and Tomás, had matured sufficiently within a year or two of my arrival to take over the fishing and to help with the small farm of about thirty acres. As I recall, the only cash which came into the family was earned by lobster fishing.

Once a week a fishing trawler arrived off shore, which was known as the *Frenchman*. The lobsters caught during the week and housed in a special floating cage in the harbour were transported to the Frenchman. Each lobster, if its two claws were intact, earned two shillings and sixpence, no doubt finishing up on some wealthy diner's plate in Maxim's or Le Tour D'Argent in Paris. The occasional larger crayfish probably fetched a little more. The family must therefore have been reasonably prosperous compared to their neighbours, who appeared to have no able-bodied young men to man the curraghs. The Clery family appeared to be almost completely self-sufficient as regards food, except for tea, sugar, salt and tobacco to fill the father's pipe, and the grandmother's *dúidín*, the little white clay pipe used by the old women in the west of Ireland.

Rita had arrived in our house in the early thirties as a governess. She, like all her family, was a native Irish speaker and Irish was the functional language of her family and the locality. As children we always spoke Irish to her, although sadly, as happened so often, it was in English that we spoke in later years when we had grown up and when I worked with her in St John and St Elizabeth's Hospital in London. She continued to speak in Irish with my father in later years. After about four years in my mother's employment she was entered into the nursing school at St Vincent's Hospital where she had a very successful career, and finished there as theatre sister. She later studied radiography and became the first radiographer attached to the Coombe Lying-in Hospital in Dublin. Like the other girls who were recruited from the western Gaeltacht by my mother as Irish speaking governesses to our family, Rita became a close friend and achieved considerable success in her later career.

The Clery family had sufficient to eat and enough fuel for comfort and domestic requirements. They were adequately clothed. There was no waste of food nor was there any garbage to dispose of. Any excess of dairy foods or potatoes was fed to the domestic animals or given to the local poorer members of the community. The two houses close to the Clery home were occupied by older couples without children and without anyone in gainful employment to support them. They were frequently the beneificiaries of the Clery family's charity.

The food in the household was wholesome, simple and entirely home produced. Large flowery potatoes, piled in considerable quantities on a cloth or towel in the centre of the kitchen table, were the mainstay element of midday dinner. They were almost invariably accompanied by odd bits of fish caught during the early morning lobster fishing foray. The only vegetable I can recall was cabbage which was grown among the potato patches in the fields. I cannot recall that we ever ate much meat but there was a plentiful supply of home made soda bread, dairy food, milk, butter milk and delicious salty home made butter. Any excess of fish caught was cleaned and thrown into a barrel of salt to be preserved for the winter months when fresh fish was not available because of the winter storms.

Morning and evening meals were simple and it was of course at that time never the custom to eat anything between meals, except for an occasional bulls eye or acid drop bought in the local shop if I was fortunate enough to have a penny.

During the first few years I slept in a bunk in one of the bedrooms but as I grew up and used go there without other members of my family, I slept with the two eldest boys in the loft above the cow shed where our rough blankets were laid on a thick layer of straw. The milking cows below may have been restless at times, and no doubt produced large quantities of methane gas, but I cannot imagine that I suffered any discomfort by sleeping in such relatively primitive conditions. Nor did the active fauna population in the straw cause me any squeamishness

While Irish was the spoken language of the family and the district, some English was spoken in the local market town of Dingle, which had been a garrison town before independence. Almost every family in the peninsula had close relatives in England and the British services, so that most people, except the very oldest, were bilingual. Many also went to Dublin and other urban areas in Ireland where the police, the civil service, the church and the teaching profession were popular and influential careers.

The Irish spoken in Kerry was somewhat different in intonation, accent and idiom than the Irish spoken in Connemara, and very different indeed from the Irish of the Donegal Gaeltacht. The differences between the spoken languages in the three areas, particularly in relation to accent, still poses a problem in achieving a successful revival of the language. Probably because I was brought up with Munster Irish, I find it, with its rich tone and resonance, to be by far the most attractive of the regional dialects.

On looking back on those years, I particularly remember the simplicity of the life, the self-containment of the family and the local community, and the traditional if not intellectual commitment to the Roman Catholic faith, or at least to its secular imperatives. In many ways the Clery family reflected the whole of Irish rural society at that time. While they did not share the poverty of many others, they did share the culture which lacked the acquisitiveness which has become a major factor in modern society and which has left us with the almost irrational preoccupation with money and personal power, and the violence and moral breakdown which this preoccupation engenders. It has brought us other problems, including an increasing obsession with sexuality, and a slow disintegration of the extended family and the social fabric as we become more mobile and more internationalised.

The Clery family reminded me of my perception of my father's and mother's antecedents, who were part of the disadvantaged Catholic population, and who, because of their greater access to education before and at the turn of the century, were about to take their places in the social, professional and political life of the country. Like the rural population in Ireland in particular, many of the members of the Clery family and their relatives emigrated to urban areas in Ireland, and to Britain, the United States and other English speaking countries. While they may have been more isolated nationally and internationally in terms of communication in its widest sense, their emigrant members were establishing links between the families at home and many countries abroad.

I used to accompany Mícháel and Tomás on their fishing expeditions. We went out early in the morning between five and six o'clock to lift the lobster pots. We were out again in the late afternoon. I guess there may have been about twenty pots in all to be visited. These pots were made during the less busy winter months. Willow or sally (*Saileach Bhan* in Irish) was widely grown in the hedgerows and was the chosen material because of the flexibility of its branches. In crafting the pots, the network of branches was held together by hessian. Whilst lobster and crayfish were the principal catch being sought, our expeditions were made particularly exciting by the diverse collection of other marine creatures which incautiously entered the pots. Congar eels and dogfish were common occupants. The dogfish were thrown overboard after receiving a bang on the head on the boat's gunwale to stop them from raiding other pots. Congar were thrown overboard to live another day, although most were so large, stretching up to six feet or more, that they could not be extracted from the pots without first cutting them into segments by a sharp knife carried for that purpose. Nobody thought of eating the eels, although to-day they are probably thought of as delicacies. Other fish, mostly pollock and mackerel, were brought home to be eaten fresh or to be salted away for the winter. Large crabs were often disposed of but were sometimes brought home for their claws. However, crabs and the numerous shell fish found on the rocks lacked the important culinary reputation and popularity which they enjoy in our present day restaurants.

We fished twice every day unless the weather was stormy. The curraghs were well designed for inshore fishing even in the choppiest of waters because of their manoeverability and easy approach to handling the pots. They were safe in heavy seas in skilled hands. The great Atlantic rollers which were a feature of the Kerry coast caused little inconvenience to the well trained fishermen. One had of course to be careful not to penetrate the thin latticework and canvas covering of the boats by awkward footwork. Although almost by tradition the men never learnt to swim, no lifebelts were available nor was it likely that they were even aware of such devices. No engine was in use and propulsion was entirely a matter of hard work with oars. Rarely a sail was erected but the nature of the fishing, with short distances between the pots, made sails of little value and awkward to carry on board.

Throwing out lines to catch fish while travelling to or from the lobster fishing grounds was another exciting aspect of these fishing expeditions. The seas were rich with a wide assortment of fish, all known by the Clery boys by their English and very often their Irish names.

The coast was rocky with high cliffs extending from the mouth of the harbour. It is not possible to forget the booming sound of the surf against the rocks and the overhanging cliffs, and the impression of one's isolation and insignificance in the immensity of the ocean and the sky. As youngsters we delighted in climbing down the cliffs to small isolated beaches, collecting periwinkles and clams, cooking these over fires of dried jetsam, and exploring caves and crevices for treasure trove.

I recall during my times there one visit to the Blasket Islands by curragh, when the mountainous seas rolling in from the naked atlantic had the boat bobbing up and down like a cork. I was crouched in the worst possible place in the boat, the bow. I found myself at one moment at the top of the world with a terrifying view of the ocean's turbulence, and the next in the deep trough of a huge black watery grave. I was greatly relieved to reach *terra firma* at Dunquin.

We used visit the Dingle Fair towards the end of August every year. This was a typical harvest celebration where there were donkey races, stalls of various sorts, and the traditional drinking of porter and eating pigs' crubeens. It was a festive occasion and I cannot recall any violence or faction fights, nor any unpleasant aspects of the festivities. I do not think that faction fights existed in that part of Ireland, at least as late as the 1930s.

On one occasion a close member of the family arrived back from Boston where he was a police officer. His dapper clothing was in striking contrast to the day-to-day clothing of the family. The visiting uncle, called an *Puncán* (the colloquial Irish word with an accent on the "a" for an American born in Ireland) came bearing all sorts of gifts, including packs of 200 Camel cigarettes and no doubt some addition to the bric-a-brac in an *seomra*. The Camels were a great talking point among the locals. The highly sophisticated habit of cigarette smoking had not yet penetrated the more remote parts of rural Ireland. The older men smoked plug tobacco and many of the older women smoked tobacco in a small white delph pipe called a *dúidín* in Irish and pronounced doodeen. The *Puncán* stayed for some days and must have lodged in the hotel in Dingle. He moved about the district like a millionaire in a shanty town, creating excitement and admiration everywhere. It is no wonder that emigration continued to be such an important part of the people's lives, not only from economic necessity, but also because of the lure of the prosperity and prestige of the great American cities and their citizens.

The girls who came to our home from the western Gaeltacht were all successful in their further careers, whether they married or not, and they maintained contact with us for many years afterwards. We spoke Irish at home but English was also spoken at least as widely. Otherwise we would have found it difficult to speak to mother, who never learnt the language, and to the domestic staff.

I cannot remember now how proficient we were in Irish but clearly we spoke enough to satisfy the needs of childish communication. During our childhood Dad always spoke to us in Irish, at least within the family group, while we spoke to mother in English. Sadly, I drifted away from the language as soon as I left school and as I progressed to more personal friendships outside the family and outside the Irish language milieu. I had none of the commitment to or affection for the language to ensure my continuing interest in speaking it. This experience was shared by all my brothers and sisters, and indeed was the fate of most people of my and subsequent generations who were taught the rudiments of the language while young but had little opportunity to use the language when they entered an entirely English speaking adult society. Since my retirement in 1988 I have been re-learning the language and regretting that circumstances in the early years failed so abysmally to make it attractive to the people of this country.

There were aspects of life in the 1930s which I recall with no little nostalgia. Life was more secure than it is to-day in a variety of ways, although we may not have been aware of this advantage at the time. Doors remained unlocked, and windows remained open during the summer nights. There were no housebreakers and anyhow there was nothing to attract such miscreants. There was a sense of security, at least in the negative sense, in that one did not have to worry about one's possessions, because one possessed little or nothing, at least of a valuable or portable nature. There was widespread poverty and destitution in the city where a substantial segment of the population lived on charity or begging, but this state of affairs was accepted as inevitable in the scheme of things, just as the poor and destitute to-day, whose unhappy state is the result of different circumstances, are accepted as an inevitable part of our society.

We lived in a close knit suburban community. We visited each other freely without formality or invitation, and it was usually only a matter of pushing open your neighbour's door. There was less loneliness then as the generations lived together and those who could afford it had indoor staff, members of whom often became permanent members of the household. Life was simpler with fewer extraneous influences.

I think the world was quieter and more serene then. I recall being awake in bed at night as a child and hearing specific sounds which to-day are lost in the cacophony of urban life. The distant plaintive whistle of the steam engine in the shunting yards of Kingsbridge, the grating sound of the tramcar turning at Kelly's Corner half a mile away, and the muted chug-chug of the canal boat on the Grand Canal on the north side of Portobello Barracks. These well remembered sounds seemed to amplify the stillness of those nights. Lying in bed, the chiming of the grandfather clock in the well of the house was more comforting than intrusive, and the passage of every quarter hour was measured by the chimes of the distant town hall clock.

I slept as a child with my brother Padraig in the blue room, facing west across the military field. As each long summer day in June and July ended the light of the gloaming in the northwestern sky faded slowly and imperceptibly into complete darkness, a natural and peaceful phenomenon which we no longer witness because of the ubiquitous lighting in our cities. The bright star-lit sky was not yet obscured by the wide diffusion of our city lights. It has been said that darkness has gone from the earth. This is certainly true, not only of our cities but also of all except the most remote parts of our countryside.

There were three bedrooms at the rear of the house where we children slept. Padraig and myself in the blue room facing west; Elisabet in the pink room facing east, and the three younger children in the large nursery, with windows facing east and west. They were large, airy and well lit. The ceilings were coved in keeping with the sloping roof, giving a feeling of warmth, comfort and security. Each room had a fireplace and a fire was provided in the winter if we were confined to bed while ill. I recall the magic of the flickering light of the dying embers when, late at night, the household was retiring. I remember the fleeting shadows on the walls and ceilings of my bedroom and the occasional quiet crunch of a boot on the gravel outside. These were memories of the guards who, in the earlier years, were there to protect Dad and the family, and who patrolled the grounds regularly at night.

We were never far from the army's presence during our childhood in Lissenfield. The house was contiguous to the five acre military field where various training exercises were carried out and regular football games were played. We had access to the field when we were young, mostly for hurling, and our milking cows could graze there when otherwise not occupied by the military. During the war, hundreds of tons of turf were stacked at one side of the field, to be available during "the Emergency" in the event of a fuel shortage. The mountain of turf is still there and apparently untouched since it was first formed. It makes a suitable grandstand for onlookers at football matches and has long ago been covered by grass and weeds. Many years ago the army authorities or the department of defence were questioned by my mother about the likely fate of the turf mountain. She were told that it would be planted with rhodedendrons to improve the amenities of the area. So far, more than fifty years later, these grandiose ideas have not been fulfilled, nor do I think that a parsimonious department of defence was ever likely to agree to such non-military extravagance.

332

At dusk we could hear the notes of the last post from the barracks, a plaintive reminder of the end of another day and a tradition which has sadly long since passed. We were familiar with the red caps, the military police, who patrolled Rathmines Road in pairs in the evenings to ensure that the soldiers were perfectly behaved and properly turned out in their uniforms and polished boots and leggings.

Signalling instruction for Padraig, military field, 1923.

On many days in the thirties we could hear the strains of the first army brass band or the pipe band, or both, as they marched along Rathmines Road to or from the city, another happy reminder of the pride we had in our peacetime army, and, to us at least, a reminder of dad's initiative in establishing the army school of music while he was commander in chief. Now there is no longer room for marching bands and it is some years since I have seen a uniformed soldier or red cap stepping it out on the street.

We grew up under different circumstances from those of to-day. In the 1930s, because of the frugality and comparative austerity of the times, and the limited spending power of even the most affluent middle classes, strict prudence was necessary in all matters of household expenditure. Clothes, equipment and other household items needed to be maintained or repaired. Nothing was disposed of until it no longer remained serviceable. Even food was not wasted. In our home at least, anything left over from the table was fed to the domestic animals or relegated to the compost heap. Clothing was not infrequently passed from one sibling to a younger one, and all clothing was repaired until no longer viable. The age of the disposable had not yet arrived. I cannot think of anything which would been disposed of until it had reached the end of its useful life. I have no doubt that the disposal habit, which is so ubiquitous to-day, will contribute to major ecological problems in the future and is already doing so.

There was always a dressmaker available to make clothes for the women and to repair or alter clothing as required. The girls learned to design and make their own clothes. Pattern books were in constant demand and the darning basket made a regular appearance as socks, pullovers and other woollen articles required repair. Rugs and sweaters were woven, shoes and boots were regularly sent to the bootmaker. From the ecological point of view, everything we eventually discarded was degradable. Plastic was unknown. The only adverse environmental problem I can recall was the heavy pollution from coal fires and steam engines, and such industry as there was. November fogs were the rule and some of these could be very dense indeed.

During our childhood we were attended by a very well known and respected general practitioner, Bill Cremin. He lived in a fine old Georgian house in St. Stephens Green West close to the corner of York Street, just across from the Royal College of Surgeons. This house is still standing and the subject of a preservation order. He was a large, solid, portly and bespectacled man whose mature and professional appearance inspired immediate confidence. He must have been a good doctor as I recall that he prescribed brown bread for most complaints and for all trivial ailments. Actual medications must have been few and must have had the advantage of being harmless and inexpensive, unlike the profusion of expensive and sometimes dangerous drugs so frequently prescribed to-day. Cod liver oil, Parrish's food (containing iron), Friars' balsam, purgatives, cough medicines, poultices and camphorated applications for lumbago and other painful conditions, were the chief items in the pharmacopoea. I suppose at the time there was little he could do apart from relieving symptoms and inspiring confidence in recovery, and eschewing unnecessary interventions

During the 1920s and early 1930s we suffered the usual children's' epidemic diseases - measles, erysipelas, chickenpox, scarlet fever, whooping cough - but fortunately we escaped the more serious endemic conditions of diphtheria, tuberculosis and poliomyelitis. Admission to one of the fever hospitals was the fate of some of us and might well have been an added hazard. Cork Street and Clonskeagh were the two fever hospitals. Mortality was high as it was in the general hospitals, which explained the reluctance of people to enter hospital at the time. To many it was equivalent to a death sentence. To me, my admission to Clonskeagh Hospital as a young child was a nightmare which left a sense of horror of hospitals on my mind for many years. Apparently, in response to my misbehaviour, a nurse had threatened to throw me down the lavatory and to pull the chain. I was so terrified that my mother had to come immediately and bring me home!

I recall no serious or prolonged illness in the house, except for an outbreak of infective hepatitis in the late 1940s while I was in London. Dad was afflicted occasionally by attacks of lumbago, a painful back which nowadays would be diagnosed as disc trouble. He invariably recovered in a day or two. Mother suffered from bunions and corns which were endemic among women at the time, almost certainly caused by improper footwear. Probably her only extravagance was her regular visits to the chiropodist. The medical profession would have made a poor living if all families were as healthy as ours.

Looking back on medicine in the thirties and forties, it is clear that, apart from the treatment of injuries and a few surgical operations, doctors had little power to alter the course of disease. There is no doubt about the substance of the old French adage dated to the fifteenth century or earlier *Guerir quelquefois, soulager souvent, consoler toujours* (cure sometimes, alleviate often, comfort always) engraved on Gutzon Borglum's statue of Dr. Edward Livingston Trudeau at Saranac Lake in New York State [3]. We might qualify this by saying that cure could be seldom rather than sometimes attributed to medical intervention and that the doctor's role was mainly in inspiring confidence, irrespective of the outcome of his or her administrations.

Nowadays we possibly cure more frequently, but in the circumstances of the wide prevalence of cancer, heart disease and other chronic conditions, we still only cure sometimes although we can prolong life more frequently and improve the quality of people's lives. This is particularly so when we take the broader view of seeking causes as well as prescribing treatment. However, we also do more harm than our predecessors through the use of drugs, surgery and other forms of intervention, but this is a subject which requires a chapter to itself. Also, we do not always alleviate, if one is to witness the prolonged and complicated interventions many patients with serious illness are subjected to in hospitals, nor is the process of dying made any easier for the patient and family by the salvage medicine which is currently so common and which did not exist when we were children.

I well remember the form of Dr. Cremin's visits. The minute or two to hear about the problem, the brief examination with a stethescope, and the occasional injection, possibly some vaccination or other. The only traumatic event I can recall during one of his visits was when he had Padraig and myself lower our trousers and he examined our genitals. He was obviously looking for paraphimosis (an excessively tight and untractable foreskin) a wise precaution in young boys if hygiene leaves much to be desired, but by that time I had clearly reached the stage of being excessively modest about this part of my anatomy. At least he did not routinely prescribe circumcision, which is an unnecessary and mutilating operation in normal boys but which was then commonly performed.

Apart from those childhood illnesses, we were a reasonably healthy lot, although Padraig, the eldest, was described as delicate at birth and received special care and attention during his early years. Predictably, he became the sturdiest of the lot, at least in the physical sense. With our extensive grounds and access to the five acre military field on the west side of the house, we had plenty of opportunity for outdoor recreation. As we grew older the tennis court became an important adjunct and was in constant use, not only by ourselves but also by our cousins, the McCullough and Monahan boys, and other school friends. Formal tennis parties were rarely held although we do have photographs in the family album of adult tennis parties in the earlier years. Dad was an enthusiastic if somewhat erratic and impetuous player as he was later when he took up golf and Bridge, while I can never recall my mother playing. In those days women were less likely to participate in outdoor sports and anyhow she was probably too preoccupied with the management of the house and grounds. Nevertheless, she was often the life and soul of our parties and social gatherings.

We were fed on simple but adequate fare, with an emphasis on boiled eggs, potatoes and vegetables, mostly the cheaper cuts of meat, (including pig's cheek!) dairy foods, bread and jam, rice pudding, apple pie and tart, tripe and our favourite in later years and Maggie's speciality, cheese and tomato soufflet, or another of Maggie's dishes, chocolate mousse. We were poorly clothed during the winter so that serious chillblains involving the hands and toes were the rule. They were aggravated by the poor heating and insulation of the house and of the schools we attended.

The regular daily or even twice daily bath or shower, so much part of our lives nowadays, and sometimes bordering on mysophobia, would have been considered a gross extravagance then and would have been thought unnecessary in terms of hygiene. As I recall, we were obliged to have a bath once every week, but to wash our hands and face every morning and evening. We probably maintained a reasonable level of cleanliness but the ubiquitous presence of a distinctive odour of poor hygiene within the community was one of the more disagreeable aspects of those earlier days and no doubt emanated from those who seldom or never took a bath.

My relationship with my father as a child was a little remote and impersonal although I was always aware of his public standing and reputation. It was only in later years, as my relationship with him matured, that I became conscious of his more unusual attributes. He was a shadowy figure in the background during our childhood in the 1930s but we were always conscious of our standing in Rathmines, and indeed in the wider Dublin community because of his public reputation. We were constantly reminded during our daily lives that we were Dick Mulcahy's children. We came into more regular and intimate contact with him later, as a diminishing house staff and our emergence into adult life brought increasing mutual interests and communication between parents and children.

I suppose the first tangible step in my achieving a mature adult relationship with my father was in 1945 when I qualified as a doctor. He had always been keen on my doing medicine and was obviously pleased and proud of the fact that I graduated as a doctor, even if my undergraduate career was distinguished more by my enthusiasm for rowing than it was by academic interests and achievements.

The world of our family remained limited to the south Dublin area and to our relations and parents' friends until the beginning of the war in 1939. By then our family life began to extend further in terms of associations and friendships as we each left school and went to University College or other third level institutions. A slow disintegration started with Elisabet going to

France for a prolonged stay in the summer of 1939 and Padraig going to Wales during the early forties as a trainee quantity surveyor. The war came in September 1939 and restricted all travel abroad for the next six years. I recall it as a time not very different in terms of our earlier life style and of our home. It was of course a time of austerity but not very different from the thirties when we knew little luxury or possessions over and above the simplicity and security of our lives. Rationing became a reality after a year or two but it was not a source of great hardship, at least as far as food was concerned. Indeed, rationing probably led to a fairer distribution of food and must have contributed to the improvement in the nutrition of the poorer people which was a feature of the emergency, particularly in Dublin and the other cities.

Travel became more difficult as the war progressed and as coal and petrol became more difficult to obtain. Trains were dependent on turf as fuel during the later years of the war. It was necessary to clean out the furnace of the locomotive every 25 miles or so because of the accumulation of ash. The fire had to be relit and the boiler brought back to full temperature before the locomotive could restart. Journeys from Cork to Dublin, a distance of 166 miles, took up to 24 hours.

On one occasion in the Summer of 1944, a group of my boat club friends, including Gerry Frost, K.P. O'Sullivan and myself, went on a cycling and camping holiday in Galway. Gerry was accompanied by his new wife, Maire Gannon. On our return to Dublin we put Maire on the train at Eyre Square in Galway. The train departed at midday as we set off to cycle the 132 miles to Dublin. We arrived at the Ballast Office in Dublin at 11.30 that evening. It is a measure of our resilience that this marathon journey was accomplished in less than twelve hours and with the heavy poorly equipped bicycles which we had at the time. We arrived safely with nothing worse than severely excoriated bottoms! We went to Westland Row station to find Maire. The train had not yet arrived nor did it until half past four the following morning. We spent the waiting hours in a dreary waiting room in the station but these hardships and tribulations appeared to cause us little trouble at the time.

Most summer holidays were spent on bicycles during the later years of the war. We cycled the hundred miles to Carrick-on-Shannon and back to attend the August week-end regatta. With Des Hogan and his brother Colm, I spent a week or ten days in Kerry and Cork, poorly equipped and camping wherever we stopped for the night. Carrying our baggage, the bicycles proved totally unreliable with frequent punctures and broken chain links. The weather was appalling and on one occasion our camp site was isolated by flash floods which inundated our surroundings and we became completely waterlogged. The final blow came when my crossbar snapped on the road back to Dublin between Midleton and Youghal. We found it impossible to stabilise the bike, despite several ingenious attempts to design a "prosthesis". I had to borrow my train fare, cadge a lift on a turf lorry to Cork, and spend the next 24 hours in the train, penniless and without food or drink.

Travel in Dublin was on foot, cycle or on the tram. Motor cars were few but anyhow few people had private cars before the war. Many articles associated with sport or leisure, such as golf and tennis balls and equipment for our rowing club in UCD, were either unobtainable or in severe short supply, but, thanks to the supplies which were still available at the beginning of the war, and to much innovation in maintenance and repair, the effects were not too dramatically felt until towards the end or after the war. I think that 1946, when the war was over and when I had gone to London, was the period of greatest austerity. In the Hospital of St. John and St. Elizabeth, where I was a resident from November 1946, food was reasonably plentiful but we existed almost entirely on whale or horse meat, potatoes, a formless mass of starch-like Yorkshire pudding, bread and margarine, with an occasional treat of tinned Spam. Cigarettes were virtually unobtainable without special contacts or without bribing the publican with free drinks. Beer was more plentiful but to somebody who had acquired a taste for Guinness, it was pretty insipid stuff.

The bicycle was our great mode of transport in Dublin. Disorderly masses of cyclists appeared on the streets and at intersections during rush hours. New bicycle equipment was scarce but ersatz spare parts and the ingenuity of the repair shops kept things going. Our local bicycle repair shop was in a broken down garage under the scouts' hall in Richmond Hill. Many a crisis was averted by Fitzpatrick, the proprietor of the shop, as our bikes showed signs of age and abuse.

We were fortunate at Lissenfield to have our own supply of fruit, vegetables and dairy food. On the whole, we were quite detached from the war itself. We were most conscious of it during the Battle of Britain, the relatively short period of six to eight weeks through the summer of 1940, when there was extensive bombing of London and other British cities, including Belfast. Every night about ten o'clock we waited with excitement and apprehension for the first of the bulletins from London. It was by far the most dramatic and heroic episode of the war, at least until the Russian front opened in 1941, and it was our first realisation that the fighting was not that remote from ourselves.

Everyone hoped and believed that the Allies would win. This conviction was strengthened when the Americans entered the war but it was virtually copperfastened when Hitler invaded Russia. By then, while we looked forward impatiently to the end of the war, we had little doubt about its outcome.

The rigours of shortages and the blackout and other restrictions increased as the war continued but I cannot say that we were more content before or since. What we lacked in affluence and acquisitions, we more than made up for in personal and collective security, and in the satisfaction of living, even if we did so frugally and perhaps at times by our wits. The quality of life may have been affected but the effects in other terms were not. Nowadays the emphasis by all segments of society is on increasing economic growth. This is the great and only sacred cow of the politicians, and who can blame them when material acquisitions appear to be the public's only concern.

Professor Murphy, when reviewing Maryann's biography [4] remarks that none of Mulcahy's children went into politics, despite the fact that he was a hero to his family. Although Padraig has been a most loyal and constant supporter of the South Dublin Branch of Fine Gael, neither he nor Sean ever appeared to me to have the slightest interest in or desire to enter politics.

I expect that I am more of a political animal, as exemplified by some aspects of my medical career. I became closely involved in the Irish Medical Association for some years and was President in 1972. I also was active in the public health field during most of my career and received a chair in heart disease prevention, the first of its kind in the world, as an acknowledgment of the health promotional and heart disease prevention research and educational work of my department at St. Vincent's Hospital. However, my interest in politics developed rather late and long after I had qualified as a doctor. I hold the view that politics and medicine have one thing in common - they are both fulltime occupations and are incompatible as joint careers. In my early university years, when an interest in politics might have emerged, I was far too immature, inarticulate and lacking in confidence to join the Finlays, the Roes, the O'Higginses and others who were obviously political material in the University in my time, many of whom subsequently reached prominence in the public life of the country.

Padraig qualified as a quantity surveyor and Sean as an electrical and mechanical engineer. Both established large consulting firms which depended at least in part on public contracts. This prevented them from identifying themselves openly with any political group. My three sisters married professional spouses and were kept busy looking after home and family. Of the three, Neilli was the only one to continue her professional work after her marriage.

I cannot say that I ever detected any evidence of an interest in politics among my three sisters. Dad never did anything to encourage us to enter politics. His anxiety was to bring about a reconciliation after the civil war, and to ensure that the next generation should not be affected by the divisions which had occurred within the Ryan family. He discouraged any discussion of politics in the house or at the table while we were young.

Both he and my mother were instrumental in our entering the university and following professional careers, and perhaps they felt that an opportunity to enjoy third level education and to pursue a professional career was one of the benefits of national independence and of the recent emergence of the indigenous Irish people.

Neither Padraig nor myself entered the army at the start of the Emergency. My parents showed no anxiety for us to do so nor indeed did they discourage us in any way. However, our first cousins the McCulloughs, the Ryans, the Monahans and the Patrick Mulcahys all contributed a recruit each to the army at the beginning of the war. All we did was join the Local Defence Force, of which Padraig became a dedicated member, while I did not allow my quasi military duties to interfere too much with my rowing and other college interests. I often wonder what these families, and indeed others, must have thought of us, bearing in mind Dad's unique involvement with the army's foundation and development. I have already noted how Dad distanced himself from the army after his resignation in 1924 and no doubt our failure to join

341

at this crucial time might be understood because of this. Anyhow, I console and excuse myself on the grounds that the frustrations Dad suffered from 1916 to 1924, and the contribution he made to the founding of a free democratic state, were sufficient to compensate for the family's later omissions. And perhaps our cousins felt that they still owed something to the country for their new found freedom!

Of the girls, Elisabet and Neilli went to UCD where Elisabet qualified in science. Before her marriage to dentist Gerard Berney, she worked first with the Birds Custard firm, and later with her aunt, Phyllis Ryan, subsequently Sean T. O'Kelly's second wife.

Neilli never finished her arts degree but instead went to Paris to study in the world of *grande couture*. She established herself in Dublin as one of our best known couturieres, with a special reputation in the use of Irish tweeds and linens. She continued her career for a number of years after her marriage to solicitor, Tommy Bacon, despite the early arrival of six daughters and a somewhat unexpected afterthought.

Maire attended the College of Domestic Economy in Cathal Brugha Street where she completed a four-year course in household management. Like her parents, she had natural managerial skills and she was outstandingly successful in running her large household in Clonmel, Co Tipperary, where she lived with her physician husband and a family of seven. Unhappily, she died from breast cancer at the early age of 56 years.

As the years in Lissenfield went by, mother became more interested in gardening. What is to-day a universal interest among home owners was then almost confined to the better off Protestant families in Ireland, and mostly to the women. Gradually the better off emerging Catholic home owners took up the hobby. Mother began to introduce a variety of shrubs which are now commonplace but which were then largely unfamiliar to us. She planted escallonia along the boundary of the military field, a distance of perhaps one hundred yards. It is as prolific as it is dense, and its care and control was to cause me many headaches after I had taken over the property in 1966.

I still have a large barrel in my home containing a magnificent and noble azalea, the Lady Alice Fitzwilliam, which mother bought in Power's nursery in Waterford in 1937. Its cuttings, which I propagate from time to time, are much in demand for their beautiful bracts of pure white bell-like flowers which appear in May and June, and spread their all-pervading sweet bouquet around the garden and the surrounding area.

Mother built a rockery along the avenue which she gradually extended around the southern and western sides of the house. Full of rock and alpine plants, it became a great source of interest and admiration, and its weeding provided her with a steady occupation as the family and household responsibilities tended to become less arduous

In later years our parents took up golf and were longstanding members of Milltown Golf Club. Dad played golf with the same enthusiasm and inconsistency as he played tennis. He was in no sense a competitive player, and his inconsistency could be attributed to his constant tinkering with his swing and his technique. He was always on the verge of the big breakthrough! However, he derived great enjoyment from the game, whether he was playing with Jack Costello, Michael Hayes or other cronies, or having a quick two-ball with mother. She also enjoyed the game and both would fly around the course in two hours flat, carrying two pencil bags with a motley set of clubs, moving briskly between shots and not wasting time with practice swings or other superfluous activities.

Mother was a late starter at golf, and then only after she could free herself from the responsibility and tedium of household management. At her age it is understandable that she was an indifferent golfer and that she remained a thirty-six handicap until the big day when, much to her own surprise and to ours, she won a competition in Milltown with an exceptionally good score of less than 60 shots net. I recall that she was elated by her success and was not at all intimidated by her new handicap of twenty or so. Her success led to her being nominated for a team to play Malahide in some interclub competition. Her euphoria was soon dampened and her golfing career was brought back to reality by the result of her match with a rather patronising Malahide lady who intimidated her to such an extent that she was beaten by a score of ten and eight!

Mother continued to play golf until she was in her early eighties. By this time she was complaining of occasional bouts of angina, particularly while playing, so she was encouraged to retire and to hang up her golf bag. She died in 1977 at the age of 92, six years after dad's death.

Dad had always been interested in exercise and was a great walker, particularly before he took up golf in his later years. Even then he would often go out for a brisk walk with mother, who was herself no mean walker. Long walks with Michael Hayes at weekends in the southern suburbs or in the Dublin hills were the rule, when the talk, I would say, might be as vigorous as the exercise itself. Not having a car and not being a driver until the late fifties, he travelled around the city as often by foot as by tram or bus. Whether walking around the city was of much aerobic value must remain doubtful, as he was so well known and easily recognised that he must have been constantly interrupted during his travels. However, he had a brisk military gait which must have discouraged many from interrupting him. He did have a car and driver while minister for education from 1948 to 1951 and from 1954 to 1957. No doubt this facility reduced his exercise but he continued his weekend walks.

Michael Hayes was his closest friend and confidante. Hayes held the chair of Irish in University College Dublin. He had been in Jacob's factory during Easter week of 1916 but escaped detection by the British after the surrender. He was chairman of the Dail from 1922 to 1932, and had put his house at dad's disposal when he was on the run during the war of independence.

Jack Costello was also a close friend and another two were Paddy McGilligan and Dr Tom O'Higgins. The latter was a brother of Kevin O'Higgins and was probably dad's greatest supporter during the years of the party from 1944 when Dad became president to the end of the second Inter-Party government in 1957.

Dad and mother used holiday occasionally with Paddy McGilligan and his wife Annie. On one occasion, in 1937 I think, they holidayed together at Paddy McGilligan's birthplace in Castletroy in the North of Ireland. Dad and Paddy played golf and both played in a competition for the Coronation Cup, a trophy presented to commemorate the coronation of King George V in 1910. Dad, as much to his own surprise as to the rest of us, won the competition. However. his victory was not without its complications. The local unionist members refused to attend the presentation and the customs officials at the border refused to allow him to take the trophy into the Free State.

344

There was very little intercourse between the South and the North during the thirties although some of the people who played an active part in the political and professional life of the South after the Treaty had come from the North at the time of the pogram there in 1922 and during earlier sectarian conflicts. The O'Learys were one such family. Simon O'Leary was a leather merchant in Belfast and lived with his numerous children on Limestone Road. His daughter Molly and his son Jack lived in Dublin. They were intimate friends of our family. We as children used visit their parents in Belfast for short holidays. I was there once, probably about 1936, and I found that Belfast left a profound impression on me as a foreign city. The buses and trams were painted red and were different in design from our own vehicles, while the public parks were a revelation to my unaccustomed eye with children's' playgrounds equipped with all types of swings and roundabouts which I had never seen in Dublin. There was an entirely different atmosphere there which I cannot easily define now but which left me with an uneasy feeling of being in a strange and forbidding land. The Sabbath was more strictly observed in the North, so that Sundays were boring and only relieved by walks to the top of Cave Hill.

Picture going was very popular among the O'Learys. While there we often went to the cinema, which we were rarely allowed or able to do in Dublin. Pictures were a major attraction and every one I saw seemed to have been an outstanding saga or classic. On one occasion my two younger sisters went to the cinema in Belfast on their own. They were terrified of violence and asked the girl in the box-office if there were any guns in the picture. They were reassured but within five minutes of the start a shooting match started. The girls rushed out of the cinema and retrieved their sixpences from the staff. Laurel and Hardy, Buster Keaton and the Marx Brothers were more to our liking, although the violence which was part of cowboy and indian films and of the great historical classics did not seem to worry us. It did not make the same adverse impression on us as cruelty and sadism does in modern films.

Jack O'Leary was a barrister at the Law Library and eventually was appointed to the sinecure position of Taxing Master. He was one of only two or three people who were served a glass of whiskey when they visited our house. He was also noted for his brilliantined hair and for the remains of this application he left on mother's antimacassars, much to her frustration. He was a fine conversationalist and was a popular visitor, despite his one shortcoming.

Mollie O'Leary worked as a civil servant in Dublin. For some time she boarded at Lissenfield and slept in the same room as my sister Elisabet. She must have been with us for at least two years. Whether she contributed to her board and lodging I cannot say. I do know she had a clerical post in the service and that she cannot have been too affluent. To us children she was remarkable because she was the only regular cigarette smoker in the house at a time when it was unusual for women to smoke.

Cigarette smoking had become a sophisticated and fashionable habit by the late thirties among the better educated. The habit was adopted by my parents, presumably because of peer example or pressure. They were never anything but harmless smokers and neither appeared to become seriously addicted. Sometime in the late thirties mother stopped. She had been informed by a highly regarded physician that one of her boys was infertile. This eminent man reached his conclusion after the child had been brought to see him for some entirely unrelated reason. The diagnosis was obviously made on the flimsiest evidence and subsequently proved to be wrong. It was a classical example of the snap diagnosis which was arrived at too frequently in those days, even by the most eminent. Mother resolved to stop smoking as a special intention to induce the Almighty to restore the child's fertility. It is likely that the diagnosis was wrong in the first place but it is quite possible that mother's faith may have achieved the necessary divine intervention.

Having heard her account of the event and of the circumstances under which the doctor reached his prognosis, I am satisfied that the opinion was entirely unwarranted on the evidence available to him. My own experience of my medical preceptors in the 1940s, when I joined the medical profession, was that dogma existed in inverse proportion to the knowledge of the practitioner. Unfortunately the tendency exists still, but to a lesser extent, among colleagues and indeed is a feature of other professions and of the frailty of human nature. Beware of the doctor who knows everything and honour the doctor who admits his or her limitations. Dad must have stopped smoking shortly after mother although I have an impression that he was less committed to the habit than she.

Casual drinking of alcohol was unknown at home in the thirties and forties, and it was rarely customary in any household to offer an alcoholic drink to casual visitors, of whom there were many in Lissenfield. Alcohol was served at formal dinner parties which were a feature of the parents' social life after things had settled down following the civil war. Dinners were events of great excitement among us children in the early years when we might be briefly received by the guests on their arrival. The number of guests were usually eight, almost invariably made up of a politician, a diplomat, a well known professional person, and perhaps a close family friend, and their spouses. I recall that one or two dinners were made the occasion to bring two single or widowed people together who might be deemed by my mother to be suited to each other in terms of matrimony. Her subterfuge bore fruit on one or two occasions.

The parents' Golden Jubilee, June 1969 at 1 Temple Villas.
left to right: Padraig, Elisabet, Risteard, Maire, Neilli, Sean.

The dinners were formal and followed a regular protocol, unlike the rather casual approach to entertainment which exists to-day. Guests arrived strictly on time, a glass of sherry was served, dinner was announced again strictly on time, with the principal guest seated on mother's right and his wife on dad's right, A glass of white wine was followed by a glass of red, and a liqueur was served with coffee in the drawing room afterwards. Strictly at the appointed hour, I think about eleven o'clock, the principal guest would stand up, indicating that it was time to go. This was the signal for all the guests to leave.

I cannot recall my parents drinking any alcohol, except at these formal dinners. As stated earlier, no drink was served on informal occasions, although I recall exceptions in the case of my uncle-in-law, Denis McCullough, and their friend from Belfast, Jack O'Leary, and later Paddy Mulcahy, dad's younger brother. They were usually served a glass of whiskey during their visits. I expect that one reason for this apparent austerity was the modest way of life imposed on us by the limited incomes of the times. The current place of alcohol as a dominant part of all social occasions, formal or informal, domestic or otherwise, is a phenomenon of the post-war period and may be related to a variety of factors, including increasing affluence, the insidious effect of modern advertising and the changing circumstances of women in our society.

In their later years, after dad's retirement and thanks to some encouragement or perhaps the example from their children, our parents took to having a night cap some evenings. Gin and tonic was their favourite drink although Dad sometimes preferred a bottle of Guinness. I am sure that this little self indulgence added to the quality of their lives in their declining years. They never developed a taste for more than one drink. T.P. Coogan, reviewing the Mulcahy biography in the *Irish Times*,[5] wrote of dad's behaviour during a meeting with him in Lissenfield. According to Coogan, Dad enjoyed a "session" of imbibing on the occasion of their meeting,. When my mother arrived home unexpectedly, he tried to conceal his drinking from her by hiding the empty bottles of Guinness. Both suggestions were quite fanciful. Coogan described the event as the only time that Dick Mulcahy was seen to lose his courage!

Things had changed in the social world as early as the 1960s. Not all guests arrive in time nowadays, dinner is often delayed beyond its stated time, and guests can stay well beyond a reasonable retiring time. Clothes too can be less formal and sometimes downright casual. The greater informality of private dinners is closely related to a less disciplined and more permissive attitude towards alcohol.

One of the great hazards of the private dinner is the delay in serving the meal by an hour and sometimes considerably more. This time is spent drinking pre-dinner cocktails, and the effects of this delay are compounded by the recent trend to employ roving professional servers to ensure that no glass is allowed to be empty, or even half empty. The waiter hovering around

348

with a large jug of gin and tonic is well known at our latter day receptions, and he must have contributed to many sore heads.

On one occasion Aileen and I invited the then Minister for Health, Sean Flanagan, and a number of other guests to dinner at Lissenfield, 7.30 for 8.0 p.m. The minister and his wife arrived at ten o'clock and naturally dinner had to await the guest of honour. At two o'clock I went to bed, leaving the minister, his wife and the remnants of the guests to be entertained by Aileen. I believe the minister was the last to leave at four o'clock. My departure upstairs was probably not noticed by any of those present.

Appendix 1

Richard Mulcahy's homily over the grave of Michael Collins, 9/8/1922

Tá ualach agus bhróin go mór ar chroíthe ár ndaoine inniu, tá ár n-aigne, mar a bheadh an Ardeaglais sin thíos ann nuair a bhíonn an t-Aifreann deireanach ráite, agus an chónra tógtha as, agus an slua mór daoine imithe uaidh - tá ár n-aigne tirim, gan fhocail, agus follamh, gan tada iontu ach solas beag an dóchais.

That there was a burden of sorrow heavy on the hearts of our people to-day, that our minds, like the great Cathedral below after the last Mass had been said, and the coffin borne away and the great concourse of people emptied from it - our minds were dry, wordless, and empty, with nothing in them but the little light of faith.

Our country is to-day bent under a sorrow such as it has not been bent under for many a year. Our minds are cold, empty, wordless and without sound. But it is only our weaknesses that are bent under this great sorrow that we meet to-day. All that is good in us, all that is strong in us, is strengthened by the memory of that great hero, and that great legend who is now laid to rest.

We bend to-day over the grave of a man not more than thirty years of age, who took to himself the gospel of toil for Ireland, the gospel of working for the people of Ireland, and of sacrifice for their good, and who has made himself a hero and a legend that will stand in the pages of our history with any bright page that was ever written there.

Pages have been written by him in the hearts of our people that will never find a place in print. But we lived, some of us, with these intimate pages; and those pages that will reach history, meagre though they be, will do good to our country and will inspire us through many a dark hour. Our weaknesses cry out to us, 'Michael Collins was too brave.'

Michael was not too brave. Every day and every hour he lived he lived it to the full extent of that bravery which God gave to him, and it is for us to be brave as he was - brave before danger, brave before those who lie, brave even to that very great bravery that our weakness complained of in him.

When we look over the pages of his diary for 22nd August, 'Started 6.15 am Macroom to Ballineen, Bandon, Skibbereen, Roscarbery, Clonakilty,' our weakness says he tried to put too much into the day. Standing on the little mantel-piece of his office was a bronze plaque of President Roosevelt, of the United States, and the inscription on it ran: 'I wish to preach, not the doctrine of ignoble ease, but the doctrine of strenuous life, the life of toil and effort, of labour and strife; to preach that highest form of success that comes, not to the man who desires mere ease and peace, but to him who does not shrink from danger, hardship, or bitter toil, and who, out of these, wins the splendid ultimate triumph.'

Mura bhfuigheann an gráinne arbhair a théidheann sa talamh bás ni bhion ann ach é féin, ach ma gheibheann se bás tugan sé toradh mór uaidh.

Unless the grain of corn that falls into the ground dies, there is nothing but itself in it, but if it dies it gives forth great fruit.

And Michael Collins' passing will give us forth great fruit, and Michael Collins' dying will give us forth great fruit. Every bit of his small grain of corn died, and it died night and day during the last four or five years. We have seen him lying on a bed of sickness and struggling with infirmities, running from his bed to his work.

On Saturday, the day before he went on his last journey to Cork, he sat with me at breakfast writhing with pain from a cold all through his body, and yet he was facing his day's work for that

Saturday, and facing his Sunday's journey and Monday's journey and his journey on Tuesday. So let us be brave, and let us not be afraid to do too much in the day. In all that great work, strenuous it was, comparatively it was intemperate, but it was the only thing that Michael Collins was intemperate in.

How often with a shout he used to get out of bed in the morning at 5 or 6 o'clock crying, 'All the time that is wasted in sleep,' and would dash around the room, or into some neighbouring room where some of us lay in the hope of an hour or two's sleep, and he would clear all the blankets off us, or would pound vigorously at the door which prudence had locked.

Crossing the square of the barracks on the Saturday morning that I mention, he told of his visit to one of the barracks in the South on his first trip there, and of finding most of the garrison in bed at 10 o'clock; and thinking of all the lack of order, lack of cleanliness, lack of moral strength and efficiency that goes with this particular type of sloth, and of all the demoralisation following on the dissatisfaction that one has with one's self all the day that one starts with an hour's disadvantage. 'Oh', he said, 'if our fellows would only get up at 6 o'clock in the morning.'

Yes, get up to read, to write; to think, to plan, to work, or, like *Ard Riogh Éireann* long ago, simply to greet the sun. The God given long day fully felt and fully seen would bring its own work and its own construction. Let us be brave, then, and let us work.

'Prophecy,' said Peter, who was the great rock, 'is a light shining in the darkness till the day dawn.'

And surely 'our great rock' was our prophet and our prophecy, a light held aloft along the road of 'danger or hardship or bitter toil.' And if our light is gone out it is only as the paling of a candle in the dawn of its own prophecy.

An act of his, a word of his, a look of his was day by day a prophecy to us that loose lying in us lay capabilities for toil, for bravery, for regularity, for joy in life; and in slowness and in hesitancy and in weariness half yielded to, his prophecies come true in us. And just as he as a person was a light and a prophecy to us individually, he looked to it and wished that this band of brothers, which is the Army, will be a prophecy to our people. Our Army has been the people, is the people, and will be the people. Our green uniform does not make us less the people. It is a cloak of service, a curtailer of our weaknesses, an amplifier of our strength.

We are jealous for his greatness. Words have been quoted as being his last words; Michael Collins is supposed to have said the fragile words, 'Forgive them.' Michael Collins never said these words, 'forgive them,' because his great big mind could not have entertained the obverse thought, and he knew those who sat around him and worked with him that they, too, were too big to harbour in their minds the obverse thought.

When Michael Collins met difficulties, met people who obstructed him, and worked against him, he did not turn aside to blame them, but facing steadily ahead, he worked bravely forward to the goal that he intended. He had that faith in the intensity of his own work that in its development and in its construction he would absorb into one homogeneous whole in the nation, without the necessity for blame or for forgiveness, all those who differed from him and those who fought against him.

He is supposed to have said, 'Let the Dublin Brigade bury me.' Michael Collins knows that we will never bury him. He lies here among the men of the Dublin Brigade. Around him there lie forty-eight comrades of his from our Dublin battalions. But Michael Collins never separated the men of Dublin from the men of Kerry, nor the men of Dublin from the men of Donegal, nor the men of Donegal from the men of Cork.

His great love embraced our whole people and our whole Army, and he was as close in spirit with our men in Kerry and Donegal as he was with our men in Dublin. Yes. And even those men in different districts in the country who sent us home here our dead Dublin men - we are sure he felt nothing but pity and sorrow for them for the tragic circumstances in which they find themselves, knowing that in fundamentals and ideals they were the same.

Michael Collins had only a few minutes to live and to speak after he received his death wound, and the only word he spoke in these few moments was 'Emmet.' He called to the comrade alongside him, the comrade of many fights and of many plans, and I am sure that he was calling around him the whole men of Ireland that he might speak the last word of comradeship and love.

We last looked at him in the City Hall and in the small church in Vincent's Hospital. And, studying his face with an eager gaze, we found there the same old smile that met us always in our work. And seeing it there in the first dark hour of our blow, the mind could not help travelling back to the dark storm-tossed Sea of Gallilea (sic) and the frail barque tossed upon the waters there, and the strong, calm smile of the Great Sleeper in the stern of the boat.

Tom Ashe, Tomás MacCurtain, Tráolach MacSuibhne, Dick McKee, Micheál O'Coileáin, and all you who lie buried here, disciples of our great Chief, those of us you leave behind are all, too, grain from the same handful, scattered by the hand of the Great Sower over the fruitful soil of Ireland. We, too, will bring forth our own fruit.

Men and women of Ireland, we are all mariners on the deep, bound for a port still seen only through storm and spray, sailing still on a sea full of dangers and hardships, and bitter toil. But the Great Sleeper lies smiling in the stern of the boat, and we shall be filled with that spirit which will walk bravely upon the waters.

Appendix 2

Dad's homily over the graves of Thomas Ashe, Peadar Kearney and Piaras Beaslai, 20/8/1967, at the time of Beaslai's death.

We come here as pilgrims, not to raise our voices nor to travel prayerfully a path traced by many prayerful feet, to seek contemplation that will fill our hearts and help us find our purpose. The path we go is firm trod, other paths spread from it. Many figures and many voices from the past are around us while we go to mark another shrine along the way.

Some of us met this path at the spot where O'Donovan Rossa was laid to rest more than 50 years ago. There we met Pearse and Griffith and Eoin MacNeill. The Pearse of 1912 and the *Barr Buadh* had turned aside from the platform of argument and appeal to face and challenge, in the uniform of the Irish Volunteers, the force, deceit and false faith that would frustrate a nation's hopes. Griffith had acclaimed and appraised the spirit of Fenianism. From the front of Charlemont House which recalls the Volunteers of 1772, MacNeill had dismissed the armed parade which had honoured the grave of Rossa and given substance to the challenge of Pearse; he had dismissed them to an unknown morrow which was to lead to the days of 1919, 1920 and 1921, when in the hands of the men of the Dublin Brigade and the General Headquarters Staff, Parnell Square was to become *Caisleán na hAiseirí*, the Dublin Castle of Ireland's political resurrection.

Our high purpose here and the power upon which we rely will be manifest if we recall our Mass at Berkeley Road Church this morning. There, for the purpose of today and to-morrow, we remind ourselves that as the glories of the Creator are being day by day made more manifest by man's work in the world, the world's horrors and dangers increase. More and more resoundingly and in unison therefore we praise God's Providence and pray for greater strength to toll away the dangers and to do our part in creating the kingdom of peace on earth, and for light and understanding to recognise and realise the Kingdom of Heaven within us.

Ever more resoundingly now at Mass we dare to pray that to this end we may be given our daily bread, and that in the forgiveness of our offences and our mistakes we may be endowed with an increase of courage, strength and hope.

More humbly and no less daringly in the quiet of our hearts we pray also:

A dhia do chuir uaiseacht iongantach sa nadúr dhaona agus tú a chruthu agus gurab iongantai na san an athnuachaint a dheinis uirthe, tabhair duinn tré rún díamhar an uisge agus an fhiona so go mbeimid rann-pháirteach i ndiadhacht an té a dheonaigh bheith rann-pháirteach in ár ndaonacht, Iosa Chriost, do Mhac, ar d'Tiarna a mhaireann agus a ríalann mar aon leatsa in aondacht leis an spiorad naomh ina Dhia ar feadh na síorraiochta.

We dare to ask that through the sacred mystery of the water and the wine of the Mass, we may be made partakers of the Divinity of Him Who partook of our humanity.

In that spirit we have come here to mark another shrine along the way - the grave where lie Tomas Aghas, Piaras Beaslai, Peadar O Cearnaigh.

On the way we have stopped to pray by the grave of Michael Collins. Expanding around it many graves recall that even in many far-flung countries today struggling for peace, Irishmen are giving their services and their labours with a dedication marked by the sacrifice of their lives. We stopped to pray by the more isolated grave of Arthur Griffith, symbolic of the effacement and the retreat in which he laboured, freely offering every drop of his often wearied blood, and every day of his doubts and questioning to be our teacher and a pointer of our way.

Here we reach another shrine. We mark a grave of significance where the memory of three mingled lives will as the days pass enlighten our memories, enoble our emotions and inspire our doings.

We praise the Providence that brings the bodies of Tomas Aghas, Peadar O Cearnaigh and Piaras Beaslai to a united grave and links their names on the one stone. Their mingled lives recall the basic gifts of Providence for man's sustenance, and the labour and faith in which Ireland received them gratefully and raised a nation.

Ashe's life and his traditions speak to us of the nature and of the quality of the basic gifts of Providence to us. *Ór fé'n aitinn, airgead fé'n lúchair, gorta fé an bhfraoch* - Gold under the furze, silver under the rushes, and famine under the heather; they tell of the tools our fathers fashioned to win the gold and silver and to banish the heather's famine, and the labour these tools involved. *An grafán, an suiste agus ag tomhas an talaimh to dornaibh* - The grafaun, the flail, the reaping hook, *an trí obair is cruaidh amuigh* - the three hardest labours ever; they tell of the companionship and society this labouring gathered, and of the song, the story, the prayer that in the passing centuries knit that society to a purpose and an achievement whose monument is Faith.

The story of Peadar Kearney epitomises for us the Dublin which in days of frustration and days of danger was our comfort and our sustenance and our protection. Its dedication to the gentle and gifted Tom Pugh marks the spirit of these days. The pages of Seamus de Burca's gracefully told story are crowded with the names of the writers, workers, artists, singers who made up Peadar's companionship. We know Peadar as the epitome of the appreciative and active citizenship of a capital which absorbed into its life and institutions everything of the grace, the culture, naturalness and gaiety that stemmed from the nation's roots.

His Soldier's Song came to discipline our footsteps, lift our chins and enline our shoulders as we helped to guard and move a people through difficult times to triumph. In our marching it mixed with the *Wearing of the Green, Sean O'Farrell, God Save Ireland,* and marches which carried no words.

In 1916, in Knutsford Jail, it became linked with our prayers. In the company of "Hail Glorious St. Patrick", "Faith of our Fathers" it helped to shake the roof and dash the walls and crash the foundation of a jail that is now gone.

Throughout the world its notes are the salute of the nations to the Irish Republic and the growing acknowledgment, a recognition of the existence of an Irish Nation. The tragic circumstances that surround it have caused the words to become a shy whisper in our own throats.

Piaras Beaslai's youth introduced him to the life and literature of Europe. He came to Ireland to seek a climate in which to anchor his soul and face a worthy lifework. He found in Gougane the inspiration for a life that included long and daring service with those who manned and held the Parnell Square *Caisleán*. While we work and wait for the flowering of the Garden of Remembrance and for the echo of its walls to re-stimulate our voices, we will hear from this grave the murmuring of the Bunsheelin river. *Ar eagla na habhann bheith doimhinn, a Rí na Foighne glac mo lámh, ar eagla na tuile bheith tréan, a Mhuire, féach agus na fág.*

And the thought will permeate all our work, *A Rí na bhFeart is agat atá Réiteach* - Oh, God of deeds, Thine is the settlement, Thine is the solution.

Source: *An t'Óglach*, Winter, 1967, pp4-5.

Appendix 3

The Biography

Dad's biography by Maryann Gialanella Valiulis[1] was published in 1992. It deals largely with his military and political careers from 1916 to 1924. It contains little material about his personal and family life and only deals in summary in the epilogue with his subsequent career as a parliamentarian from 1924 to his retirement from politics in 1961.

Maryann's biography underlines the vital, if somewhat low, profile of the GHQ staff in the war of independence and it underlines the more important aspects of Mulcahy's contribution to the foundation of our State. There are other aspects of GHQ and the chief of staff's role which are important and which are included in the biography, but dad's influence in guiding army policy and establishing a peace time army to conform with the principles of a democratic state was his greatest single contribution.

Maryann describes him as a forgotten hero, by which she maintains that his reputation as a soldier politician and one of the major contributors to achieving Irish self-determination, widely appreciated during and immediately after the foundation of the State, was overshadowed by the exploits and reputation of Collins who did not survive the revolutionary period. It was also adversely affected by the army mutiny. Maryann puts forward these and other reasons for this decline in his reputation, a subject which is discussed in my earlier text.

She writes about the gradual drift from the conservatism of his non-political family to his increasing attraction to nationalism and separatism, and to an exceptional commitment to Irish culture. She justifies her decision to dwell on the 1916-1924 period because this was the time in his life when he made his unique contribution to the foundation of the state and to the political nature and final structure of the independent nation. At this time too his reputation as a soldier and leader reached its height.

The biography was originally conceived after Maryann had written her earlier thesis on the army mutiny [2]. She thus became familiar with dad's prominent role in the army leading up to the mutiny, and later expressed an interest in the part he played in the foundation of the Irish Free State and the Irish Army. For many years my family had been under pressure from friends and colleagues of dad's to have a biography written, just as he had frequently been requested to prepare an autobiography during his lifetime. Indeed, in the early sixties he was induced to cooperate with the late Mary Purcell to write his memoirs. He commenced to do so in his usual systematic way, but after preparing two chapters about his early years, which are available in UCD archives, his distaste for the task led to his neglect of the project. I have no idea how he managed to explain his lack of cooperation to Miss Purcell. After his death, we had always intended to approach a biographer but had failed to identify a suitable candidate until Maryann Valiulis arrived on the scene.

The biography was published 21 years after his death. It was co-published by the Kentucky University Press for the American market. It is the product of ten years of research, if one is to include the four years devoted to researching Maryann's first monograph *Almost a Rebellion* which was published in 1985. The bedrock of the research material used by Maryann is the large Mulcahy collection of war of independence, truce, civil war and Cumann na nGaedheal papers which are lodged in the archives of University College Dublin. Maryann had access to other papers in the University archives and papers in the National Library, the military archives, the Royal Irish Academy and elsewhere.

The publication of my father's biography seemed an appropriate occasion to add some personal details about his life and that of his family. While I have no reason to be unhappy with Maryann's perception of his military and political career and of her interpretation of his motives and actions, there are several reasons why I should add to her account of his life. The biography is largely confined to the years 1916 to 1924 and there are certain insights into a man's character which can best be conveyed by those who knew him best. On the other hand, I am also conscious that familiarity and consanguinity can also lead to biases which can distort the truth.

Neither I nor my brothers and sisters were too concerned about the omission of the more personal aspects of dad's personality or family life from the biography. We thought it fulfilled an important purpose which was to record the particular role he played in organising and directing an army, both in military and ethical terms, which would successfully stand up to British aggression, which would not alienate the local population, and which would play its role in establishing a free and democratically elected parliament.

I thought it an innovative idea to have a member of the subject's family review the biography along the lines of a professional reviewer. It provides an opportunity of amplifying some of the aspects of his life and times which emerge in the text. Some additional information may be of interest, particularly in relation to dad's relationship with and recorded opinions of some of his contemporaries in the national movement. His public personality, portrayed with unusual clarity by Maryann, and an appreciation of which provides an understanding of much of his career, naturally impinged much on his family, through his natural austerity and self-discipline. While this was part of his public persona, his family and more intimate friends were aware of his other attributes, his qualities of graciousness, warmth, consideration and informality. An account of the family circumstances and background will serve to identify the man and will add to Maryann's account.

Whatever views may have been expressed about the biography by reviewers and by other individuals, it was generally agreed that it was a most scholarly work, particularly rich in the use of documentary sources. It was its high academic standards that gave the greatest satisfaction to us. The integrity of the author was apparent from her objective account of his role and his personality, an assessment which was not free of criticism at times. By her objectivity and her frank interpretation of the events he was involved in, she avoided the adulatory approach which so often takes from the value of biography while at the same time she managed to encapsulate his personality in a remarkable manner, although some would and did say that the personality portrayed by her was the one which was perceived by those who met him in his public life, and that his more affable personality attributes were only apparent to his family and his intimates.

While a few statements and conclusions in the book may require qualification from the vantage point of personal experience, the comments of some of the professional reviewers of the biography need examination. Anybody who is familiar with the art of reviewing books is only too aware of the temptations that afflict reviewers and of the irritations that can beset authors. According to the poet James Beattie, writing about book reviews:

> In giving an account of new books, I would aim rather to inform
> the public, than give vent to my own admiration or dislike; and
> be brief and modest in panegyric, and in censure very sparing

363

and very merciful, except where the work animadverted upon appeared to have been written with a bad intention,. To publish a dull book is a misfortune rather than a fault. .... Reviewers are apt to begin their account of a book with some commonplace observation of their own. This, I think should be avoided, except where it is necessary to prepare the reader for understanding what is to follow .... A review ought to consist of three parts and no more - an account of the author's plan; a specimen of his manner; and a brief character of his work [3]

The temptations afflicting reviewers can be based on failure to read the manuscript, on disagreement about facts about which the author may be more familiar than the reviewer, on indulging in "ego trips" which distract from the main purpose of a review, and which may be based on the reviewer's fixed ideas and prejudices, and on preoccupation with trivial or anecdotal details. As a frequent reviewer of medical papers and books, and as the author of papers and books subjected to review, I am only too well aware of the reviewers foibles and of the sensitivity and limited insights of authors.

I found most of the reviews to be disappointing in that they missed the chief messages to be derived from Maryann's scholarship. It was clear that some of the reviewers had not read the book or at least had not sufficiently acquainted themselves with its contents to be aware of its main substance. In other cases, the reviewer indulged in ego trips which were largely irrelevant or dealt in unnecessary detail with trivial aspects of dad's life.

Maryann's biography is an important contribution to recent Irish history. It emphasises the role of the general headquarters staff in organising the Irish forces in the Anglo-Irish war and in achieving such success as they did achieve. The role of the GHQ staff has been neglected by historians and writers of the times. This is almost certainly because the early Beaslai biography of Collins became an important source document about the war of independence for subsequent writers and historians, but it makes no mention of the GHQ staff as such and deals almost entirely with the Collins exploits.

The biography refers to some aspects of Mulcahy's career between 1916 and 1924 which have also been neglected by reviewers and historians and which had an influence on our subsequent history. These were his insistence that the army should maintain high ethical standards, even under the stresses of increasing British harassment and atrocities and a bitter civil war, and that the army should remain subservient to the Dail and the will of the people.

Dad's devotion to democracy ensured that his primary motivation during his time in the army and his many years in politics was based on a deep commitment to the supremacy of the people's will [4]. This is apparent from the following excerpt written by him many years later when proportional representation was under threat by the Fianna Fail party.

> I think it could be said that even today, democracy, as we understood it from Griffith's dream and teaching back in 1908 etc, has its work cut out for it to maintain the concept it had then for us, of freedom and dignity and the sense of personal responsibility and worth, and the understanding of communal or society power that we associated with the idea of a parliament based on proportional representation [5].

Throughout his army career from March 1918, when he became chief of staff, to March 1924, when he resigned from the ministry of defence, he was dedicated to organising and maintaining a military force along strict ethical lines. He was also committed to the philosophy that the army must at all times remain subservient to parliament and the people. This philosophy, which I believe is the message to be derived from Maryann's biography, is clearly apparent from his papers and tape recordings [6], and from his subsequent history. It is encapsulated in the phrase he used in his homily over Michael Collins' grave:

"Our army has been the people, is the people, and will be the people."

Appendix 4

I have used three documentary sources in writing about my father. They are his papers lodged in the archives of University College Dublin, his 460 page annotation of the Beaslai's *Michael Collins and the Making of a New Ireland*, and his tape recordings made between 1961 and 1970

(1) The Mulcahy Papers

In writing about his 1916-1924 period I have deliberately avoided referring to the Valiulis account nor have I read or quoted from her biography while I was writing these notes. Hence, some of what I write about in this section may reflect what is already published by Maryann. I have included additional material which will confirm the view expressed by many of his contemporaries that, through his intimate contact with the leading politicians and military figures during these eight crucial years and his large collection of war of independence, truce, civil war and Cumann na nGaedheal papers, he was probably the best qualified surviving participant to write about these historic times.

One of his correspondents writes "as well as being the maker you will also be the narrator of modern Irish history" [1] and Paidin O'Keeffe exclaims that the people of Ireland know that some day the truth will be written, and this can be by only one man, that is, Mulcahy, and, in seeking divine support for his opinion, he adds "God help us"! [2]. The same views were expressed by Col Gerry Ryan, the IRA leader in Tipperary [3].

Having being trained in the post office service, as part of his organisational skills he was a stickler for detail. He was also an assiduous collector of papers. His later war of independence papers, and his truce, civil war and post-civil war papers were presented to the archives of University College Dublin in the late 1960s where they form a substantial part of the University's collection of early twentieth century material [4]. His earlier war of independence papers were captured by the British in November 1920 and were later destroyed by fire during a doodlebug attack on a British army installation in London during the last world war.

The index of his papers is divided into sections and runs to 93 pages of typed A4 paper. The earlier papers dealing with strictly military matters were originally lodged in Portobello Barracks when he retired from the army after the civil war in May 1923. They were removed by him when he was preparing his submission to the army mutiny enquiry. They were never returned to the army but were carefully maintained by him at his home, Lissenfield House, until they were presented to the University in the late 1960s. They were in excellent order and fully archived in his own style, so that the task of the staff in the archives department was made substantially easier than is customary in such situations.

When he retired from politics in 1961 at the age of 75 he was a little disconsolate and unhappy to be out of the main stream of things in Fine Gael and Dail Eireann. He had retired reluctantly and partly due to family pressure. He found himself at an unaccustomed and unwelcome loose end. His dilemma was my reason for suggesting that he should consider putting his large collection of papers in order, and that he should write his autobiography or at least put on paper an account of his career in the army and in politics.

His memory of events was remarkable, as was his recall of people. No doubt in this regard he was greatly assisted by his copious collection of papers. However, during his active years in politics up to 1961, he did not concern himself with past events and constantly expressed the view that, rather than waste time and energy in recalling the past, the problems of the present were more than enough to occupy his time and his talents.

With a part-time secretary, a typewriter, and an inexhaustible supply of tapes of every size and description, he threw himself enthusiastically into the task of recording and archiving his collection of papers, and of recounting the background of his early military and political career

(2)   Annotation

His annotation on Beaslai's "*Michael Collins and the Making of a New Ireland*" was dictated in 1961 and 1962. The annotation runs to 460 pages of A4 typescript. It was done at my suggestion because I was aware of the heavily bluepencilled volumes of the Collins biography in his library and of his dissatisfaction with many of Beaslai's opinions and accounts. The index of this annotation was completed by me in 1995. Each quotation I have included is referenced by Beaslai's volume number and the annotation page number. The annotation was dictated initially on tape and subsequently transcribed by his secretary, Chriss O'Doherty. His comments have not been edited in any way, nor have any changes been made in punctuation or syntax apart from an occasional change to clarify meaning. The style and syntax is distinctly that of the spoken, not written, word but is no less readable for all that.

The annotation with its index is available in the UCD archives. The index is also on floppy disc. Dad's comments in the annotation will complement the information available on his tapes. Information from the annotation can also be sought indirectly by consulting the index of the Beaslai biography and referring to the appropriate page in the annotation, although Beaslai's index is incomplete. I have included some extracts from dad's annotation in the tape material where these extracts are relevant to the recordings.

The index of the annotation includes the names of participants, and key subjects and events. The subjects chosen are those of principal interest. There is inevitably some overlapping between some of these. Some subjects might appear to be incompletely indexed because of the use of different headings. An example is "IRA, including Volunteers". Some references to the IRA/Volunteers appear under other army headings. This may apply to other subjects as well.

The names of all participants are included, except for casual references to individuals who would be of little interest to the researcher. References to the names of people who are included are infrequently omitted when they appear in a context which is irrelevant to them or which adds no useful information about their roles. Sections of particular interest or of a comprehensive nature are included in bold type and underlined.

Dad's military career and the role of the GHQ staff were overshadowed by the publication of Beaslai's life of Collins in 1927. While he was writing the biography Beaslai never consulted Mulcahy. This was surely remarkable in view of dad's intimate association with Collins from 1917 onwards. Nor did Beaslai consult the senior members of the Irish Free State army who had been attached to GHQ and to Collins's group during the Anglo-Irish War. These included Sean McMahon and Sean O'Muirhile. Despite Beaslai's failure to consult with several important figures who worked with Collins, his book was perceived to be a history of the Anglo-Irish war and became the source material about the war for other writers and historians.

Reference to the 460 page annotation of the Collins biography bears testimony to the many errors of fact and omission which Dad perceived it contained and which could only be attributed to Beaslai's failure to adequately research his subject, at least if one is to accept his biography as a comprehensive account of the Anglo-Irish war.

A history of the Collins biographies by Beaslai and Rex Taylor has been published by Deirdre McMahon [5]. From her detailed account of the commissioning of the Beaslai biography by the government in 1923, it is clear that the work was undertaken in the midst of considerable controversy. If it had not been for the encouragement and support of the Collins' family, it is unlikely that the biography would ever have been written. The biography was written by Beaslai between 1923 and 1925, and published in 1926.

The biography's limitations as a history of the war is clear in that it was largely devoted to Collins military and political contributions, and made only casual reference to other members of the GHQ staff, and the considerable routine work of the staff during the War. Beaslai fails to mention the formal setting up of the GHQ staff at the time of the conscription threat in March 1918. It might be construed from his account (and of course from the Jordan film of 1996) that, from October 1917 to the end of the war in July 1921, Collins was the prime influence in organising the army leading the resistance to the British. GHQ is not included in the index of the book, although some of the members are, but then generally in the context of the Collins role.

The Beaslai biography was influential in leading to certain misconceptions about the war of independence, such as the chief of staff position, where my father is described as the assistant chief of staff and Brugha as the chief of staff. On the occasion of the 75th anniversary of the first meeting of Dail Eireann in 1974, a government publication describes Cathal Brugha as chief of staff, confirming the error contained in Beaslai's book, and Mr Albert Reynolds in 1994, in his address on the same occasion, stated that Michael Collins and Cathal Brugha directed the war of independence. Brugha was never chief of staff nor did he ever attend staff meetings.

Apart from the tape recordings, perhaps dad's single most important contribution was to dictate this annotation. It is a valuable critique of the

Beaslai biography and goes a long way to amplify the Collins story, as well as qualifying or even contradicting many aspects of Beaslai's account. He is highly critical of Beaslai's account of the war of independence, not only because of his many errors of fact, but also because he maintained that Beaslai's experience was confined to the Collins intelligence group, the Squad and the Vaughan's Hotel area. He goes on to say:

> If this work of Beaslai's were carefully examined to see what particular parts of the country he deals with, it would be found that he had little general picture of the country as a whole. To some extent, or perhaps to a large extent, this restriction in outlook is related to his rather concentrated connection with the Vaughan's Hotel citadel and .... [6]

> Except for the fact that we probably will find in the Murthuile papers, that some of those people who congregated at Vaughan's Hotel or at Devlins had their minds working rather in an IRB enclosure of a very limited and personal group kind, and didn't see the work of those outside that group. [7]

Dad refused to review the biography when invited to do so by the publishers in 1926, as did my mother. His reasons for doing so were clear. He did not wish to rekindle any fresh controversy after the bitterness of the civil war and the subsequent mutiny, and he was consistent in avoiding any public reference to the personalities involved in the struggle and to the many conflicts which arose. He stated that a comprehensive commentary by him would not be much shorter than the biography itself. He also refused to review the second abridged edition which was published in 1937.

> One of my deficiencies may be that I find it easier to do things with a shut mouth, and that it would be very difficult even with a natural or developed sense of publicity, to note what things ought to be publicised in the days of '22, '23 and '24. [8]

Beaslai was one of the thirteen members of the GHQ staff portrayed in the painting by Leo Whelan now hanging in McKee Barracks. He had no military function during the war of independence but was the editor of the clandestine paper of the army, *An tÓglach*. Despite dad's criticism of Beaslai's biography and his views about the author's limited knowledge of the work of the Volunteers during the war of independence, it was quite characteristic of dad's loyalty to his colleagues in the army that he gave the homily at Beaslai's graveside and paid him a most gracious tribute for his sterling work as editor of *An tÓglach*.

(3) The Tapes

Another document I completed lists the tapes which he recorded between 1961 and 1970. I have summarised the contents of each tape, and, for the convenience of research students and others, I have included many names of persons and events as key words. A summary of the tape contents is stored on a floppy disc and is available in the University archives. The information contained on the disc can be retrieved by punching in the key words. If anything, the Beaslai annotation is a more comprehensive source of his recollections and opinions than the tapes although the tapes are of particular interest because of his interviews with my mother, myself, a number of historians and media correspondents, and with a few of his contemporaries who lived through the revolutionary period. I have added a number of my own observations at various stages in the summary of the tapes which were relevant to his interviews.

When I began medical practice as a physician in Dublin in October 1950, I started using a tape recorder to dictate letters and papers which were then transcribed by my secretary. I would dictate directly on to tape, although conceptualising and dictating at the same time required some experience and practice. I was almost a pioneer in using a tape recorder, at least among my colleagues in the medical profession, and indeed many of my colleagues continued to dictate directly to their secretaries for decades after that time.

My interest in using tape recorders must have been derived, at least to some extent, from my father's long interest in this means of communication. His interest in the early years started in 1925 when he attended the Inter-Parliamentary Union Meeting in New York, and first saw the dictaphone there. He refers to this visit on tape [9-11]. He had a machine imported for his own use and he proceeded to record documents and speeches, and had some contact with Delargy of the Folklore Commission I have a photograph of a group using the dictaphone to collect songs and stories from a *seanachaoidhe* in the Aran Islands. He also recorded songs and stories for *An Fear Mór* at Ring College in Co Waterford. In the late 1930s he was using a wire recorder which had been manufactured in Chicago. There is a reference to his first contact with a recording machine, a phonograph in the possession of Father O'Flynn in Ballingeary, which was a primitive forerunner of the modern dictaphone [12].

According to the dates of the various tapes, they were recorded between 1963-1970. However, Dad was using a tape recorder as early as 1961 but he probably did not start recording conversations until after he had dictated the annotation about the Beaslai biography, which he did in 1961 and 1962. He also did some earlier recordings but, like the annotation recordings, these may have been obliterated after they were transcribed by his secretary, Chriss O'Doherty. These transcriptions are available in the University archives.

The tapes which were recorded in the earlier years contain the most important material because the most important areas of discussion were dealt with then. In the earlier stages too Dad still retained the sharpness of mind and the occasional terse sentence which were typical attributes of his during his more active years.

In the later tapes, during his last years, his speech and his thought reactions are slower, his speech is more hesitant and inclined to slurring, and he becomes preoccupied by certain themes about which he becomes repetitious and almost obsessional. By this time he was almost blind and was showing early signs of intellectual deterioration as part of the ageing process. The themes which preoccupied him include, among others, Dev's perceived failure of leadership during the war of independence, the shortcomings of the Fianna Fail regime, the shortcomings of the historians who wrote about the 1916-1924 period, and his sensitivity to criticism of Collins and Griffith. While Dad might occasionally in his earlier years be encouraged by visitors to talk about some of his exploits during the war of independence, particularly his numerous escapes from the British Forces while he was on the run, he had little inclination to talk about the recent past in Ireland, at least until I became his confidante after his retirement. His reluctance to talk about the past is well summed up in the letter he wrote to the publishers of Beaslai's biography of Collins when he, and later my mother refused to review the publication. A remark made by him more than once was "Haven't we enough to do with the country in the state it is without the futility of going back over the past!"

Dad expressed strong and trenchant views about historians in general and Desmond Williams in particular [13,14]. His views of the shortcomings of historians are scattered about in several places in the later tapes, and were based on the historians' interpretation of certain aspects of the history of the War of Independence and its aftermath which conflicted with his own experience and opinions. His criticism of Williams was largely based, I believe, on the latter's view, expressed in a Thomas Davis lecture at the time of the fiftieth anniversary of the civil war, that de Valera and Collins were equally responsible for the civil war. There is little doubt that Williams had a point in implicating Collins but this view grated on dad's sensitivity about Collins and his apparent view that Collins could do no wrong.

During the recordings Dad showed himself to be a good listener, to have the patience of Job and to have a terrier-like persistence when seeking the information he desired. He also maintained his sense of humour. Of all the speakers on the tapes, he is probably the most articulate, if one allows for his circumlocutions and fondness for metaphor. The best tapes are those which were recorded in the early sixties and those which were recorded by Dad on his own, or in conversation with myself, Prof Kevin Nowlan and a few others who spoke as clearly as he and who were as articulate as he was. His own delivery is excellent, particularly during his earlier recordings.

Because Dad recorded a great number of interviews with many different people, it is inevitable that there is a considerable amount of repetition, particularly when he is describing his own participation in the events of the time.

The tapes were a miscellaneous lot of different sizes and manufacture. Because of the difficulties of having them duplicated on better quality tape in Ireland, they were brought to the United States by Maryann Valiulis where two copies were made. Shortly after they were duplicated, the original tapes, with the indexes prepared by Dad, were accidentally destroyed. The two duplicate sets were returned to me in 1992 about the time of the publication of dad's biography. In 1993 I started to prepare a summary of their contents and I completed an index of their key words. I transferred a summary of the contents of the tapes and the important key words on to the the word processor, so that information can be easily accessed. I added further material about my father and the revolutionary period as I was going through the tapes. Most of this added material was derived from his annotation of Beaslai's biography of Collins. In such cases the appropriate page of the annotation is referenced. Many of the tapes have been transcribed and the transcriptions will be found in the university archives, particularly in that section marked P7b/176-200. Reference to the tapes in the text of the memoir shows the tape number and side.

The tapes' quality of reproduction is mixed. Relatively few are sufficiently well recorded to be suitable for direct transmission by radio, although excerpts, suitably edited, would be satisfactory for this purpose. There are substantial problems created by the absence of information about the identity of some of the people interviewed by Dad, a problem compounded by the loss of the original tapes and his detailed index. There is also the problem of the poor delivery of some of the interviewees, and the unstructured arrangements when three or more people are taking part in a conversation. In the latter case, the conversations are difficult or impossible to interpret because of repeated interruptions or when two or more participants speak at the same time. During some conversations the speakers may be badly seated in relation to the microphone, and are therefore difficult to understand. Unfortunately, because I did not listen to the tapes when they were initially recorded, it did not occur to me at the time to supervise their production.

There are a few points to be made about the tapes and their arrangements. Because the original tapes were destroyed, and because the material was transferred on to new tapes, continuity of material has to some extent been lost. There are 178 tapes included in the series I have archived which, because of initial confusion on my part, are not in proper sequence. To add to the problem, nos 74-98 are duplicates and were inadvertently included, although they belong to the second set which is still in good sequence. One, no 178, was not part of the original set but was recorded independently by my sister-in-law, Rosemarie Mulcahy, who interviewed my mother at a relatively late stage in her life.

The use of key words will allow the student to find the various subjects which are included, even if the material is scattered about in different tapes. In some cases I have listed the tapes dealing with certain specific subjects. It would simplify the use of the tapes if the second set were archived and tape nos 74-98 in the first set were included. It took me the best part of two years to archive the first set of tapes so that my reluctance to archive the second set can be easily understood.

The names of some of those who have been interviewed are not always mentioned nor is the source of some documents identified. Because of the considerable amount of work involved in the preparation of the tape abstracts, and of the tedium of the work, some details of value may have been omitted. Also, because of my lack of experience of this type of archiving, I have not adopted a very satisfactory methodology. For example, all the names of people mentioned have not been included in the key words. I have only done so sporadically but I believe none of the more important people have been omitted.

I have where possible provided information about the dates when the recordings were made. This is important, if only because Dad became unduly prolix, repetitive, and sometimes slightly irrelevant in his last few years when he was approaching the mid-eighties and when his intellectual capacity and his judgement may have begun to deteriorate.

I was probably straying from my original purpose by including material from dad's annotation and other sources with the tape abstracts, and also by including my own comments from time to time. This additional material may distract the research worker, but it may add some interest to the 147 page document.

The initials RM throughout the text refer to me. When referring to my father I have used Mulcahy, my father, or Dad, using the more familiar term when discussing matters of a more personal nature. I have used R when quoting conversations with him.

References

The references are numbered and recorded at the end of the text for each chapter.

Tape references: e.g. 48B = tape number and side.

Annotation references: e.g. v1 26 = volume number of Collins biography and page number of annotation.

References to Mulcahy papers: e.g. P7b/182.

References to cabinet papers, 1919-1922 & 1948-1952 e.g. CPs 9/1/21.

The tapes, annotation and Mulcahy papers are available in the archives of University College, Dublin. The cabinet papers are available in the National Archives.

Comments within the text in square brackets "[ ]" are the author's.

Introduction

1   Maryann G. Valiulis. *Portrait of a Revolutionary: General Richard Mulcahy and the Founding of the Irish Free State.* Irish Academic Press, Dublin, 1992.

2   Maryann G. Valiulis. *Almost a Rebellion: The Irish Army Mutiny of 1924.* Tower Books, Cork, 1985.

3   Terence de Vere White. *Kevin O'Higgins.* Methuen, London, 1948.

4   137A

5   Piaras Beaslai. *Michael Collins and the Making of a new Ireland.* Phoenix, Dublin, 1926.

Chapter 1 - Background and Family

1   Pb7/12. *Sister Miriam Teresa Bulletin,* v15, 3/10/1960.
2   P7b/10
3   35A
4   35B
5   41B
6   72A
7   73A
8   73B
9   75A
10 75B
11 76A
12 143A
13 143B
14 144A

Chapter 2 - A Summary of his Career.

1   88A
2   3B
    71B
4   72A
5   85B
6   88A
7   143A
8   143B
9   72B
10 144A
11 114B
12 93A
13 P7a&b.182.
14 7A
15 160B
16 P7b/182, pp27-46.

Chapter 3 - Richard Mulcahy's Opinions and Writings about the Period 1916-1924.

3.1 The Rising, Knutsford and Frongoch

1   V1 8
2   71A
3   Joseph Lawless, *The Capuchin Annual*, 1966, p309.
4   Joseph Lawless, *An t'Óglach*, July,1926, p4.
5   V1 15 *(The Constabulary Gazette)*
6   10B lists full recordings.
7   *An t'Óglach*, April 1961.
8   V1 25
9   170A
10   Michael Tierney, *Eoin MacNeill, Scholar and Man of Action, 1867-1945.* Ed. FX Martin, Clarendon Press, Oxford, 1980, p266.
11   139B
12   92A
13   V1 20
14   V1 16
15   140A
16   116B
17   117A
18   V1 1-8A
19   V1 1-6B

3.2 Return from Frongoch and Army Leadership

1   32A
2   69B
3   4A includes details of GHQ staff members.
4   V1 95-100
5   6A
6   6B
7   77A
8   44A includes reference to O'Muirthile's memoirs.
9   V2 15-16 includes O'Muirthile's memoirs
10   41B

11 V2 41
12 26A
13 81A
14 82A
15 82B
16 V1 95-100
17 V1 126
18 V1 48,49
19 V1 51
20 V2 173
21 *An Cosantóir*, v 40, 1980 pp 35-39;67-71;99-102.
22 70A
23 80A
24 107B
25 121A
26 128B
27 C.C. Trench, *Irish Independent*, 8/8/1992
28 V2 89,103,117
29 V2 43
30 V2 32

3.3 The War of Independence : Army Policy

1   137A
2   P.S. O'Hegarty, *The Victory of Sinn Fein*, The Talbot Press, Dublin 1924, p 166
3   7B
4   80A
5   V1 130
6   V1 69
7   127B
8   V1 29
9   42A
10   42B
11   53A
12   63A
13   63B
14   68B

15 69B

16 127B

17 154A

18 Michael Collins, *The Path to Freedom,* Talbot Press, Dublin, 1922, p61.

19 7A

20 152B

21 V1 33

22 V1 30

23 V1 102

24 V2 36,80

25 48B

26 P7a/196

27 Desmond Ryan. *Sean Treacy and the Third Tipperary Brigade*, Kerryman, Tralee, 1925.

28 V1 89

29 V1 103,104

30 V1 123

31 V2 36,37

32 V2 161

33 91A

34 97A

35 V1 92

36 David Fitzpatrick, *Politics and Irish Life, 1913-1921, Provincial Experience of War and Revolution,* Gill and Macmillan, Dublin, 1993, p93.

37 ibid p206

38 ibid p208

39 i68B

40 76A

41 23A

42 V2 96

43 V2 288

44 CPs 10/6/1920

45 158B

46 V1 32

47 P7v/182

48 P.S. O'Hegarty's. *The Victory of Sinn Fein*, The Talbot Press, Dublin 1924.

49 Ibid p171

50 128A
51 140B
52 32A
53 3A
54 26A
55 26B
56 69A
57 88B
58 89A
59 V1 24.

3.4 The First Dail and Sinn Fein

1   V1 61
2   120A
3   120B
4   53A
5   15B
6   93B
7   V1 85,86
8   135A
9   91A
10   148B
11   149B
12   Michael Laffan, *The resurrection of Ireland : The Sinn Fein Party 1916-1923.* Cambridge University Press, in press.
13   92B
14   93A
15   140B
16   V2 133
17   54B
18   64A
19   66A
20   134B
21   CPs 15/9/21
22   Cps 29/9/21
24   CPs 25/7/21; 4/8/21
25   CPs 27/8/21; 9/9/21

26 67A

27 P.S. O'Hegarty. *The Victory of Sinn Fein.* Talbot Press, Dublin, 1924, p51.

28 54A

29 CPs 24/1/1922

30 V2 28

31 70A

32 122A

33 128B

34 141A

35 157B

36 158A

37 76B

3.5   The Truce

1   92A

2   128A

3   134B

4   118A

5   122A

6   158A

7   158B

8   P7a/5

9   6A

10 CPs 24/11/21

11 16B

12 17A

13 139A

14 P7b/182

15 CPs 29/9/21

16 V2 166

17 V2 165

18 157A

19 V2 254

20 32A

Chapter 4 - Richard Mulcahy Writes about Military and Political Colleagues, and refers to the Genesis of the Civil War.

4.1 Michael Collins

1   V2 256
2   70B
3   51A
4   86B
5   66A
6   65A
7   52B
8   55A
9   154A
1 0   154B
1 1   118B
1 2   V1 35
1 3   111B
1 4   V2 113
1 5   V1 94
1 6   V2 73
1 7   27A
1 8   V1 7
1 9   V2 164
2 0   V1 118
2 1   V2 45
2 2   V1 33
2 3   V2 80
2 4   36B
2 5   V1 134
2 6   V1 135
2 7   V1 136
2 8   V1 38
2 9   V2 36-37
3 0   V1 39
3 1   V1 43
3 2   V2 20
3 3   V2 175

34 67A

35 V1 95

36 V2 239

37 V1 117

38 V2 176

39 V2 147

40 V2 174

41 V2 162

42 V2 72

43 V2 159

44 134B

45 135B

46 160A

47 137A

49 John Regan, *Looking at Mick again : Demilitarising Michael Collins.* History Ireland, v3, no3, pp17-22

50 Padraic Colum, *Arthur Griffith*, Browne and Nolan, Dublin, 1959 p179

51 Ibid, p215

52 4B

53 65B

54 134A

55 134B

56 135A

57 63B

58 66B

59 V1 21

60 26A

61 61B

62 P7b/189. pp51-54

63 Calton Younger, *Ireland's Civil War*, Muller, London, 1968, p435.

64 Piaras Beaslai, *Michael Collins and the Making of a New Ireland*, Phoenix, Dublin, 1926, p437

65 Ulick O'Connor, *Oliver St. Gogarty*, Mandarin, London, 1990, p190

66 109A

67 *An t'Óglach*, Winter, 1967

68 P7a/178

69 156A

70 P7a/196

4.2 Arthur Griffith

1 V2 108
2 59B
3 94B
4 Padraic Colum, *Arthur Griffith*. Browne and Nolan, Dublin, 1959, p53 57A
6 V2 159
7 66A
8 91A
9 91B
10 134A
11 V2 159
12 M.J.McManus, *Eamon de Valera*, Talbot Press, Dublin, 1944, p161
13 Beaverbrook, *The Decline and Fall of Lloyd George*, Collins, London, 1963, pp82-123.
14 V2 163
15 V2 164
16 V2 147
17 V1 108
18 V2 6
19 Oliver St. John Gogarty, *Arthur Griffith and Michael Collins Memorial Issue*, Martin Lester, Dublin 1924, p54
20 V2 96
21 7A
22 66B
23 V1 82
24 122B

4.3 Eamon de Valera

1 156B
2 V2 4
3 158B
4 127B

5   V2 108
6   V2 124
7   V2 139
8   John Murphy. *Sunday Independent*, 17/8/1992
9   Maryann G. Valiulis, *After The revolution: The Formative Years of Cumann na nGaedheal.* personal communication
10 V1 49
11 122A
12 158B
13 136B
14 53B
15 118A
16 118B
17 121B
18 7B
19 V2 171-2
20 V2 173
21 Reference not found but probably in report of the private session of the Dail on the 26/8/1921
22 92B
23 Dorothy Macardle, *The Irish Republic.* Gollancz, London, 1937, p548
24 V2 200
25 Piaras Beaslai, *Micheal Collins and the Making of a New Ireland*, Phoenix, Dublin, 1926
26 V2 130
27 V2 143
28 CPs 8/12/21
29 V2 190-1
30 V2 138
31 V2 1
32 V2 3
33 V2 6
34 V2 67
35 V2 74
36 V2 109
37 134B
38 66A
39 V2 6-8
40 Michael Collins, *The Path to Freedom.* Talbot Press, Dublin, 1922, p33

4 1 CPs 30/11/20

4 2 CPs 13/12/1920

4 3 V1 129

4 4 V2 97

4 5 V2 103

4.4 Cathal Brugha

1   32A

2   66B

3   29A

4   139A

5   139B

6   140A

7   144A

8   62A

9   69A

1 0 V1 132-3

1 1 V1 94

1 2 69B

1 3 V2 41

1 4 76B

1 5 61B

1 6 66A

1 7 63B

1 8 33A

1 9 111B

2 0 V1 77

2 1 V2 56-7

2 2 V2 7

2 3 V122

2 4 166A

2 5 61A

2 6 112A

2 7 158B

4.5 Dick McKee, Liam Lynch and others.

1   V2 85
2   V2 87
3   Ernie O'Malley. *On Another Man's Wound*, Rich and Cowan. London, 1936
4   162A
5   V1 44
6   42A
7   42B
8   V2 81
9   V2 233
10 V2 123
11 V2 128
12 23A

Chapter 5 - Further Factors in Genesis of Civil War.

1   V2 220
2   V2 248
3   V2 250
4   91B
5   V2 244-6
6   46A
7   112A
8   112B
9   113A
10 Tom Garvin.1992, *The Birth of Irish Democracy*. Gill and Macmillan, Dublin, 1996.
11 61A
12 23b
13 141A
14 J.J. Lee. *Ireland 1912-1985 : Politics and Society*. Cambridge University press, Cambridge 1989 .
15 116A
16 33A
17 57B
18 63A

19 Michael Tierney. *Eoin MacNeill, Scholar and Man of Action, 1867-1945.* Ed. FX Martin, Clarendon Press, Oxford, 1980, p266

20 53A

21 93B

22 V1 61

23 161B

24 Tom Garvin, *The Anatomy of a Nationalistic Revolution: Ireland 1858-1928.* Comparative   Studies in Society and History. v28, Cambridge University Press, 1986

25 151B

26 167B

27 *Irish Independent*, 9/12/21

28 92B

29 V2 252-81

30 118A

31 39A&B;40A&B

32 40A

33 P.S. O'Hegarty. *The Victory of Sinn Fein*, The Talbot Press, Dublin 1924, pp54-58.

34 16A

35 16B

36 57A

37 88A

Chapter 6 - Post-Treaty and the Army Mutiny

1   94A

2   94B

3   77A

4   108A

5   109A

6   161B

7   P7b/182. See: John F. Larchet, *The Army School of Music.* Corrigan and Wilson, Dublin, 1923.

8   10B

9   88a

10   160A

11   160B

12 P7a/201

13 *The Kilkenny People*, 6/10/1923, quoting an article from *Collier's Magazine.*

14 141A

15 P7a/196

16 138A

17 138B

18 163A

19 163B

20 Pb7/182/27-46

21 136B

22 137B

23 12f7B

24 20A

25 48A

26 97B

27 98A

28 106A

29 106B

30 Terence de Vere White, *Business and Finance*, 7/7/1967,pp28-9

31 48B

32 1A

33 159B

34 Terence de Vere White. *Kevin O'Higgins*. Methuen, London, 1948.

35 61A

36 164A

37 27A

38 Maryann G. Valiulis. *Almost a Rebellion : The Irish Army Mutiny of 1924*, Tower Books, Cork, 1985..

39 136A

40 46A

41 V1 46

42 88B

43 89A

44 P7/D/3

45 137A

46 Michael Tierney. *Eoin MacNeill, Scholar and Man of Action, 1867-1945*. Ed. FX Martin, Clarendon Press, Oxford, 1980, p266.

Chapter 7 - The Years 1924-1932

7.1 Political Wilderness

1 P7B/12
2 25B
3 106A
4 110A
5 110B
6 111A
7 138A
8 160A
9 160B
10 20A
11 P7B/35-50
12 137A
13 137B
14 P7b/182/27-46
15 25B
16 *Irish Times*, 11/5/86.
17 *The Sunday Press*, 11/5/1986
18 P7b/62-89
19 21A
20 P7b/23
21 P7b/87

7.2 Cumann Na nGaedheal

1 Maryann G. Valiulis, *After The revolution: The formative Years o;f Cumann na nGaedheal.* (Personal communication)
2 138A
3 138B
4 67A
5 160
6 Michael Tierney. *Eoin MacNeill, Scholar and Man of Action, 1867-1945.* Ed. FX Martin, Clarendon Press, Oxford, 1980, p355
7 82B
8 P7/C/99

7.3 The Irish Language

1   160B
2   Michael Tierney, *Studies*, March 1925.
3   Richard Mulcahy, *Studies*, March 1925.
4   CPs 9/1/21
5   CPs 20/2/20
6   111A
7   138B
8   25B
9   John Coolahan, *Irish Education : its History and Structure*. IPA, Dublin, 1981, p45
10 ibid p81
11 *Claidheamh Soluis*, November 29, 1902, quoted by Michael Tierney in his biography of Eoin MacNeill, p85

Chapter 8 - 1932 and After: Opposition and Inter-Party Government.

1   29B
2   12A
3   6A
4   Mike Cronin. *The Blue Shirts and Irish Politics*, FCP, Dublin, 1997. p195
5   163A
6   137B
8   Prof John Murphy, *Sunday Independent*, 17/8/1992
9   57B
10 58A
11 58B
12 25B
13 44A
14 CPs 11/10/48
15 CPs 19/8/48
16 Patrick Lynch, personal communication
17 CPs 9/11/48
18 CPs 12/11/48/
19 CPs 14/11/48
20 CPs 7/1/49

2 1 CPs 3/5/49
2 2 160B
2 3 96A
2 4 Patrick Lynch, personal communication
2 5 CPs 4/11/49
2 6 CPs 14/11/50
2 7 CPs 6/4/51
2 8 Brian Maye's *Fine Gael - 1923-1987*, Blackwater Press, Dublin, 1993
2 9 151A
3 0 David McCullagh. *A Makeshift Majority*. IPA Press, Dublin, 1998.

Chapter 9 - Later Years and Last Days

1 5B
2 Piaras Beaslai, *Micheal Collins and the Making of a New Ireland*, Phoenix, Dublin, 1926
3 Michael Tierney. *Eoin MacNeill, Scholar and Man of Action, 1867-1945*. Ed. FX Martin, Clarendon Press, Oxford, 1980, Chap 5, *Year of Ferment*.
4 P7a/196
5 Sinead McCoole. *Hazel - A Life of Lady Lavery, 1880-1935*, Lilliput Press, Dublin, 1996, p151.
6 Padraic Colum, *Arthur Griffith*. Browne and Nolan, Dublin, 1959 p 269
7 *Free State or Republic?* by Padraic de Burca and John F Boyle. Dublin:
8 P7b/27
9 159A
1 0 55B
1 1 55A&B;56A&B
1 2 P7b/17/13 ????
1 3 P7b/17/15
1 4 P7a/201
1 5 P7b/17/6
1 6 John Murphy, *Sunday Independent*, 17/8/1992.

Chapter 10 - Min and Ryan Family.

1 22A
2 22B

3 83B

4 484A

5 Charles J. Travers. *Sean MacDiarmuida*, Breifne, Cumann Seanchais Breifne, 1966

6 Ryan, Mary Josephine. *The Irish Rebellion of 1916 and its Martyrs.* Ed: Maurice Joy. Devlin-Adair, New York, p378

7 P7b/182

8 84B

9 78A&B

10 113A

11 112A

12 112B

13 109B

14 Proinsias O Concuain. *Scéal a Bheatha a Insint ag Seán T. O'Ceallaigh*, O'Gormain, Teo. Gaillimh, 1963

15 Richard P. Davis. *Arthur Griffith and Non-Violent Sinn Fein.* Anvil Books, Dublin, 1974, pp24-28

16 66B

17 116A

Chapter 11 - The Family at Lissenfield

1 48a

2 76A

3 *Familiar Medical Quotations.* M.B.Strauss (ed), Little Brown, 1968, p410.

4 John Murphy, *Sunday Independent.* 17/8/1992.

Appendix 3 - The Biography.

1 Maryann G. Valiulis, *Portrait of a Revolutionary - General Richard Mulcahy and the Founding of the Irish Free State.* Irish Academic Press, Dublin, 1992.

2 Maryann G. Valiulis, *Almost a Rebellion - the Irish Army Mutiny of 1924.* Tower Books, Cork, 1985.

3   Forbes M., *Beattie and his friends.* Altrincham: Martin Stafford,1990: p128, first published in 1904.

4   157A&B

5   V2 114

6   9 A

Appendix 4 - The Mulcahy Papers, Annotation and Tapes.

1   174A

2   176B

3   90B

4   149B

5   Deirdre McMahon, *Michael Collins and his Biographers: Piaras Beaslai and Rex Taylor.* Bullan, v2, no2, Oxford, 1996, pp55-66.

6   V2 81

7   V2 35

8   V1 46

9   12A

1 0   95B

1 1   160B

1 2   75A

1 3   4 A

1 4   V2 262

INDEX

A

Adams, Gerry, 257
Adye Curran family, 303
Aherne, Dr Leo, 115
Aiken, Frank, 120–1, 172
Aknefton, 237–8
alcohol consumption, 346–8
Alexander, Lord, 249
American Association for the Recognition of the Irish Republic (AARIR), 146
An tOglach, 46–7
an tSagairt, Siobhan, 17–18, 32, 164
Anglo-Irish Treaty, 1921, 22, 45, 92
    debates, 61–2, 118–20, 124, 189–90
    influence of women, 181–3
    negotiations, 94, 105, 124, 125–8, 138–43
    opposition to, 100, 136–7, 143–4, 154, 160–1, 167–75
    political failure, 180–1
    ratified, 179
    rejection of, 112–13
    RM's views on, 176–8
Archer, Liam, 182
archives, 367–76
arms decommissioning, 151, 183–4
Army Comrades Association, 235–6
Army Council, 47–8, 262
Army Mutiny, 22, 74, 110, 188, 191–3, 197–205, 219–20, 222, 262, 271
    enquiry, 209
Army School of Music, 185, 187–8, 198, 318
Ashbourne, Co. Meath, 21, 26–7, 111, 118
    monument, 261
Ashe, Thomas, 21, 34, 43, 58, 102, 118, 132
RM homily, 357–60
Auxiliaries, 60, 65, 162, 296

B

Bacon, Tommy, 342
Ballingeary, Co. Cork, 17, 32, 43, 224
Ballykinlar Camp, 29

Ballyvourney, Co. Cork, 43
Bantry, Co. Cork, 17–18
Barrett, Donal, 20
Barrett, Josephine, 14
Barrett, Richard, 194
Barrett, Stephen, 240
Barry, Tom, 91
Barton, Robert, 77, 88, 137
Beaslai, Piaras, 28, 44, 81, 104, 156, 158
  Collins biography, 161
    RM's annotations of, 23, 52–3, 141–2, 145–9, 263, 368–72
  Collins's death, 114–15
  on Frongoch, 38, 41–2
  and RM, 46, 47
  RM homily, 118, 357–60
  on Treaty, 106
Belfast, 153, 345
  boycott, 81–3
Berney, Gerard, 342
Black and Tans, 60, 65, 296
Blasket Islands, 329
Bloody Sunday, 1920, 46, 159, 163
Blueshirts, 235–6, 237
Blythe, Ernest, 178, 214, 223, 224, 225, 230, 266
Boilbester, Mr, 266, 267
Boland, Harry, 47, 75, 76, 104, 112, 113, 178
Bolands Mills, 28–9
Bolton Street technical college, 19
Bord Pleanala, An, 305
Boundary Commission, 204, 209, 220, 222
Brase, Fritz, 115, 187–8, 198
Breen, Dan, 62, 64, 167
Brennan, Michael, 182
Brennan-Whitmore, W.J., 39
Bridge, 295–6
British Army, 13, 20, 65, 87–8, 90
Brown, Fr Paddy, 298
Browne, Dick, 32
Browne, Noel, 248, 252–6

Broy, Ned, 104
Brugha, Cathal, 27, 132, 149, 150, 165
  assassination plan, 155-6, 160
  and Collins, 84-5, 97-100, 106-7, 113-14, 156-7, 173-4
  on executive, 43
  and IRB, 74
  minister for defence, 22, 50-1, 52, 58-9, 69, 79-81, 83
  and RM, 66-7, 70-1, 88-91, 173, 174, 199
  RM on, 153-61
  sacks RM, 84
  and Soloheadbeg ambush, 60, 64
  and Treaty, 127, 137, 181
Brugha, Rory, 153
Burke, Denis, 223
Burke, Liam, 221, 223
by-elections, 240, 251-2
Byrne, Alfie, 234

C
Carrigtwohill barracks, 61
Casement, Roger, 29, 98
Catholic Boy Scouts, 319-22
Catholic University, 6
Central Statistics Office, 256
Childers, Erskine, 81, 89, 133, 143, 149, 165-6, 168, 171-2
  execution, 194-6
Christian Brothers, 5, 9, 12, 225
Cistercian Order, 14-15
Civil Service Appointments Commission, 216-17
Civil War, 14, 22, 45, 90, 94, 99-100, 110, 112, 121, 129, 132-3, 154, 159-62, 195, 285-6
  Cabinet confined, 193
  effects of, 227-8
  executions, 137, 194-7
  influence of women, 181-3
  Lynch, 164-6
  political failure, 180-1
  preliminaries to, 185-91
  reasons for, 167-84

responsibility for, 112, 134–8
RM's role, 263, 265–6, 271
Clann na Gaedheal, 145–6
Clann na Poblachta, 240, 254
Clann na Talmhan, 258–9
Clare, County, 62, 160
Clarke, Tom, 28, 275, 277, 288
Clery, Rita, 325, 326
Clery family, 324–30
Clonskeagh Fever Hospital, 335
Clune, Archbishop, 83, 149, 151, 152, 153, 176
Coffey, Diarmuid, 196
Colaiste Mhuire, 225
Colivet, 28
Colliers Magazine, 189
Collins, Michael, 49, 54, 62, 94, 132, 162, 164, 202, 209, 215, 237, 238, 262, 297, 303. see also under Beaslai, Piaras
administrative ability, 100–2
army split, 136
Belfast boycott, 81–2
Bloody Sunday, 159
and Brugha, 85–8, 106–7, 113–14, 156–8, 173–4
and Civil War, 112–13, 180
Custom House fire, 68
and de Valera, 104, 107–9, 133, 138–9, 143, 147–8, 149, 150
death of, 22, 112, 114–18, 129, 175, 191
first Dail, 178
Frongoch, 38–9, 42–3, 44
funeral of, 186
and Griffith, 103–4, 105
Griffith funeral, 119
horseplay, 102–3
intelligence director, 45, 46–8, 95, 104
and IRB, 74–5, 114
Nichevo on, 118–20
Phyllis Ryan on, 293
post-Treaty, 185–91
and RM, 56, 60, 69, 81, 93–122, 128, 243, 244, 271
RM homily, 351–5

and Stack, 85–8, 106–7, 113–14
and Treaty, 106–7, 136, 137, 181, 183
Truce, 84–5, 91, 152, 153
Collins, Sean, 243
Collins Barracks, 190
Collins-de Valera Pact, 105
Colum, Padraic, 111, 124, 128–9, 130, 267, 288, 315
Commission of Defence, 89
Commonwealth, 178
Compton-Smith, Major, 61–2
conscription, 58–9
Constitution, 1922, 193
Coogan, T.P., 348
Coolahan, Dr John, 229
Coolidge, President, 211
Coosan Camp, Athlone, 20
Cork, Bishop of, 217
Cork, County, 43, 162, 163–4, 167, 169, 179, 180, 224
Cork city, 27, 28, 40, 61
Cork Street Fever Hospital, 335
Corry, Eoghan, 233–4
Cosgrave, Liam, 240–1, 258, 259
Cosgrave, Mrs, 203
Cosgrave, W.T., 22, 23, 137–8, 178, 187, 198–9, 203, 212, 219, 235–6,
    241, 271
    executions, 195–6
    losing support, 223
    party organisation, 221–2
    refuses RM appointment, 211–12
    retirement, 216
Costello, John A., 111, 229, 237–8, 243, 257, 271, 343, 344
    declaration of republic, 246–50
    Mother and Child Scheme, 255–6
    political career of, 250–2
    Taoiseach, 239, 243, 244–5, 258–9
Costello, General Michael, 182
Coughlan, Sean, 321
Coyle, Eoin, 270
Craig, Sir James, 82, 109, 149, 174

Craig, Maurice, 305

Cregan, Mairin, 291

Cremin, Dr Bill, 334, 336

Cremin family, 11

Cronin, Mike, 236–7

Cumann na mBan, 172, 181, 277, 278, 283, 293

Cumann na nGaedheal, 22–3, 135, 138, 178, 193, 210, 271, 288
  effects of Army Mutiny, 204
  election, 1927, 212–13
  and Irish language, 228
  in opposition, 233–42
  successes and failures, 218–23

Curragh Camp, 175, 192

Cusack, John, 270

Custom House, 67–8

D

Dail Eireann, 22, 51–4, 62–4, 78, 104, 112, 131
  Custom House attack, 67
  FF enters, 219
  first cabinet, 146
  members of, 178–9
  RM backbencher, 209–11, 214–16
  support of de Valera, 133–4
  suppressed, 58–9, 61, 83
  Treaty debates, 118–20, 137
  War of Independence, 75–8

Dalton, Emmet, 44, 46, 114–15, 202

Davis, Richard P., 288

de Valera, Eamon, 19, 22, 83, 131, 205, 244, 257, 291, 298
  and Army split, 92, 136–7
  attack on RM, 236–7
  on Brugha, 97
  Civil War, 112, 134–8, 160, 165–6, 168–9, 173–4, 194, 202–3, 261
  and Collins, 96, 107–9
  Custom House attack, 66–8
  declaration of republic, 249
  Easter Rising, 28–9
  Fianna Fail, 188

and Griffith, 125–8
and IRB, 114
Lincoln escape, 73, 75, 77
and Lloyd George, 133, 140
personality, 56
PR abolition, 240
president, SF, 43, 51, 77
reaction to Treaty, 84, 100, 136–8, 143–4, 173, 175, 179–81
RM's funeral, 270
RM's views of, 131–53, 215, 261
Second World War, 238–9
and Sinn Fein, 79–81
straitjacket of republic, 175–80
Treaty negotiations, 106, 126–7, 138–43
Truce, 80, 85–6, 88
US trip, 70, 84, 113, 124, 128, 135, 145–51, 156–7
de Vere White, Terence, 195–6, 198, 200
Deasy, Liam, 103, 163
demobilisation, 188, 191, 192–3
Democratic Programme, 76–7
Derby, Lord, 109, 149
Derrig, Thomas, 228, 229
Devoy, John, 145–6, 278
Dillon, James, 138, 239, 241, 244, 245, 246, 249, 256
Dimbleby, Richard, 306
Dingle Peninsula, 323–30
dinner parties, 346–9
Document No. 2, 142–3
Dominican Order, 10
Donegal Men's Association, 215
Donnelly, Jimmy, 311
Donnelly, Simon, 29, 161
Doorly, Bishop, 182
Douglas, Harold, 245
Doyle, Peadar, 243
Dublin, 62, 234
Dublin Brigade, 26, 38, 43
Dublin Grand Opera Society, 318
Duggan, 47, 88

Dumay, Bertha, 32
Dungannon Clubs, 287–8

E
Easter Rising, 1916, 10, 12, 13, 93, 105, 131, 284, 288, 291, 344
  Brugha, 153, 154
  Frongoch, 40
  Kerry, 81, 98
  Min Ryan on, 275–8
  RM's role, 19–21, 62
  RM's views on, 25–9
education, council of, 230
Education, Department of, 228–9, 238, 255
emigration, 330
Ennis, Co. Clare, 5, 13
Erne hydroelectric scheme, 257
External Relations Act, repeal of, 246–50

F
Farmers' Party, 219, 236
Farnan, Dr, 132
Farrell, Brian, 182
Farrell, Paul, 55
Fianna Fail, 172, 211, 214, 220, 285, 298
  enters Dail, 219
  and Inter-Party governments, 251, 255
  Irish language, 226, 228–9
  Jim Ryan in, 291
  name of, 188
  organisation of, 221
  in power, 1932, 22, 23, 235, 303
  RM's views of, 215, 242–3, 244, 261
Figgis, Darrell, 111, 133
Fine Gael, 23, 138, 216, 221, 233, 234, 258–9, 271, 340. see also
  Inter-Party governments
  established, 236
  leadership, 237–8
  RM president, 239–42
Fingal Brigade, 25–7

Finlay, Thomas, 251
First World War, 20
Fitzgerald, Alexis, 245, 254
Fitzgerald, Billy, 251
FitzGerald, Desmond, 138, 220, 223
Fitzgerald, Oliver, 254
Fitzgerald, Paddy, 254
Fitzgibbon, Constantine, 94
Fitzpatrick, David, 64–5
Flanagan, Sean, 349
Fletcher, Dr, 114
Fogarty, Dr, bishop of Killaloe, 207–8
  letter to, 70–3
Fogarty, Father, 34, 35, 36
Forster, E.M., 315
Foyle Fisheries, 257
Free State Army, 14, 22, 185–97, 262–3. see also Army Mutiny
French, Lord, 63
Friend, General, 34
Frongoch, 21, 36, 38–42, 93, 100, 288, 291–2
Frost, Gerry, 338

G
Gaelic Athletic Association (GAA), 58, 83
Gaelic League, 18, 21, 43, 47, 58, 83, 132, 154, 227, 264
Gaeltacht Commission, 18, 178, 224–32, 262
Galvin, Kathleen, 115, 117, 130
Galway, County, 18, 160
Galway County Council, 152
Gannon, Maire, 338
Garden of Remembrance, 263
Garvin, Tom, 173
Gavan Duffy, George, 121, 288
Geary, Roy, 256
general elections
  1918, 177
  1923, 188–9, 200, 220
  1927, 204, 212–13, 219
  1932, 221, 235

1937, 234
1938, 234
1943, 234
1944, 234
1948, 241
1954, 258
German Plot, 58, 100, 108, 125
Glavey, Betty, 285
Gogarty, Oliver St John, 114, 115, 128, 130
Good Friday Agreement, 257
Government of Ireland Act 1920, 136
Greene, Graham, 315
Gregg, Bishop, 196
Griffen, Cardinal, 306
Griffen, John, 20
Griffith, Arthur, 18, 43, 78, 79, 123, 133, 136, 209, 283
  acting president, SF, 128, 148, 149–51
  arrest, 83, 109
  Belfast boycott, 81–2
  and Brugha, 98, 156, 158, 174
  and Collins, 103–4, 105
  Colum biography, 267
  Dail president, 145
  and de Valera, 125–8, 138–9, 143, 144, 160
  death of, 94, 112, 129–31
  dual monarchy, 153, 177
  economic policy, 129, 204, 220, 223
  first Dail, 76–7
  funeral, 118, 119
  and Hobson, 288
  RM's views of, 122–31
  and Treaty, 84, 106, 107, 125–8
  Treaty debates, 137, 181
  Truce, 86, 87, 152
  War of Independence, 62, 69, 70, 73

H
Hailsham, Lord, 236
Hales, Tom, 137, 155, 167, 194

Harbison, Eleanor, 317
Harbison, Jock, 316–17
Harding, Mr, 55–6
Harding, President, 147
Harris, Grandpa, 10
Harris, Maria, 5–6
Harris, Samuel, 5–6
Harris, Thomas H., 5
Hayes, Michael, 55, 138, 176, 182, 211, 213–14, 214, 216, 221, 343, 344
Hayes McCoy, 62–3
Hearne, John, 250
Henderson, Mr, 152
Hinkson, Mrs Katherine Tynan, 122
Hobson, Bulmer, 18, 287–8
Hogan, 223
Hogan, Colm, 338–9
Hogan, Des, 289, 338–9
Hogan, Paddy, 22, 192, 197, 213, 214
Holland, Frank, 115, 117, 196, 268
Home Affairs, Department of, 72, 73
Home Rule, 12, 20, 77
Hughes, 220
Hunter, Tom, 35–6

I
Industrial Development Authority, 256
Industry and Commerce, Department of, 256
Inishannon, 60, 63
Inter-Parliamentary Union Meeting, 211–12
Inter-Party Governments, 237, 241, 258–9
  first, 242–59
Irish Bulletin, 179
Irish Hospitals' Sweepstakes, 222
Irish Independent, 243
Irish language, 17–18, 19, 178, 264, 265, 314, 315–16
  family use, 323–30
  Gaeltacht Commission, 224–32
Irish Medical Association, 253–4, 340
Irish National Society, 78

Irish Parliamentary Party, 178, 179, 316

Irish Press, 233, 236

Irish Republican Army (IRA), 14, 191, 235

  Collins in, 93

  election 1918, 112–13

  and IRB, 74–5

  relations with Sinn Fein, 68–75

  split, 92, 112, 136–7, 167

  Stack appointment, 85–6

  Truce, 84–92, 143

  War of Independence, 57–75

Irish Republican Brotherhood (IRB), 103, 112, 114, 145, 277, 287, 288

  and Army, 74–5

  Army Mutiny, 191, 201–2

  Brugha in, 153, 154–5

  Easter Rising, 27–8, 98

  election 1918, 112–13

  Frongoch, 39, 42, 100

  idea of republic, 175–6

  RM joins, 18, 19

  and Treaty, 105

Irish Sisters of Charity, 7, 9

Irish Times, 188, 237–8, 266

Irish Volunteers, 18–22, 20, 26, 43, 47, 58, 78, 135, 145, 178, 283

  Brugha in, 154–5

  de Valera criticism of, 147

  Executive, 43, 49–50, 93

  GHQ, 44, 45, 48, 50–2

  RM Chief of Staff, 45–54

  split, 168–9, 173–4, 185–91

J

John XXIII, Pope, 159

Johnson, Thomas, 76, 211

Jones, Chris, 304

Justice, Department of, 211

K

Kearney, Peadar, 118
  RM homily, 357–60
Keavey, John and Ellie, 236
Kelliher, Sean, 17
Kelly, John, 94, 257
Kennedy, Hugh, 251
Kent, Eamonn, 154
Kerry, County, 18, 27, 28, 81, 90, 98, 179, 180, 227, 277
  Gaeltacht, 323–30
Kiernan, Kitty, 117
Kilkelly, Mrs, 67
Kilkenny, County, 162, 195
King, Sean, 35
Kinnane, Dr, Archbishop of Cashel, 64
Knutsford Jail, 13, 21, 29–38, 39, 288

L

Labour Party, 179, 219, 220, 221, 258–9. see also Inter-Party governments
Laffan, Michael, 78
Langley, Liam, 20
Larchet, John, 185, 187, 198
Larchet, Mrs, 198
Larkin, Jim, 234
Lavery, Cecil, 250
Lavery, Sir Hugh, 114
Lavery, Lady, 266
Lawless, Col Joseph, 26–7
League of Nations, 147
Lee, Professor Joe, 174
Legge, Hector, 249
Leitrim, County, 218
Lemass, Sean, 172
Lester, Sean, 20
Lewes Jail, 42
Limerick, County, 160, 162
Limerick city, 27, 28
Lincoln Jail, 73, 146
Lissenfield House, Rathmines, 302–5, 310–12

Lloyd George, David, 65, 80, 107, 126–7, 133, 135, 140, 153, 189
Local Appointments Commission, 216–17
Local Defence Force, 341
Local Government Department, 72
Lovett family, 323–4
Lown, Bernard, 131
Lynch, Fionan, 98, 138, 201, 211
Lynch, Liam, 54, 86, 121, 163, 164–6, 194
Lynch, Patrick, 229, 245, 249–50, 254, 256
Lyons, F.S.L., 248, 249

M
Macardle, Dorothy, 141
MacBride, Sean, 244, 245, 248, 249, 250, 254
McCann, Pierce, 20, 37
McCartaigh, T., 42
McCartan, Dr Patrick, 288
McCarthy, Fr Desmond, 265, 266, 272
McCullagh, David, 259
McCullough, Denis, 28, 125, 185, 198, 297, 316, 348
  Dungannon clubs, 18, 287–8
  Frongoch, 37, 40, 41, 42
  and godson, 289–91
  president, IRB, 277
McCullough, Domhnall, 307
McCullough, Donncha, 289
McCullough, Mairtin, 289, 307
McCullough family, 311, 336, 341
MacCurtain, Tomas, 40, 42
McDermott, Sean, 21, 25, 28
MacDermott, Sean, 105, 154, 277–8, 288, 294
McDonagh, Joe, 113
McDonnell, Dr, 59
MacEntee, Sean, 171–2, 250, 263
MacEoin, Sean, 74, 77, 85, 182, 202, 240, 267
McGarry, Sean, 43, 45, 77
McGilligan, Patrick, 138, 162, 223, 229, 246, 344
McGrath, Joe, 197, 198, 201, 205, 222
Machtig, Sir Eric, 250

McKee, Dick, 45, 46, 47, 49, 53, 159
  RM's views of, 161, 163–4
McKelvey, Joseph, 194
McKenzie (scout), 321
McMahon, Deirdre, 135, 196, 250
McMahon, Peadar, 182
McMahon, Sean, 44, 45, 46, 47–8, 53, 74, 202
McManus, M.J., 126
MacNeill, Eoin, 121, 138, 176, 177, 204, 222
  Civil War, 202
  Easter Rising, 28, 29, 40, 278
  Irish language, 178, 224, 230, 264, 265
  on RM, 208–9
  War of Independence, 69, 70, 83, 151
McQuaid, Dr J.C., Archbishop of Dublin, 253
Macready, General, 87–8, 189–90
MacSwiney, Terence, 20, 40, 42
Magennis, Dr Jim, 130
Maggie (housekeeper), 270, 314, 336–7
Manchester, 34–5, 106
Mann, Thomas, 315
Manning, Maurice, 215–16
manuscripts commission, 224
Marcus Aurelius, 308
Markievicz, Constance, 79, 82
Mathew, Fr Theobald, 10
Maugham, Somerset, 315
Maxwell, General, 39
Maye, Brian, 256
Meade, Dr Harry, 130
Meath, County, 62
medicine, 335–6, 340–1, 346
Mellowes, Liam, 44, 46, 87, 91, 99, 108, 168, 172, 180, 185
  execution, 194
  Four Courts siege, 162
Military courts, 221
Milltown Golf Club, 343
Milroy, Sean, 77
Monahan, Jim, 7

Monahan family, 336, 341

Moore, Colonel, 67

Morrin, 'Pops,' 191–2

Morrissey, Dan, 243

Mother and Child Scheme, 252–6

Mount Sion, Waterford, 5

Moville, Co. Donegal, 251–2

Moylan, Sean, 85

Moylett, P., 149

Mulcahy, Aileen, 304–5, 349

Mulcahy, Elisabet (Mrs Berney, daughter), 9, 281, 307, 313, 322–3, 332, 337–8, 341, 342, 346, 347

Mulcahy, Elizabeth (mother), 5, 6, 8, 11

Mulcahy, Elizabeth (Sr Senan, sister), 7, 9

Mulcahy, Kitty (sister), 7, 8, 9–11, 12, 14

Mulcahy, Maire (daughter), 203, 307, 322, 323, 332, 341, 342, 347

Mulcahy, Mary Josephine (Min, wife), 48, 172, 198, 302, 304, 347. see also Ryan family
  army benevolent fund, 262
  Army Mutiny, 203
  and Collins, 95, 110, 111
  death of, 343
  gardening, 342–3
  golf, 343
  life and family of, 275–87, 292, 296–9
  married life, 301–2, 310–11
  and McDermott, 277–8, 294
  personality, 294–6

Mulcahy, Mary (sister), 6–7, 8

Mulcahy, Nano (Sr Otteran, sister), 7, 8

Mulcahy, Neilli (daughter), 307, 316, 322, 332, 341, 342, 347

Mulcahy, Nell (Sr Angela), 6, 7, 8, 10, 13, 14, 271

Mulcahy, Major Paddy (brother), 13, 13–14, 348

Mulcahy, Padraig (son), 298, 304, 307, 311, 316, 322, 333, 338, 340, 347
  career, 341
  childhood illness, 336
  Gaeltacht, 323, 332
  scouting, 319, 321

Mulcahy, Patrick (father), 5, 8, 11, 12

Mulcahy, Richard, 8, 20, 44, 85, 88, 89–90, 182, 198, 200, 243, 302, 347.
see also Easter Rising; IRA; Irish Volunteers
1924-32, 207–32
ancestry, 5–6
archives of, 367–8
Army Mutiny, 197–205
backbencher, 209–13
Blueshirts, 237
and Brugha, 91, 113–14
career summary, 17–23
Chief of Staff, Volunteers, 49–50
Civil War, 189–90, 195
Collins's death, 117–22
and constituents, 216–17
death of, 268–73
education, 5, 12–13
election, 1918, 177
exercise, 343, 344
family life, 6–11, 301–49, 305–13, 318–19, 337
finances, 310
Gaeltacht Commission, 224–32
Griffith funeral, 118, 119
health of, 335
homily for Ashe, Kearney, Beaslai, 357–60
homily for Collins, 351–5
Inter-Party government, 242–59
literary interests, 314–16
Minister for Defence, 22, 75, 80, 262
Minister for Education, 11, 226, 228–9, 238, 255, 259, 261
Minister for Local Government, 22, 216–18, 217
musical interests, 318
nationalism of, 264–7
Nichevo on, 118–20
O'Higgins funeral, 214
in opposition, 233–42
personality, 56
president, FG, 23, 223, 233, 237, 239–42
religion, 306–7
resigns from army, 22, 188–9

   resigns from ministry, 207–8

   retirement, 261–73

   security guards, 210–11

   speaking style, 215, 233

   takeover of Collins Barracks, 190

   tapes, 372–6

   and Treaty, 176–8

   Truce, 84–92

   view of Collins, 93–122

   view of Griffith, 122–31

   War of Independence, 54–6, 57–75

   and IRB, 74–5

   and SF, 68–74

   writing style, 233

Mulcahy, Rev. Richard, 265

Mulcahy, Richard (great grandfather), 11

Mulcahy, Dr Risteard (son), 17–18, 307, 347

   childhood, 305–13

   cycle trips, 338–9

   fever hospital, 335

   holidays, 323–30

   Lissenfield House, 303–5

   relationship with father, 337

   scouting, 319–22

Mulcahy, Rosemarie, 278, 322

Mulcahy, Sam (Dom Columban, brother), 6, 14, 14–15

Mulcahy, Sean (son), 7, 278, 297, 307, 311, 322, 332, 340, 347

   career, 341

Mulcahy family, 279, 307, 322

   and army, 331–3, 341–2

   clothing, 333–4

   diet, 336–7

   finances, 310–12

   governesses, 322, 323–4, 326

   holidays, 323–30

   illness, 334–6

   Irish language, 323–30

   literary interests, 314–16

   music, 316–18, 317–18

    physical affection, 305–6
    and politics, 340–1
    religion, 306–10
    Second World War, 339–40, 341
    travel, 337–9
Mullins, William, 20
Mulloy, Sheila, 291
Murchu, 211
Murphy, Humphrey, 167
Murphy, Professor John A., 134–5, 172, 242, 271, 340
Mussolini, Benito, 237

N
Nash, John, 303, 305
National Aid Association, 93, 100
national anthem, 187–8
National Defence Conference, 238–9
National Executive, 43, 45, 50–2
National University of Ireland, 11–12
Nationalist League, 219
Ned (gardener), 311
'Nichevo,' 118–20
North Tipperary Brigade, 63–4
Northern Ireland (NI), 58, 148–9, 175, 248, 344, 345
   anti-partition campaign, 257–8
peace process, 183
Norton, William, 244–6, 249
Nowlan, Prof. Kevin, 67

O
O'Beirne, Mr, 187
O'Brien, William, 76
O'Caghlaigh, Professor Cormac, 214
O'Conluain, Proinsias, 284
O'Connell, Bob, 254
O'Connell, Comdt J.J., 39–40, 41, 42, 44, 46, 47, 53
O'Connell, Professor, 182
O'Connor, Matt, 191, 192
O'Connor, Paddy, 196

O'Connor, Rory, 43–5, 44, 47, 53, 162, 168, 172, 180, 185, 203, 238
  execution, 194
O'Connor, Ulick, 115, 270
O'Donnell, Peadar, 39
O'Donoghue, Florrie, 163, 167
O'Donovan, Seamus, 44, 46
O'Driscoll, Mrs Collins, 235
O'Duffy, Eoin, 44, 45, 85, 86, 87, 235–6, 237
O'Farrell, T.J., 239–40
O'Flanagan, Fr Michael, 113, 150, 152
O'Flynn, Fr Christie, 227
O'Grady, Standish, 315
O'Hegarty, Diarmuid, 43, 62, 112, 113, 154, 164
O'Hegarty, P.S., 57–8, 70–3, 76, 82, 113, 181, 182, 288
O'Hegarty, Sean, 94, 167
O'Higgins, Kevin, 137, 138, 178, 223, 251, 344
  and army, 90, 110
  Army Mutiny, 191–2, 197–201, 202, 203
  assassination, 210, 219, 221
  executions, 194–6
  funeral of, 214
  party organisation, 222
  and RM, 22, 213, 266, 272
O'Higgins, Mrs, 203–4
O'Higgins, Tom, 191, 192, 258
O'Higgins, Dr Tom, 29, 235, 344
O'Keeffe, Paidin, 79, 80, 98, 110, 125, 148, 156, 157
  on Collins, 112–13
  Truce delay, 151–2
O'Kelly, Phyllis, 95
O'Kelly, Sean T., 169, 281, 297, 342
  career of, 283, 284
  marriages, 95, 172, 181, 282, 283, 285, 291
  president, 64, 261, 291
  RM's views on, 261
O'Leary, Jack, 345–6, 348
O'Leary, John, 128–9
O'Leary, Molly, 345, 346
O'Leary, Simon, 345

Olympic Games, Paris, 223
O'Mahoney, John, 113
O'Mahony, John, 40
O'Malley, Donough, 230
O'Malley, Ernie, 137, 161, 162, 194
O'Malley, Michael, 290
O'Muirthile, Sean, 35, 47, 74, 154, 164, 202
O'Rahilly, The, 277
O'Reilly, M.W., 40, 41, 289
O'Sullivan, Gearoid, 44, 45, 47, 53, 164
O'Sullivan, John Marcus, 214, 223, 228
O'Sullivan, K.P., 289, 338
O'Sullivan family, 11
Our Lady's Hospice, 269, 297

P
Pakenham, F., 127
Parks Grove, Co. Kilkenny, 5
partition, 135–6
Peace Conference, 70, 77, 284
Pearse, Mrs, 296
Pearse, Patrick, 21, 25, 28, 77, 105, 284, 296
Pembroke Nursing Home, 268
Phoenix magazine, 234
Plunkett, Count, 125, 151
Portobello Barracks, 190, 209, 303, 311, 331–3
Post Office, 13, 17, 18, 19
Power, Jenny Wyse, 79
Price, Eamonn, 44, 45
proportional representation, 240

R
Ranelagh Road, 293, 297
rates collection, 217–18
Reid School of Music, 317
Reading jail, 39, 40
Redditch, Jimmy, 114
Regan, John, 110–11
religion, 306–10, 327–8

religious orders, 11

republic
  declaration of, 246–50
  straitjacket of, 175–80

Rice, Edmund Ignatius, 5

Richmond barracks, 34

Robbie affair, 89

Robinson, Seamus, 162

Rockwell College, 13

Rooney, 126

Royal Academy of Music, 317

Royal Institute of Public Health, 216

Royal Irish Academy, 216

Royal Irish Constabulary (RIC), 21, 63–4, 65, 66, 261
  Ashbourne capture, 26–7

Royal Ulster Constabulary (RUC), 251–2

Rugby, Lord, 250

Russell, Sean, 44, 46, 86

Ryan, Agnes, 37, 297

Ryan, Betty, 286

Ryan, Chris, 290, 294

Ryan, Desmond, 62

Ryan, Gerry, 115, 234

Ryan, Jack, 279, 286–7, 291, 298, 299

Ryan, Fr James, 280

Ryan, Dr Jim, 172, 255, 283, 285, 290–1, 294

Ryan, Joanna (Sr Stanislaus), 280, 283–4, 299

Ryan, John, 281–2

Ryan, Liz, 299

Ryan, Fr Martin, 279, 281, 282, 286, 299

Ryan, Mary Josephine (Min), 335, 336. see Mulcahy, Mary Josephine

Ryan, Mary Kate (Kate, Kit, Mrs O'Kelly), 172, 280, 282, 284, 285, 294, 297, 299

Ryan, Maureen, 297

Ryan, Michael, 286–7, 291, 300

Ryan, Molly, 285, 287, 300

Ryan, Nell, 285–7, 298, 299–300

Ryan, Phyllis (Mrs O'Kelly), 28, 181, 275, 277–8, 285, 291–2, 294, 342

Ryan family, 12, 111, 236, 275, 276, 279–83, 283–7, 341

children, 283–97
Treaty split, 278, 280–1, 285–7
Rynne, Stephen, 160

S
St Vincent's Hospital, 326, 340
Sauersweig, Comdt, 198
Savage, Michael, 63
Sceilg, 227
Scoil Colmcille, 228
Scoil Muire, 228
Scotch accounts, 97, 99, 107, 108
Scott-Moncrieff, George, 15
Second World War, 237, 238, 338, 339–40, 341
sex education, 305–6
Shortall family, 287
shorthand, 19
Sinn Fein, 18, 19, 57, 133, 143, 156, 172, 220, 283
  constitution, 141
  Dail members, 178–9
  election 1918, 112–13
  executive, 43, 52, 70, 125, 131, 135
  and first Dail, 75–8
  Griffith acting president, 148, 149–51
  harassment of, 58–9
  history of, 78–84
  and IRB, 74
  and peace process, 257
  relations with Army, 68–74
  straitjacket of republic, 175–80
  War of Independence, 98, 100, 112
Slattery, Elizabeth. see Mulcahy, Elizabeth
Slattery, James, 6
Slattery, John, 10, 208
Slattery, Joseph, 10–11
smoking, 330, 346
Smuts, General, 149
Smyllie, R.M., 118–20
social class, 319–20

Soloheadbeg ambush, 60, 62, 63–4
South Tipperary Volunteers, 61
Spike Island, Co. Cork, 91
Squad, the, 46–7
Stack, Austin, 20, 79, 150, 161
    army staff, 45, 46, 89
    and Collins, 97–8, 106–7, 113–14, 174
    Easter Rising, 27, 81
    jail visit, 106
    and Treaty, 127, 169
    Treaty debates, 137
Staines, Michael, 38, 40, 41, 43, 82
Stephens, James, 315
Sunday Independent, 246, 249
Sutton, Eliza, 283
Sweeney, Joe, 182

T
Taisce, An, 305
tapes, 372–6
TB campaign, 255
Teeling, Frank, 161
Thackaberry, Frank, 321
Thornley, David, 248
Thurles, Co. Tipperary, 5, 6, 12–13
Tierney, Michael, 27, 176, 204–5, 225–6, 230, 264–5
Tipperary, County, 162
Tipperary, South Riding, 234
Tobin, 47, 201, 202
Tralee, Co. Kerry, 17
Travers, Very Rev Charles J., 277
Traynor, Oscar, 68, 172, 234
Treacy, Sean, 62, 64
Trench, C.C., 53–4
Truce, 29, 48, 67, 68, 76, 83, 134, 156
    arms decommissioning, 183–4
    delayed, 151–3
    GHQ staff, 50, 53
    RM on, 84–92

RM's role, 77, 80, 110, 132, 143, 157, 271
Trucileers, 90

U
Ulster Volunteer Force (UVF), 20, 58
Unionists, 178
United States of America, 210
   de Valera trip, 70, 84, 113, 124, 128, 135, 145–51, 156–7
   Mulcahy in, 211–12
   plan to send Collins, 108–9
University College Dublin, 21, 75–6
Ursuline Order, 6–7

V
Valiulis, Maryann, biography by, 138, 237, 255, 264
   Army Mutiny, 193, 201
   Army split, 165, 185
   Civil War, 134, 135, 189, 263
   Collins, 60
   comments on, 234, 265, 272
   Cumann na nGaedheal, 218–19, 222
   description of, 361–5
   leadership of FG, 240, 242
   reviews of, 271, 340
   Treaty, 176, 178
   Truce, 84–5, 87–8, 143
   War of Independence, 54, 57, 66, 301
Vaughan's Hotel, 46–7
Volunteer Convention, 1917, 132
Volunteer Dependants Fund, 21

W
Walsh, Dr, Archbishop of Dublin, 125–6
Walsh, J.J., 222–3
War of Independence, 90, 93, 98, 110, 191, 202, 344
   army policy, 57–75, 68–74
   Dail Eireann and SF, 75–8
   de Valera and Collins, 108
   de Valera criticisms, 147

moral right of, 179
RM's role, 21–2, 45–54, 50–1, 53–4, 96, 190, 261–2, 271, 280, 296
role of IRB, 74–5
Truce delayed, 151–3
Waterford, 5
Waugh, Evelyn, 315
Wexford, County, 18, 90, 280–1
Whelan, Leo, 48–9
White, James, 49
Williams, Prof Desmond, 112
Wyse Power, Jenny, 181, 284

Y
Younger, Calton, 114, 115